D0400586

PROCEED WITH CAUTION

PROCEED WITH CAUTION,

WHEN ENGAGED BY MINORITY WRITING

IN THE AMERICAS

DORIS SOMMER

HARVARD UNIVERSITY PRESS

Cambridge, Massachusetts

London, England   1999

Copyright © 1999 by the President and Fellows of Harvard College
All rights reserved
Printed in the United States of America

Library of Congress Cataloging-in-Publication Data

Sommer, Doris, 1947–
   Proceed with caution, when engaged by minority writing in the
Americas / Doris Sommer.
      p.   cm.
   Includes bibliographical references and index.
   ISBN 0-674-53658-4 (alk. paper). — ISBN 0-674-53660-6
(pbk. : alk. paper)
   1. Spanish American literature—Minority authors—History and
criticism. 2. American literature—Minority authors—History and
criticism. 3. Literature—Philosophy. 4. Difference (Psychology)
in literature. I. Title.
PQ7081.S687   1999
860.9'98—dc21   98-50383

To my resilient and loving parents,
Julius and Adela Sommer, for whom
English is a seventh language. "Second
language?" people ask indulgently. "No,
seventh."

CONTENTS

ADVERTENCIA / WARNING

[African American] music makes you hungry for more of it. It never really gives you the whole number. It slaps and it embraces, it slaps and it embraces.

—TONI MORRISON

Fuck off, now. Go away and let me sleep.

—JESUSA PALANCARES

I'm still keeping secret what I think no-one should know. Not even anthropologists or intellectuals, no matter how many books they have, can find out all our secrets.

—RIGOBERTA MENCHÚ

You who read this act of contrition should know that by writing it I seek a kind of forgiveness—not yours. The forgiveness, rather, of those many persons whose absence from higher education permitted me to be classed a minority student. I wish that they would read this. I doubt they ever will.

—RICHARD RODRIGUEZ

Be careful of some books. They can sting readers who feel entitled to know everything as they approach a text, practically any text, with the conspiratorial intimacy of a potential partner. Readers bent on understanding may neglect another kind of engagement, one that would make respect a reading requirement. The slap of refused intimacy from uncooperative books can slow readers down, detain them at the boundary between contact and conquest, before they press particularist writing to surrender cultural difference for the sake of universal meaning. The very familiarity of universalism as measure of literary worth, while its codependent term, particularism, sounds new to literary studies,[1] shows how one-sided interpretation has been, even when we read "minority" texts. If learning makes the distance between writers and readers seem superficial or circumstantial, mere interference on the way to understanding, particularist writing puts circumstance to work, resurfacing the stretch and marking it with stop signs. Those signs go unnoticed and have no rhetorical names, because the study of rhetoric has generally assumed cultural continuity between writer and reader.[2]

Naming some figures of discontinuity is one purpose of this book: to contribute toward a rhetoric of particularism that will appreciate artful maneuvers for marking cultural distance. Why should distance be marked? Shouldn't limits be overcome through empathy and learning? Because overcoming them makes the writer ultimately redundant. One will do. Contemporary criticism is hardly scandalized by readers who disappear authors, even when texts resist. The reduction cheats readers too, as they override the specific charm or bite in some books. Particularism's seductive and defensive tangle with universalism produces the formal experiments and aesthetic thrill that can be lost on readers who rush toward one term or the other. More seriously, we miss opportunities for genuine dialogue with texts and with citizens in public arenas, because presumptuous habits of reading cannot prepare us to listen.

Limits of intimacy and access are not the same as the difficulty, ambiguity, or complexity that demand and reward interpretive labor. Limits should be easy to read as disruptions of understanding, "absences so stressed, so ornate, so planned," says Toni Morrison, "they call attention to themselves; arrest us with intentionality and purpose." Paradoxically, arrest is also a point of entry "into the question of cultural (or racial) distinction." It is the slap that interrupts the embrace of communication to open up space for improvising.[3] Absences can incite the fill-in work that keeps a reader self-important; but they can also interfere with comprehension (which still means grasping, seizure) to release readers from the exorbitant (and unethical) but usually unspoken assumption that we should know the Other well enough to speak for him or her. Released and relieved from that obligation, we may wonder at the persistence of our desire to overtake otherness. Noticing the aggressive desire will be the point, before we rush to redirect energy. Stopping short is a step in the syncopated rhythm of engagement offered by particularist books, perhaps with no ultimate resolution. There is a danger, of course, in demurring entirely. Cultural relativists claim a freedom from desire that amounts to irresponsibility, and colonizers decline to know the Other for fear that knowledge would compromise their control. Yet literary studies proceed as if control were not a political concern but only an illusion that serious literature challenges by frustrating readers' expectations and explanations.[4] The challenge, I am saying, has been more hermeneutical than ethical, more a goad than a reason to worry about heady approaches to texts and to the world.

Worry should be part of the work, if we learn to read the distance written into some ethnically marked literature. A variety of rhetorical moves can hold readers at arm's length or joke at their pretense of mastery, in order to propose something different from knowledge. Philosophers have called it acknowledgment. Others call it respect.

The chapters that follow are invitations to develop an unlikely program of training in the modesty and respect that make engagement possible. These are premodern postures that postmodern negotiations will need to revive. I call the program unlikely, even if sensitive leads have already shown how to tread with one step in and one step out of competence.[5] In our enlightened traditions learning still assumes a substantive object or a self-authorizing method, not a vulnerable comportment. We learn something. But the particularist books that detain us require something besides the epistemological desire that drives readers toward data, and something beyond the impulse to overrun oppositions before they can do their productive work. Amassing data or dismissing them, either way, we have typically wanted to share so much ground and so many games with the author that we can pretend to assume whatever he or she assumes. This Whitmanian rush of easy intimacy wants no dialogue and stays lonely; it imagines democracy to be a natural and unitary spirit of the people, something to celebrate. If, however, a backward glance at our histories in this hemisphere shows that democracy is a painstaking process, a war of positions, then those of us who are learning the signs of positioning can hope to become participant-observers.

The lessons in listening for surprises and pausing before they are neutralized; the training to stretch our expectations of difference and to recoil from quests for mastery—these may be universal markers of literature worth discussing, but today they are particularly productive and audible from some ethnically colored authors and from culturally self-conscious white ones. Astute about their own social circumstances, these writers set manageable limits around readers who mistake a privileged center for the universe, and who need obstacles to notice the circumstances of conversation. One limit can show a reader that his monolingualism is unequal to a bilingual perfor- mance; another frustrates the expectation of a talking cure when a trauma story wisely refuses to satisfy impertinent curiosity. At some points, secrets mark limits of intimacy whether or not they guard information; at others, benighted white narrators nervously defer to or defend against colored competitors. In all these cases, writers can maneuver texts into unantici- pated passes that make even bullish readers stop to ponder the move. The performances can wrest control from readers who may become enchanted by the surprising turns and feel disoriented, dependent, even relieved from the burden of competence.

The power adjustment is a prerequisite to possible dialogues. Because, if universalist readers think they can know more and interpret better than the particularist authors they target, dialogue may turn into a posthumous challenge after the author is pronounced dead. Without setting limits, can an ethnically marked, "minority," or unconventionally gendered writer hope really to engage an authoritative reader? In writers whom postcolonial theory calls subaltern, agency or "subject-effect" is felt mostly in the con- struction of boundaries. Without them, the imperial I would fill up more space.

The title of this preface is inspired by one such colonial subject, the first mestizo chronicler of Peru. Known by the oxymoronic name of El Inca Gar- cilaso de la Vega, he inherited an unstable mix of indigenous royalty and Spanish nobility. In masterful Spanish, Garcilaso performed wonders with prefaces. His magic was to multiply the conventional first move, adding one prologue after another to keep readers at the threshold. Caution is the redundant message: the prologue-dedication of his history, "To the Most Serene Princess," is followed by a "Preface to the Reader" that discounts Spanish historians because they know so little about Peru. Then, still hold- ing back—so that the stance itself is a performance of control—Garcilaso adds his "Advertencias" about the general language of the Indians that Spaniards will never master, despite some laudable exertions by Jesuits. Now "advertencia" is the standard term for preliminary advice to the reader, although here it is pluralized to multiply the barriers. But the popular English translation neutralizes the word into "notes" ("notices" would be better), perhaps to associate it with "advertise," a term of open and welcoming information. In Spanish, though, the association is more legal than commercial, more cautionary than welcoming. Advertencias are warnings.

If one stops to think about it, the rhetorical restraints and barbs at aggressive appropriations are all plausible. But we have seldom stopped to think about the ravages of facile intimacies; we have not paused to hear the invitations to tangle that are issued between wariness and refusal. Particularist literature would logically vie for central importance while holding off universalists who would claim coauthorship. But our tradition of criticism takes the underdeveloped practices of "reader response" theory as basic and unobjectionable. The "strategies of containment" that claim our attention here would defend cultural difference as a value in itself.[6] It is what Jean-François Lyotard calls the differend, the stubborn residue that survives on the margins of normalizing discourses. Acknowledging that residue is the precondition for democratic negotiations. Difference safeguards particularist identities against seamless assimilation, a word that rhymes with neutralization and sometimes also with physical annihilation.

Is inhospitality toward the reader, or his demotion, surprising? Then it merits a pause long enough to learn new expectations. Mistrust is a feature of some literary seductions, but we have too often, and blithely, missed the persistent signs. Educated readers usually expect to enter into collaborative language games with a range of writers, as if asymmetrical relationships flattened out on the smooth surface of print culture. But particularists can counter those expectations with less flattering and more promising games. Instead of summoning collaboration in stories that become ours by dint of effort, they invite us to play variations on follow-the-leader. Perhaps we can learn to step differently, to respect distances and explore the socially enabling possibilities of acknowledging our own limits.

The unyielding responses of a rhetoric of particularism studied in this book are: Garcilaso's *circumlocutions,* so exquisite that even strident readers become dizzy and docile (Chapter 3); *deferring translation* to target dangerously smug self-authorization (Chapter 4); the political agency of *withholding information* (Chapter 5); the contrasting strategy of unstinting availability that bores adventurers—the *"featherbed resistance"* that Hurston described (Chapter 6); Toni Morrison's staged confrontation of *intimacy versus information* (Chapter 7); counterpoising a clueless Cuban narrator with the eloquent slaves whom *whites cannot hear* (Chapter 8); and performing the *nervousness of a biographer* whose jazzman subject keeps dismissing the biography (Chapter 9). The *haunting rhythm of difference* is the theme of Vargas Llosa's *The Storyteller* (Chapter 10), as it is the theme throughout these readings. That same circular rhythm puts the general considerations up front in Chapter 1, available for readers who want to consider the implications of a particularist rhetoric for literary theory. Those who prefer not to detour into theory can proceed to Whitman's embrace (Chapter 2) and then to the slaps that interrupt it.

The challenges are legible and audible from so many directions that the focus here on literature from the Americas, mostly Spanish America, shows the limits of my own circumstances and interests. Like Sander Gilman's *Jewish Self-Hatred*, this book could have followed many different leads from literary traditions that others know better than I. Gilman's focus on Jews is almost fortuitous, autobiographical, he says, since any "marginalized" culture produces self-hatred to the extent that minorities participate in a majoritarian culture that hates them. During my own childhood in Brooklyn, we had a bad name for Jews who were so embarrassed by ethnicity that they chose not to claim it. They were "white Jews," troubled and untrustworthy. Whatever utopian or democratizing ideals may have tempted us all toward assimilation, "whitening" was, to many of us, a hasty price for a distant prize. So instead, like Garcilaso and like the Jewish philosopher of love whom he chose to translate, we preferred to weave back and forth, glad to fit into universal culture when we could, but loath to give up the anchor of a "native" condition.

My "mosaic" New York sometimes showed volatile cultural conditions that demanded acknowledgment and negotiation. Years later, I circle back to the first step, to listening for the limits of culturally embedded positions. More steps should follow from this, but it would miss my point about attentive engagement to predict what they would be. Instead, I want to stay at the first stage as an exercise in stamina for tolerating the reluctance that we have rushed to overcome. The intention is—of course and paradoxically—to refine readerly competence, not to dismiss it. The improvement will be substantial. It will be to notice the tropes of particularism as invitations to engage, to delay and possibly to redirect the hermeneutical impulse to cross barriers and fuse horizons. If we manage to include among our reading requirements the anticipation of strategic refusals, because differences coexist and do not reduce to moments in a universal history of understanding, this will be no minor adjustment, but a halting yet more promising approach.

A RHETORIC OF PARTICULARISM

1

Las palabras se hacen fronteras, cuando no nacen del corazón
hablemos el mismo idioma y así las cosas irán mejor.

[Words can become barriers when they don't come from the heart
Let's speak the same language, and that way things will go better]

—GLORIA ESTEFAN
 and EMILIO ESTEFAN, JR.

"At least grant that while phrases from ordinary language are equivocal, it is a noble task to seek out univocality and to refuse to entertain equivocation."

"That's Platonic, at the very least. You are preferring dialogue to differend. You are presupposing, first of all, that univocality is possible; and second, that it constitutes the healthiness of phrases."

—JEAN-FRANÇOIS LYOTARD
 The Differend

"Universalism is not what it used to be," said an irritated colleague when he heard a slogan from Miami played to a salsa mix: "Hablemos el mismo idioma."[1] The words translate as "Let's Speak the Same Language" in the bilingual booklet that comes with the CD, an ecumenical accompaniment to make good on the call for racial rainbows and musical fusions *(colores de un arcoiris, acordes de un mismo son)*. But there's no denying the irritation that Gloria Estefan can cause, because her monolingual appeal to get beyond differences is pitched to decidedly Latin locutors. After the first few lines, the song disinvites some listeners who may have wanted to sing along, when the "us" turns out to be "los Latinos." Some of us are literally put off, even though Estefan had accounted for differences from the very first lines

1

of her call to unity. She admitted that differences constitute her as a subject (*A pesar de las diferencias que me hacen quien soy*), as she enjoined us think about how much we have in common (*respiramos el mismo aire, despertamos al mismo sol, nos alumbra la misma luna, necesitamos sentir amor*). But when the "us" comes into question, her rhythm of moving from many to one falters, skips a beat, freezes it in a *syncope*, a term that Catherine Clément takes from musical notation (and from its medical meaning of "apparent death") to name a political or philosophical interruption of predictability. "The queen of rhythm, *syncope is also* the mother of *dissonance*; it is the source, in short, of a harmonious and productive discord . . . Attack and haven, collision; a fragment of the beat disappears, and of this disappearance, rhythm is born."[2] The pause between strong beats in Estefan's song, between unity and selective solidarity, is a break for reflection. But readers who may feel the sting of exclusion do not necessarily stop to think about it. They may be too quick on the uptake.

Estefan's pitch for pan-Hispanic solidarity rehearses what Puerto Rican Willie Colón, Panamanian Rubén Blades, and Cuban Celia Cruz have been intoning for years, a "trans-Latino" identity that now characterizes urban centers like "the New Nueva York."[3] Improvising on the themes of sameness and difference, the way that musical mixes make salsa from different national styles, Latinos are also saying that universalism is not what it used to be. They are saying it with relief, because they had fit so badly into milky homogenizations. "Racism as Universalism" is one assessment of the colorless abstraction.[4] But there is new hope for universality, say defenders of the public sphere and pragmatists, if democracies can tune in to discord in order to develop an "interactive" politics. Discord among culturally and economically disparate subjects reveals the gaps that separate them, which are the space of democratic negotiation.[5] Without gaps, negotiation would be unnecessary. And because of them, listening is not easy; it requires patience at the *syncope* of communication in a country where citizens do not always speak the same language. Even when they do speak English, the range of culturally inflected accents fissures the language community, happily, because our accents safeguard American diversity from the meanness of one standard sound.[6]

Theodor Adorno appreciated the "negativity" inside communities as boundary markers that resist the individual's "greedy thirst for incorporation" of difference into sameness.[7] If there were no difference, there could be no recognition of one subject by another, but only the kind of identification that reduces real external others into functions of a totalizing self. Yet the gap that allows for enough autonomy to make mutuality possible also risks misrecognition and violence. The risk is worth taking, because without it we allow the violence of forcing sameness on others: either they are forced to fit in or they are forced out.[8] That necessary risk of breakdown, which democracies defend as the negative (autonomous) moment of mutuality, surely gives some universalists pause about the possibility of a coherent culture and a cohesive polity. They fret that "difference criticism" can overwhelm the space for dialogue.[9] But pause is not a bad thing; it interrupts the person who speaks for someone else and makes for time to listen.[10]

Ernesto Laclau argues provocatively, along with some critical legal scholars, that universalism is promising today because it depends on difference.[11] The idea has survived classical philosophy's dismissal of particularity as deviation, and it has outlived a European Enlightenment that conflated the universal (subject, class, culture) with particular (French) incarnations. Today's universalism is a paradox when compared with that of the past, because it is grounded in particularist demands. They unmoor universalism from any fixed cultural content and keep it aware of an "always receding horizon."[12] Dissonance, then, isn't noise. It is a function of the syncope, of the "performative contradiction" that can sing "Hablemos el mismo idioma" (a universal theme in a particularist key) and risk liberal improvisation between the "apparent deaths" of the polity. Democracy works in unscored counterpoint. Precisely because citizens cannot presume to feel, or to think, or to perform alike, their ear for otherness makes justice possible.[13] That is why political philosophy and ethics, from Benjamin and Arendt to Bakhtin and Levinas, caution against empathy, which plays treacherously in a subject-centered key that overwhelms unfamiliar voices only to repeat the solitary sounds of the self.[14]

LOOK AND SEE

Literature, we are used to saying, is what exceeds or defies habitual patterns of communication, because it notices difference and requires continuous translations.[15] The unfamiliar is what students of literature are supposed to see and hear, ever since Russian formalism sensed the strangeness that distinguished literature from ordinary language, and especially since deconstruction blurred the distinction. Then we noticed that ordinary speech, and even philosophical reasoning, are surprisingly unstable. Perhaps our training to sense textual differences, either as strangely literary or as characteristic of language in general, can be made sensitive to textual markers of the political differences that keep democracy interesting and honest. To be less sensitive than the exercise requires is hardly to promote a liberal education.

Signs of democratizing difference and contingent translations are everywhere, unless we continue to ignore them. One that first stirred me was Rigoberta Menchú's peculiar insistence that she was keeping secrets in her 1983 testimony about Guatemala's war on Indians. Why proclaim silence instead of being quiet, I wondered, as if announcing secrets mattered more than keeping them? One result of this practice was that no amount of information she shared could establish a mood of intimacy or conspiracy with me as a reader. Maybe that was the point of her performance, I began to think: to engage me without surrendering herself. A formidable lesson.[16] It sent me back to recover certain omissions from literature and (self)ethnography, in areas that I began to recognize as purposefully unyielding and disturbing. Notice the absence of intimate details from slave narratives, Garcilaso's dizzying tour of Peru, Toni Morrison's refusal of confession in *Beloved,* the subject's rebuffs to the narrator in Elena Poniatowska's testimonial novel, the incompetence of white narrators who tell stories about black slaves (in *Cecilia*), even the cold shoulder that Richard Rodriguez turns to his Anglo allies. The list of examples that drew me back and brought me up short is almost arbitrary; I happened to have read them. Some of these examples, and others, are developed in this book, but anyone can think of different or overlapping lists.[17] The point is that signs of refusal to fit into a reader's agenda are transmitted, and we should stop to notice.

Anthropologists have, for some time now, been noticing and commenting on the gestures that informants use to draw observers in and to keep them at a distance.[18] Withholding information or supplying false leads are standard moves, whether or not ethnographers record them; others include reminders of the outside limits to information, and even requests for contributions to a community's welfare. For example, the Brazilian mothers interviewed by Nancy Scheper-Hughs about infant mortality for *Death without Weeping* (1991) obliged her to help build a hospital for them and their children.[19] Long ago, Zora Neale Hurston could have shown us how to anticipate informants' balancing acts, between polite defensiveness and demands for reciprocity. How telling that it has taken us so long to respond.

Attention to unanticipated gestures does not, though, always make a difference. Scholars can declare the best intentions to hear surprises, while their work neutralizes the shock value. Consider James Scott's well-received study of *Domination and the Arts of Resistance*.[20] "Hidden transcripts" of disgruntled subalterns stay behind the scenes for Scott. They let off steam but start no fires. A lead from literary criticism might have prepared him to expect disruptions of master narratives. Walter Benjamin had followed that lead to anticipate breaks in secular, predictable histories. It was Baudelaire's intuition of correspondences between eternal beauty and its modern guises that inspired Benjamin to expect irruptions of messianic presence that pierce through "empty and homogeneous" secular time. What most lulls us to ignore the irruptions, Benjamin complained, is the empathy of historians (like Scott) who posit an overall consistency in human experience.[21]

But the literary lead does have a legacy in postcolonial history. By contrast to unflappable historians of empire, Ranajit Guha shows that colonial stories are susceptible to disruptive readings. The masters' discourse that fixes the terms of "dependent" transcripts for Scott turns out, on Guha's reading, to be itself derivative and dictated by the speech of organized resistance. Instead of asking if subalterns can speak, Guha gives a (perhaps idealized) interpretation of the official transcript of colonial India to reconstruct the dynamic language of peasant insurgency.[22] If speech acts are interventions in the world, surely, he concludes, mass insurrections amount to a powerful kind of speech. Discourse is always a response. It can, and typically had been, argued that India's peasants responded to England's domination. But Guha chooses to focus on a more promising point in the endless dynamic of speech and response. Once the English came, it was the peasants who set the political agenda; the masters were obliged to answer with the paradoxically dependent "prose of counter-insurgency."[23]

Why is it that literary criticism can remain almost cold to the cues that it offers to self-critical anthropologists and to postcolonial historians?[24] Perhaps we too can take advantage of insights into contingent objectivity and into the sheer performativity of language. Literature participates, of course, in the levels of secrecy that characterize hegemonic societies. My rather obvious point is that those areas of secrecy make differences for readers and writers. Learning and teaching to read literature in ways that acknowledge difference can be the most basic training for the democratic imagination. Yet children usually learn one-sided approaches that ask them to identify with favorite characters, without also asking what interferes in the process. And critics continue to "collaborate" with authors, rather than to pause at their uncooperativeness. We get what we expect to get, as philosophies of representation remind us. But we can learn to expect more dissonance than our current practices allow. We can learn—if, that is, we admit unwieldy and even unrewarding data.

"Don't say: 'There *must* be something common, or they would not be called games'—but *look and see* whether there is anything common to all," Ludwig Wittgenstein counseled. "For if you look at them you will not see something that is common to *all,* but similarities, relationships, and a whole series of them at that. To repeat: don't think, but look!"[25] Wittgenstein seldom insisted so vehemently. He must have been worried that colleagues and students would continue to force patterned expectations on data, crushing the circumstantial use of words which is what matters most for meaning. Allow surprising evidence to speak, exhorted the man who was as alive to the unchartable variations that language games could play as he was impatient with philosophy's obstinate desire to find patterns and to fix meanings. Just as wrongheaded as reductive empiricism was the habit of misreading the world as multiple corruptions of ideal "concepts," an unfortunate term that suggests the superiority of abstract "simples" over an endlessly interesting range of circumstantial meanings.[26] Once we register the damage wreaked by propositional reductions, "We feel as if we had to repair a torn spider's web with our fingers."[27]

With this haunting image he repeats, again, the injunction to notice the delicate contingency of human meanings. This is an ethical warning; it is about doing damage, after all. In a different circumstantial variation, Emmanuel Levinas will repeat the injunction to respect Otherness, instead of presuming to incorporate it into a knowable self. But here I want to pause at Wittgenstein's worry about the vulnerability of meaning. Vulnerability is no excuse for condemning language as untrustworthy, or for scoffing at its efforts to make connections between thought and things. He was impatient with a radical skepticism that made excuses for not dealing responsibly in the world.[28] Observing the contingent use-value of meaning "is not to say that we are in doubt because it is possible for us to *imagine* a doubt."[29]

This antifoundationalist position doesn't need to forfeit purpose. Goals and values, and also culturally particularist postures, can be useful, as Wittgenstein would remind us. Perhaps we might consider them to be not grounds for meaning but a heuristic, a device for thinking, a philosophical fiction that enables a worthwhile game.[30] Aristotle had defended rhetoric in general for just this heuristic capacity; the language games that Plato (along with the idealists who followed him) reviled could, his best disciple countered, be devices for pursuing truth and ethical behavior. Without imaginative devices, how can one think of political progress?[31]

Idealism and essentialism have often behaved pragmatically, rhetorically, as persuasion and intervention, Stanley Fish observes. So he reads Catharine MacKinnon's insistence that pornography is rape as an effective performance, rather than as the essentialist argument she alleges. It seems therefore hasty and impractical for him to dismiss as "untrue," for example, the "theological" utopianism he finds in Roberto Unger's Critical Legal Studies. Utterances, as Fish knows from Austin and Wittgenstein, are not merely to be judged as true or false; they are acts and invite effects. Why, then, does he demand a truth value of political performance? If MacKinnon actually did agree that her stance were a productive fiction, as Fish says she should, her performance might fall flat. And why dismiss Unger's enabling ideals, as if they lacked the rhetorical efficacy allowed to MacKinnon's performance? Are women persuasive even when they are not reasonable, whereas men are not?

Language games can fail because of our underdeveloped skills for hearing differential meanings. This is Wittgenstein's scruple. Among the signs we miss, or dismiss as "false," are the particularist postures and accents that invite improvised engagements. When a writer makes a statement, the received significance may very well skip the intended meaning (a distinction that Iser adapts from Frege),[32] and the web meant to catch us may show nothing but a hole. It is obviously true that we read from within what Fish calls "interpretive communities" to make culturally conditioned sense of what we read. But the boundedness is flexible and permeable to competing codes of interpretation, Fish assures us, so that solipsism as a personal or even a communal redundancy is a false demon. Therefore, he counsels "not to worry."[33] The advice is sound if we allow codes to compete with each other and alert literary critics to delicate webs of language. But given what interpretive communities are (where MacKinnon may be instructed but Unger eliminated), and given the damage we can do by forcing what Lyotard calls ethically sacred difference into our communitarian paradigms,[34] I think that Wittgenstein's is the sounder advice here. Worry.[35]

SEEK AND HIDE

Some books make worry a reading requirement. If we care to notice, they would raise doubts about our competence, intentionally. Intentionality is no longer the scandal it used to be when New Criticism dismissed it as irrelevant, and deconstruction showed it going astray. Toni Morrison underlines the deliberateness of lacunae in African American writing. And Stanley Cavell remembers that even formalists (starting with Kant) saw "purposiveness" in art. "What counts is what is *there,* says the philosopher who distrusts appeals to intention. Yes, but everything that is there is something a man has *done.*"[36]

By marking off an impassable distance between reader and text, and thereby raising questions of access or welcome, resistant authors intend to produce constraints that more reading will not overcome. I am not referring to the inexhaustible ambiguity of literature. Ambiguity has long been a consecrated and flattering theme for professional readers. It blunts interpretive efforts to invite more labor, allowing us to offset frustrated mastery with a liberating license to continue endlessly. Nor do I mean resistance as the kind of diegetically empty, "clogged," or even bored refusal to narrate that Flaubert apparently pioneered when he would stop a story to contemplate some digressive detail.[37]

The issue is neither undecidability nor novel pauses to titillate "reader-flaneurs."[38] It is the rhetoric of selective, socially differentiated understanding. Announcing limited access is the point, whether or not some information is really withheld. Rebuffs may not signal a genuine epistemological impasse; it is enough that the impasse is claimed in this ethico-aesthetic strategy to position the reader.[39] The question, finally, is not what "insiders" can know as opposed to "outsiders"; it is how those positions are being constructed as incommensurate or conflictive. Even readers who share enough social space with a writer to claim privileged understanding may too hastily fill in the gaps these texts would demarcate.[40]

The habitually overlooked markings could direct readers toward a productive "incompetence" that admits areas of unavailability.[41] Incompetence here is not the kind lamented by Alan Bloom and others as a failure of education, but a paradoxical goal; it is to acknowledge the socially circumscribed limits of interpretation, the distances and the refusals that some texts have been broadcasting to our deaf ears.[42] Is there a reading lesson that enjoins limitation? It sounds so unfamiliar in current literary criticism, which doesn't pause but approaches, explores, interprets, freely associates, understands, empathizes, assimilates. Rigoberta Menchú stops the approach with her secrets. Richard Rodriguez frustrates it when he gives deliberately empty English information.[43] And Toni Morrison holds back readers who demand to know a story but will not witness it.

This kind of obstinacy to interpretation discriminates between the authorial community (which will not read Menchú, is avoided by Rodriguez, and has no monopoly on Morrison) and the authorial audience of perhaps predominantly curious outsiders. It targets those who would read in the presumptuous register of "If I were a . . . ," and forget how positionality affects knowledge.[44] Asking about the place from which one speaks, the locus of enunciation, is a question sometimes put to narrators and characters, but hardly ever to readers. The asymmetry of positions restricts a reader's travel from one place to the other, despite the fantasies of mutuality that imagine efforts to understand an ethnically inflected text compensate for a writer's burden to perform in an imperial language.[45] "Ideal" or target readers for particularist texts are, then, hardly the writer's co-conspirators or allies in a shared culture, as we have presumed in our critical vocabulary.[46] They are marked as strangers, either incapable of or undesirable for intimacy. Discrimination here admits that social differences exist in social positionality, and that different degrees of understanding are consequences, or safety requirements.[47] From the demarcated positions on a chart where only the powerful center can mistake its specificity for universality, these "marginal" or "minority" texts draw boundaries around that arrogant space. Instead of pandering to "competent" readers with guided tours, the texts, in a "Cordelia effect" (like Bartleby's too), cripple authority by refusing to submit to it.[48] Mario Vargas Llosa's fictional informant turns away; Elena Poniatowska's heroine bores her readers to distraction; Julio Cortázar's black musician contradicts his meticulous biographer, just to keep him nervous. Even assimilationists (Garcilaso and Rodriguez) play this game; they flaunt their "exoticism" to become the center's unconquerable object of desire. All of these writers place traditionally privileged readers beyond a border. From there readers can be "ideal," paradoxically, because they are excluded.

Readers have felt excluded before, in esoteric traditions, for example, or dadaist affronts, or in the elitism that made the other (Spanish) Garcilaso and his baroque followers so intriguingly hard to get. And recent skepticism about meaning in language may promote games of interpretive hide-and-seek as writerly reticence goads readerly suspicion. But unlike elitist and esoteric restrictions, which give way to readers in the know, no initiation is possible into a resistant text. Impossible, when one target audience is constructed as outsider and another is complicitous in the exclusion. Esoteric writing may set controls that amount to demands for dedication; and skeptical subterfuges of meaning may inscribe endless detours for modernist literature. But particularist texts draw a different map of restrictions. Rather than a labyrinth or a prison-house of language, it is a walled city that announces no trespassing. Readers can enter only if they accept unfamiliar invitations that reach out in order to keep us at arm's length.

CANNIBALISM IN THE CLASSROOM

Competent readers are unaccustomed to rebuffs, so unaccustomed and ill-prepared that slights go unnoticed.[49] Years of training in literary traditions understandably add up to a kind of entitlement to know a book, possibly with the possessive and reproductive intimacy of Adam who knew Eve. As teachers and students we have until now welcomed resistance as coy, teasing, a summons to test and to hone our competence. We may pick up a book because we find it attractive, or because mimetic desire kindles a murderous urge to displace a model reader. Always, we assume in our enlightened secular habits that the books are happy to have our attention, like wallflowers lined up for a quick turn or an intimate *tête-à-tête*. If the book seems easy, if it allows possession without a struggle and cancels the promise of flattery for an expert reading, our hands may go limp at the covers. Easy come, easy go.

The more difficult the book the better. Difficulty is a challenge, an opportunity to struggle and to win, to overcome resistance, uncover the codes, to get on top of it, to put one's finger on the mechanisms that produce pleasure and pain, and then to call it ours. We take up an unyielding book to conquer it and to feel enriched by the appropriation and confident that our cunning is equal to the textual tease that had, after all, planned its own capitulation. Books want to be understood, don't they, even when they are coy and evasive? Isn't part of the game to notice that coyness is a cover-up for practically nothing, a distancing effect that stimulates our desire? Evasiveness and ambiguity are familiar interpretive flags that readers erect on the books they leave behind. Feeling grand and guiltless, we proceed to the next conquest.

"I am only interested in what does not belong to me. Law of Man. Law of the Cannibal," is the gluttonous way Oswald de Andrade put it. Appropriation of the other is what our New World cultures feed on, says the Brazilian modernist, so long as the other offers the spice of struggle, because cannibals reject bland and boring meat.[50] In his digestion of Montaigne's essay, Andrade suggests that Europe too is constituted by ingesting its others. Walter Benjamin also comments on the literary cannibalism at home. "The reader of a novel seizes upon his material more jealously than anyone else. He is ready to make it completely his own, to devour it."[51] "Eating the Other" is also bell hooks's description for white appropriations of minority cultures.[52] Infinitely expanding Walt Whitman didn't mince words: "All this I swallow . . . and it becomes mine, . . ."[53] Andrade's point is, after all, that devouring alterity is what makes us modern (or just human, for Freud), as we participate in an Occidental culture nourished on novelty. Therefore, provocations by Whitman and Andrade and the queasiness of Benjamin and bell Hooks can stand in for other, more contrite, admissions of plunder.

But how contrite is Roland Barthes's self-consciousness, in *Pleasure of the Text*? It pushes reader-response theory to its eroticized limits, to an orgasmic release from the very text that gave him pleasure. Here, the Benjaminian "aura" of art, capable of reciprocating an admirer's gaze, passes over to the viewer and stays to enhance only him.[54] "The text is a fetish object, and *this fetish desires me*."[55] Dependent and eager to please, the text "must prove to me *that it desires me.*" As reader and object of desire, the solicited partner for an intimate entanglement, Barthes performs tirelessly in his extended essay to reciprocate. The result is a book composed of flirtatiously neurotic intermittence, deliciously anticipated but unpredictably syncopated interventions at gaps in the body of conventional criticism. Barthes might have taken advantage of his own point about the neurotic rhythm of desire to notice and to name the ways a text's desire for the reader is punctuated by apparent deaths of intimacy. But he hardly noticed this, probably because he was flirting with Flaubert and Sade instead of exposing himself to particularists. Abrasions that heighten pleasure are, for him, an effect of reading, not the result of a text's abrasiveness.[56] In any case, Barthes's unabashed hedonism sounds scandalous against the drone of academic theories; and it rubs dangerously against the sensitive skin of correct comportment in today's American academy. Is it really foreign though, to more common strains of reader-response theory that flatter readers as objects of textual desire, as partners, collaborators, coauthors?

For critics as different from one another as Georges Poulet is from Wolfgang Iser, the focus has been on the readers' agency. Whether agency is understood as interiorizing (not to say cannibalizing) the text in Poulet's version,[57] or as talking back to set the text into dialogic motion in Iser's classic studies,[58] readers are necessary and equal partners in the shared pleasures of aesthetic production. Poulet claims passively to "accede" to a text,[59] but only after initiating his own surrender to the helplessly dependent objects that crave his attention:

> Books are objects. On a table, on shelves, in store windows, they wait for someone to come and deliver them from their materiality, from their immobility. When I see them on display, I look at them as I would at animals for sale, kept in little cages, and so obviously hoping for a buyer. For—there is no doubting it—animals do know that their fate depends on a human intervention . . . Isn't the same true of books? . . . They wait. Are they aware that an act of man might suddenly transform their existence? They appear to be lit up with that hope. Read me, they seem to say. I find it hard to resist their appeal.[60]

Book shops cum pet stores make a flimsy cover-up of love for sale.[61] Once the reader-prince commands a performance and succumbs to his own sensitivity, the rest of his essay follows the rhythm of reciprocal possession. The first move is to purchase a partner and to feel thereby chosen by the book; the next is to appreciate its "offering, opening itself . . . It asks nothing better than to exist outside itself, or to let you exist in it. In short, the extraordinary fact in the case of a book is the falling away of the barriers between you and it. You are inside it; it is inside you."[62] As the entanglement proceeds, Poulet manages some distance, taking a breath for reflection on a breathless activity. ("On the other hand—and without contradiction—reading implies something resembling the apperception I have of myself . . . Whatever sort of alienation I may endure, reading does not interrupt my activity as subject.") But the repeatable rhythm of contact and consummation concludes by celebrating abandon to the writer who "reveals himself to us *in* us." Celebration is in order because, far from diminishing the reader as ventriloquist or vehicle, abandon returns him to princely primacy. "The work lives its own life within me; in a certain sense, it thinks itself, and it even gives itself a meaning within me" a meaning that finally does not belong to a particular work. It is a haunting "transcendence" that is perceptible when criticism can "annihilate, or at least momentarily forget, the objective elements of the work, and to elevate itself to the apprehension of a subjectivity without objectivity."[63]

Poulet's immodest dance with the death-of-author idea suggests one limit of reader-response criticism, where self-centered ludicism overcomes the specificity of texts.[64] Another site of trouble is the underdeveloped place where reader response meets political imperatives. The trouble brewing here comes from the inordinate difficulty that educated readers have in recognizing themselves as textual targets.

A case of missing the aggressive point is Ross Chambers' *Room for Maneuver: Reading Oppositional Narrative*. It begins with an admirably ethical inspiration for "Changing the World." Chambers wants to open a space beyond the action-reaction dynamic, a Foucaultian spiral of power and dissent that changes nothing. To pry open the dyad and achieve real resistance, Chambers employs a fulcrum or a third term between the narrator and narratee. It is the reader, a neatly dialectical solution to unproductive tensions. Readers, as indirect objects of discourse, are available for the kind of sentimental re-education that could amount to a political change of heart.[65] The question raised by this bloodless *Aufhebung* is whether getting away unscathed leaves one's retrograde desires in place.[66] For example, despite Chambers's intentions to redirect desire, his self-appointed role as coauthor-collaborator remains unchallenged. And the possibility of sustained hostility toward the reader vanishes in the dialectical magic of helping hands. Not that Chambers ignores the initial tension, but that he decides too quickly that it is a dead end, that readers are capable of self-criticism while they occupy an (ad)vantage point above the fray.[67]

We have almost lost a truly humbling tradition of theological readings that Stanley Fish, among many others, used to practice. *Surprised by Sin* may anticipate his later reader-response approach, but it certainly links back to Christian hermeneutics. The book locates the reader in Milton's *Paradise Lost,* but not to illustrate coauthorship or complicity, nor to perform the eroticized *pas de deux* that erases the text for Poulet, nor to request readers' arbitration (as in Chambers.) Milton sets traps for his readers; he cajoles them into thinking they can understand something of God's divine pattern, and then dashes their presumption. Christians should know that God is unknowable, and the text plays on our stubborn expectation of enlightenment to counter it abruptly, aggressively, repeatedly. "Milton consciously wants to worry the reader, to force him to doubt the correctness of his responses, and to bring him to the realization that his inability to read the poem with any confidence in his own perception is its focus . . . Milton's programme of reader harassment begins in the opening lines . . . without Milton's *snubs* we could not be jolted out of a perspective that is after all *ours.*"[68]

Down-to-earth versions of this harassment are what particularist texts offer to readers who can make an intentional difference in this world. The messiness of asymmetrical histories and the responsibilities they imply are the lessons here, not the metaphysical mysteries of a predestined world and an otherwordly Maker. Anxiety about wordly, racially marked otherness motivates writers like Cirilo Villaverde, Julio Cortázar, and Mario Vargas Llosa, who bear a hemispheric resemblance to Melville, Twain, Poe, and Cather.[69] All these writers play on the expectations of enlightened modern readers, for whom the amount of energy expended should predict the level of mastery gained. But labor theories of readerly value will miss the specific use value of these books. What Milton's poem denounces is the reader's presumption that (self-) improvement is possible. And the particular lives of black and Indian protagonists also shun the unsolicited labor of their white narrators and readers. Like Milton, other self-conscious authors insist repeatedly that we miss the point by striving after it so confidently.

I am saying that refusal need not be entirely coy, not simply a spur to desire. It is also a barricade against the rush of sentimental identification that lasts barely as long as the read. Refusal insures an indigestible residue from voracious mastery.[70] To the extent that particularist writing is provocative, it is calculated to produce the desire that will then be frustrated. A challenge for Palancares or Rodriguez, Menchú or Morrison, is how to be interesting without promising the dividends of ownership. They wish to produce enough desire for refusal to smart, because the objective here is to engage unfamiliar, perhaps unfriendly readers, not to be ignored by them. And through a convenient metalepsis that readers of René Girard's work may notice,[71] refusal itself can produce desire. Some books claim authority, if only to deauthorize others. Before they can refuse attention, they have to elicit it. And they do so by a slight to our vanity as competent critics. Irritated by the snub by an illiterate Guatemalan Indian or a Mexican washwoman, coming face to face with the reserve of the Black novelist or a Chicano conservative, we may wonder what kind of superiority in the Other accounts for our interpretive demotion.

Their tactic is neither to chastise our egotism nor to implore our ethical self-effacement, as Emmanuel Levinas does. His dismissal of history in favor of ethics cannot attend to the historically embedded demands the particularist writers make. Yet they do not plead for recognition by creating individual subjectivities associated with empowered men, the way some feminists have done. A limiting or boomerang-effect of both the self-effacing and the self-affirming gestures is that they reinscribe privilege for readers who choose to be moral or welcoming. The writers I read here exhibit no abjection nor essential superiority. Instead, they assume that they are in control of their subject and that access to it is limited. With telling asides about the reader's difference from the narrator, with truncated allusions and purposeful incomprehensibility, their texts refuse to flow. The readings they permit, between stop signs and warnings against trespassing, can teach critics a self-doubting step too lame for conquest.

A RHETORIC FOR RECOGNITION

Learning to read these reticent texts will require noticing signs that make a political as well as an aesthetic difference. As scandalously unexpected as Flaubert's narrative sidetracks, the refusals of familiarity should produce the kind of gaps between text and reader that Gérard Genette describes as literary figures, if we recognize them.[72] Wittgenstein made the general point that signposts mean something "only in so far as there exists a regular use of signposts, a custom."[73] And Thomas Kuhn showed that perception depends on existing paradigms.[74] Failing to notice the signs means that our vocabulary of conventions continues to lag behind literary production, and readers override the restrictions they have never been taught to respect. The tautological result has been that signs of resistance remain obscure and unexpected, as unremarked and invisible to readers as ethnicity and gender might be for conservative politics. Anticipating resistance is part of the remedy.[75]

Sometimes the tropes will be easy to read, such as the epistemological limitation, declared silence, and denied intimacy already mentioned. But recognition of polite evasiveness or defensive distractions will take both practice and the sensitivity that comes with expectation. Zora Neale Hurston gave this lesson to would-be collectors of African American folklore, and very possibly to readers of African American literature as well.

> They are most reluctant at times to reveal that which the soul lives by. And the Negro, in spite of his open-faced laughter, his seeming acquiescence, is particularly evasive. You see, we are a polite people and we do not say to our questioner, "Get out of here!" We smile and tell him or her something that satisfies the white person because, knowing so little about us, he doesn't know what he is missing. The Indian resists curiosity by a stony silence. The Negro offers a feather-bed resistance. That is, we let the probe enter, but it never comes out. It gets smothered under a lot of laughter and pleasantries.
>
> The theory behind our tactics: "The white man is always trying to know into somebody else's business. All right. I'll set something outside the door of my mind for him to play with and handle. He can read my writing but he sho' can't read my mind. I'll put this play toy in his hand, and he will seize it and go away. Then I'll say my say and sing my song."[76]

These moves may sound like defense mechanisms, and the label is apt because the military metaphor suggests tactics for coping in a hostile world: "calls for delay, strategic retreat, regrouping of forces, abandoning of untenable positions, seeking fresh intelligence, and deploying new weapons."[77] Is Hurston suggesting that defensive tropes work *because* they are unperceived and do not provoke an insistence to trespass? Yet she calls attention to the tactics, saying, in effect, that whites can never know blacks except through (her) mediations.[78] Is her self-defense simply self-promotion as a black informant? Is it a friendly caution against useless prying? Or is it a characteristically polite hint that the "knowledge" of whites in dealing with blacks is hopelessly naive? If she tells us we cannot know while she tells us how we might go about it ("hitting a straight lick with a crooked stick"),[79] readers should notice the double move to engage and to deflect outsiders. And if reliable knowledge cannot be gotten, control is impossible.

"Outsider," it will be objected, is not a fixed or impermeable category. The claim of an insider's authenticity is always suspect, as Henry Louis Gates, Jr. argues in his "Lesson of Little Tree," about the book that passed for a Native American autobiography and turned out to be a white man's fiction. The revelation was a scandal. It outraged a public that had assumed it was reading the real thing. The lesson of passing, Gates concludes, is that "No human culture is inaccessible to someone who makes the effort to understand, to learn, to inhabit another world."[80] This availability makes some minority critics angry, because ethnic cultural content is eaten up by white consumers who are careless of the people they cannibalize.[81] But particularist texts are different from displays of cultural content that can be consumed. Particularism offers opacity, not to watch it evaporate or to congeal in shows of transparent authenticity, but to mark difference. It plays "signifying" games of double consciousness that deal uneven hands to monocultural readers. In *The Signifying Monkey,* Gates described the game of doubling discourses, drawing a boundary between black virtuosity and white monolingualism that keeps white readers safely on one side, so limited that they miss the point of missing.[82] Mexican-American doubling also draws circles around narrow readers, as in Gloria Anzaldúa's deft performance. Boundaries enable her virtuosity, though she complains that they cut a community until it hemorrhages.[83]

Frederick Douglass, for one, knew that outside and inside were not fixed positions and that different views of slavery came from unequal experiences, not from essential differences. The free human being, black or white, "cannot see things in the same light with the slave, because he does not, and cannot, look from the same point from which the slave does."[84] Douglass also noted that he could hardly have commented on that experience were he not already outside it. Likewise, Hurston knew that coming home to Eatonville with a "spy-glass of Anthropology" made her a bit exotic there.[85] And certainly Menchú suffers the irony of betraying norms of her community in order to preserve it, becoming an "outsider" in order to stay inside.

Remembering Douglass here suggests that responsible incompetence and degrees of readerly underachievement may teach us to remark the resistant signs of an older tradition of African American literature that knew how to distance its "ideal" abolitionist readers. Writing often at the unrefusable request of white allies and supporters, slave narrators could not afford to appear uncooperative. Yet many readers will recall how Harriet Jacobs interrupted her intimate confessions of *Incidents in the Life of a Slave Girl* (1861) to stop at the color line. You "whose purity has been sheltered from childhood, who have been free to choose the objects of your affection, whose homes are protected by law, do not judge the poor desolate slave girl too severely!"[86] And readers may find it significant that Cuba's Juan Francisco Manzano changed his mind about what to write for abolitionist Domingo del Monte. The slave had agreed to record his memoirs for the man whose support could mean freedom for the author, but a second letter explained that candor about certain incidents would be impossible.[87] Was Manzano perhaps chastening the liberal white reader who presumed to understand a slave's pain?[88] The general point Douglass made about noticing the position from which one speaks will surely evoke more refusals, if we learn to recognize them.

To notice the unstable boundaries between the self who writes and the other who reads is not to vitiate the opposition. It is to repeat what any military strategist knows: the lines of battle change while the conflict continues. Subject positions, we know, are not fixed through time. But in the war of positions that reading so often is, historically specific circumstances matter.[89] If we are used to assuming the virtues of overstepping the frontier between self and other, or to confusing deconstruction with assimilation, we may need to consider the differential effects of liberal and universalist principles when the Other is magnanimously absorbed into the greater Self.[90] The condescending generosity, for example, in Tzvetan Todorov's *The Conquest of America,* provokes conflicting responses. Universalists are guilt-ridden about the Aztecs who were unequal to the more advanced Spaniards; and particularists are angry at the invidious comparison that laments the disaster by explaining its inevitability. Like Mexico's first Jesuit chroniclers and catechists, Todorov assumes that the catholic or universal Self already inhabits the particularist pagan Other, and that history is a process of necessary accommodations.[91] In *The Morals of History,* he argues the same point more carefully. Clearing away the relativism identified with Montaigne, because relativism leads to solipsism ("I say others the better to say myself"), Todorov favors Montesquieu, who held on to universal values that he tried to coordinate with particular cultural norms. Sometimes they fit badly. Respect for Aztec and Incan cultures, Todorov glosses, made Montesquieu predict their doom. The only thing that could have saved them was what they could not possibly have had: European rational philosophy. "If a Descartes had come to Mexico . . ."[92]

It may surprise some well-meaning readers to find that particularists do not imagine their cultures to be static, nor do they welcome offers of "universal" Reason and assimilation. The ecumenical gestures to reduce otherness to sameness suggests that difference is a superable problem, rather than a source of pride or simply the way we are in the world.[93] A liberal embrace that squeezes out difference, to make partners equal insofar as they are the same, is a gesture that Walt Whitman helped to confuse with democratic process (see Chapter 2). Some writers resist this embrace and similar gestures that would clone citizens from one ideal type.

Difference works in "strategically essentialist" poses more often than in the intransigent postures associated with "differences criticism."[94] But even "intransigence," as I said, can be read as performance. If the essences were really stable, they might be unstrategically available for appropriation or dismissal (as in "Little Tree"). Interchangeability can be commonplace and ironic. This is the point that Werner Sollors brilliantly exposes for the United States, where ethnic difference is claimed for cultural "particulars" that repeat from one group to the next, more like bridges than boundaries.[95] My point, however, is that boundary tropes do not vanish with the irony of overlapping contents. They continue to distance readers simply by claiming to do so, as Mary Waters concludes.[96] The tropes show family resemblances to what Greeks called *metis*, "an aesthetics of the ruse that allows the weak to survive by escaping through duplicitous means the very system of power intent on destroying them."[97] Puerto Ricans call the art *jaibería*. It is the knack for avoiding fixed and dangerously head-on positions, advancing sideways like the weak but wise crab *(jaiba)*.[98] A subtle intransigence, it undercuts control by acceding to one position and then to another. Refusing to stay in a fixed place can be confusing to interlocutors, who then become anxious and more controlling. But the gain is some space and time to maneuver. These texts will not be caught by a possessive intimacy that wants to pass for love. Real love, Levinas says, "is a relationship with what forever slips away,"[99] because love needs what Winnicott simply called the external body.[100]

I remember that Edward Said interrupted a question about the possibilities for a more intimate appreciation of the East, for curing the blindness he denounced in *Orientalism* and taking in the real thing. "How should we achieve a better understanding of the Arab world," the sincere colleague was asking. "How can we avoid the mistakes, get closer to knowing, and . . ." Said interrupted to ask why Westerners suppose that the "Orient" wants to be understood. Why did we assume that our passion was reciprocated? Did we imagine that the desire was mutual, or that we were irresistible? Could we consider the possibility that our interest would not be satisfied? I think his provocation was intended to put a brake on the dangerous spiral of knowledge and power decried in *Orientalism*. Knowing the Other, in the empirical sense of the colleague's question, had been the target of his critique. Perhaps getting close entails respect from afar, and relationship needs the limits that keep two from collapsing into one. Evidently, the reader who wants to know more and better did not get the point.

To ask if the subaltern can speak, as Gayatri Spivak had asked, misses a related point. The pertinent question is whether the other party can listen.[101] Privilege gets in the way of hearing even a direct address. ("They just don't listen well," minority educators complain about their white colleagues.)[102] Spivak denounced Foucault and Deleuze for simplifying subaltern subjectivity in order to speak for it, yet she concluded, as simply, that "The subaltern cannot speak." Only the privileged classes can; for the insurgents' acts exceed language.[103] A disappointing deduction, to be sure. Language seems so heavy with established meaning, so securely in elite control, that others cannot affect the master code, as James Scott argued. But Spivak changed her mind after reading Ranajit Guha more seriously.[104]

Subalterns write creative literature as well as active history. My own expectation of challenges to elite language came from reading texts that send presumptuous readers on discursive tangents away from the self-criticism that can move in a vicious circle around readers at the center. The tangents lead to places that some readers have not visited. But before considering the general or theoretical questions that resistance raises for literary interpretation, our habitual resistance to resistance is worth considering from another perspective: that of feminism.

FEMINISM, IRRESPECTIVE OF DIFFERENCE

During decades of campaigns for self-empowerment, feminists have demanded that women and their books "break the silence." The enlightened assumption was that the truth will set us free, that we can achieve a "feminist dream of a common language"[105] *(el mismo idioma)*. Silence is not simply a prison in this asymmetrical world. Sometimes it is a tactic. Long ago, Sor Juana Inés de la Cruz vowed obedience when the Church demanded her silence, then she explained it all at great length in a published letter.[106] Her ingenious baroque insubordination is matched by Rigoberta's public secrecy, which turns an informant into a leader. Those who can learn to listen will hear creative refusals to talk.

To listen, we will have to resist the reflex that Adrienne Rich, among many others, celebrated in her classic and cumulative statement of 1975: "[W]e are breaking silences long established, 'liberating ourselves from our secrets' . . . How do we make it possible for another to break her silence?"[107] By this point of women's movements (and of this introduction) readers should doubt whether all women are equally served by candid disclosures. This goes against the grain of white feminists who cringe at hierarchies and prefer to blur the lines.[108] Consider philosopher Drucilla Cornell. She urges women—all women—to overcome apparent social limits. Limits are merely disabling fictions, she claims on the authority of Wittgenstein. And she coyly uses Lacan's rather empty concept of "the feminine" to imagine endless meanings for woman. Liberties have been taken with Wittgenstein too, in Cornell's slide from one discourse to another. He distrusted psychoanalysis and any style of thought that distinguished between deep and surface phenomena, between ideal and real, sublime and secular.[109] Meaning, he insisted, was the particular use that words have inside limited circumstances. So Wittgenstein would hardly have authorized Cornell's disregard for limits. Boundaries are flexible and rules change constantly, but they are, literally, the enabling circum-stances of meaning.[110]

Wishful overreading of Lacan and Wittgenstein fuels Cornell's empathy for other women.[111] Limitlessly, she hopes for "mimetic identifications [as] a rhetorical and artistic device for both the engagement with and the displacement of the boundaries that have limited our imagination."[112] The trouble is that metaphoric identification is a murderous trope that reduces two to one. Paul de Man noticed this danger and named autobiography the strong case of metaphoric substitution, as readers take the place of writers[113] in the disappearing act of linguistic fungibility.[114] Rigoberta Menchú shored up the boundaries that Cornell would demolish to offer a metonymic association in place of a metaphoric overlap.[115] Metonymy is a figure for coalitions, imaginative enough to see commonality yet modest enough to respect differences. Cornell's imagination wants more, an empathetic, ethical, "Levinasian" impulse that leaves aggression behind as barriers fall away. But empathy is the egocentric energy that drives one subject to impersonate another, the calamitous dismissal of politics by feeling.[116] And in this interpretation Levinas has been evacuated too, along with the sacred difference of the Other that his work tirelessly defends. Cornell's expansive subject is precisely the target of his critique.

For another glaring example of violation by sentimentality, consider the editors of *Autobiographical Essays by Native American Writers,* who insisted that their contributors reveal and publish intimate information: "While our presentation of autobiographies of contemporary Native American writers may seem to testify to the congeniality of the autobiographical form to Indians today, the reality is finally much more complex. Thus, a contributor . . . movingly wrote in a covering letter: 'You should realize that focusing so intently on oneself like that and blithering on about your own life and thoughts is very bad form for Indians.'" In response to her reticence, the editors proudly report that they persisted and prevailed.[117] The example recalls African American women who increasingly bring their experience more plainly into focus. Barbara Smith explains that part of the process is calling attention to the pain and the personal costs of telling.[118]

Some texts refuse to repay irresponsible curiosity. They know better. Silence can be a tactical civility or a willed repression of a trauma narrative, a defense against humiliating or panic provoking memories. "Silent, except for social courtesies, when they met one another," Morrison writes of displaced blacks; "they neither described nor asked about the sorrow that drove them from one place to another."[119] The unspoken agreement to force forgetting into collective therapy, the common acknowledgment that memories of degradation may trap rather than free us, these recall passages of Holocaust literature,[120] for example, Eleonora Lev's "Don't Take Your Daughter to the Extermination Camp":

> The thing I always try to keep secret from her—out of shame, out of fear of hurting—is the rabid dog, the drooling, worm-infested beast, eyes inflamed, who races about madly in a corner of my mind . . . What do you do when you visit a gas chamber, what do you do? . . . For years you've been imagining, haven't you, that studying the technical details would help you understand, digest it, lance the inner abscess which fills with pus each time anew. Why did you imagine that?[121]

UNLEARNING MASTERY

Lev's rhetorical question undoes her enlightened faith in knowledge. Sometimes learning requires unlearning, and that is not easy. Critics on several fronts still hail the conquest of knowledge. One front is a tradition known broadly as hermeneutics. Its strategies perform something like a clean-up campaign after confrontation with texts. Hermeneutics has typically advocated an empathetic quest to identify with a work, as if displacing the author were the same as being in his or her place.[122] The reflexive variety, associated with Hans Georg Gadamer, does acknowledge the interpreter's prejudice as the starting point for interpretation, the ground from which we move toward the otherness of a text. But philosophical hermeneutics calls the approach and encounter by gentle names, such as dialogue or fusing of horizons. Gadamer does not often worry about what is burned away when we fuse the "alien [into] our own."[123]

> [A]ll human orientation to the world is an effort to conform "the *ato-pon*" (the strange), that which does not 'fit' into the customary order of our expectation based on experience. Hermeneutics has only called our attention to this phenomenon. Just as when we progress in understanding the *mirabilia* lose their strangeness, so every successful appropriation of tradition is dissolved into a new and distinct familiarity in which it belongs to us and we to it.[124]

Readers of particularist texts should fret about the loss of strangeness and difference. We may worry enough to offer a version of hermeneutics that locates what we *cannot* know, in both epistemological and ethical senses. It seems that only the epistemological meaning has been operative in other revisions of the hermeneutical project. But resistant texts erect ethical constraints.

To follow Gadamer one more step, though, we should note that his thinking agrees with structuralists like Gérard Genette, who argues that interpretation needs a recognizable and shared rhetorical system. The challenge for readers of "minority" literature is to develop that system to include tropes of multicultural communication that block sharing. Without rhetorical specificity, we will continue to overlook the intentional absences that are also points of entry, as Morrison called them. "Where, indeed [Gadamer asks], but to rhetoric should the theoretical examination of interpretation turn?" It is concrete and "'positive' as against the 'negative' of linguistic interpretation."[125] Genette's version makes structuralism the safeguard against (deconstructive) fragmentation.[126] And the best (most easily interpreted) deployment of rhetoric, reaching back to Aristotle and Plato, is achieved by speakers whose grasp of truths leads to unerring choices of persuasive figures, and whose profound knowledge of others' souls makes incursions possible.[127] From hermeneutics' reliance on rhetoric, and from rhetoric's reliance on the projected interpretation of listeners, Gadamer deduces their mutual interpenetration. "There would be no speaker and no art of speaking if understanding and consent were not in question, were not underlying elements; there would be no hermeneutical task if there were no mutual understanding that has been disturbed and that those in a conversation must search for and find again together."[128]

Disturbance presupposes an earlier calm, the way that the act of searching and finding presupposes equality and mutuality. In the classical tradition, Gadamer assumes that the purpose of rhetoric is to achieve familiarity, that rhetoric is always a bridge, and interpretation is always a positive, community-building practice. Why assume any of this? Are the differences between writer and reader only provisional obstacles? Can they be overcome through mutually legitimating conversation, as Jürgen Habermas believes? (Levinas will say that the essence of conversation is apology, where the subject asserts itself but inclines before the transcendent Other.)[129] Must rhetoric only build bridges, or can it also locate narrow contiguities? Dilthey's skepticism about the possibility of coherence returns like a repressed warning against coercive unity.[130] For him, the hermeneutical enterprise bowed to history and produced divergent worldviews, mutually incomprehensible and unbridgeable.[131]

My concern, therefore, is with facile conflations of understanding with identification between reader and text. Gadamer himself tries (with mixed success) to maintain a critical distance from the text, so that fusion of horizons remains an engagement with difference rather than its elimination.[132] In that spirit, my project to locate limited engagements fits into a broadly hermeneutical project. The focus on a rhetoric of particularism could disturb our underexamined hermeneutical habits, if we are able to acknowledge certain perverse tropes that resist melting. Rather than persuade readers to share judgments and interests, the recalcitrant figures draw the limits of sharing.

This is the moment to recall the public promise of contingent, debate-driven universality.[133] Some skeptics dismiss any use for universality, even as an enabling fiction. Lyotard, for example, considers it a *normative* language and proposes that we unlearn it. He despairs of the justice based on universal principles, because decisions often boil down to favoring one litigant and harming the other. The process is unequal to the "differend," when no single rule applies equally to the opponents.[134] Lyotard's guidance beyond postmodern "aimlessness" (through Wittgenstein's flexibility into Levinas's sense of obligation, to arrive at Kant's respect for Judgement [#197] takes politics out of the neat Hegelian line of history where any event will seem predictable. In fact he accompanies Levinas beyond narrative altogether, as if stories always pointed to final solutions. But Lyotard's postmodern defense of particularist "phrase regimes" has a precedent in history, and Marianne Constable hopes to revive it. It is an old English example of *non-normative* "universalism," the proto-pragmatic "mixed jury."

In medieval England, from the Norman conquest to political consolidation, law developed as a polyglot practice without adding up to a common law. Medieval Saxons, Jews, Germans, Danes, and others were not obliged to "speak the same language" in any literal way, but were enjoined to deal fairly with one another in light of the "personal" law that modern law would soon override. Prudent listening for the "differend" was a medieval practice, long before it became Lyotard's postmodern hope. Its mechanism was the mixed jury, which combined local subjects and foreigners as members of the same tribunal in order to hear cases between litigants from different communities that could not be subject to one existing rule.[135] The mixed jury predates the contradiction between nation and republic that Lyotard locates at the inconsistent core of modern polities.[136] Constable suggests that American law, so mired in procedure by now, would do well to retrieve and adapt medieval respect for cultural specificity as a vehicle and safeguard for justice.

SOME BEG TO DIFFER

All books do not beg to be understood in the same way, just as all sentences cannot be read as either true or false. My point is not to rehearse religious or radically subjective critiques of the Enlightenment; in their separate ways, traditional objections to knowledge seem to emerge from the troubled relationship between human beings and Being, between the individual and an inexplicable cosmos.[137] At issue here is the differential, nonuniversal effect of understanding particular writers. It is the relationship of one human being to the other, in the spirit of Levinas's polemic against self-centered ontology. Ontology "reduces the other to the same, [and] promotes freedom—the freedom that is the identification of the same, not allowing itself to be alienated by the other."[138] If the notion of an author behind a text, a flesh-and-blood person to be reckoned with, seems naive for those of us who understand the evaporating effect of writing, we should hesitate before dismissing the ghost. Incorporeal and vulnerable precisely to our dismissive habits, authors nevertheless take positions which a responsible reading ought to respect. To locate position and difference is not to account for the difficulties of a text, or worse, to explain them away. It is to establish the kind of regard that interferes with assimilation.

Social differences by their nature are not entirely comprehensible. To imagine otherwise is to miss the lessons we have been teaching ourselves about some traps of (nonreconstructed) essentialism. If experience and positionality help to constitute the subject, how can readers presume fully to understand particular writers? Good-enough reading will fall short of fullness. Restrictions won't daunt us if we simply strive for traditional competence and remain content with our best efforts and partial successes. But who is to judge success? Is partial failure not to be reckoned? Without stopping at these questions, readers skip over differences in a collective culture of denial. Surely we have the responsibility to pursue understanding of others, and we are morally bound by that understanding, despite the hands-off recommendation of cultural relativists. But I am underlining the residues of pursuit. The will to understand can become willfulness or greed in the guise of an embrace. Desire for knowledge and power is a collusion that has occupied critical theory at least since Theodor Adorno's *Negative Dialectics*. The paradox of striving for complete understanding is that it misunderstands the particularity of its object. To understand is to establish identity; and this requires conceptualization that generalizes away otherness. Identifying, therefore, turns out to be a trap at two levels (as we saw in the case of Cornell): empathetic identification violates the other person; and ontological identification eliminates particularity for the sake of unity.[139] Long ago, and in worlds foreign to Adorno, people have known enough about self-defense to be discreet, laconic, oblique, or silent about their identity.

Unlike Adorno's skepticism about achieving knowledge in the downward spiral of history "after Auschwitz," and unlike Foucault's resignation to the complicity between knowledge and power,[140] Levinas's refusal to seek knowledge of the Other is meant to safeguard sociality. "Knowledge is always an adequation between thought and what it thinks," the self and the comprehensible world. It forces data into a good fit. But sociality is different; it means respecting an imperfect fit as a sign of alterity and an opportunity to escape loneliness.[141] For Levinas, existing relationships need not reproduce themselves endlessly. The totalizing desire to know can be tempered by a subject's stamina for infinity and otherness. And his work strains to locate "a non-allergic relation with alterity"[142] by validating the break-in that disturbs the ego's coherence.

In some important ways, Levinas's passionate voice makes a difference. He has been warning Western readers about the self-promoting solipsism of a philosophical tradition (including hermeneutics) that strives to overcome mystery with clarity. Ours is a culture that presumes to reduce the experience of Self and Other into a neat totality. If everything fits into the One, of which the ego is an expression, then the Other fits inside the self with no remainder, no loose, particular, or incompatible features. It is the promise of ultimate fit that drives traditional universalism forward. "This primacy of the same was Socrates's teaching: to receive nothing of the Other but what is in me, as though from all eternity I was in possession of what comes to me from the outside—to receive nothing, or to be free."[143] Levinas takes this hubris of philosophy as the target of an ambitious dismantling campaign that reaches back to a time before Plato neutralized and coopted the Other, in order to recognize him as inaccessible alterity, mystery, divinity.

This profound lesson resonated with my reading of some Latin American books. They had prepared me to read Levinasian sentences like these: "If the other could be possessed, seized, and known, it would not be the other. To possess, to know, to grasp are all synonyms of power."[144] "The void that breaks the totality can be maintained against an inevitably totalizing and synoptic thought only if thought finds itself *faced* with an other refractory to categories."[145] But were I to conjecture a reversal of encounters, I doubt that reading Levinas first could have predicted the engagements of particularist texts.

Levinas professes humility to an absolute Other, not to a particular strategist. Renouncing history in favor of ethics, as if obligation were simply imposed by the Other's existence, Levinas leaves no room for a process of moral perfectibility, for learning by stages from the Other.[146] He exhorts us to venerate the mystery of a face that we see and that sees us, not to respond to particularly situated and messy human demands. Therefore his message can go astray. In Levinas's sustained performance of the subject he strains to dislodge, the appeal goes from and toward the subject, who should have been diminished by confronting absolute Otherness.[147] There seems no point outside the tradition from which to launch a critique against it. Archimedes cannot move the world since he cannot stand outside of it. And Levinas remains in his own world, I worry, because he doesn't consider specific language games that keep distances and avoid identification. Instead, he stares at alien ground on which the Other remains largely imaginary, always already known as mystery. The result of contemplating the Other as pure positivity (perhaps the construct of his own speculative powers) is ignorance; there is no response to another's warnings.

This is important. To the extent that Levinas acknowledges the enigma that limits his ability to know, he is the ideal "incompetent" reader that resistant texts need. Speech (unlike vision which appropriates the other) does not fill the gaps between interlocutors but continually marks their separation.[148] However, to the degree that the Other is "absolute," so is his speech. It is not particular and leads to no human engagement about issues like land distribution, or affirmative action, or civil rights, but appears somehow beyond mundane struggle. Unable himself to give up the endless speech of submissiveness, Levinas may have suspended the Other's chance to talk by imagining him as divinely nonviolent enough to keep silent. If the face is characterized by the ability to speak,[149] why does it not speak a particular demand from a humanly limited position? Perhaps Levinas is not listening.[150]

It is one thing to read an inscrutable face and to conclude that attempting to understand would be a violation; it is another (though related) thing to hear a foreign accent set the terms for respectful distance. In Levinas, different voices do not jar the subject. The consistency of his (admittedly disarmed) posture is suspiciously like that of Spivak's Foucault and Deleuze, and like that of other Eurocentrist theorists from Montesquieu to Barthes, Kristeva, Lyotard, and Derrida too, all of whom Homi Bhabha criticizes for using the Other as a stable "horizon of difference, never the active agent of articulation."[151] The Other looks and sounds like Billy Budd with his angelic stammer, or like Jesus silenced in "The Grand Inquisitor," both of whom Arendt censures for "their incapacity (or unwillingness) for all kinds of predicative or argumentative speech, in which someone talks *to* somebody *about* something that is of interest to both because it *inter-est*, it is between them."[152] Nevertheless, the voice hushed by the holiness of a foreign face does talk back once Levinas acknowledges more than one Other. This is when it is necessary to call on Justice to mediate between competing claims on the subject.[153]

Levinas's subject of philosophy, though, seems more mesmerized by an unfathomable Other than engaged in judgment. He prefers an ethical bearing to specific responses to human resistance. And the asymmetry of a meek self (prostrate before the transcendent, divine Other) can turn out to be a mirror inversion of the older asymmetry of the voracious subject before its objects of knowledge. The result of recognizing oneself as the Other's other, as the potential object of another (asymmetrical) desire, is not always humility.[154] Underlying the humble stance is the presumption of a greatness that can be humbled. But what gesture would follow if a subject could not presume advantages over another? Would humility be ethical? Or would historically under-represented subjects do damage to themselves and to democratic process if they deferred to powerful interlocutors? Levinas doesn't consider this possibility. Given the human capacity for violence, self-effacement is the condition for a relationship which begins with "After you, sir!" No doubt intended as a variation of the selfless "Here I am" in Abraham's exemplary dedication to God,[155] Levinas's "After you" assumes that the speaker could claim priority but chooses not to. His self-limitation assumes privilege, not debt;[156] it suggests what Jewish mystics called *tzimtzum*, to describe God's loving self-diminishment to make room for creation.

A break, a destabilizing irruption outside the self, is what I learned to miss in Levinas from having read particularist books.[157] Perhaps this is an unfair disappointment, if it derives from the paradox of writing self-effacingly. Levinas continues to write, to fill pages with such admirable humility and keeps filling more pages, taking more effort and attention. Philosophy continues to speak of the Other who remains speechless. Literature, not philosophy, is where difference plays its open-ended gambits, to follow Sacvan Bercovitch's important distinction.

When others speak, their appeal, I have been saying, is not an entreaty;[158] it brooks no subordination and wants no empathy or murderous mutuality from the reader.[159] By appeal I mean attractiveness, the books' capacity to play on our desires and to frustrate them with a limiting subject-effect. The life and death game is to stop us short. Sometimes I think that Rigoberta Menchú, Jesusa Palancares, the nameless narrator of *Balún Canán*, and

Richard Rodriguez write at length about their apparently private selves precisely to withhold the anticipated intimacy and sting readers with the rebuff. Their most provocative performance may be the cold-shoulder effect. Noticing this effect evidently allies me to reader-response critics who locate the ways a text teaches the reader how to read.[160] More boldly, we might say that concern for readerly responses asks how texts engage readers through seductive education; that is, how writing intervenes in the world.

In my last book, in which I asked how national romances helped to consolidate Latin American nations, I could trace the strategies of making the texts slip allegorically between passion and patriotism.[161] There we could assume that readers are invited as participant observers in the love affairs that engendered countries. Identification with the frustrated lovers whose union could produce the modern state was precisely the desired effect on the tenuous citizenry of newly consolidated countries. It was a mirror effect that survived mass distribution to required readers who were taught, in the embrace of compulsory education, that their differences from the elite lovers did not really matter. My project, in other words, was to explore foundations on their own ideal terms, with a foundational theory that conjugated imagined communities with dreams of love.

But to read particularist fictions in *their* ideal terms needs a paradigm shift. A theory of narrative foundations for inclusive communities cannot read books that show and stretch the cracks at the base of society. To read these books, our critical vocabulary will strain after anti-foundationalist terms. It will be a struggle, because their characteristic tropes have evidently been unremarkable. In the vicious hermeneutic circle of familiarity and predictability, the unanticipated lessons these texts could teach seem hard to grasp. How can the books teach reading effectively, if our training strives to overcome their lessons? There is so much that one must ignore anyway, especially in long works, that it would be easy to continue our inattention.[162] If training assumes that learning is a progression, that one always learns something, how does interpretive reticence make sense? At our most circumspect we have been assuming, with the New Critics and then with deconstruction,[163] that ambiguity cannot be conquered. But an ethical distance from the object of desire? Confessed ignorance of that object? No trespassing signs that suggest cautious approaches? We have yet to recognize those purposefully offputting enticements.

THE TRAPS
OF TRANSLATION

FREELY AND EQUALLY YOURS, WALT WHITMAN

2

melting everything else with resistless heat,
and solving all lesser and definite
distinctions in vast, indefinite spiritual,
emotional power.

—WHITMAN
Democratic Vistas

As he stares at you from the cover in your hand, can you resist Walt Whitman? The very first lines of "Song of Myself" are thrilling with excitement. Writer and reader apparently feel, think, want, know, and are the same, at least potentially, as they gaze at one another. Rushing from the *I* to the *you*, Whitman seems to break out of the social isolation that Bakhtin denounced in lyric poetry, in which the speaker's voice is deaf to dialogue.[1] Whitman says he is not isolated or privileged, only fascinating to the degree and in the same ways that you are.

> I celebrate myself, and sing myself,
> And what I assume you shall assume,
> For every atom belonging to me as good belongs to you.[2]

Is this a challenge to match his colossal self-confidence and to merit him as a partner? Or is it a warning against being overcome? Skeptical readers may worry that the invitation doesn't offer dialogue but rather comes on like an assault. And his willing partners often take Whitman's exorbitant claims as intentionally unstable, a license to talk back and undo him. America's literary history shows how powerfully his partners have responded to the provocations.[3]

Here, I want to stop at the disarming, suctioning energy of his poetry, which threatens to prevail before it provokes. The other writers I will discuss don't simply discount Whitmanian claims as too extravagant to be serious; nor do they accept an invitation to compete in universalizing terms. These terms (symmetry, mutuality, boundlessness) are precisely the ones at issue for particularists. Whatever else Whitman's fantasy of a cosmic self manages to do, it is likely to do some damage to the personal and cultural boundaries people normally set. Even if we deconstruct his disarming desire to show how the poet anticipates (plans?) his own undoing when he oversteps personal limits, the desire to overstep is contagious. Why should he, or we, want to disarm the other, whether it were possible to do that or not? Whitman doesn't stop to ask why; he hurries past questions.

Personal boundaries disappear in the practically orgasmic embrace of the first lines, before Whitman's partner can make a move. The ec(static) symmetry wastes no time in pursuit. The Other's difference doesn't endlessly slip away from Whitman, the way it does in Levinas's formulation of love. Difference is captured. A Levinasian lover says: you are always before me, in time and in space you are literally my priority.[4] But Whitman doesn't prioritize or differentiate. Without a before and after, his frame is an eternal now that holds the self steady against falling out of phase and revealing the separateness that makes one vulnerable to the Other.[5] If we refuse Whitman's invulnerable hold and forfeit the thrill of our own reflected greatness, he may dismiss us as no readers at all, and we are free to put the book down. But if we continue to hold on to the book/man, we risk yielding to his totalizing terms.

Particularists don't deal in these apparently even exchanges. By definition, they assume asymmetrical relationships that will not boil down to interchangeable positions, so they become sticking points in Whitman's totalitarian effort. In this chapter, I take Whitman's assumptions in "Song of Myself" literally, and I read them (in the tradition of Quentin Anderson and of C. L. R. James)[6] as a condensation of liberal democracy's founding ideas. The focus will be specifically on Whitman's unstable but compelling solution to liberal democracy's fundamental contradiction between demands for (liberal) personal *freedom* and the requirements of public (democratic) *equality.* The energy he brings to brace them together, and his—at least rhetorical—success, provide the universalizing heat that glows so intensely through "Song of Myself" to light up liberating movements in poetry and politics at home and abroad. That energy also fuels a range of rhetorical refusals to be melted down. Whitman radiates a menacing kind of appeal for particularists, because his non-negotiable universalism effectively cancels them out. To appreciate their refusals, we should first acknowledge his magical vaporization of conflict to produce an American aesthetics of transparency that seems effortlessly inclusive.[7] In its midst we may hardly notice the resourceful gestures of those who demur, preferring to safeguard their cultural and political distinctions even after they come to America.[8]

Whitman is known as the poet of American democracy. It is easy to agree with this characterization, but hard to know what this means. Considering the political disagreements among us, to "justify" *America* and *democracy* obviously means many things, some would say almost nothing. Whitman managed to stretch these words so wide and so thin that they have accommodated wildly divergent styles and stark differences of interpretation. Thinness of character may be America's trademark, to follow Philip Fisher's comments about a Whitmanian culture of the lowest common denominator. Wai Chee Dimock makes a similar point in her Rawlsian interpretation of Whitman, the democratic spirit that equalizes citizens by being blind to the unequal goods and talents that luck distributes unfairly.[9] America (modernity itself), unburdened by divisive particularities, ranges over a map imagined to be empty.[10] Whitman's America is "national by subtraction," to borrow Roberto Schwarz's irony about an ideal Brazil, because immigrants and natives leave their differences behind to enter Whitman's inclusive catalogues. Schwarz contrasts the cultural anemia of ideal nationalists, left and right, to the richness of creative "cannibalism"; it makes most Brazilians unabashedly American consumers of Europe, Africa, and everywhere else.[11]

Whitman's "loose drift of character," like his America (and nationalist Brazil), is another empty form, free of contentious substance. It made him available to everyone, left and right. Emma Goldman and Eugene Debs claimed him as a comrade,[12] while Ezra Pound and T. S. Eliot finally called him father, "pig headed" though he was.[13] The same is true for Whitman's international disciples, the Communist Maiakovsky and the Futurist Marinetti, for example, and South Americans left and right.[14]

Essayists and poets as commanding and varied as Jorge Luis Borges, Pablo Neruda, and Octavio Paz, among many others, would tease out different and competing Whitmans from the amorous tangle declared in the opening lines of "Song of Myself." The irresistible engagements are more often ideological than erotic. José Quiroga notes that Latin America's gay poets of love can be indifferent to Whitman, perhaps because he stifles desire with possessiveness, and because his more delicate poems, either censored or neutralized, didn't travel well. Emilio Ballagas, Xavier Villarrutia, Salvador Novo, José Lezama Lima, and Néstor Osvaldo Perlongher, Quiroga says, leave Whitman to more rugged tastes for grandiloquence and speculation. Homoeroticism prefers the unsettling refinements of seduction over the controlling barbaric yawp.[15] But Arnaldo Cruz Malavé doesn't discount the seductiveness of control, nor Whitman's iconic value in Latin America as the patron saint of homoerotic cruising.[16]

Effortless mastery helps to explain what made Whitman irresistible to ideologues, the object of a political competition for his legacy, left, right, and center of America's self-definitions. His political availability for radically different positions pits contestants in a struggle for his legacy that seems starker in Latin America than in the North. Perhaps Whitman remains a bit exotic for Spanish Americans, available material for strong misreadings. The geographic distance and foreign traditions put the Latin Americans beyond having to wrestle with Whitman, as Pound felt he had to. Instead, Spanish-language poets could choose to claim him. And those who did took advantage of his Americanness to declare it their patrimony, to use it freely in one strident direction or another.

A PAUSE FOR PARADISE

One way of accounting for the range of Whitman's heirs is to note that he espoused radical ideas in favor both of personal liberties and of institutional equality. He did so expressly in order to neutralize the conflict between them. Later readings would tug at the static balance in one direction or another. But when *Leaves of Grass* (1851) was first published, just after the liberal European revolutions of 1848 that flared into collective radicalism, and one precarious decade before irreconcilable conflict erupted in the

American Civil War, a balance seemed more desirable than choosing either liberty or equality.[17] That same balance between individualism and social responsibility motivates Nathaniel Hawthorne's *The Scarlet Letter* (1851), and Sacvan Bercovitch convincingly argues against readings that mistake its equanimity for indifference to politics.[18] The obvious ideological overlap between these contemporary, immediately popular, and lasting books suggests a general culture in the Northeast that became hegemonic after the war. Hawthorne and other like-minded contemporaries (including Emerson, Thoreau, Melville) might therefore have provided useful counterpoints to a rhetoric of particularism.

My choice of Whitman has to do with his broad appeal North and South, which probably owes to his genre, the short poetic fragments that switch from one rhythm to another between pauses for breath, in a syncopated assault on readers provoked to respond. Fascinated or irritated (or both), generations have responded. By contrast, as Bercovitch shows, Hawthorne's prose is subtle and ambiguous. It accommodates the tension between liberty and equality through a dialogue (or dialectic) between individual development and the social growth that individualism both needs and promotes. Ambiguity is the result of Hawthorne's rhythm, which affirms one value and then the other in a balancing act that moves through stages of historical sublation. Whitman's essays sometimes attempt that rhythm.

But "Song of Myself" elides prosaic tension altogether, and it preempts the dynamic that tension could have generated. Instead of Hawthorne's balancing act, Whitman's poem performs a vanishing act. Liberty and equality have no argument with one another in the persona of the fully enhanced social self, Walt Whitman. Drawing others to embrace him freely, and being available to each reader equally, he cancels contradictions with the overwhelming force of his love for each reader. Whitman did create an aesthetics for liberal democracy, as his admirers say, but to my mind the achievement is doubly paradoxical. First, because democracy here is an effect of Whitman's narcissism, the multiple reflections of his ideal self in each equally significant citizen (and each section of the poem). And second, in a less evident paradox, the gaps that Whitman left between the fragments probably do more for democracy than the words he wrote. The poem works in what Barthes would call the intermittances between short, renewable, moments of intensity. Between those moments, a reader can catch her own breath, and reflect.

Reflection on the words "America" and "democracy" seems programmed right into the looseness of Whitman's poem, which is open, capacious and uncontrollable, as if to invite everyone in. He chose not to fix or to finish the poem in the etymological sense of making perfect, because no living thing ever reaches the stasis of perfection.[19] Some readers have been annoyed by the sloppiness. For example, Mark Van Doren disapproved of it in a 1945 essay that continues to introduce the *Portable Walt Whitman:* "Whitman had the illusion, common to prophetic natures, that everything he said must be right because he said it. Poetry has a special way of exposing the error, for it demands its own kind of rightness, regardless of any other. Whitman did not regularly take the trouble to be right as a poet. He has paid the penalty."[20]

Whitman's own 1855 Preface mentions the rawness and dissonance of some of his work, but not to excuse it. This is a manifesto for rawness in a new American poetry that isn't always just right. The self-consciously unfinished quality is taken up again in a Preface of 1872, in which, after several editions that added to, deleted from, and rearranged the book, Whitman finally defends the coherence of *Leaves of Grass.* Yet he insists, sounding like a Derridean reader of his own texts, that writing goes on in "the surplusage forming after that volume." Of the current "supplementary volume" he confesses uncertainty, since "there is no real need of saying anything further. But what is life but an experiment? and mortality but an exercise? . . . If incomplete here, and superfluous there, n'importe—the earnest trial and persistent exploration shall at least be mine."[21] Whitman's model allows for variations that should turn the reader into an accomplice who fills in the ellipses between the fragments. Democratic poetry happens every time a reader takes up Whitman's invitation to be his equal. If Americanness meant kissing old models affectionately but unflinchingly good-bye, as he does in the first paragraph of the 1855 Preface, then his heirs should do the same to him. "He honors most my style who learns under it to destroy the teacher."[22] On the next page he repeats, "I teach straying from me." Then he adds coyly, "yet who can stray from me?"

What choice do we really have when straying is a version of staying? The spaces that Whitman left open look like sites for dialogue, but they may be the flat and predictable mirror-like surfaces that leave only room enough for readers to return the poet's expression. By supplying this perfect self-sufficient image Whitman, as a generous lover for each of us, elicits our desire for him. And by appealing to us through a laconic and fragmentary book, Whitman invites the reader/lover to be coauthor. The empty spaces in the poem suggest room for a free and equal exchange that should get past the traditional hierarchy of writer over reader. But his rhetorical mechanism does more than affirm the ideal equality of American subjects. It *stamps* an equal value on each reader when it stamps out difference, as if Whitman were the national mint.

Stamping is literally the name he gives to the poet's work of nation-building. "[A]s . . . it is strictly true that a few first-class poets, philosophs, and authors have substantially settled and given status to the entire religion, education, law, sociology, etc., of the hitherto civilized world, by tinging and often creating the atmospheres out of which they have arisen, such also must *stamp, and more than ever stamp,* the interior and real democratic construction of this American continent, today, and in days to come."[23]

Can Whitman's coinage circulate as the community of differences that defines a liberal democracy? Or have exchangeable commodities been reduced to interchangeable value (in the spirit of Tocqueville's critique of democracy)?

LIBERALISM AND DEMOCRACY: NO CONTEST

Cloning ready-made liberal democratic citizens from Whitman's self-image avoids the complications of negotiating between partners in conflict. Liberalism and democracy live in fundamental tension with one another: one promotes liberal economic competition, and the other constrains competition in the name of a democratic common good. In a standard shorthand for the continuing feuds about personal and family planning, the theorist associated with modern liberalism is John Locke, and Jean-Jacques Rousseau is identified with classical egalitarianism.[24] John Rawls, for example, can simplify the terms of the "conflict in democratic thought" by juxtaposing "the tradition associated with Locke, which gives greater weight to what Constant called 'the liberties of the moderns,' freedom of thought and conscience, certain basic rights of the person and of property, and the rule of law, and the tradition associated with Rousseau, which gives greater weight to what Constant called 'the liberties of ancients,' the equal political liberties and the values of public life."[25]

Whitman didn't fret about the conflict, as I have been saying. He finessed it, and seemed as true to Locke's natural property rights as to Rousseauvian egalitarian political rights (although after the incendiary year of 1848 he did "recoil" from the revolutionary consequences).[26] My point is that Whitman embraces each separately and so passionately that their differences flatten out, just as he embraces and flattens each reader. Whitman says he competes so well in the liberal market that competitors have no chance; and he insures such uniform equality that one voice can speak for all. In essays like "Democratic Vistas" a postwar Whitman will admonish his countrymen to internalize the spirit of democracy, without which its institutions are superficial and vulnerable. That spirit would produce a culture to displace the feudal, aristocratic, romantic habits of feeling that were limiting the legal and political strides toward democracy.[27] In these later essays Whitman would attempt to set liberalism and democracy into a dialogic and mutually dependent rhythm, the way Hawthorne coordinated them in *The Scarlet Letter*. But "Song of Myself" fixes liberal democracy's partners (or agonists) in an uncannily static and perfect moment; it declares no contest in their free and equal children.

Young Whitman was less moved to admonish citizens than to celebrate democracy beyond all doubts and arguments about how to achieve it. He leaves struggle and movement behind (just as he abandons European vestiges of hierarchy, dichotomy, and prosody), to step into the eternal present nondialectical tense of America. In the Preface, the poet "is no arguer . . . he is judgment."[28] And later he insists, "Backward I see in my own days where I sweated through fog with linguists and contenders, / I have no mockings or arguments . . . I witness and wait." That is why the "talkers" and "trippers and askers" are irrelevant. "Writing and talk do not prove me, / I carry the plenum of proof and every thing else in my face, / With the hush of my lips I confound the topmost skeptic."[29] Some readers have been coaxed into mistaking the energy of celebration for dynamism, his static and utopian *Jetztzeit* for development, the resonance of a single voice for the harmony of a nation. We may intuit a better future from Whitman's happiness, but the image comes in an unmovable present.

FREELY

Lockean liberalism seems boundless in "Song of Myself," where free commodity exchange is the mechanism for everything worth having. In Whitman's America, competition among equals, specifically among independent producers, was assumed to benefit each individual and to allow for the personal growth that promoted social development. Therefore each citizen could celebrate a fellow citizen's success without feeling envy. If aristocratic literature pitted good against evil, insider against outsider, Whitman's liberal poetics passes freely between selfishness and sociality. This is what Hannah Arendt admired about America's revolutionary tradition. It was the gradual result of a contractarian culture that began with the compacts Puritans wrote to bind each to the other. Through respect for personal property among independent producers, Americans as pragmatists were bound to appreciate the negotiations of politics that protected market relations. The *event* of colonization, she observed, not an abstract ideal of the New Jerusalem, imposed the logic of contract on the relatively autonomous polity in the wilderness. Practice preceded theory in America; a century and a half of colonial history was the inspiration for Locke's revolutionary *Treatises of Civil Government*.[30] Arendt's admiration for liberalism is part of her Cold War-inspired polemic against the French Revolution and its legacy of sacrifice for egalitarian ideals. Her stark formulation of the difference can help us to locate Whitman.

Obviously, he is on the liberal side, celebrating himself as the embodiment of America's "experiment in commercial politics," as Waldo Frank called the United States.[31] The 1855 Prologue provokes Old World English by putting "cheap" in apposition to "divine." Whitman doesn't stint as the model producer and consumer of endlessly available commodities. The trouble is that he is so unstinting and successful that competition is impossible, since the freedom of exchange always favors him. Whitman gives himself to us, sometimes claiming to expect nothing in return. But he doesn't forget, even if we do, that gifts are made to circulate; in some form they ultimately return to the giver. And in Whitman's case the profits he expected were enormous:

> What is commonest and cheapest and nearest and easiest is Me,
> Me going in for my chances, *spending for vast returns,*
> Adorning myself to bestow myself on the first that will take me,
> Not asking the sky to come down to my goodwill,
> Scattering it freely forever.[32]

Again he will expect us to reciprocate, though he protests disinterestedness: "Spread your palms and lift the flaps of your pockets, / I am not to be denied . . . I compel . . . I have stores plenty and to spare, / And anything I have I bestow."[33] Even if the gift economy he indentures us into is not the market of dollars and cents,[34] Whitman demands just the same, perhaps more, to give returns on his generosity. And the economic vocabulary he uses to represent social relationships underlines the market as their legitimate site. In this way, Whitman's exchange reproduces that precarious economic ideal of antebellum America: to preserve free market trading among independent producers without promoting unequal capitalist relationships.

His offer is irresistible for at least two reasons. First, we members of a market society cannot refuse an offer of the cheapest and most basic commodity. Whitman is as plentiful as the grass and the fresh air that he prefers over the cloying atmosphere and prosody that he leaves behind immediately after the first lines ("Houses and rooms are full of perfumes"). He offers himself up to unlimited takers for the very reasonable price of simply recognizing his worth. The second reason is that his worth is limitless. He is the most common and also the vastest and most satisfying item on the market. We both want him and want to believe that we merit him. Whitman assures us that both desires are fulfilled. For one thing, he is already ours, and for another the erotic exchange that he touches off with his initial offer makes his partners fully equal in their obligation to give vast returns for his love. By representing erotic exchange in market language, then, Whitman involves each reader individually in a relationship that enacts the ideal of free and equal access to an American market where the best commodities are the cheapest. Each reader is a perfectly adequate buyer, because Whitman is so "reasonable" and because we all equally have the resource for exchange: our selves. Thus we enact and affirm the Lockean, liberal ideal of political equality through equal opportunity in a free market. The Prologue promises the same ideal, of reducing differences to uniformity, and Whitman delivers in the convincing rhythm of his apparently arbitrary catalogues, where the most extreme differences of social class, profession, origin, and gender level out through the steady and ardent incantation that melts down differences into pulsing, regular, variation on sameness.

At the same time that he gives aesthetic form to the equalizing force of the free market, Whitman is also flooding the market (of ideal American comrades) by offering himself so cheaply ("Outbidding at the start the old cautious hucksters"[35]) and by insisting that he be bought. No room for competition here, even though the thought of an intellectual or cultural monopoly seemed abhorrent to him. But for Whitman, a thought is different from a deed. Protest is not poesis. As a poet, he wanted to "be marked for generosity and affection and for encouraging competitors . . . without monopoly or secrecy . . . glad to pass any thing to any one . . . hungry for equals night and day."[36] The trouble, I repeat, is that generosity does little to encourage competition. Whitman's "gift economy" undermines the very free market that he assumes in his erotic transaction. In other words, his apparently disinterested offer of love threatens to overcome all the healthy independence that Whitman says he admires in a partner.

Whitman becomes the monopolizer, the arch-capitalist whose best and cheapest wares reduce competitors to mere consumers of an imaginary fulfillment of conflicting desires (for market freedom and for political control). Whitman's ideal democracy, however, continued to be based on the mass participation of independent producers, even after many of America's workers had already become wage-laborers. America is most firmly knit by "the aggregate of its middling property owners . . . ungracious as it may sound, . . . democracy looks with suspicious, ill-satisfied eye upon the very poor, the ignorant, and on those out of business."[37] Whitman's disdain for capitalism in its rapacious and centralizing aspects was common to most of the political and economic thinkers of his day. Capitalism was the cancer that would reintroduce hierarchy and class antagonism to undermine the participatory government that made America special. The antebellum South was understandably more tolerant of a class society, as long as distinctions were color-coded and precluded the slave "underclass" from political participation. But the northern "American School" of Economics condemned the "capitalist" southern planters for demeaning labor and thereby threatening the wages commanded by free white workers. Whitman says clearly that the fate of the white working class is or should be the real concern of northern abolitionists.[38] The Civil War may well have been fought, as Allen Kaufman argues, over the compatibility between democracy and class distinctions. Could democracy be consistent with class society or not?[39] Whitman was sure it could not be, but he leaves nothing to chance or competition when he gets his readers to buy into the ideal of equal Americans.

EQUALLY

The threat of class and other social divisions is so unspeakable for Whitman that he enthralls us before we can speak of it. As a strict egalitarian, he overcomes even the differences his ideal market thrives on. In his essays he stops to worry about social contradictions, but only long enough to resolve them with the force of feeling. On the one hand he endorses John Stuart Mill's definition of democracy as a polity with varied character and full play of differences. But on the other hand, differences represent obstacles to be overcome by the equalizing force that Whitman calls love or sex in his poems. In "Democratic Vistas" he calls it the "tremendous Idea" of the true nationality, "melting everything else with resistless heat, and solving all lesser and definite distinctions in vast, indefinite spiritual, emotional power."[40] Why does Whitman assume that "distinctions" must be "solved," as if they were problems? And even if we grant that some mediation is in order, what does it mean for democratic practice to equalize by "melting everything else with resistless heat?" Whitman's ardor may be burning up the very partners he celebrates, just as his generosity threatens to monopolize a free market ideal.

With resistless heat is precisely how Whitman comes on to his reader in *Leaves of Grass*. He is the hottest item imaginable; he knows that our desires are infinite (Lockean) and promises to respond to them all (à la Rousseau). His seduction, as José Martí would say, is as irresistible as rape. True, we are free to look away, and some readers manage to escape through indifference. Others feel the imperious heat as harassment of their particularism and refuse to be overwhelmed. But Whitman's pledge is that to know him, to be him, is to know and be our best possible selves. The first lines he gives us blur the differences between curiosity and vanity, interest in others and self-interest, and ultimately between democracy and imperialism.

Years after the Mexican War, and right after the short Spanish American War (named that in the United States when it snatched the glory away from Cuba's War of Independence), Uruguayan José Enrique Rodó expressed a collective concern about one thing leading to another. "As fast as the utilitarian genius of that nation takes on a more defined character, . . . so increases the impatience of its sons to spread it abroad by propaganda, and think it predestined for all humanity. To-day they openly aspire to the primacy of the world's civilization, the direction of its ideas, and think themselves the forerunners of all culture that is to prevail."[41] Passages from Whitman's "Democratic Vistas" of 1871 sound as if they were among Rodó's sources: "When the present century closes, . . . The Pacific will be ours, and the Atlantic mainly ours. There will be daily electric communication with every part of the globe. What an age! what a land! Where elsewhere, one so great? The individuality of one nation must then, as always, lead the world. Can there be any doubt who the leader ought to be?"[42] To be fair, Whitman's expansionism didn't sound much different from Cuban annexationism until 1870. Desperate to be rid of Spain, Cubans who feared the instability of independence had been urging the United States to annex their island, since "the peoples of America are destined to form one nation and to be the wonder of the entire world." But by then it became clear even to the politically timid Cuban junta in New York that the United States had dishonorable intentions.[43]

If we allow Whitman to give himself to us, we guarantee his own returns and give up our particular desires for his universal will. It is a political alchemy worthy of Rousseau: one general will results from melting down the will of all.[44] La volonté de tous had meant consent in classical political philosophy. It was deliberative, as opposed to inspired, and it presupposed a state structure that allowed for interpersonal deliberations. The general will eliminates the public sphere when it consolidates collective consent into a single voice. Hannah Arendt targets Rousseau as the inspiration for the terrible ardor of the French Revolution, as the author of Robespierre's slogan about the people having one will *(il faut une volonté UNE),* and as the father of the fiction about leaders' virtuous sentiments being good political guides. In all this, Arendt alleges, Rousseau helped to confuse responsible action with feeling responsible. And since feeling is a fickle guide to action, he promoted the endless doubts about personal virtue that set the Revolution's leaders against each other and against themselves. Arendt objects to this tradition (in France, in Russia) as self-destructive and hopelessly elitist. Leaders claimed their authority to speak for the masses because the people were always wretched and humble;[45] leaders presumably (should) stay in power because the masses (should) stay wretched.

Where is Whitman in Arendt's contrast between Rousseau and Locke, equality and liberty? Evidently he is in both traditions, the "and/also" option that Bercovitch reads into Hawthorne's ambiguity. But Arendt's choice of American hero to stand for the country's collective values is Thomas Jefferson, author of the purposefully ambiguous Declaration of Independence. "His famous 'felicity of pen' blurred the distinction" between public happiness and private rights, she says, when it substituted the "property" of civil rights with an implicitly public "pursuit of happiness." The implication was spelled out at the Virginia Convention of 1774, when Jefferson stretched the purely private (Lockean) rights of the Old World to fit the colonists' quest for "public happiness."[46] In the Declaration, Jefferson restores the private dimension by suppressing the adjective "public"; yet a trace remains in the very substitution of private property by an unmarked happiness that straddles private and public spheres. Jefferson declared its pursuit to be a sacred right of Americans. But he doesn't say if this is a civil or a public right.

Whitman must have appreciated the purposeful confusion of public and private. In fact, he perfected the trick by collapsing the difference altogether with (a Rousseauvian) flourish. Whitman gives each claim limitless weight as if liberty and equality did not disrupt or contaminate one another. Rather than preserve one term inside its apparent opposite, with the deconstructive irony of pragmatic statesmen like Jefferson, Whitman makes them both vanish with the heat of his enthusiasm for simple ideals. He doesn't conciliate the terms so much as he cancels one term by the other: liberty overrides equality (I am the best product on the market and I monopolize all other sales), and equality overrides liberty (you are the same as I so I will talk for us both). He takes the words, and his partners, so passionately to heart that they are overcome.

THE LEVELER'S APPEAL

Whitman's assault, or appeal, acknowledges a distance between himself and the beloved (reader) indirectly, in the rush of energy meant to cancel the distance. Of the several techniques that he uses to court and to conquer, the most seductive may be his direct appeal to a single (private Lockean) reader: "This hour I tell things in confidence, / I might not tell everybody but I will tell you."[47] The fact that Whitman will be just as available and intimate with anyone else who picks him up does not contradict the terms of his offer. The important thing is that he calls us into the relationship as individuals, not as a mass of people. The (Rousseauvian) compact is constructed through our particular mergings with Whitman; it was not there before. In the beginning was the gift, offered in Whitman's intimate tone.

Jorge Luis Borges noticed the metaleptic mechanism of Whitman's apostrophes to the reader: "We are touched by the fact that the poet was moved when he foresaw our emotion."[48] Here is an example: "Prodigal!, you have given me love! . . . therefore I to you give love." When Borges suggests that we compare this effect of intimacy to other poets, he underlines Whitman's successful break with a European bardic tradition each time he asks, or demands, permission from each of his readers to represent him or her. The American bard does not take for granted the privilege to be our collective voice by virtue of his superior sensitivity: he bids for the contract with each reader. I said that Whitman slyly begins with an offer of himself rather than with demands; then he continues with a calculated modesty. If his "unoriginal" thoughts "are not yours as much as mine they are nothing / or next to nothing." Later he will add more aggressively: "All this I swallow . . . and it becomes mine," and "I have embraced you, and henceforth possess you to myself."[49] This direct appeal is hard to resist because his self-importance is contagious. The enthralled partner may be speechless, but happy, perhaps, to let unstoppable Whitman celebrate them equally.

The formal innovation of Whitman's free verse works together with direct address to put the reader into the poem as if s/he were equal to Whitman's language, since its register sounds so close to everyday speech. The verse threatens to lapse into a prose of the street variety, which in its time displeased English-speaking conservatives more than it did the Spanish Americans. Translation and a possible indulgence towards exotic art tempered the rudeness. In fact, Whitman traveled South in double displacements of language, because (except for Martí) his first fans and translators were reading him in Italian, or French, or German versions that obviated the problem of staying true to the text.[50] This mediated Whitman did not always flaunt the prosaic "decomposition" that is evident in English. In English, the break with tradition was dramatic; it tended to cancel the privilege of poet over reader, of regular scansion over the flexible patterns of common speech, and it generally legitimated the ordinary by blurring the boundaries between life and art. Gerard Manley Hopkins confessed to recognizing the similarity between his and Whitman's experiments in scansion; he identified them as using the prose rhythm of iambs, anapests, and a combination of these. "Extremes meet and . . . this savagery of his art, this rhythm in its last ruggedness and decomposition into common prose, comes near the last elaboration of mine."[51] The effect of social plenitude that Whitman achieves is, to a considerable degree, produced by the free verse that levels American language to a "degree zero."[52]

Whitman, the leveler of style and the architect of an American poetics, appears impatient with dichotomies: poetry vs. prose; man vs. nature; production vs. reproduction. The leveling is also the product (or cause) of Whitman's self-consciously disordered catalogues, as well as the permutable fragments of "Song of Myself." He sometimes manages to relax oppositions by bracing the binary terms into a pleasing metaphor that reads like a natural found object. Take the title of his book. The substitution of the common word "blades" (of grass) by the more civilized or writerly "leaves" is as clever as Jefferson's replacement of "natural" property rights with social happiness. In both cases the competing terms survive, not in a dialectical sublation but in slippery translations from the natural private sphere to the civilized public sphere. Whitman's written leaves are his product as much as they are nature's. And what is nature if not the work of another coquettish Author for whom grass may be the "handkerchief of the Lord, / A scented gift and remembrancer designedly dropped, / Bearing the owner's name someway in the corners, that we may see and remark, and say Whose?"[53] Or, the grass may be the pubic "curling" hair of graves, transpiring from breasts of young men and laps of mothers. One reading of leaves doesn't cancel multiple others.

The image of leaves for nature's messages was rather commonplace in the period, John Irwin shows. For Transcendentalists leaves were the ultimate hieroglyphic of Nature's writing, because they reveal the simplicity of relationships that show correspondences between levels of creation. Thoreau turned the natural image into a challenge for civilization: "The Maker of this earth but patented a leaf. What Champollion will decipher this hieroglyphic for us, that we may turn over a new leaf at last?"[54] Whitman simply assumed that he was the man. His leaves, unlike Thoreau's, were not a "metaphysical reading" of nature; they were themselves natural products. Irwin suggests that Whitman's poetry attempted to return language to the childlike natural signs that were popular in the "hieroglyphic Bibles" of his day.[55] But the critic fails to notice that Whitman made an astounding change in the figure. His leaves are no longer arranged in the top-down model of the trees that his contemporaries were gazing up at. They composed the level ground underfoot.

HE LOVES YOU TO DEATH

Gilles Deleuze and Felix Guattari did notice the change, and they loved Whitman for it. The down-to-earth equality of his *Leaves* promised to bulldoze Europe's stubborn philosophical dualism and the hierarchies it sustained. Not even Nietzsche could promise as much, because his "cyclical unity of the eternal return" endlessly reinscribed familiar problems.[56] The way out, they say, is to re-spatialize our political imagination: move from thinking in terms of circles or poles or dialectical spirals to thinking in terms of the Whitmanian "rhizome." The figure is "an underground stem" that proliferates laterally without any center or goal, so that each growth is equal to and connects with all others. And their primary example is the grass; specifically Whitman's *Leaves of Grass*. This radically American work allegedly sets the model for the "successive lateral shoots" that can loosen Europe's fixation on deep roots. (Deleuze and Guattari might also have gone back to Jefferson's ideally repeatable Cartesian plots of land.)[57] The problem for Deleuze and Guattari, just as it was for Whitman (and Jefferson), is that proliferation assumes a model or a typical element that is endlessly repeated. Who establishes that element, however humble, common, and cheap? And how can its endless repetition accommodate the different styles, interests, desires that Deleuze and Guattari had defended in *Anti-Oedipus* against the standardization of Western culture? They seem to imagine that by dismissing philosophical fathers, an empty space can be cleared for establishing nonhierarchical relationships. But they forget, in their slash-and-burn zeal, that even a rhizome is originary and proliferates to pattern everything its way.

THE CONTEST FOR HIM

Whitman's persona and poetry are underfoot everywhere in South America and have been enlisted in support of competing ideologies ever since José Martí celebrated him as the model citizen of a New World. "Let us hear what this hardworking, contented people sings; let us hear Walt Whitman. Self-assertion raises this people to majesty, tolerance to justice, order to happiness."[58] José Martí's "Walt Whitman" is a paean to America written in 1887 from New York and published in both Mexico and Buenos Aires. It was in fact aimed at the emerging citizenry of Latin American republics, urging it to engage in constructing a bold, capacious and unencumbered culture. The essay sent thrills up and down the Southern continent. Successive and cumulative responses would canonize Whitman as the bard of the Other America, "Our America" in Martí's famously defensive formulation of 1891. But Martí himself was too close to Whitman's America to ignore the connections between its generous spirit and its limitless appetite. He had been living in the United States for years, gathering support for Cuba's independence struggle and reporting on American politics and public culture. Whitman, for him, was quintessentially American and therefore the object of both desire and dread. Martí submitted to Whitman's seductions with an ardor that feared its own gasping for breath. "Sometimes Whitman's language ... sounds like a stolen kiss, like a rape, like the snapping of a dried-out parchment in the sun ... his verses ... gallop on devouring the land; at times they neigh eagerly like lustful stallions; at times covered with lather, they trample clouds with their hoofs."[59] Whitman makes real dialogue unnecessary, although, like the rapist, he demands a partner.

"Whitman, Left, Right and Center" was the title for my own projected study of ideological and stylistic competitions among three of the area's star poets: Pablo Neruda (defending an egalitarian Whitman), Jorge Luis Borges (for a mystical Whitman, above distinctions) and Octavio Paz (with Whitman's liberal contradictions).[60] What remains of that project, besides this version of an introductory essay,[61] are titles for chapters that announced themselves almost imperiously, as if commanded by the shade of Whitman.

One title was "Paz and Whitman: Bearing the Contradictions," although it was never clear how to spell "baring" because the homonym suggests the Oedipal slippage between claiming and denouncing one's inheritance. To embrace self-love and to reject it for the general good is a contradiction, but the double gesture probably marks us as Americans. It also puts Paz at the center of Whitman's disciples, between Neruda on the left and Borges on the right. The Mexican poet, nonetheless, cannot help but recognize the predatory tendency in expansive democracy in Whitman's editorials during the Mexican American War. He had cheered the U.S Army as it conquered, and then continued to cheer when Congress annexed half of Paz's country. Another Mexican, Mauricio González de la Garza, became so furious at Whitman's continuing appeal in Latin America that he collected and commented on the hateful articles in *Walt Whitman: racista, imperialista, antimexicano.* Here is a sampling of Whitman's pronouncements:

> The more we reflect on the matter of annexation as involving a part of Mexico, or even the main bulk of that republic, the more do doubts and obstacles resolve themselves away, . . . The scope of our government, (like the most sublime principles of Nature), is such that it can readily fit itself, and extend itself, to almost any extent, and to interests and circumstances the most widely different . . . greediness is not ours. We pant to see our country and its rule far-reaching, only inasmuch as it will take off the shackles that prevent men the even chance of being happy and good . . . We have no ambition for the mere physical grandeur of this Republic. Such grandeur is idle and deceptive enough. Or at least it is only desirable as an aid to reach the truer good, the good of the whole body of the people. [June 6, 1846]

> What has miserable, inefficient Mexico—with her superstition, her burlesque upon freedom, her actual tyranny by the few over the many—what has she to do with the great mission of peopling the New World with a noble race? [July 7, 1846][62]

But Paz's own double loyalties to personal and to political freedom lock him into an anxiety of influence with the bard who celebrated that very contradiction as it drove America forward.

The chapter on Borges, "I Am You, You Are Me, So We Are Neither," would have developed Borges's Schopenhauerian pessimist "misreading" of Whitman. This was not the poet of democracy's multiple and discreet wills, nor the heroic Nietzschean Whitman who had, by then, become a cliché in Latin America. Borges's banal and ironic Whitman undoes stable, coherent identities by repeating himself one persona after another. He is modest and mystical, aware that personalities are interchangeable permutations that render historical change both impossible and unnecessary.[63]

I called the more developed essay on Neruda "How Neruda Rights What Whitman Left Out," a pun on the conservatism of Neruda's "left" or popular democratic poetry. He writes in the gaps Whitman left open. True, Neruda could rise (or descend) to Whitman's celebration of the commonplace, as in the *Elementary Odes* to his "Blue Wool Socks" or to "A Watermelon." But passages in Neruda's colossal *Canto general* (1950) showed an admiration for the master that displaced Whitman's narcissism with the hierarchical secondary narcissism of hero worship. And sometimes Neruda smuggled back the primary kind of self-love, as in "Somos muchos" (We Are Many), a united-front title that introduces a multiple, fascinating, singular poetic self.

Whitman's poetry drowns the difference between self and other; it translates so effortlessly between personal and collective terms that disciples don't stop to ask directions. Pablo Neruda didn't worry about the difference between a dialogue of equals and the equality of repetition. In fact, he destroyed his teacher by resuscitating older hierarchical models which Whitman had dismissed in his Preface. The *Canto general* (satirized as "The Earth" by the narrator's prolix rival in Borges's "The Aleph")[64] will write in and close off the spaces for the poet's interlocutor by repairing America's fragmented "epic" to look like a familiar romantic narrative. "Arise with me,

American love," and "I come to speak through your dead mouth,"[65] set Whitman's rawness right. Ironically, the Chilean Communist marshals tradition against the earlier and more revolutionary aesthetic, until what is left of Whitman is the right of paternity, something he claimed never to want. Neruda uses this patriarch to affirm the usefulness of epic over Whitman's own poetry of "pure possibility."[66]

This irony is prepared by the cultural politics of the Communist Popular Front of the mid 1930s, when the Party abandoned radical internationalism to take advantage of anti-fascist positions in Western democratic traditions. One of those openings was Walt Whitman. He was being promoted as the hemisphere's Poet of Democracy by Roosevelt's regime in its own efforts to shore up wartime alliances through Pan-Americanism. The Left stopped condemning Whitman as a chauvinist, even jingoist, and started to rehabilitate his career:

> But from 1929 to 1935 when Communism was at its most active and revolutionary phase in the United States, Whitman was frequently regarded as both a precursor of progressive poetry and a victim of his own lack of militancy. The 'dialectics of history' now rendered *Leaves of Grass* ineffective and even dangerously likely to cool the revolutionary ardor of the masses . . . This was the attitude of the Rebel Poets, a group formed to protest the execution of Sacco and Vanzetti . . . As late as 1935, when the Party was already soft-pedalling militancy and rebellion in favor of Democratic Front slogans, Spiers still condemned Whitman's Hegelian view of historical development as mystical and falsely dialectic.[67]

By then, Stalin's thaw toward liberal democracies encouraged most American radicals to warm to their country. "Communism itself was advertised as 'Twentieth Century Americanism,'" and the home branch of the Party exhumed local heroes including John Brown, Nat Turner, and Walt Whitman.[68] Americanism became synonymous with democracy, as Whitman had always maintained, when struggles for national liberation became part of Communism's internationalism. For obvious reasons, the American Whitman attracted Chilean Neruda, for whom the novelty of nationalist alliances with internationalism was a political tradition. In Chile, Communists and Socialists had formed a Popular Front before World War II, and renewed it after the collapsed coalition government outlawed the CP and exiled the Party members from 1948 to 1952.[69] In 1947, Communist Senator Neruda had insured his own persecution by publishing a critique with the coyly Whitmanian title, "Carta íntima para millones de hombres."[70] He went into hiding, and then travelled to read from his work throughout the Americas, Europe, and the Soviet Bloc.[71] In general, one can say that South American Communist parties, dedicated as they were to national economic development, saw themselves as successors to liberal democracy, however contentious the wars of succession would be.[72] At the First Latin American Communist Conference (June 1929, in Buenos Aires) the International's delegate set the goal: "Not a liberal state, then, but the democratic dictatorship of workers and peasants, will be born from the bourgeois-democratic revolution."[73] The national delegates listened approvingly, each thinking of his or her particular country.

Of course Whitman attracted other Spanish Americans too, Borges, for example, who struggled against Neruda over Whitman's dead body. In 1969 Borges published an exquisite translation of selected poems from *Leaves of Grass* and sent a dedicated copy to President Richard Nixon.[74] (This is the conservative Borges, whose impartiality during Argentina's "Dirty War" of the 1970s offended many admirers of his writing.) Four years later and two years after the poet and the revolution had died, Pablo Neruda's *Incitation to Nixonicide and Praise for the Chilean Revolution* (1973) was published posthumously. Neruda opened the attack with the following fastidiously rhymed invocation: "Comienzo por invocar a Walt Whitman":

> Es por acción de amor a mi país
> que te reclamo, hermano necesario,
> viejo Walt Whitman de la mano gris.[75]
>
> [Because I love my land
> I claim you, my necessary brother,
> old Walt Whitman of the grey hand]

Not all the contests for Whitman in Spanish American poetry are quite this dramatic. Fernando Alegría tracks the bard's appearances in *Walt Whitman en Hispanoamérica* (1954), to take account of this "phantom's" haunting the hemisphere and to ground it in a history of translations, biographies, and inspirations for Spanish-Language poets (sometimes coming circuitously through Europe).[76] Later, Enrico Mario Santí would tighten some loosely descriptive connections in Alegría's book, and develop the competition I had sketched among Paz, Neruda, and Borges.[77] For some, Whitman is the precursor of revolutionary poetry; for others he is a nihilist, and yet others feature Whitman as the father of an American mystique of individualism.[78] The disagreement is a competition for political and aesthetic stakes.

Whitman is not any one of the above; he is all of them. He and some contemporaries cultivated freedom of contention and took sides only in order to save that freedom during a breaking point in American history, when the stakes were the Union. Readers, including the aged Whitman himself, eventually lost confidence in America's experiment to coordinate the basic values of freedom and equality. That is why C. B. McPherson could eulogize an already dead effort in *The Life and Times of Liberal Democracy*.[79] And disciples who read mid-twentieth century ideological movements back into Whitman's poetry purposefully miss the obvious point that his democratic liberalism has no direct heirs. Paz unabashedly admits that tradition is not inherited, it is conquered *(La tradición no se hereda, se conquista)*.[80] At most we can say that the vanishing act Whitman performed on the tension wire between freedom and equality survives only as an imaginary "possible utterance" that gives a nonmimetic direction for future poets.[81]

Whitman's democracy, where all are equal because all are identical, is politically precarious, poised between the freedom to embrace comrades and the imperialist thrust that takes everything in. A snap of dry blades is what interrupted Martí's admiration for Whitman and what echoes in Rodó's decision not to complicate his criticism of North America with any mention of a Whitman he could not help admiring.[82] Rodó's admiration had made him regret that Spanish America's most important poet, Rubén Darío, was not "el poeta de América," the poet to whom Darío had condescended in the "Preliminary Words" to *Prosas profanas* (1896), "Democrat Walt Whitman." But by the time he wrote *Cantos de vida y esperanza* (1907), dedicated to Rodó, even precious symbolist Darío invokes Whitman's spirit in an angry ode "To Roosevelt."[83] Whitman's persona here, and elsewhere, became a topos in Spanish America for freedom and equality (paradoxically, in struggles against the expansionism that the man promoted), even when his stylistic innovations were lost in translation. Whichever use he serves, as heroic mask or as rude lover, he has one message, which is redundant: it says, we are all equal because you are, or should be, the same as I am. Whitman will love you, but he may love you to death. While his practically irresistible and equalizing direct address offers an alternative to the bardic tradition, Whitman achieves a comparable authority each time a reader submits to "My flesh and blood playing out lightning, to strike what is hardly different from myself."[84]

SOME STRAY

I doubt that Whitman's democratic ideal was what conditioned his sexual preference for lovers hardly different from himself. But I do think that his homosexuality helped to figure ideally horizontal relationships, beyond the differentiating foreplay of domination and coyness. Homoerotic love was certainly a scandalous language for politics at the time, and perhaps for this very reason it provided a rhetoric for the strict reciprocity of equals. After the revolutions of 1848, radically egalitarian democracy must have seemed a scandal too. "Dash me with amorous wet," Whitman challenged the ocean, "I can repay you." If the seduction that initiates Whitman's reader makes him a corporeal equal ("For every atom belonging to me as good belongs to you"), then that reader/lover is figured as another man. And the absolutely equal love between comrades spills over into Whitman's utopian vision of a society bound by affection:

> If I worship any particular thing it shall be some of
>   the spread of my body;
> Translucent mould of me it shall be you,
> Shaded ledges and rests, firm masculine coulter,
>   it shall be you,[85]

This manly love, as an allegory for nonhierarchical relationships, appealed to Edward Carpenter among other English homosexuals in the nineteenth century.[86] Nevertheless, we noted that it could leave gay readers in Latin America cold. Perhaps they imagined what Reinaldo Arenas lived to experience after he escaped Cuba's homophobic repression. Free and equal sexuality turned out to be boring compared to the transgressive rhythms of seduction, conquest and submission; it was more like gymnastic exercises to build the body than the asymmetrical risk of love.[87]

Another Anglo-American gay writer who responded to Whitman was D. H. Lawrence. He even offered a developmental gloss for the allegory of manly love: after the first two stages of human love (the cohesion of family/clan and the powerful sexual bond between man and woman), homosexuality fulfills these in a kind of Hegelian realization of human(e) capacities; it is a love beyond purpose,[88] possible only when freedom is wrested from necessity. Lawrence gleefully noticed that Whitman had evacuated the women to somewhere beyond the poem where they could be still and bear children.

What Lawrence failed to notice is what may have put off some gay readers of Whitman; it is that the men are also evacuated, or eviscerated, "stamped" and flattened into mirror reflections of the poet. Lovers lose the difference that love depends on, in Levinas's philosophy and in Winnicott's psychology; they also lose the distance that excited Whitman's initial rush of energy. Of course Levinas assumes that love's difference includes heterosexuality (in unredeemably sexist stereotypes, Luce Irigaray complains);[89] but distinctions can of course be marked in a variety of ways between men, between women. Whitman preferred not to mark but to erase distinctions. If he is America's Everyman, it is not because he was typical, but because he devoured everyone else.

The poem you hold in your hand gapes like an open window through which Whitman draws you in.[90] "Whatever I assume you shall assume." The shiny surface of the page is not a mirror, because it shows Walt Whitman staring out and inviting the reader in. Yet the poem's resemblance to a mirror allows for Whitman's supreme conjuring trick of identifying the reader with (as) himself. In the Preface he literally invites us to look at the poem as if it were a mirror: "You shall stand by my side and *look in the mirror with me.*"[91] Later, each reflected face repeats the divine model: "In the faces of men and women I see God, and in *my own face in the glass.*"[92]

One way to appreciate Whitman's maneuver is to think of his "Song" as a simulation of Lacan's mirror stage of development. Readers glimpse an ideal self in the poem and reenact a formative scene when, as babies, we presumably first stared at a pleasingly coherent image in the mirror. But this time, it is Walt Whitman who stares out and says, I am you. Speechless (prelinguistic) partners can be born-again citizens, equal to each other because they are identical to one image. Whitman returns readers to the founding moment of personal identity in order that we find him there, one at a time.

The repetition (of readers, of fragments) enacts the interchangeability of parts that American manufacture was developing in the nineteenth century, and that has been worrying this essay from the beginning. Whitman's poem works by substituting one subject or scene for another (as in Tocqueville's bad dream of democracy), by stamping out qualitative difference and stamping equal coinage of citizens. Something like a midwife for modernity, or like a New World Zeus (the old one gave birth to Athena and Dionysus as pieces of himself),[93] Whitman delivers America, citizen by (free) citizen, like an infinite machine of (equal) interchangeable parts. His rhyzomatic republic spreads, weed-like, around him in repeatable images of Narcissus admiring himself in identical counterparts.[94]

Whitman's America clears differences away as obstacles to democracy. It expands endlessly, overriding boundaries of culture and history, sometimes violently (as in the Mexican-American War) and other times with indifferent tolerance (as in his chaotic catalogues). Readers can be grateful for the reprieve from limitations, but some will refuse to be redeemed from the differences that constitute them as particular citizens, capable of sustaining debates in a public sphere. They may resent being set free only to follow the leader. So they take Whitman at his word when he says, "I teach straying from me."[95] To his coy afterthought, "yet who can stray from me?," they respond with the coyness of purposeful misreading, as if Whitman were not asking a rhetorical question but posing a challenge.

MOSAIC AND MESTIZO:
BILINGUAL LOVE FROM HEBREO
TO GARCILASO

3

La verga es proporcionada a la lengua en la
manera de la postura, y en la figura, y en el
estenderse y recogerse, y en estar puesta en
medio de todos, y en la obra; que assi como
mouiendose la verga engendra generacion
corporal, la lengua la engendra espiritual;
y el beso es comun a entrambos, incitatiuo
del uno al otro.[1]

—LEÓN HEBREO
    Diálogos de amor (translated from Italian
    into Spanish by Inca Garcilaso de la Vega)

The "Inca Garcilaso." His very name is an oxymoron that braces two imperial languages without reconciling them. It also condenses a personal history
of impossible translations between mother tongue and fatherland, a history
of borrowed and inexact belongings. As part of the New World and as a participant in its Spanish renewal, Garcilaso is a guide back to a broken-off past
and forward to a modern empire. The bilateral movement is practically in
his blood. His name announces a story of passionate crossings, violent
contact, reversals, and doubled identities. A royal Peruvian mother and her
aristocratic Spanish conqueror managed to produce a remarkable child in
1539, just after Francisco Pizarro's easy triumph over an internally divided
empire. But the Castilian's desire never developed into marital love for the
Quechua princess (by 1549 he married a Spanish girl),[2] perhaps because the
passionate parents never learned each other's language. Their son's chosen

name commemorates the double nobility of his bifurcated heritage, and the incommensurable clash.

Christened Gómez Suárez de Figueroa in 1539, the future author of the *Royal Commentaries of the Incas* (1609), as well as of *La Florida* (1605) and *Garci Pérez* (1596), would sign his books with the more illustrious name of his deceased father, which he had earlier been signing anyway as scribe and confidant. The son hoped, no doubt, to take the place, and the pension, that the conqueror's name promised in Spain's legal order. When Captain Sebastián Garcilaso de la Vega died in 1559, leaving the beloved bastard enough money and unmistakable instructions to study in Spain, the young man left ancient Cuzco for the new world of the conquerors.

Like one of his father's generation of warriors who crossed the ocean to win glory and privilege, Garcilaso embarked on adventure, but apparently in the wrong direction. The mestizo fought bravely in Spain's War of Alpujarras to put down rebels of Moorish descent, but never advanced very far as military defender of the Empire, whether in rank or in the ever more pressing issue of salary. Spaniards were evidently reading him wrong, as a halfbreed, a misfit, an unauthorized outsider. In response, Garcilaso would spend his next career showing that each half was a whole, that he was an insider both here and there, and that with both Peruvian and Peninsular parents of noble lineage, he was doubly authorized as a privileged participant in both worlds. With unquestionable authority, then, he put down the ungrateful sword and began to wield a more promising pen that would endorse his self-authorized name: El Inca Garcilaso de la Vega.

Writing became Garcilaso's career in a kind of internal exile, after his attempt to win an inheritance fell flat, ostensibly because of his father's double-dealing with the Crown. Captain Sebastián had insisted he was loyal to the Spanish Crown, but histories documented a "treacherous" loyalty to Gonzalo Pizarro. The brother of Peru's leading conqueror had been loath to cede his privileges to anyone, including the King of Spain, who had decided to curtail the conquerors' control by limiting their entitlements. During the civil war that followed, the mutinous Pizarro saved his life by escaping on the horse that Sebastián offered him. Garcilaso was sure that the allegations of treason were exaggerated, that his father's service to the state far outshone the small (literally chivalrous) stain of horse-lending that the courts first ignored, but stubbornly inspected once the pension was claimed. The son persisted for years on behalf of, and in, his father's good name. He was also entitled to something, or should have been, as an Incan aristocrat. Another countryman, Guamán Poma de Ayala, was making his own appeal on precisely those grounds, and lamented his people were so undone by the Spanish conquest that they failed to engage its opportunities for legal petitioning.[3] Hence Garcilaso's persistent engagement was neither desperate nor naive. In fact he proudly points out that his defense of Incan nobility had practical results for others.[4] The label "mestizo" was therefore not simply a stamp of corrupted blood. "I call myself mestizo openly, and do myself honor thereby," writes the slightly defensive chronicler.[5] But more often than not, extra-marital mestizo "heirs" inherited more legal hot air than anything else. Whatever legitimate or hopeful appeals Garcilaso could voice as the beloved son of his heroic father, they were muted by louder concerns in Spain's courts.

The country was waging an internal crusade to establish *pureza de sangre:* "natural children," as illegitimate offspring were delicately known (are legitimate children unnatural in baroque Spanish?) were vulnerable to legal dispute, especially in the case of a visibly mixed-blood bastard. The authorities had their reasons, and Garcilaso mentions some, by name. His ex-schoolmates Juan Arias Maldonado and Pedro del Barco are two such reasons. These Hispanized mestizos had led significant interregional rebellions in Peru during the rash of resistance between 1562 and 1567.[6] And the rebellions would recur for a long time, sometimes fueled by the past glories that Peruvians read in the *Commentaries* themselves. The most notorious outbreak was the war against Spain led by the direct descendant of the last Incas, Tupaq Amaru II, who had been reading the indigenous history before his campaign of 1780 and 1781. In a recent study, José Mazzotti interprets the sometimes aggressively Andean tone of the *Comentarios reales* to argue that they have a dual appeal: along with the evidently European bias that celebrates the improvements of Spanish civilization over the already formidable achievements of the Incas, there is a Peruvian perspective. It is pitched to insiders as an expert guide to political and cultural survival.[7]

A memorable passage in Garcilaso's writing attempts to legitimate the very term for bastard, *hijo natural,* precisely as homeboy with undeniable rights and privileges in his father's house. Significantly, the passage describes his own reception in tolerant Portugal, not in Spain. In Portugal, "la primera tierra que vi cuando vine de la mía, que es el Perú" (the first land I saw when I came from my own, which is Peru) generous and Godfearing people of the islands and the capital received him "como si yo fuera hijo natural de alguna de ellas" (as if I were one of their homeboys).[8] As a gesture of appreciation (and an appeal for support) to the Portuguese, Garcilaso dedicated *La Florida* (1605) to Teodosio de Braganza, explaining that many of the Duke's countrymen had accompanied Hernando de Soto on the famous, if inconclusive, expedition.

How could the Incan immigrant have imagined that another natural child of Lisbon was León Hebreo, Garcilaso's literary and philosophical mentor? And for a still more striking coincidence, Hebreo's father had ties with the very same Braganza family that Garcilaso was courting. Those ties turned out be so damaging that they forced León's family to flee from Portugal back to its earlier Spanish homeland. Had Garcilaso been thinking about Hebreo's bilingual career when he prefixed an Incan title to a Spanish name, it might have been obvious that bicultural claims would cause some problems in Spain.

Foreign royalty appended to Spanish nobility was a destabilizing supplement to the paranoid purity of Spain's Inquisitorial discourse. Garcilaso would learn to take advantage of the instability that follows from adding supplements to systems that seemed coherent; he wrote his *Commentaries*, after all, as sustained supplements to official histories in order to overload their simple "truths" with complicating detail.[9] But first he was the victim of his own overloaded name. His cultural as well as legal claims to Spain foundered on the dangerously doubled identity of an Incan youth who declared that he was at home in Spain. The bilingual signature did more than claim entitlements for the Inca Garcilaso; it also gave some unimpressed authorities signs of divided loyalty and inconstancy. The ambitious young man evidently chose to meet that danger by wielding the doubly dignifying name. That he took pride in the family name is obvious. Garcilaso de la Vega was not only the venerated captain in Cuzco, so generous and popular that he became the target of invidious reports by rivals and of elegantly written responses by his son the scribe. The name also belonged to perhaps the best poet of the Spanish Renaissance, and to other relatives who were famous bards and ambassadors: the Marqués de Santillana, Fernán Pérez de Guzmán, Pero López de Ayala, the Manriques. No wonder the overseas scion of such poetic and political glory chose to activate that lineage, using the kind of sympathetic magic that changes one's luck with a merely nominal adjustment.

"As his name is, so is he," goes the Hebrew saying.[10] A Hebrew expression to describe the Inca Garcilaso's belated, even nostalgic self-fashioning is not entirely out of place here; Spain is the place of frustrated homecomings where the category of alienated national had become almost synonymous with Hebrews, and Hebreo was literally the name of the exiled Spanish Jew whose book Garcilaso would translate from Italian into Spanish as his apprenticeship in writing.[11] León Hebreo's *Dialoghi d'amore* (1535) is a Neoplatonic treatise in two voices that shuttles between classical and Mosaic codes of belief, as the lover Philón reads the codes allegorically and explains their compatibility to his wise Sophía, too wise ever to be satisfied. She never gets enough of his talk, and so finds endless difficulties in his exposition so that he can continue endlessly to engage her.

MOSAIC MAN

The name Hebreo was no more native to the man who became one of Italy's foremost philosophers of love than was Italy itself. For eight years before the edict of expulsion in March 1492, the man later known by that name had been living at the court of the Catholic Kings Ferdinand and Isabel. His famous father, Isaac, had become minister of finance and political adviser to the monarchs, and the son himself was probably their royal physician. That was before ethnic and religious differences became absolutely intolerable in Spain, and the court doctor could still take pride in his legitimate name: Yehuda Abravanel, of the long line of poetic and political Abravanels as illustrious as the Garcilasos, a line that allegedly reached back to King David and forward to the true Messiah.[12] The family's Spanish roots were deep, probably going back to the beginnings of Jewish settlements there, after Rome sent the Jews in flight from Judea. Documented credentials reach back to at least 1284, when Hebreo's namesake, Don Yehuda of Seville and Córdoba, began to serve Sancho IV (1284–1295) as royal tax collector, a job he continued for Fernando IV (1295–1312). By the end of the fourteenth century, with the first Inquisitorial rumblings, the patriarch, Don Samuel Abravanel, decided that if he could no longer be Spanish and Jewish, an

65

apparently threatening and therefore threatened combination, he would solve the contradiction by converting. Samuel was henceforth known as Juan Sánchez de Sevilla.[13] The family members who remained Jewish didn't remain in Spain for very long; they moved to neighboring Portugal, which was then fighting for independence from Castile. The Abravanels settled in Lisbon, where they entered into the service of King Alfonso V. Don Isaac was born in 1437; his son Yehuda in about 1460. Eventually, after three generations of Portuguese prosperity, King John II accused Isaac of conspiracy. The patriarch barely escaped to the precarious security of Spain, the same year that Christopher Columbus arrived there. It was 1484. Everyone knows what happened to the Jews only eight years later.

Spain rid itself of a people who had come to identify so stubbornly with that unnatural mother of a country that for centuries thereafter they would distinguish themselves from Balkan and North African neighbors as "ispanioles." After the expulsion, young Doctor Abravanel—already into his second exile—translated himself in every sense of the word. He moved to another country, and traded his Hebrew name, Yehuda, for its Spanish counterpart, León. As for the particularly distinguished Sephardic surname, he gave it up altogether for a generic label, "the Jew." Hebreo's modern Hebrew translator says that the author's name could have referred to almost any one of the many Jewish men exiled in Italy. If our only information were the man's name, as it appears in the first published edition of his work, it would be impossible to establish his identity. We know what it was thanks to some biographical details, mostly from Don Isaac's mention of the family in prologues to his prolific work (mentions that exclude Don Samuel the convert),[14] from Claudio Tolomei's letters (Venice, 1566),[15] and from the detailed title of the first Spanish translation of the *Dialoghi*. It is a version by Guedella Yahiya, a third-generation exile and friend of the Abravanels, one that Garcilaso would almost surely not have known. The translation was published in Venice in 1568, and dedicated (strangely?) to Spain's Felipe II as defender of the Catholic faith: *Los Diálogos de Amor de Mestre Leon Abrabanel Médico y Filósofo excelente. De nuevo traduzidos en lengua castellana, y deregidos a la Maiestad del Rey Filippo.* For some reason, the Jewish translator insisted to his ideal imperial reader that the book's argument developed very "católicamente,"[16] even though the author had clearly refused to be limited to that kind of approval. He left instead.

The Catholic Kings would have been happy to retain doctor Yehuda and financier Isaac, happy to overlook the stain of ethnicity in the glow of professional services during this first wave of forced conversions or flight, before "limpieza de sangre" became a patriotic requirement. What good options would the royal clients have had, anyway, at a time when money matters and worldly medicine seemed to be monopolies of miscreants? Faculties of medicine, we may remember, were the first to admit Jewish professors.[17] Don Isaac counted on his usefulness, no doubt, in that famous scene (as Cecil Roth describes it)[18] when he threw himself before his royal masters and pleaded with them, in vain, to rescind the decree of expulsion. Instead, Ferdinand and Isabel offered the family "a dispensation"; that is, they offered to sponsor the family's conversion. Other illustrious Jewish subjects were doing it. In the Introduction to his *Commentary on the Book of Kings*, Don Isaac doesn't mention them. He is silent about the many thousands of last-minute conversions, including that of his personal friend, Rabbi Abraham Shneiur, head of Spain's Jewish congregation, whose decision to change cult rather than country precipitated so many other capitulations.[19] Instead, Isaac describes a seamless scene of exodus, as "one man says to the next, 'Let us stay strong in our faith, and hold on to God's Law, however we are pursued by enemies. If we survive, so be it; and if we die, we will die without breaking our covenant."[20]

This kind of determination withstood even Ferdinand's plots to keep the Abravanels at home, as hostages if need be.[21] The king had arranged to have Yehuda's baby son kidnapped, in order to hold the family nearby; but they foiled the plan and sent the child and his nurse to Portugal, where he was apparently seized and baptized anyway. Twelve years later, on the eve of what would have been a bar mitzvah, Yehudah wrote a rending elegy about the depth of his loss.[22] Rather than live the ignominy of one who descended from David and yet joined the camp of Israel's enemies, Isaac and his son chose loss and exile. The young doctor's prescription against cultural death by purification was a life of conscious contamination. He would thrive as a Spanish Jew. Since he refused to erase his Jewishness in order to stay at home, he used his home language to broadcast his "infidel's" identity, signing his name as "Jew" (Hebreo) in bold Spanish strokes.

The point would not have been lost on Hebreo's mestizo translator. El Inca Garcilaso, of the ethnically mixed name and culturally conflicted heritage, could well have recognized the self-exiled Spaniard as a figure for himself. Abravanels had been intimates of the Iberian kings, their compatriots of countless generations. Hebreo was a homeboy, even if he was hounded out as a foreigner by fanatics. He had a cultural claim on Spain, the kind of claim Garcilaso was making when he assigned himself the paternal name.

The overlapping circumstances make for an almost uncanny echo between the "Italian" writer and his "Castilian" interpreter, as if one life simply evoked a surprising intimacy with the other. The intimacy seems metaphorical, a result of fortuitous similarities between terms that belong to different and unconnected discourses, Incan and Jewish. But metaphors, we know, sometimes win their shock effect by losing their memory of historical connection. They become metaphors when the metonymic moment is forgotten. And forgetting is just what the Spanish Empire demanded of culturally complicated subjects such as the Incan prince and the Jewish "aristocrat." But these "mosaic" subjects preferred not to forget their pre-Hispanic pride. They were therefore related, not through the stories of presumed continuity, made popular by European chroniclers who imagined that Israel's lost tribes were being found in America where they still dressed, ate, and prayed like Christianity's forebears, but through a shared history of Spanish reconquest, consolidation, and new conquests.[23] "Comenzaron las conquistas de indios acabada la de los moros, porque siempre guerreasen españoles contra infieles . . ." (The conquest of Indians began when the conquest of Moors finished, so that the Spaniards would always make war against infidels . . .), in Gómara's famous formulation.[24] Garcilaso would complain that the "unpure" of blood (mestizos and conversos) were treated worse than criminals.[25] It was a univocal story of forced inclusions and simplifications that produced some wonderfully dissonant, or dialogic, refusals to be simple.

MOVING TARGETS

Garcilaso's choice of material for his writerly apprenticeship may be circumstantial, but the circumstances surround both of Spain's estranged sons. The Inca's enduring *Traduzión* of Hebreo's *Dialoghi* (Madrid, 1590) was the first document to bear the mestizo's newly coined and culturally compound signature, no less complicated than Hebreo's label of intimate foreignness from Spain. Why Hebreo, of all people, should have provided the mestizo with a master text was a question from the very beginning. The first recorded response is ill-tempered and incredulous. It appears in the Inca's prologue to Part II of his *Royal Commentaries* (1617), the part about Spain's conquest of Peru, including his father's participation. The book is dedicated to the surviving, and to the thriving, inhabitants of the new order, "a los indios, mestizos, y criollos de los reinos y provincias del grande y riquísimo imperio del Perú" (to the Indians, mestizos, and creoles of the kingdoms and provinces of the great and very rich empire of Peru). The anecdote Garcilaso tells is about his recent move to Córdoba, where he got a friend to arrange an invitation from Don Francisco Murillo, the venerated schoolmaster. The old man was laid up in bed, sick with the gout, when he received Garcilaso, who gave his host a copy of the recently published translation of *Diálogos de amor*. The very title and signatures provoked Don Francisco: "What business," he asked, "does an Antarctic native of the New World, born over there underneath our own hemisphere, someone who sucked the general language of Peru's Indians along with his mother's milk, what business does someone like you have to interpret Italians to Spaniards? And even if I grant that you have enough presumption to try it, why didn't you chose any old book instead of the one that Italians are proudest of and that Spaniards know least?" The self-invited guest replied that, as a soldier, he had learned to gamble for glory. The greater the odds, the more glorious is victory.[26]

Garcilaso obviously won the little skirmish with Murillo, to judge from the story's tone. But the reception shows how skeptical Spain was about its unbidden child; and it also tells us something about Italy's intellectual standing during the century that spanned Hebreo's composition and his translator's Peruvian chronicles. It is not that Italy was easily forgotten as the center of Renaissance philosophy, poetry, and linguistics, but that it had since fallen out of political favor in Spain. At the beginning of the American conquests, and through the next generation of inquisitorial guidance under Cardinal Cisneros, Spain was quite open to syncretic Italian humanism and even to Northern, self-reflexive Erasmism. But by 1525 the Church was outlawing the religious excesses (*éxtasis*) of the "alumbrados" on the one hand, and on the other it was showing general signs of future unfriendliness to the secularizing humanists whose haven, everybody knew, was Italy.[27]

Italy surely boasted internationally celebrated authors in the period; from Dante to Machiavelli, Petrarch to Pico della Mirandola, Italian names fairly dominated the modernizing libraries of Europe. If Italian books naturally held out a hope of intellectual legitimacy for Garcilaso, it is still unclear why the novice would chose to win credibility through León Hebreo's *Dialoghi*. Surely better known books were in greater demand of translation. And if a further disincentive can be deduced from Murillo's condescending banter, it is his objection to choosing Hebreo when Italian literature hardly lacked for brilliant native writers. "Leo the Jew" was obviously not an Italian original, although the country earned his loyalty as the period's haven for religious and political exiles.

To the war-weary Jews of Spain and Portugal, while much of Europe was marching fully armored towards external conquests and internal control, Italy was a refuge; it lingered at home, in the service of truth and beauty. Naples was a haven, at least during the peaceful pauses in the contest between France and Spain (marked by the French invasion of 1494 and by King Ferdinand's integration of the city into Spain's Inquisitorial empire in 1509), and Hebreo's family would shuttle back to Naples from forced displacements to Genoa, Barletta, Venice, and perhaps Florence. By 1520, while the Inquisition remained resolute at home, in the outpost of Naples its Viceroy Gonzalvo de Córdoba was more flexible; he appointed Leon the Jew as personal physician with special privileges.[28] In Italy other authorities were hiring Jewish refugees too, especially as doctors and teachers. Among them was a young professor from a family of doctors, Elijah Delmedigo, appointed at age 23 as lecturer of philosophy at the University of Padua. There he taught Pico della Mirandola, who later became an admirer and friend of "Leone Ebreo."[29]

One very good reason for Garcilaso's choice of the *Dialoghi* is the book's content. I mentioned its Neoplatonic ideas about the basic universality of all cults and about a perfectible world created by love. Logically, and through dialogic probing, the book coordinates the competing tenets of classical, Christian, and Jewish philosophy as useful versions and developments of one accommodating truth. The challenge that the book sets and meets is to appreciate the interlocking allegorical meanings of disparate traditions. A good interpreter, in other words, need not have divided loyalties; he can weave among them. Some of Hebreo's sources must have surprised certain Jewish readers, despite the attractions Christianity held for Kabbalists.[30] In fact, his inclusion of John the Baptist, along with Enoch and Elijah, as immortal souls[31] evidently amazed some readers enough to assume that Hebreo was no longer what his name said, because the man must finally have converted. It certainly surprised a transcriber of Ibn Yahiya's early Spanish translation (writing the Spanish in Hebrew characters as the Sephardic Jews usually did); it surprised him enough to assume that John was there because of a Christian interpolation (an opinion Carl Gebhardt would share).[32] The scribe therefore excluded Saint John from the list, as did the early translator into Hebrew, Rabbi Yosef Baruch of Urbino.[33] It is a wonder that exception wasn't taken to what precedes the Baptist in Hebreo's text: I mean the trinitarian logic of dialectical thinking that coordinates between the one truth and a three-part movement of the intelligence that begins with unity, develops apparent contradictions, and returns to a coherence.[34] At the same time, Philón finds authority in the Sacred Scriptures, which are synonymous with Mosaic Law.[35] Because of the zigzagging, though, *Mosaic* begins to work like a pun, pointing backward to an exclusive relationship between God and his particular people, and forward to a universal design made of many peoples.

The Neoplatonic and universalizing ideas in Hebreo's book surely pleased Garcilaso enormously, as Enrique Pupo-Walker notes,[36] while he downplays (along with José Durand[37] and Aurelio Miró Quesada)[38] the translation's literary significance as a mere warm-up exercise for Garcilaso's original works. Later, Susana Jákfalvi-Leiva argued that translation, between codes and between cultures, is precisely the art that Garcilaso would exercise throughout his career; the *Diálogos de amor* are not an excisable appendix to his literary corpus, they are its very heart.[39] Sabine MacCormack concurred, calling Hebreo's philosophy an Ariadne's thread that would soon lead Garcilaso through the labyrinth of competing histories of Peru; his entire career as commentarist on indigenous religion is seen as a long development of the pre-Christian apologetics learned from León.[40] Garcilaso the humanist fits quite naturally in his company, agrees Margarita Zamora, for linguistic and philosophical reasons; she shows that the two outsiders dwelled inside a humanistic culture that valued ethnically marked experts for their authenticating knowledge, even when those marks were a political liability.[41] These rereadings suggest that Hebreo's most lasting lessons were not necessarily in philosophical ideas, but in the art of writing. Garcilaso's training through translation is by now a standard signpost of criticism, yet the question of style is often merely remarked and passed by. I want to tarry there.

Style is something different from philosophical probing and linguistic legitimation. What exactly did Hebreo's text offer the Inca in terms of technique? If his target was to cultivate Castilian flair in his Spanish translation, any other foreign book might have provided similar opportunities. But Hebreo's book must have caught Garcilaso's attention for a range of reasons, technique being among them. Understudied as it is, Hebreo's technique was perhaps the main attraction for Garcilaso. At the very least, whether or not he modeled some of his own maneuvers on the *Diálogos,* they offer Garcilaso's readers a telling repository of those repeatable techniques. Hebreo had an imitable manner of a man on the move.[42]

More than a storehouse of ideas, Hebreo was also a poignant figure for a new Christian's peregrination and passion. And more even than giving Garcilaso a pretext for translation across equally legitimate languages and lores, Hebreo was also a modern writer about cultures of antiquity. Despite his sometimes tortured Tuscan prose, Hebreo managed to produce a chatty style that brought celestial love down to earth and circled it back again.

Beginning with either textual interpretation or circumstantial information, many readers have already noticed more than one coincidence between the Inca and the Jew. As if responding to Murillo's taunt about what possible connection there could be between an Antarctic Indian and an Italian master, a chorus of commentators answers with all sorts of ideas. This wide range of commentaries, to which I add my own piece, found this connection frankly surprising. For example, in an exhaustively historical and comparativist introduction to his own 1983 Hebrew translation of the *Dialoghi,* Menaham Dorman is evidently moved by the unforeseen parallels between Abravanel and the Inca. Other Spanish versions simply don't compare in accuracy or in elegance with the 1590 *Traduzión,* nor do the French or Latin translations of the period. Dorman may have had no notice of Garcilaso before, and yet the spiritual affinity with Abravanel is unmistakable. The "new (world) Christian" and the Jewish humanist were treading the same interpretive and syncretic waters between Spain and the areas it both feared and disdained. Similar conclusions had already come from the Spanish-language critics mentioned above. For Hispanists, Hebreo is no surprise; not one of them stammers, even for a moment, with Dorman's sense of wonder. Don León is simply a standard name in the Spanish canon ever since Marcelino Menéndez y Pelayo published his still standard *Historia de las ideas estéticas en España* (1883–1891). In it the Jewish philosopher occupies much of Chapter 6 as a necessary name in the Spanish history of ideas. No matter that the man had to leave Spain (the country has always been too complicated to reduce its culture to one intolerant strain), or that he wrote in Italian (it is full of Hispanisms, which suggest a Spanish pretext): Hebreo is ours, legislated the lasting historian of Spanish letters.

STYLISH DEMOTIONS

It was his style that probably did the most to seduce the Peruvian reader. By style, I do not mean the uneven quality of Hebreo's language, a clumsy Tuscan that has nurtured endless speculations about a pre-Italian original manuscript in Spanish, Hebrew, or Latin.[43] Instead, style here refers to Hebreo's peculiarly coy and flirtatious dialogical movement. The lesson about how to get ahead by sometimes stepping back and putting down may not have been entirely new to Garcilaso the ex-soldier, but its literary application was apparently what he needed to initiate his writing career. The translator would be just as coy in this own *Comentarios* as Hebreo was in philosophizing about love, maybe more so. He probably outdid his teacher's technique. He had to, because Garcilaso, unlike Hebreo, could not assume that knowledge or wisdom were already the objects of spiritual lust. From a Spanish perspective, at least, Incan glories and the surviving Incas themselves may have been matters of relative indifference. Unlike Philón's declaration of feeling with the opening line of the *Dialogues:* "El conocerte, o Sophía! causa en mi amor y desseo" (To know you, O Sophía!, awakens in me love and desire), the Inca begins his *Commentaries* with caveats and cautionary delays. To know his beloved arouses the lover in Hebreo. But Garcilaso's reader knows next to nothing about Peru, and therefore cannot love his Andean interlocutor.

73

How will Garcilaso make us want him? A worthy disciple of his coy master, Garcilaso performed a kind of metaleptic reversal of feeling. By stepping away from his reader he sought to induce love; by assuming our hunger for knowledge, he supplied it in small, appetizing, portions. Just to be sure that we want it, he kept full familiarity unreachably in view. After offering points of contact, he stepped away, translated himself (literally moving from one place to another), waiting for us to make the next, predictably dependent, move. Garcilaso noticed that Hebreo had written for an active reader, one who would follow along, philosophizing with the author. The reader of the *Comentarios* must also know how to follow; that is, the reader, aware of hazards, will appreciate the complex trajectory of an expertly guided exploration.

Multiple preliminary admonitions about the linguistic and historiographic foreignness of Peru warn us about underestimated hazards. Then chapters 1 and 2 keep delaying us, this time with moralizing detours into circumspection. The first chapter affirms God's universal creation in order to catch Christians as blasphemers if they mistake His holy unity for two hierarchically organized worlds. The second chapter sets the limits of the author's own writing, in effect to counsel general modesty that refrains from speculating about geography (or anything else) before exploration advances. Finally, chapter 3 of *The Royal Commentaries* begins with "How the New World Was Discovered." The conventional heading promises familiar ground. Then a supplementary story erodes familiarity and our ground begins to shake:

> In about 1484, to within a year or so, a pilot born in Huelva, in the county of Niebla, called Alonso Sánchez de Huelva, had a small ship with which he traded by sea and used to carry wares from Spain to the Canaries, . . . he ran into a squall so heavy and tempestuous that he could not withstand it and was obliged to run before it for twenty-eight or twenty-nine days without knowing his whereabouts, since during the whole time he was unable to take an altitude either by the sun or by the north star. The crew suffered great hardships in the storm, for they could neither eat nor sleep. After this lengthy period the wind fell and they found themselves near an island . . . The pilot leapt ashore, took the altitude and wrote a detailed account of all

he saw and all that befell him at sea on the outward and inward voyages ... Of seventeen men who left Spain, no more than five reached Terceira, among them the pilot Alonso Sánchez de Huelva. They stayed at the house of the famous Genoese Christopher Columbus, because they knew he was a great pilot and cosmographer and made seamen's charts. He received them kindly and entertained them lavishly so as to learn the things that had happened on the long and strange voyage they said they had undergone. But they arrived so enfeebled by hardships that Christopher Columbus could not restore them to health . . .[44]

What is this? It cannot be about America's discovery, can it? Who is this obscure Alonso who comes out of a foggy place (Niebla means "fog"), a mere merchant pushed and pulled against his will by natural forces from the Canaries to the Caribbean? Was America discovered by mistake? And barely alive back in Spain, the unknown victim of his own uncontrollable voyage is cared for and questioned—to death—by Columbus. And why is this unanticipated and rather damaging, undignified, story narrated in so straightforward, so deadpan and unapologetic a style? For we know better: unless we are holding out for a Viking version of the discovery, a version that evidently didn't translate well into imperial Spanish, everyone knows that Columbus discovered America in 1492. We know how he and his men mounted three little ships with their charmingly girlish names and then sailed to glory, thanks to the Admiral's bold intelligence, and thanks also to Queen Isabel for deciding to take a chance on the daring man.[45]

Given what we know, we might have imagined that the title of Garcilaso's early chapter would introduce the standard facts in order to give the *Royal Commentaries* a conventional or formulaic beginning, following a century-long practice of writing histories of the Indies, both official and independently submitted histories. But Garcilaso is apparently after a different kind of validation, and a different relationship with his reader. Instead of fitting into the conventions, he operates alongside them. His genre is not history; it is "Commentaries" on other chronicles. And instead of flattering his readers with affirmations of what we know, this mestizo informant offers the kind of dangerous, supplementary, information that destabilizes the epistemological framework we had taken for granted. What do we know for sure about the discovery after reading Garcilaso? In fact, it is perfectly plausible that we know next to nothing, but that Columbus knew quite a lot about the New World before he sailed to "discover" it. "But if it had not been for the news that Alonso Sánchez de Huelva gave him he could not have promised so much and so exactly what he did promise merely out of his own imagination as a cosmographer."[46]

Many years later, in a novel of 1979, Alejo Carpentier speculated about Columbus's contrition at the end of a life that exploited multiple sources of unacknowledged information, information gleaned from merchant maps and from rowdy bars where drunken salts spiced their talk with the unconventional details that couldn't have come from adventure books. Carpentier concludes that a sailor on the southern coast of Spain would have been either deaf or indifferent, not to have known about the New World. Columbus was neither. And even Garcilaso's contemporaries might have sensed that informed ambition motivated the "Discoverer," given all the ignominious controversy about his rights to titles and privilege. Why not, then, imagine that a rather simple but resourceful Spanish sailor came out of the fog to show the way? Is there any reason to defend Columbus? Does it enhance Spain's glory to think that the credit goes to a Genovese opportunist of indefinite national belongings, a man who had failed to convince the Portuguese princess to risk capital on what was probably still a vague project before 1484? Disappointed, Columbus left for Spain in that same year, when the Abravanels were escaping Portugal and Alonso was gathering the information that would make Columbus a risk worth taking. "[L]ike a wise man keeping the secret" of that information, Garcilaso explains that Columbus was also smart enough to report it "in confidence to certain persons who enjoyed great authority with the Catholic monarchs."[47] Carpentier's Columbus ejaculates the empowering secret to a queen who had, until then, been condescending to her lover.[48]

The point is not that the supplementary story about Alonso the sailor was unknown to other historians. Garcilaso does not, in fact, invent it. He says that the primary source is his father's conversations with fellow conquistadores. Apparently, people in the business of discovery and conquest were wise to Columbus, because they could fill in some missing pieces of his simplified and self-serving account. But Garcilaso had other sources too. He even cites one laconic mention of a sailor in Father José de Acosta's history of Peru. There were other mentions, too, all of them undeveloped in standard histories. Rumors of an unnamed precursor of Columbus appeared in Fernández de Oviedo's official history of 1535, where the story is almost parenthetical, like an unauthorized or an apocryphal curiosity. Francisco López de Gómara's equally official 1552 report favored the rumor, but failed to supply much corroborating detail. That is one reason Italy's contemporary Girolamo Benzoni rejected the tale as so much invidious Spanish chauvinism, designed to discredit a Genovese genius.[49] The controversy lasted, at least until Washington Irving took sides with the Admiral and against Alonso, in his *Life of Columbus* (1828). But Garcilaso's intervention doesn't seem to take sides; it has a deliberately objective tone, as if the details were neither debatable nor potentially damaging. Where other historians used indefinite pronouns and vague timing to conjure up a character and a period, Garcilaso supports his information with proper nouns and precise numbers. He identifies names, places, dates, cargoes, without losing his way among conjectures and speculations that can carry other historians off to unfounded conclusions, as Alonso was carried off his course. The Inca's concreteness has the effect of inverting suppositions of rumor and truth. It underlines the anecdote and puts the standard story under erasure. With this sleight of hand, he also suggests that his own unsolicited expertise is superior to any official authority. Whatever other historians were guessing at, Garcilaso knows in detail; and whatever readers thought we knew starts to dissolve, from the beginning. Here is a local informant who will talk, if we relax our habitual posturing and learn to listen properly.

In an introductory "Word to the Reader," Garcilaso had already apprised us of the corrective nature of these "commentaries and gloss." They were intended to develop existing, but laconic, histories of Peru written by Spaniards who had an understandably limited knowledge of the country, compared to this native son of Cuzco. The "commentary" on Columbus is already a hint of the sabotage these additional details can wreak on standard histories. After the preliminary "Proemio," Garcilaso adds "Advertencias" (warnings) about the language of Peru. Spaniards need to be cautioned, he explains, about particular phonetic and grammatical features of the general language imposed by the Incas throughout their empire, because the foreigners do not yet (nor can they possibly) know the language with a native's mastery. Jesuit Father Blas Valera can be trusted, not so much because he is the author of a learned history in Latin, but because he is a mestizo local. Garcilaso refers respectfully, and often, to Valera's frayed and sometimes fragmentary pages. By contrast, not even the exemplary Jesuitical discipline and dedication of Acosta can compensate for his foreignness. Less careful practitioners have imagined that competence can be casual and incomplete, enough to evangelize, for example. But Garcilaso knew that compromises with competence lead to error, both epistemological and evangelical error.[50] This mestizo master of his mother's tongue, the man who wished to be respected by Andalusia's admirable linguists before composing these commentaries, knew the ravages of getting words almost right. Inexpert translations were misshaping the memory of a glorious Incan past, they were perjuring reports of current practices in Peru, and they were mistaking the eloquent difference of the country by normalizing it in Spanish.[51] These were no less than historiographical sins. Just as seriously, inarticulate priests were moving Indians to laughter rather than to lofty feeling. A mistaken noun or a misused verb, uttered with the most saintly intention, were sure obstacles to the salvation of new souls. Snickering Incan subjects were used to more elegance and precision in authoritative discourse.[52]

European readers may defer to some of Garcilaso's almost pedantic preambles about language and cultural differences. He is evidently establishing his own, homegrown, expertise in these first pages. They may even concur with his righteous reminders in chapters 1 and 2 about Catholic universality and about the necessarily slow progress of human understanding. But to concede ignorance about Peru doesn't seem to be enough; to level the audience's differences with the mestizo before God and before natural science doesn't sufficiently humble it either. No; Garcilaso tips the balance in his own favor when he demonstrates superior knowledge about Spanish history, and when the demonstration is made in such enviable Spanish style. Garcilaso's almost unequaled style in the period (some critics say that only Cervantes wrote better)[53] and his expertise in linguistic analyses outperform readers on their own intellectual ground. "*Yupanqui*," he explains, "is a verb in the second person singular of the future imperfect in the indicative mood"; *ayusca* is a past participle; and Spaniards have entirely misunderstood the proper noun *Viracocha*, which could not possibly be a compound word "sea of fat," because in combinations of nominative and genitive, the genitive always comes first.[54] To the corrosive logic of the narrative supplement he adds the academic training of a European expert in linguistics and comparative historiography, until the reader can hardly hold on to any intellectual advantage over this socially marginal mestizo. The imbalance can be irksome, if not downright offensive. Even more annoying are his repeated delays of narrative information.

Why do we need to be held off for so long? Does Garcilaso imagine us to be incapable of judgment? Why dig so many moats around Incan information that would drown us if we presumed to cross over unattended? Are the moats meant to create a job for the local maker of interpretive locks? These would not be locks to keep us out, obviously, but the kind that regulates a flow and raises us, little by little, to a navigable level. And once we get there, exactly where are we? The native guide first floats us a story of dubious historical value, a tall tale about sailors that neither Oviedo nor any other Spanish historian took seriously. The very next chapter, chapter 4, gives us the tragicomic "Just So" story of how Peru got its name: when the first Spaniards asked an Indian where they were, the unarmed informant, scared to death *(pasmado y abobado)*, first fainted and then, sure that he was the blameless object of their insistent questioning, identified himself as Beru and pointed to the place they found him, Pelu (river). Confusing one sound with another, as the Spaniards always did, they invented the misnomer Peru for the far-flung empire of four corners, Tahuantisuyu. "The Christians believed what they wanted to, imagining that the Indian had understood them and answered accordingly, as if he spoke Spanish as they did."[55]

It is one thing for Garcilaso to allege this sort of European arrogance and even ignorance about Incan matters, in his preambles and throughout; he can logically claim authority about his own culture, whether or not that culture mattered much to Spanish readers. For centuries, they have noticed the self-authorizing gambit of the insider who makes cultural capital out of his circumstances. But it is quite another thing for the Inca to dismiss basic European knowledge about the conquest in the Columbus chapter. There, his American authenticity was no advantage at all; in fact, it would disqualify him from academic debates about Spain by the same logic of local grounding that granted him expertise about Peru. Yet the story is plausible and not easy to dismiss. Its authoritative presentation demanded a hearing at least long enough to broaden official history beyond the cult of sudden heroes. The dangerous supplement has its own destabilizing logic; it undermines authority instead of substituting one master for another. Garcilaso may not become our expert, even if he effectively challenges others; but whether or not his story convinces its readers, its very objectivity of tone offers an alternative narration and keeps open the floodgates of interpretation and choice. Not only has the native guide argued for his inimitable expertise, in terms that would make any competition literally misguided. This politically frail and economically precarious product of Spain's conquest has also managed to make us doubt whether we know anything at all, even the most basic information of a European tradition. By the end of chapter 3 (with its caveat on Columbus), and chapter 4 (about Spanish linguistic impertinence), a possibly presumptuous reader has been weakened by stages, the way an overbearing bull is bled into docility before the matador can lead him gracefully into new paces. Perhaps now the reader will stoop to follow a skillful guide.

Do Garcilaso's authorizing strategies contradict one another? They certainly seem to. Can he logically affirm the knowledge that comes from a privileged insider's position on one page, and on the next page destabilize the knowledge associated with tradition and power? No, not logically. But there is an advantage to shuttling from one tactic to another, an advantage beyond limited questions about consistent argumentation. As if he were planting a clue, Garcilaso tells a story that reads like a parable of misfired and insufficient questions, the kind of misguided interrogation that demands an inquiry beyond convention and into the sort of "commentaries" that his book generally supplies. The story is about a murder investigation in the course of which a *curaca* (a regional, non-Incan, dignitary) supplied extra information to Spanish authorities. He overrode their limited procedure in the service of truth, since the facts of the case would have continued to escape the interrogators if he responded only to the questions they thought to ask. "Saying one part and hiding another" would have amounted to a cover-up and a lie.[56] One lesson to take from this is that supplements are necessary, not ornamental. But another, less direct, message is that real informants can make surprisingly independent moves; they can slip into a controlling spot by inverting the hierarchy of Q and A. It may be more consistent to tailor answers to questions, but consistency is not always the chronicler's most effective technique. Sometimes chronic alternations of viewpoint and argument work better. Garcilaso's shuttling between ethnic grounding and deconstructive displacement is, in short, strategic. He is difficult to catch, or to contain. This insures his authority and superior agility over his slightly disoriented and overwhelmed readers. If Garcilaso writes himself into a problem, he keeps on writing, so that even a contemptuous reader gets enough countervailing information to be contaminated by complexity and doubt.

FLIRTATIOUS WISDOM

Garcilaso's writing strategy could have been inspired by Hebreo's philosophical Sophía, if we take her taunts and instigations as a collection of narrative devices that Garcilaso appropriated. He had other sources, certainly, for learning how to put one version of history under erasure by writing another; there were plenty of competing and contentious historians who preceded him. To cite just two of the most familiar examples: Bartolomé de las Casas had countered Fernández de Oviedo's official disdain for dying Indians with the pious outrage of *History of the Indies* (written 1527–1566); and Bernal Díaz del Castillo's eye-witness testimony filled in López de Gómara's bureaucratic version of Mexico's conquest (1552) with a corrective *True History* (1570, published 1632). Sophía is not a practitioner of corrosive commentary; rather, she is practically an instructor in its performance. Her few discursive gestures thematize a whole lifetime of lessons for Garcilaso, some of which might not have suited the other, venerable historians.[57] Sophía instructs her interlocutor in the pleasures of discourse. She tells Philón to unsay *(desdezir)* a mistake, if he has made one. (For a future philosopher of ethical erotics, Emmanuel Levinas, anything that is said, thematized, and congealed, must always be unsaid.[58] On second thought, she notices that her lover is so glib that his best way out of a discursive difficulty is to supplement it with more discourse; he can either erase, or he can overwrite, either unsay or say more. "Ya puedes dezir lo que se te antojare, que según veo, bien sabes el modo de rescatarte." (You can now say whatever you like, because as far as I can see, you're the master of rescuing yourself.) In either case, she incites more talk. Did Sophía give Garcilaso some of the ideas for his unstoppable style? I am referring to three basic and characteristic strategies of Garcilaso's *Comentarios:* (1) supplementing; (2) unsaying; and (3) inciting expert talk. We have already seen something of the first, practically generic, strategy; that is, adding comments and rewriting standard histories. Second is the play between *dezir* and *desdezir,* a move and double move of telling and almost taking it back. For example, Garcilaso will introduce an indigenous theme, advance toward giving it a Christian name, and then retreat, a bit, toward the first term.[59] Lest this procedure seem to traduce the truth, Garcilaso adduces the speculation of Spanish authors who shuttle between cult and religion. And then he steps back, just far enough to provoke the reader's chase. He coyly drops the handy interpretive thread of *praeparatio evangelica*[60] that has been sewing honest pagans into a Christian fabric; he drops it just long enough to make a reader stutter and bend down, perhaps, to recover the connection. "De lo que hemos dicho puede haber nacido lo que algunos españoles han querido afirmar, que comulgaban estos Incas y sus vasallos como los cristianos. Lo que entre ellos había hemos contado llanamente: aseméjalo cada uno a su gusto." (What we have said could have given rise to what some Spaniards have wanted to affirm, that these Incas and their vassals had Communion like the Christians. What was among them we have openly recounted: each can assimilate it to his taste.)[61] Taste and judgment, the Renaissance relativist knows, are often products of one's circumstances. In Quito, for example, roosters are said to chant "Atahuallpa" in mourning for the martyred king from that region; but in Cuzco, roosters (and rowdy children) shriek the name in mockery of Atahuallpa, murderer of his brother Huáscar the legitimate Inca. "Cada uno dice de la feria como le va en ella" (Each tells of the fair how it went for him)[62] is the homey Spanish proverb that Garcilaso's readers ought to have recognized.

Third of the strategies mentioned is Garcilaso's sometimes studiously naive, nearly coquettish, posture that beckons an affectionate interlocutor to speak more. The source of loving lore here is Garcilaso's Incan uncle, as it was Philón for Sophía. To make room for the speaker, an infantilized (feminized) Garcilaso wisely retreats at points from the insider's vantage that he usually assumes. It would have made him privy to secrets about Incan mummies that Spaniards could never know,[63] for example; and it made him the overseer for Indians who couldn't trust the foreigners in business transactions.[64] Garcilaso defers occasionally to his uncle's authority, to dramatize how knowledge must submit to those who know more. The Hispanized nephew has, nevertheless, brought the baggage of his technical superiority to the questions he asks, perhaps as a figure for future and presumptive Spanish readers of the *Comentarios*. Cagey as ever, Garcilaso gives his uncle the floor but keeps one foot forward, confident of the lasting advantages of his own writerly craft that will preserve memory far better than the Inca's ephemeral techniques of knotting colored strings and streamlining stories for easy oral relays.[65] Just as cagey, though, his uncle responds to the provocation with apparently endless detailed information, and with a royal indifference to the child's effrontery about memory needing script. What possible advantage could anyone bring to a superior informant?[66]

Many pages later, the boy will ask how so few Spaniards could have conquered so many Indians in a sophisticated Incan Empire. Garcilaso's slip into a Spanish perspective anticipates the obvious question for foreign readers already convinced of their own superior intelligence and prowess. The provocation incites a sarcastic response. Do you think that Spain could have conquered, the uncle sneers, if Peru hadn't anticipated the change in regime? Huaina Capác's last prophecy and exhortation "fueron más poderosas para nos sujetar y quitar nuestro Imperio que no las armas que tu padre y sus compañeros trajeron a esta tierra" (were more powerful in subjecting us and depriving us of our Empire than the arms your father and his companions brought to this land).[67] And when the youth, practically packed off for Spain and evidently thinking from that distance, wonders why his family is not mourning the death of Atahuallpa's son, the uncle turns on him, furious at the reckless mistaking of a traitor for a king.[68]

The unsolicited supplements that undermine what we know, the recursive shifting from pagan to Catholic and back again and from Iberia to the Andes, are some techniques for keeping a bullish reader dizzy and docile. Garcilaso has others, too. For example, he practically (re)moves the very ground from under us, when he says that two distant provinces or cities can have the same name. (Go know that another Chelm really does exist!) If Spaniards attribute certain marriage practices to the Incas, it is because they confuse one province with its namesake.[69] Spaniards thought they were learning about cannibalism happening near Cuzco but were mistaken, Garcilaso corrects, because they were being told about a remote regional homonym during the primitive pre-Incan period. Provinces could have the same name, it seems, if they shared a professional mission. This is what happens in Rucana and Rucana, "ambas de un nombre" (both of the same name), two different places that provided royal bearers for the Inca.[70] The geographic doubling that shuttles readers from one place to another blurs familiar information into a disorienting double vision. The device may mean something more than a simple corrective to the epistemological limitations of a European identity principle. It may also be designed purposefully to disorient and to dizzy a reader. Thrown off balance, an otherwise bullish traveler stays submissive and permits an agile guide to weave gracefully back and forth. If I am reading control out of this nominal doubling and displacement, it is because Garcilaso suggests as much in a passage that praises Incan political strategy. One winning tactic of the empire's political control was the *mítmac,* which amounted to shifting newly conquered populations from familiar territory to unknown parts.[71] First the Inca's enemies lose the war, and then they are lost in a vast, unknowable empire that only the royal house can truly comprehend.

Bi-directional translations, identical place names that send us coming and going, alternating and almost equally pitched praise for Spaniards and for Incas—these are practically signatures of Garcilaso's style. An unkind observer might call him a "weaver," in the sense that Gonzalo Pizarro's merciless field marshal used the term *tejedor* to slander soldiers who went back and forth during the civil war between Pizarro's men and the Spanish Crown.[72] Whether or not Garcilaso's father was such a warrior of wavering, or pragmatic, loyalties, the son's later military service to Spain was unimpeachable, if minor. But his literary tribute of a lovingly detailed Incan world lasted a lifetime, and it surely increased the value of His Majesty's conquests. Once the Inca substituted his sword for a pen, he showed himself to be an expert weaver indeed. Without forsaking one side for the other, he alternated ceaselessly between languages and loyalties.

Accusations of opportunism tarnished his reputation for a while, especially a generation ago, when he was being unfavorably compared to other Andean chroniclers of the period, notably to Guamán Poma de Ayala and to Juan de Santacruz Pachacuti Yamqui, who were said to be more racially and culturally "authentic" than the Hispanized master of Castilian style.[73] No wonder the Spaniards loved him; he pandered to their pride in overpowering Peru, militarily and culturally. Spanish contemporaries were, in fact, evidently impressed enough with his work to pass it through the Inquisitorial censor and to publish it. But they knew they had made a politically delicate decision by the time of Tupaq Amaru's rebellion in 1781. After that Garcilaso's book was banned in America. Some years later, the South American liberator José de San Martín remembered why: the *Commentaries* could teach Americans to be proud of a great indigenous civilization, and he was sure that a local printing of the work would stimulate the struggle for emancipation.[74] A successful strategist himself, San Martín may have appreciated Garcilaso's pragmatic parries with the powerful. Sometimes this means choosing when to be heroic. Certainly early Spanish historians had sometimes preferred discretion over daring.[75] Garcilaso promises to be bolder, but evidently that didn't mean being foolhardy. Thus he follows the advice of his own translation:

> Philón—Aunque no es de hombre virtuoso dezir mentira (puesto que fuesse provechosa), no por esso es de hombre prudente dezir la verdad, quando nos trae daño y peligro; que la verdad, que siendo dicha es dañosa, prudencia es callarla y temeridad hablarla.

> [Philo: Although it is not for a virtuous man to tell a lie (merely to seek advantage), this is not to say that a prudent man should tell the truth, when it will bring harm and danger; because a truth, which when told is hurtful, is prudently kept quiet and spoken with temerity.][76]

The wise are not stupid, Sophía's philosophical lover explains. They neither welcome disaster nor mistake the neglect of basic needs for sanctity. It is more pious, obviously, to provide alms than needlessly to beg them.[77]

Garcilaso was good at avoiding disaster, and at shoring up basic needs. As a weaver, doubling back and forth sometimes in the same sentence, he was prudently mending a torn text, rent between Spain and Peru, a fabric that could, potentially, protect him. Indians were expert at weaving together their own torn garments, Garcilaso tells us, and they would laugh at the holes and clumsy stitching that scarred Spanish clothing.[78] His business was not turning coats but weaving a coat of many colors. The privilege of a doubly noble heritage that Garcilaso hoped to display was also, perhaps, a demonstration that racial and cultural threads are stubbornly colorfast. They don't easily run into an assimilated monochrome that could camouflage difference. Although his was not always a safe style of self-presentation, especially when it could provoke powerful Spaniards and offend the already damaged pride of Incan survivors, it suited him handsomely. He wove so beautifully complicated a text that both sides would want to see themselves in its flattering lines.

The lines crossed, but they never twisted into a synthetic mestizo unity. More and more, today's readings of Garcilaso's "mestizaje" are changing it from a composite term to an internally divided word.[79] It is not only that his two worlds are finally irreconcilable, juxtaposed rather than fused, but that Garcilaso himself meant different things when he called himself mestizo, as Antonio Cornejo Polar explains. Sometimes the word stood for his particular mix of noble blood, and other times for the marginalization he shared with the misfits of both worlds.[80] Garcilaso's work has sometimes been celebrated as an agenda for resolving cultural tensions, but his best readers (including Cornejo, Jákfalvi-Leiva, and Mazzotti) notice that the tensions persist throughout the text, unabated.

Garcilaso locates himself both at the authentic root of American civilization and at the modernizing vanguard of European culture. His course is justified by an Incan creed that, like the Old Testament, delivered people from idolatry and prefigured salvation. (Huaina Cápac's personal testament condenses the story, when the dying Inca urges his empire to obey a superior civilization about to arrive.) Through his easy and elegant Spanish, sometimes replacing Blas Valera's worn Latin letters with modern speech,[81] Garcilaso stations himself inside the Crown's colonial enterprise. Spanish was the language of empire, just as grammarian Antonio de Nebrija had predicted in his 1492 prologue to the language's first manual. Christianity did not need Spanish, as the Jesuits and other evangelizing orders knew very well from their work in Latin and in several local languages.[82] But conquest did demand a unified code, comparable to the "general language" that the Incas imposed in each newly conquered and capably controlled territory: not the exclusive and elite language spoken among Incan royalty, but a consistent and uniform colloquial language. Spaniards might perfect their own best tool of empire, Garcilaso suggests, by emulating that consistency.

Style, then, in Garcilaso, is something different from the dialogic conventions of Hebreo's genre, which others have already appreciated. One feature of dialogue is that it can drive an argument forward, and this was obviously a handy frame for Garcilaso's long-term defense of his trammeled rights. Yet if the dialogic genre were Hebreo's main asset, his translator might have chosen a more classic, Socratic-type dialogue by someone else, of the kind that sets an objective and presses on to win. Dialogue need not, of course, be a genre for winning points; it can also explore them, which is what Hebreo did and, as some have noticed, what Garcilaso learned from him. He learned to manipulate a bi-vocal figure for his doubled identity, and thereby to frame his transactions and translations from one world to another. Two voices engaged in understanding one another, and the universal principles that affect them both, would indeed be ideal vehicles for Garcilaso's cross-over efforts from one position to another. But neither forensic force nor equalizing reciprocity is the main characteristic of the particular style that Hebreo practiced and that Garcilaso perfected.

Hebreo's dialogues don't drive; they ramble and circle. His interlocutors don't use one another as foils for reaching a truth that favors one and dismisses the other; they charm one another with intelligent talk and probing questions. Philón talks. Sophía questions. One answer raises more queries, and objections bring opportunities for more speculation. In fact, the dialogue never ends; it just stops. Hebreo announced another conversation to follow his three-part work, but that final, fourth, dialogue has never been found. Perhaps it was preempted by the unstable environment. Writing projects can get lost in geographic shuttles and political see-saws.[83] But the unfinished form is noteworthy for more than its possible traces of circumstance; it makes sense in a Neoplatonic treatise about the continuing process of perfecting the world. How could a final, grammatically "perfect," word be pronounced before the process is finished? Whatever Garcilaso may have learned about legal argumentation from these dialogues, it was not how to reach closure.

As for noticing the possibility of ideal reciprocity in the genre, its opportunities for translating from one position to the other, there is nothing of the sort in Hebreo. The translations between codes transpire only in Philón's voice. He develops classical myths into allegorical analogies with Scripture; he follows the thread that ties human desire to universal love. Sophía tells us nothing, it seems. She just taunts the man, goads him, keeps him chasing after explanations, and after her. To focus on the balance of voices in an open-ended dialogue like this one, as opposed to the Socratic sort, is to miss the particular style here. It is playful, or nervous; and the only balance it produces between the interlocutors is a balance of power. He has all the answers, but she keeps dodging any conclusive assent. Whatever legal and logical connections he can master, Philón is finally a slave to the law of desire.

> No te puedo resistir, o Sophía! Quando pienso averte atajado todos los caminos de la huyda, te me vas por nueva senda. Conviene, pues, hazer lo que te plaze; y la principal razon es que soy amante y tu amada; a ti toca darme la ley, y a mi guardarla con execucion.

> [I cannot resist you, O Sophía! When I think I have cut off all the paths of your flight, you escape through a new route. It makes sense, then, to do what pleases you; and the principal reason is that I am a lover and you are the beloved; it is up to you to give me the law, and up to me to keep and execute it.][84]

Hebreo's most original lessons are in coquettish instability. Renaissance intellectuals dared publicly to admire women's physical and intellectual charms; certainly Hebreo did. He dedicated his book to Madonna Laudomia Forteguerri, and admired, along with everyone else, his captivating cousin Doña Benvenida Abravanel, the center of intellectual salons and spirited conversation, who married his younger brother Samuel. Guedella Ibn Yahiya, that first and almost forgotten Spanish translator of Hebreo's *Dialogues,* confessed that the book had changed his own misogynist mind and had inspired a short work he later wrote, "In Praise of Women."[85]

Coyly, but unmistakably, Sophía's lessons are thematized in Hebreo's book. Her loving quip about Philón's intellectual agility shows it to be unstoppable: "Ya puedes dezir lo que se te antojare, que segun veo, bien sabes el modo de rescatarte" (you can well say whatever you like, for I can see you know how to rescue yourself). Endless talk that solves the very problems it raises (as if problems were a desired opportunity to keep talk alive), and the slippery wisdom that keeps intelligence on the chase by subordinating knowledge to desire, are Hebreo's basic elements of style. They describe the book's constant maneuvering between engagement and estrangement. Together, the lessons teach an inexhaustible logic of errancy that evidently inspired Garcilaso.[86] That the translator was attentive to the alternating rhythm of the book is clear from his comments in the prologue-letter to Don Maximiliano of Austria: Hebreo did not write for passive readers, but "for those who would accompany him, philosophizing together." Garcilaso's very process of translation, in bits and pieces for his own recreation, suggests that Hebreo's almost playful rhythm of pursuit must have been at least as alluring as its philosophical conclusions about the ultimate coherence of competing systems of belief.[87]

TWO TONGUES

Hebreo was the master dialectician of desire, the model of a literary practice that urged correspondences and cast them as ever higher degrees of love. When Sophía wonders why desire does not flag after the act of love is consummated, Philón answers, rakishly, that she obviously lacks experience in the matter. Desire of the flesh may be sated by contact with the flesh, but a lover's desire has no rest—a reply probably aimed at the nontranscendent philosophers associated with Maimonides and Averroes, who put sex at the center of worldly activity.[88] When desire is born of intellectual as well as corporeal attractions—like the multiple charms with which Peru could captivate her conqueror in Garcilaso's historical seductions—corporeal copulation frustrates the lovers more than it fulfills them. Physical love is so limited a form of penetration that it only whets an appetite for a more complete union. Bodies are vehicles, but they get in the way.[89] Heretical as this sounds, the philosophical content of Hebreo's book sometimes seems besides the main point for his interlocutors, the point being simply to keep talking. The diachronic-dialogic frame shuttles a reader between responding to a lover's command and attending to the always insufficient words that renew the command. That frame continually shows through the philosophical (synchronic and thematizable) meanings that Philón apparently masters.[90] And the diachrony, the proximity through time, is what keeps the lovers together. Philón and Sophía crave one another's conversational contact, they can't get enough of one another, because whichever tongue happens to be working (either the one between the lips or the one between the legs, in Philón's (porno)graphic analogy[91] borrowed from *Sefer Yezirah*),[92] the limited and frustrating contact it makes with the beloved only goads desire. When Philón seems to have sewn up all the arguments, Sophía wisely points to a loose thread in a badly stitched text. The exasperated and exhilarated man in love concedes, and continues to talk.

Can it be merely accidental that the dialogues do not end? The fragmentary form, as I mentioned, makes philosophical sense, since it participates in an unfinished Neoplatonic process of perfecting the world. But the form makes another kind of tactical sense, too. It gives an open-ended shape to the lesson of continuity in the dialogues, a lesson of avoiding closure, of maneuvering in and out of the intellectual gaps, in this way producing more talk and keeping the lovers together. Philón's intellectual superiority is acknowledged in every one of Sophía's endless questions. He has all the ideas, all the explanations; he makes all the theological and philosophical connections between cultures; his tongue is the source of information. He is also the more sublime lover, as a man who can use a nether tongue for giving love. "Ten paciencia, o Sophía!, que mas perfetamente ama el varón, que da, que la hembra, que recibe" [Be patient, O Sophía!, because the man, who gives, loves more perfectly than the woman, who receives].[93] And the capacity to engender both ideas and babies with the two tongues makes his "bilingual" love analogous to a parent's selfless love for a child and God's divine love for creation.

Sophía is, in fact, quite patient with his unflattering comparison between their respective levels of intelligence and generosity. Her advantage over him is entirely different. She is as wise as her name, Hebreo shows us repeatedly. How can that be? What virtue can she possibly have in a philosophical dialogue about love that casts her counterpart as the only expert? The answer is strategic: Sophía embodies the virtue and the wisdom of tactical evasion. She can humble a superior intellect by simply refusing to be overwhelmed. Sophía is ever on the alert for discursive lapses, those promising opportunities to talk and to stay, to safeguard, in Levinas' vocabulary, the eroticized and ethical proximity of incomplete Saying from the cold and asocial finality of the Said.

Although Philón is the uncontested male giant of scholarship, pretty little Sophía can lead him by the nose. Like a delicate but dauntless choreographer of bulls, she is wisdom itself, perfecting the powerful intellect by engaging it in a continuing program of graceful exercise. Desire is what makes Philón submit; it weakens his will, constrains his self-confidence, and puts him to work. It would seem that Garcilaso learned to double as Sophía when he learned, in his own work, to maneuver around a privileged and powerful reader who could be taught to desire and to defer to the guide.

Garcilaso's seduction reaches an almost perverse level of refinement. It both offers satisfaction and undercuts it. Sophía's coy evasions and Philón's passionate pronouncements, her destabilizing questions and his intellectual reparations, both echo through one dialogic style. Reaching farther, Garcilaso's characteristic shuttling and weaving (between viewpoints, languages, cults, and countries) not only unhinges any intellectual mooring a reader may have had; it also makes the author the moving target of his reader's unsated desire. And insatiable desire, we know from Hebreo, is one sure sign of love.

CORTEZ IN THE COURTS

4

—The judge wants to know if you stole a horse.
—I stole a horse?
—The defendant says he stole a horse.
—Ask the defendant why he stole the horse.
—The judge wants to know why you stole the horse.

—I needed a horse?
—The defendant says he needed the horse.
—Ask him why he needed the horse.

—The judge asks what you needed the horse for.
—Me? A horse? I needed a horse *oyf kapures* (for a sacrifice; meaning, for nothing; I didn't need it).
—The defendant says he needed the horse for ritual purposes.

(Yiddish joke)

On May 5, 1992, the day after children came back to school in smoldering Los Angeles, a front-page article in the *New York Times* showed a dark child drawing houses aflame and people being assaulted. These were his memories of the riots that followed a local court's acquittal of four white policemen who brutalized Rodney King. On the same front page, another legal decision made the news. The Supreme Court overturned the guarantees for fair hearings established by the 1966 amendment to habeas corpus (here is the body). That amendment had acknowledged the possibilities of error, ignorance, or bias, when it entitled state prisoners to a retrial at the federal level, if "the material facts were not adequately developed at the state-court hearing." This legal refinement had enhanced the law dramatically: "Of the 400 habeas corpus petitions granted each year, more than 40% of all the death penalty cases were overturned." A corollary was the 1978 Public Law No. 95-539, the federal Court Interpreters Act, which stimulated state and municipal courts to also guarantee translations when needed. Laws like these were transforming the American courtroom.[1]

Some resented the change. Years later, the Supreme Court ruled in favor of simplicity over carefulness. Perversely, it allowed translation to replace testimony in *Hernández vs. New York* (1991), by absolving a District Attorney from charges of racism after he disqualified two possible jurors because they were Hispanic. Spanish speakers would have heard statements directly and upset the equanimity of a court that heard only English translations.[2] Any legal difference between testimony and interpretation evaporated entirely in the May 4, 1992, decision, reported by the *Times* alongside fresh images of race-riots. In *Keeney v. Tamayo-Reyes* the Court ruled out obligations to remedy misunderstanding when it found no reason to retry a Cuban convict of manslaughter, even though his lawyer had failed to offer crucial evidence. Instead, the lawyer offered Tamayo-Reyes a no contest plea, so badly translated that the defendant did not understand what he was signing.

The *Times* article did not editorialize on a connection between the Washington ruling and West Coast unruliness. In both cases, justice parodied its own ideal of indifference. The Los Angeles judges chose to be blind to the videotaped violence of white authority against a single black man; and a week later, our highest court decided to be deaf to the demand for translatable justice: if English is a problem for subjects of the law, it is *their* problem, not one that the law should consider. Blind and deaf, but not dumb, the country's courts continue to promulgate rules that resent intrusive minorities, as if discouraging blacks and Hispanics from expecting real equity were a guarantee of white privilege and property. While the angel of vengeance ravaged the city named for more benign spirits, and while one city after another girded itself against a potential scourge, Supreme Court judges were counting the nickels and dimes of legal proceedings, cutting the short-term costs of retrials, not the long-term material and social costs of injustice.[3]

Sometimes a life is lost in translation. Mistranslation (or visual underexposure) can misfire in a series of casualties, including a ricochet effect back onto the benighted or befuddled source. These are the dangers suggested in the juxtaposed articles of May 5th. Errors can be fatal enough, even when intentions are sound. But the high court's indifference to error is high arrogance. It says, in effect, that English is the only legally binding language. The decision will probably not foster a utopian, inclusive, polity that speaks the same socially binding language. Instead it is likely to have the opposite effect: it will inflict legal binds on virtually indefensible "outsiders."

A melting pot fantasy that dissolves the differences it might celebrate is a double bind familiar to American law.[4] Rather than trace the twists of that history here, I want to fix on a particular scene of contradiction (and of misfired translations), a scene that has been played and replayed ever since Gregorio Cortez shot the sheriff in Karnes County, Texas, on June 12, 1901, and then escaped a small army of Rangers for ten days.[5]

VERSIONS OF THE MAN

The first English versions were newspaper articles about the killing and the characters. The *San Antonio Express* of June 23 reported that Cortez had until then respected the law during the eleven years he and his brother lived in Karnes County. And two days later, alongside indignant complaints that the man should have been lynched as soon as he was brought to San Antonio, the same paper ran a front-page piece on the Mexican's good looks and confident manner:

> He is tall, slender, and lithe, with the lean muscular appearance of one who has passed through a trying physical ordeal . . . His hands and feet are small and well shaped. His head is large and of good shape. It is covered with hair, of which any society "exquisite" might be envious—black as night and tumbling in heavy curls all over his head. His face is long and aquiline, all the features being regular . . . The eyes are brown and bright, but not fierce or unduly prominent in repose . . . his teeth are regular and white . . . He was easy in his manner and showed no embarrassment . . . it was apparent that Cortez understood English, and later demonstrated that he could speak it . . . he coolly proceeded to give the officers a detailed statement . . . He talked unaffectedly and was at pains to make himself clear, often repeated statements over and over to make himself understood. Where his statements seemed at variance with the facts as known by the officers, he argued the point and usually succeeded in removing the doubt.[6]

The ambivalence of the Anglo public is patent, but it goes as unacknowledged and uncommented in the *Express* as does the pattern of legal blindness and deafness in the recent *Times*. Demands for the Mexican's blood competed with calls for brotherhood, because some outsiders cast Cortez as a dark-skinned demon while others read him as romantic victim. The subsequent story of trials, appeals, and retrials—lasting a dozen years until Governor Colquitt finally pardoned Cortez on July 14, 1913, would bear out the romantic reading. As early as an *Express* article of October 10, 1901—where much is made of the murderous mistranslations that led to the shooting, followed up by a reversal of the guilty verdict at the Texas Court of Criminal Appeals on January 15, 1902—English speakers have had occasion to pause over the decisive details that we will review here. But the newspapers' reaction to Cortez's release retained the initial ambivalence about the case; one local paper ran a restrained review of the history, while another editorialized on the "Dangerous Murderer Pardoned."[7] In English, the story kept shuttling between one account of criminality and another of unaccountable victimization.

But in Spanish it stayed at a pitch of epic heroism. First *El Regidor* and then *El Imparcial*, both of San Antonio, published the news, along with appeals for justice, for funds, and for reliable lawyers. As far away as Mexico City, *El Popular* repeated the plea for fairness and funds.[8] And the news ran ahead of the papers through the *corridos* about Cortez. In Texas, at the turn of the century, news could circulate in corridos, popular, usually anonymous, Spanish ballads that sang the news, commemorated heroes and lamented lost loves, often in patriarchal patterns (which nevertheless leave women some room to maneuver).[9] Called "the people's newspaper,"[10] the corrido often begins by precisely dating, and usually locating, the event.[11] Still a popular practice in Mexico and on its frontiers, singing corridos is as close to medieval "trovar" as one can imagine. Its composers-singers are literally called *trovadores ambulantes*, traveling troubadours.[12] And few ballads have traveled as wide, as long, or in as many variants as the "Corrido de Gregorio Cortez." This staple of border balladry takes advantage of the news to repeat postures of resistance that were already legendary, as if the facts were a confirmation of fabled Mexican courage and capacity, rather than particular news items.[13] The earliest extant version, offered for sale as "The

Mexico City Broadside," became a regular in the minstrels' repertoire; it begins, classically, by timing and placing a verifiable event:

> Como decimos, así es,
> en mil novecientos uno,
> el día veintidós de junio
> fue capturado Cortés.
>
> En junio día veintidós
> por telégrafo supieron
> que a Cortés lo aprehendieron
> entre el Sauz y Palafox.[14]
>
> [I tell it like it is,
> in nineteen hundred and one
> on the twenty-second of June
> they captured Cortez.
>
> Through the telegraph box
> on June the twenty-second
> they knew Cortez was arrested
> between Sauz and Palafox.]

Many versions followed, as did debates about the accuracy of detail. All this activity shows the ballad's endurance. A 1929 recording ends in tragedy, when Christ-like Cortez allows himself to be betrayed; another sets him free after eight years in prison.[15] These and others were collected by Américo Paredes, a man whose interlocking careers as singer, poet, journalist, and folklorist bring home the generic connections between reporting the news and recording (in both senses) corridos. In a 1958 book that predated and helped to establish what we now call Chicano studies, Paredes framed his own resistance to Anglo bigotry by retelling the story of this legendary resister to an audience of a linguistically limited academy, whose influential interpreters of border tensions, such as J. Frank Dobie and Walter Prescott Webb, had been arguing the superiority of Anglo-Texans over allegedly degenerate Mexicans. Paredes outperformed—or outgunned—them. "*With His Pistol in His Hand": A Border Ballad and Its Hero* is a book entitled by the phallic posturing of a selected verse from the Cortez corrido, and ably aimed at the new Texas Rangers on patrol in academic walkways. When it appeared, after some concern for reprisals at the University of Texas Press, an ex-Texas Ranger actually threatened to "shoot the sonafabitch who wrote that book."[16]

More than merely an inspiration, the book was an important source for a 1983 movie, *The Ballad of Gregorio Cortez*, starring Edward Olmos (of *Zoot Suit* and *Miami Vice* fame), directed by Robert Young, and produced by Moctezuma Esparza, with support from Robert Redford's Sundance Institute, PBS, and the National Endowment for the Arts. It was originally produced for television, but Olmos made personal efforts to have it distributed to theaters.[17] The movie is significantly named for the corrido, rather than for the bald events, and so puts itself in the category of repeatable and enduring popular revisions of history. This version opens on a locomotive belching smoke as it transports Cortez from one prison to the next, we later learn, while the sound track mixes train whistles with Paredes's own voice singing two verses from the corrido, his "Variant X."[18] The movie, a popular medium for this update of the ballad, is meant to appeal to (some will say primarily) Anglo audiences as well as Hispanic. For both, it dramatizes more than injustice and defiance; it also stages the vagaries and the violence of bad translation. By focusing on the film we can linger over the differences between this extended fiction and the contemporary reports in newspapers and in popular ballads. The fiction, we will see, organizes the facts of the matter into the unmistakable motifs of a fractured polity. After seeing and hearing the movie, it would be hard to miss the pattern of refusals to translate justice into practical terms, hard to miss the connection between the right and the center of the *Times* front page.

Fiction makes good use of opportunities for dwelling on newsworthy problems of translation. One example is Mario Vargas Llosa's novelistic gloss on his own journalism. In newspaper articles of 1983 he had confronted Indians' cultural intransigence as an obstacle to Peru's national unity; but five years later, *The Storyteller* (1987) would circle in slowly and self-consciously on the cultural devastation visited on Indians by Peru's intolerant desire for unity. The care and the graceful pace of his ponderings will be taken up in a later Chapter. But here I mention his success in moving from "objective" reportage to self-implicating fiction, because it speaks to the same kind of contemplative opening that the film offers to the news about Cortez.

Developed beyond other versions of the Cortez legend, the movie is a meditation on the presumptive arrogance of English-speaking law enforcers. Histories tell the same story, notably the detailed history that Paredes offers, complete with misfired translations and, unfortunately, better aimed bullets; and the versified variants had been repeating the story for years. But only the film elicits a particular effect on the audience, a guilt-provoking effect of self-conscious collusion, or at least of acknowledged nescience. For all the deadpan humor that Renato Rosaldo points out in Paredes's text,[19] the written version plays no joke on the reader. On the contrary, it splices in the linguistic ironies of the story as it unfolds. Paredes does not withhold correct translations. He shares information openly, and welcomes English language readers as intimates of the misunderstood Mexicans.

But the movie does hold back reliable translation by playing the bilingual scene of confrontation and shooting of the sheriff without subtitles. It thereby withholds intimacy with a reserve that parallels Gayatri Chakravorty Spivak's remarks about Mrinal Sen's almost contemporary movie of North India, *Genesis* (1986). Like the *Ballad,* Sen's film withholds translation, strategically. It constructs an aesthetic object that is suddenly unavailable to outsiders who had been reading English captions until a dramatic moment, when a woman sings, without subtitles.[20] This is not to say that Sen's movie excludes English-only viewers, any more than does *The Ballad of Gregorio Cortez,* but that the target audiences are doubled. The films include us all, but border people who live on the line in English only will see the films very differently from the bilingual straddlers of two worlds.

TARGET AUDIENCE

Put a bit provocatively, *The Ballad* sets a trap for its Anglo viewers and eludes their efforts to grasp its meaning until the end, when reasons for the initial violence and for the hour-long chase scenes are finally cleared up in court. Meaning escapes monolinguals for as long as Cortez manages to escape his pursuers. The film depicts the Mexican's regional mastery, so embarrassingly superior to that of 600 Texas Rangers, at the expense of a similarly embarrassed Anglo audience. The movie, in other words, makes us worry about more than what we watch; it corners us into considering who watches and from what position on the language divide. And for all the incongruities of interpretation possible on either side, this film—like resistant texts—performs the necessary gesture of highlighting an impassable incongruity between the sides.

Let us listen to the scene of initial conflict, as Boone Choate presumes to negotiate the divide. Sheriff Morris had taken him along to Cortez's ranch, Choate explains later to a reporter from the *Express,* because "I talk Mexican. I been around 'em most of my life." Then the film cuts back to translator Choate and the sheriff driving up in a surrey as Gregorio sits on the porch stoop, arms around knees, while his brother Romaldo stands in the foreground. The surrey drives in, Gregorio stands up, thrusts hands in pockets, leans against a post, and listens:

CHOATE: Buenes tardees.

ROMALDO: Buenas tardes.

MORRIS: Ask him his name.

CHOATE: Como ste . . . como seyames?

ROMALDO: Romaldo.

MORRIS: Ask old Romaldo if he knows Gregorio Cortez.

CHOATE: El cherife quiere hablar con Gregorio Cortez.

ROMALDO: [looking back] Te quieren.

GREGORIO: Gregorio Cortez, a sus órdenes, ¿en qué les puedo ayudar?

CHOATE: [to Morris] He didn't tell him you wanted to talk to him. He told him you wanted him.

MORRIS: Ask him if he's traded in a horse lately.

CHOATE: El cherife quiere saber si has cambiado un caballo ahora.

GREGORIO: No. Un caballo, no.

CHOATE: He says he hasn't traded a horse.

MORRIS: I understand "No," Boone. Uh, tell him another fellow said he did.

CHOATE: El cherife . . . dici . . . que . . . ya hablamos con . . . con el otro, que no hay que mentir.

[Gregorio walks off the porch toward Romaldo, who turns around toward him.]

ROMALDO: Vinieron por el cambio . . . esos rinches.

GREGORIO: [To Romaldo] Sí. [To Morris] No estamos mintiendo. No cambiamos un caballo, era una yegua [Romaldo laughs], pero hace dos días.

CHOATE: They ain't gonna tell you nothing.

MORRIS: Well, you habla him that he's under arrest. [gets down from surrey]

CHOATE: [with sly smile toward Gregorio] El cherife dici que te va a arestar.

GREGORIO: ¿Por qué? No hemos hecho nada. No nos puede arrestar por nada.

CHOATE: Nooo? [Morris faces him for clarification] He says no man can arrest him.

MORRIS: Boy [he cocks his gun toward Gregorio], get back in that surrey.

[Morris shoots Romaldo as he is running, and Gregorio shoots Morris, walks up close to his writhing body and shoots again, with a long stare of contempt and defiance.]

An Anglo audience is no doubt upset by the violence of an American sheriff who shoots a Mexican for helping his brother resist arrest, perhaps on some trumped up charge. And the uneasy feeling is probably compounded by the fury Morris triggers in Cortez. But a bilingual audience also knows enough to laugh with Romaldo and to wince over Choate's incompetence, enough to feel the violence more poignantly, as a tragedy of humorless arrogance in translation. Bilinguals will notice, immediately after Choate's boastful "I speak Mexican," that he can hardly speak at all. From the mispronounced greeting to the last and fatal mistranslation, he is both funny and infuriating. Here are the same exchanges as insiders hear them:

CHOATE: *Gid afternood.*

ROMALDO: *Good afternoon.*

MORRIS: Ask him his name.

CHOATE: *What yer . . . what's yer named?*

ROMALDO: Romaldo.

MORRIS: Ask old Romaldo if he knows Gregorio Cortez.

CHOATE: *The sheriff wants to talk to Gregorio Cortez.*

ROMALDO: [looking back] *They want to talk to you.*

GREGORIO: *Gregorio Cortez, at your service. How may I help you?*

CHOATE: [to Morris] He didn't tell him you wanted to talk to him. He told him you wanted him.

MORRIS: Ask him if he's traded in a horse lately.

CHOATE: *The sheriff wants to know if you traded a horse now.*

GREGORIO: *No, not a horse/stallion.*

CHOATE: He says he hasn't traded a horse.

MORRIS: I understand "no," Boone. Uh, tell him another fellow said he did.

CHOATE: *The sheriff ... says ... that ... we already talked to the other guy. ... that you shouldn't lie.*

[Gregorio walks off the porch toward Romaldo, who turns around toward him.]

ROMALDO: *They came about the trade ... those rangers.*

GREGORIO: [To Romaldo] *Right.* [To Morris] *We are not lying. We didn't trade a horse/stallion. It was a mare.* [Romaldo laughs] *But it was two days ago.*

CHOATE: They ain't gonna tell you nothing.

MORRIS: Well you habla him that he's under arrest. [gets down from surrey]

CHOATE: [with sly smile toward Gregorio] *The sheriff says he's gonna arrest you.*

GREGORIO: *Why? We haven't done anything. He can't arrest us for nothing.*

CHOATE: Nooo? [Morris faces him for clarification] He says no man can arrest him.

MORRIS: Boy [he cocks his gun toward Gregorio], get back in that surrey.

One deadly joke is on the sheriff, of course, who gets shot for thinking that "no" effectively summarizes a much longer sentence. He presumes that the object of his interrogation can answer only yes or no, that Cortez is too simple to engage in word games and to show himself a master of language. By today's standards, the sheriff's very style of indirect interrogation is asking for trouble. After a long history of misunderstandings between law enforcers and citizens, today's bilingual courtroom requires judges, prosecutors, and lawyers to address defendants and witnesses directly. In Texas, to be specific, "The interpretation shall be conducted in the first and second person, as if the interpreter did not exist. The non-English speaking client should be informed of this, so as to avoid confusion. For instance, the question should be 'What is your name?' NOT 'Ask him what his name is.' Likewise, the interpreter shall respond for the client 'MY name is . . .' NOT 'He says his name is . . .'" California passed a similar law in 1981: "All questions by counsel examining a non-English speaking witness should be directed to the witness and not the interpreter. For example, do not say, 'Ask him if . . .'" Nevertheless, Susan Berk-Seligson notes that attorneys and judges still lapse into addressing the interpreter, just as Morris addressed Choate. And interpreters, true to their title, often shape the exchanges more than simply translate them.[21]

The force of the movie's fatal humor falls mostly on Choate, the subject who presumes to know and to translate. By extension it falls on those of us who follow the false leads of his translations. In answer to Gregorio's dignified courtesy *(a sus órdenes, ¿en qué les puedo ayudar?),* Choate counters with innuendo about Romaldo's alleged misrepresentation. Then the sheriff's suggestion about contradictory reports escalates to a charge of lying. And Cortez's informative banter about the mare who doesn't fit into Choate's limited masculine signifier, along with more information about the precise timing of the admitted trade, is traduced into a report of intransigence. Finally, *nada* is confused with *nadie* to twist Gregorio's legal logic about grounds for arrest into unnuanced resistance of the law.

It would be impractical to object to the inevitable linguistic damage done in translation's move from one language to another, literally from one side to the other. To hear quotes misplaced or misused is hardly surprising, given what deconstructionists have been telling us about the iterable quality of language, its decontextualized life, and the attendant problem of shifty signifiers.[22] My move here is merely to notice the points at which the sides are inscribed or circumscribed, to discover when translation pays tolls or is forced to stop. Instead of bringing us to the other side, Choate's translations derail understanding. Patient reconstruction of the linguistic detours that lost their way finally do rescue comprehension, just as the Rodney King trials finally do convict two of the four policemen. The Texas court eventually did authorize a competent translation by Carolot Muñoz, who had been active in the general effort to free Cortez.[23] But by then the man had spent twelve years in prison. His health was broken, and he died soon afterwards.

In legal terms, nevertheless, the outcome seems to make one theme of the story and of the movie (and of the King trials) clear: the fight was worth the effort. U.S. lawmakers have had to acknowledge the potential universality of their own law, and they will have to assume the burden of halting, tentative, translation. From this promising perspective, the desire of the film is to produce competent viewers and interlocutors from within an English-speaking audience that is, by definition, not ideal.

MISSING MEXICANS

This "happy ending" is what many Chicano critics object to. They complain that the film abandons the Mexican perspective of the original corrido. It never mentions the Mexican newspapers that exonerated the hero and the Mexican community that raised funds for his legal defense. Instead, the movie highlights English-language journalism and English-language law. Cortez is no longer the subject of his own story, but an object on screen, practically mute, reduced to almost bestial simplicity, close to the land, closer to his horse. He is the object of a story for the *San Antonio Express* by Bill Blakely, a reporter so smart and skeptical about the Texas Rangers' intentions and tactics that he finally solves the mystery of a mare taken for a horse. What has happened to Cortez? Rosa Linda Fregoso makes this point, as do other Chicano scholars, when she objects to the "subordination" of the hero as the most striking feature of the film.[24] Silencing him, "denying a subject voice in the narrative to the central agent of the historical event," she says, "corresponds to the elision of the Chicano point of view"; and this is unforgivable in a film that on the face of it denounces the subjugation of Mexicans. The fundamental error, Carl Gutiérrez-Jones had said, is that the film frames Cortez inside an Anglo-Texan legal framework; Anglo law makes Cortez the object of its (colonial) gaze, presumably an exotic, primitive exhibit for general Anglo viewers who share that legal discourse.[25] And where are the Chicano viewers? Historian Tatcho Mindiola protests that they have been shut out, along with their hero and his Mexican supporters, by the movie's Anglo perspective.[26] Guillermo Hernández objects to the film's omissions: of Mexican journalism, of community support, of the fact that

Cortez knew English: "Whatever the reason and intention of the filmmakers might have been, the consequence of this dramatic choice is the representation of Gregorio as an inarticulate and stoic victim whose tragedy would not have occurred had he enjoyed the benefits of bilingual education."[27]

In the move from the corrido to the film, Mexicans have been translated out of the picture for these Chicano critics, who demand more visibility and more positive representations of Mexicans on the screen. And they have a point, despite other points one could make about the advantages of "unmarked" nonrepresentational engagements and about the political limitations of essentialism. Visibility is an important mark and means for legitimacy, as activists for gay and cultural rights will tell you. The movie may well be playing to Anglos, however self-critically. Certainly the English-language newspapers were enthusiastic about it.[28] But if the movie fails "to be" Chicano in any essential way, it does not fail utterly. For one thing, it enacts the cultural difference between Anglos and Chicanos, drawing a line of comprehension that calls to mind English-language law, with its insiders and outsiders. Viewers inevitably identify themselves as either bilingual insiders or as English-only "targets" of bilingual jokes. For another thing, even though Mexicans are not telling this version of the story, they have left a linguistic residue so thick and insoluble that it purposefully mires the Anglo version until the specificity of Spanish is acknowledged. Bilingual Cortez wasn't holding out for nothing.

His refusal to use English speaks to a desire that exceeds the "happy" legal ending of the film. That desire suggests a "Mexican" perspective that critical Chicanos may have missed, insofar as it hesitates before, instead of welcoming, Anglo understanding and interference. Even "badly formed" and misunderstood phrases have meaning. This is a Wittgensteinian point that helps Lyotard to account for speech that refuses exact translation. The meaning is precisely the refusal to move from one language regime to another, the insistence on untranslatability that situates the speaker at a distance from the addressee.[29] Truer to the heroic spirit of the corridos than to the extended and exonerating history of legalities, this more prickly perspective prefers to keep resistance alive. Instead of encouraging correct translations from the local language into imperious universals, the film's alternative desire is to refuse collaboration, to paint a fresh coat of local color on the stop signs in translation's way.

Why else does Cortez strike the unmistakably proud and unyielding posture that Edward Olmos repeats in the movie? Hands stuck in his pockets, leaning with theatrical ease on the post of his porch, Olmos's Cortez is a studied model of pride and courtesy, as if those attributes played on the courtly etymology of his name. Why else would he concede to the artifice of translation if he knew English, except to keep the sides distinct? And why does he speak in a conspicuously Mexican singsong, underscored by Romaldo's Pan-American register, except to claim pride of place as a proper Mexican on his own property? Politeness and pride are his displays of superiority, gestures of formal hospitality to strangers in the land. Paredes would write similar gestures into a short story about "Little Joe," composed just after World War II but published only recently, probably written in response to caricatures of Mexican American soldiers in novels like Norman Mailer's *The Naked and the Dead*. Paredes's hero is quiet and seems menacing to the bigger men in his squad ("That little guy, he don't look like much, but don't cross him, I'd hate to do that"). But Joe's calm is a mark of his courtesy, as Ramón Saldívar notes.[30] And courtesy, as I am reading it here, can be a passive-aggressive measure of his cultural superiority, even if the gringos cannot read it.

THE CONCEPT OF LAG-TIME

From this perspective, then, even the correct translation of the event, bringing out Cortez's cooperation that Anglo viewers of *The Ballad* will appreciate, may reveal a kind of intransigence after all. Distance survives translation. We know that presumption and ignorance are finally indicted in court, as the bandit hero of the corridos is convicted, retried, reindicted, removed from one prison to the next, and finally pardoned. But after almost a century, his audience remains divided. Part of it continues to sing and to hear his ballad, and to be immediately *in* on the film's jokes. Another part stands as far outside the humor of codes in collision as did the legal system that gradually admitted its own limitations. The difference is hardly forgettable, especially now that the Supreme Court has admitted that its limitations don't much matter.

English, it will be understood, is different from Spanish; it can ignore the distinction between male and female horses and seem laughably simple to a

Mexican victim of moving borders. Cortez resists the language and the law-lessness of those who took half of Mexico's territory in the 1840s war. The Republic of Texas, we know, is a particular case of national banditry. It had seceded from Mexico in 1836, after Americans settled there and outnum-bered the Mexicans ten to one. Mexican Tejanos fought for independence alongside the newcomers, but then found that they had merely traded one master for another. By 1845 the United States annexed Texas, as the first gobble of territorial gluttony, and two years later Mexico was half its former size.[31] With characteristic ambivalence, the war was unpopular for many Anglos, who saw little justification for annexing the dusty land and just as little gain. The effort was driven by an expansive army and hawked by ideo-logues who meant to save Mexicans from their own benighted habits (per-haps with the same kind of confidence in universally valid law and language that motivates our current High Court). Walt Whitman was one such hawk, to the horror of his friends. Remembering Whitman here is almost in-evitable on both sides of the shifty border; he is the enduring voice of Amer-ica's liberal embrace. Benignly, we sometimes celebrate him for equating progress and democracy with America, but translated to Mexico the enthu-siasm reads differently. *Walt Whitman: racista, imperialista, anti-mexicano* (1971) by Mauricio González de la Garza collects some of the bard's newspa-per editorials to show the belligerence of that equation. In one, Whitman celebrates Taylor's victory in Monterrey as "another clinching proof of the indomitable energy of the Anglo-Saxon character" (*Brooklyn Eagle,* October 13, 1846).[32] *Democratic Vistas* (1871) will show an apparently more accommodating Whitman, less worried about ethnic and linguistic differ-ences, because the war was already won. American nationalism was "melt-ing everything else with resistless heat, and solving all lesser and definite distinctions in vast, indefinite spiritual, emotional power."

Gregorio Cortez (the man, the myth, and the movie) resists the heat. And his exemplary performance of polite intransigence hints at a whole range of devices that comprise a rhetoric of particularism. His proud pose, the movie makers seem to say, should prepare for meaningful communication with powerful interlocutors who come to see that they have been speaking out of turn. Texts like *The Ballad of Gregorio Cortez* resist the dominant culture by staying intentionally cool before the Whitmanian warmth. An-nouncing limited access is the point, not whether or not some information is really withheld. Cortez, after all, withholds nothing. His resistance, ironically, is really a compliance in the local language; but the choice of language puts the sheriff, the judges, and the viewer in their linguistic places.[33] Cortez constructs the positions of "insiders" and "outsiders" as tragically incommensurate. If he did, in fact, know English, he refused to let on, or to let the sheriff in. And professional readers like Paredes, who share social space with Cortez-like performers or protagonists, enough to claim privileged understanding and explanatory powers, may rush to fill in the gaps which the texts' authors would demarcate.

The book you are reading now is an exercise in reading such pauses and residues from translation, in order to locate the ethical and political limits of comprehension. This attention to the tempo of communication has some relationship to Homi Bhabha's concept of lag-time, which names the temporal gaps between a center and peripheries that cannot (or will not) catch up. Bhabha does some urgent work of underlining the asymmetries and complicating the notion of empty or homogeneous modern time that he attributes to Walter Benjamin (although we should say that Benjamin named the bourgeois temporal tidiness in order to blast it apart with the interruptions of *Jetztzeit*).[34] For me, the notion of time-lag describes a particular asymmetry: not the inequalities Bhabha decries against the drone of institutionalized multiculturalism,[35] but the rhythmic variations in speech, even when we speak the same language. Time-lag can apply to a syncopated musical notation, a deferred reaction to stress, or a delayed apprehension of meaning, the skipped beat in conversation that also marks the rhythm of a joke; time-lag can be the signature of one language through the medium of another. We share a polity, after all; differences among speakers exist in time as well as through time, without necessarily stopping the conversation. Blockage comes, instead, from rushing to fill the gaps, through facile understanding or through empathy.

The year 1998 is an auspicious time for tuning-in to the counterpoints of Our Americas.[36] It commemorates the Spanish American War that set a new rhythm for inter-American relationships. The commemoration comes after a pause for reflection that began in 1995, when people took time out to remember three different masters who did not fit their own times. One was Sor Juana Inés de la Cruz, a nun who was too brilliant and too bold for her colonial Mexico, but who was at the center of a modern nation during her third centennial. Also in 1995 a century had elapsed since the death of Jorge Isaacs, a universal but unhomogenized figure for the nineteenth century. He was a fissured, mosaic star, a Colombian Jew, and the century's only Latin American novelist to thrill readers far beyond his own country. In his own life, though, Isaacs's Hebraic habits made him almost inassimilable at home.[37]

But the year's most significant centennial was probably the one that honored José Martí, author of many works including the Cuban War of Independence (that ended, in so many ways, with the Spanish American War) and of the essay "Our America" (1891). What "Our" means in his celebration of indigenous and African strains in New World Hispanism is a problem, for two reasons. First, the possessive pronoun neutralizes internal differences and claims ownership in monocultural ways that now seem unproductive. Martí's nineteenth-century nationalism needed to focus on victory by squinting at Cuba, compressing its complexity into a thin but homogenous *cubanidad*. The other problem is that the discriminating pronoun "Our" is so shifty, so available for competing positionalities and equivocal meanings. In a New World where commercial, cultural, and political border crossings define so many lives, boundary words like here and there, mine and yours, now and then are hardly stable signposts. They are, as always, shifters. Merely to translate "Nuestra América" as "Our America" is to deform the possessive claim by the treachery of displacement. It is to move from a defensive position right into the enemy's camp.[38]

Strategists will know that mobility is not only a cause for worry; it is also an opportunity to gain ground. Perhaps Nuestra América, in the genre of Estefan's solidarity song and in anticipation of a new Generation of '98, has a future history here, up North. Translation, of course, literally means switching ground. And following particular guides is an important precaution, if we hope to avoid the muddle of mistaking "Hispanics" for a homogeneous group. The very repetitiousness of efforts at solidarity is a cue to the divisions among constituencies usually identified by national origin.[39]

PUERTO RICAN SHUFFLE

I want to follow Puerto Rico's lead here; it can be the strong case of a nation that maneuvers along the faultline of grammatical shifters, in the space between here and there, now and then, Our America and theirs. It is a case of an entire population that is on the move, or potentially so, so much so that Luis Rafael Sánchez jokes about Puerto Rican national identity being grounded in the *guagua aérea* (air bus) shuttling up and down the Atlantic puddle.[40] Literally a nation of *Luftmenschen,* half is provisionally on the Caribbean island, and half on and around that other mad-hatter island, which has become a homeland that Tato Laviera calls *AmeRíca.*[41]

Laviera's genius is to skip a beat, to syncopate the syllables of a seamless label and unravel it, by reading the English sign for America with an eye for Spanish. In Spanish this country looks like "Améríca," because without a written accent on the "e" to give the word an irregular stress, America would use a default, unwritten, stress on the "i." Laviera's hyper-corrected reading displaces the logic of diacritical marks from one language to another and performs a time-lag of translation. The alleged omission of an accent mark is an opportunity, an invitation to read the country in syncopation as AmeRíca, a time-lagged sound whose visible signs reform the country's look too. With a foreign stroke if you read it in English (just as superfluous for Spanish, where the written accent is excessive in the default position), and with an intrusive capital "R" that splits and then fuses a conventional name into a convincing compound, Laviera's orthographic encroachment and strategic pause push both standard languages slightly out of bounds. The result is a practically providential metaphor: AmeRíca transforms what for English or Spanish is just a word into a *mot juste* in Spanglish. It proclaims doubly marked mainland Ricans as the most representative citizens we've got. AmeRícan is saying I'm a Rican.[42]

Puerto Rican independentists resent the doubling, and they resist being taken for endless rides in the guagua aérea. They were protesting America's empire even before the 1917 U.S. decision to confer, or to force, citizenship on the island. At that time, José de Diego published a protest simply and unequivocally titled "No." "Crisp, solid, decisive as a hammer blow, this is the virile word that should inflame our lips and save our honor in these sad days of anachronistic imperialism." "Yes" may be useful for some things, he coyly admits after this first sentence, but in politics "We must learn to say NO: arch the lips, relax the chest, tense up all the vocal muscles and powers of will, and shout out that O of the NO! It might resound through America and the world, and to the very heavens, more effectively than the roar of guns." An understated reason for NO being the only word with real political purchase is that its value doesn't get lost in translation. De Diego considers the alternative "sí," its brevity and harmony in Romance languages contrasting with the clumsy Latin equivalent,[43] and presumably with the cacophonic "yes" in English. Spanish and English words of affirmation do not match up, and the asymmetry opens up a space, a trench like the one we might notice between NAFTA (North American Free Trade Agreement)—sounding so explosive in European languages—and its Mexican counterpart, TLC (Tratado de Libre Comercio)—so misleadingly friendly in American English. When a Spanish speaker hears that English "yes," does s/he sometimes wonder at the insistent sibilant "s" at the end, where it might have stayed discreetly underpronounced in Spanish, wonder if the word might be a hiss of disapproval or the totemic sound of a serpent stalking its prey? And is it possible that an English listener might hear in a Spanish "sí" not a simple endorsement but an invitation to look at something unsettling? "No," by contrast, is as smooth and hard, as virile as a bullet; it may in fact be the only word that is so firm and impervious to interpretation. "No" is not vulnerable to ventriloquism, nor does it suffer from jet-lag in the endless translations of Puerto Ricans from one place and language to another. Mercifully, one word, one possession at least, doesn't tarnish or expire on the trips. NO remains intact and unambiguous.

Is it really so dependable, though? The very coherence of the word, its travel-friendly symmetry, is a kind of betrayal. The problem with "no" is precisely that it translates so easily, that it is as natural here as there, and the same in the past and present. It fooled Sheriff Morris, for example, into thinking that he understood Cortez. The very word that refuses intimacy with empire suggests that intimacy. "No" is a weapon of self-defense that turns into a deconstructive trap, a roar of virile resistance that can sound like the moan of irresistible seduction. "No" treacherously adds a supplement, despite de Diego's painstaking pronouncement. It is the message of translatability, the essence of a supple and pragmatic war of positions. "No" plays in a *fort da* rhythm that keeps universalism and particularism in contrapuntal improvisation. It refuses intimacy and therefore names it as a goal; it offers satisfaction, but undercuts it. The rhythm engages a shared language but speaks with particular patterns of stress.

To consider what America, AmeRíca, or La Merica may mean,[44] is first to hear where the accent falls. The difference, for another example, between two words for home in two homelands so often in conflict, is this: the Dominican "bohío" (indigenous hut) has a stress in the middle, while the Haitian "Boyó" (one of the names considered for the country) is two beats with a stress at the end.[45] Does America name exceptionalism, in a paradoxically repeatable project from one American country to another, as in early versions of American Studies and in José Vasconcelos's *La raza cósmica* (1925), which named Mexico's synthetic mission to the world? Or is AmeRícan part of *La raza cómica,* as Puerto Rican theorist Rubén Ríos Avila suggests when he reads missions as a kind of madness?[46] It is useful to learn to hear the local accents and the sometimes purposeful mispronunciations that legal theorist Mari Matsuda defends.[47] We may also notice that Américo is the name of the father of Chicano studies—Américo Paredes— who in 1958 warned Texan readers, "With his pistol in his hand," that they were on shifty ground, a land alternately called the Southwest and el Norte.

Translation makes for ambivalent naming in American history. For nineteenth-century founding fathers in the Southern Cone, America meant a project because it was everything they wanted to overcome: the indigenous *pampa,* emptiness, desert, an impossible grounding for a *respública,* that would first have to be filled before it could bear modern values.[48] "Gobernar es poblar," was the slogan of generations, to govern you first need to populate the territory.[49] But the word "pampa," according to El Inca Garcilaso's seventeenth-century *Commentaries,* means public space itself, and the public women who create a hub of erotic and economic interest in the suburbs of ancient Incan cities.[50]

Reading Peru's bilingual chronicler of the oxymoronic Quechua Castilian name, we may wonder what it is that we *do* know about America. It is next to nothing of indigenous cultures, but also embarrassingly little even about the Europeans' "discovery." Who, then, are the heroes of American history? How many histories is it? El Inca Garcilaso wrote one as a commentary on standard Spanish versions, and signed it with a name that added a dangerous supplement to monolingual and monorhythmic measures of worth; it was an emblem of the dangerous doubling that monolingualism makes possible while it insists that we speak the same language. Translation produces excess, as in the possessive pronoun that shifts belonging from Nuestra América to Ours, and even the simplest NO of uncompromising refusal can get stuck in the slime of translation's surplus. But for English and Spanish speakers to avoid translation would be to imagine a cultural emptiness on the other side of one Imperial language, to mistake, for instance, New York (Nous York, in an Air Canada advertisement) as unusably foreign, or El Norte as simply Gringolandia. Ambiguous and staccato translation is not only a limit of understanding; it is also an asymmetry that cures squinting because it enables winking at the counterpoints of AmeRícan negotiations.

Asymmetries keep alive what ethicist Emmanuel Levinas calls the Saying, that is, the mystery and transcendence of social intercourse; they don't allow language to kill the desired other by getting his meaning right through understanding or empathizing. The ambivalence, for example, of Gloria Estefan's exhortation to speak the same (Latino) language in a bilingual booklet suspends the copula between the speaker and her identity, just as the ambivalence of Cortez in the Courts forces English-language law to pause and consider its own limitations. These moments preserve America from being "Said" in an essentialized, definitive or dead way. The word remains a range of staggered be-longings, desired, virtual, but wisely and prophylactically unconsummated connections. They safeguard Saying Our America, in all its rhythmic accents, shifty attributions, and impossible refusals.

TAKING A LIFE

NO SECRETS FOR RIGOBERTA

5

The language-game of reporting can be
given such a turn that a report is not meant
to inform the hearer about its subject matter
but about the person making the report.

—WITTGENSTEIN
Philosophical Investigations

Rigoberta Menchú's testimonial astonished me when I read it over ten years
ago. Her secrets stopped me then, and instruct me now in other contexts,
whatever the validity of the information or the authenticity of the informant. Why should she make so much of keeping secrets instead of just keeping quiet, I wondered. And why do these cultural secrets matter, if they have
no apparent military or strategic value in her denunciation of Indian
removal politics in Guatemala? Here is an exposé that refuses to share information. The dissonance raised a question about Rigoberta: was she an
authentic witness to abuse, a vehicle for truth beyond her control and vulnerable to a compromised and infuriated government? Or was she being
coy on the witness stand, exercising control over apparently irrelevant
information, perhaps to produce her own strategic version of truth? The
difference is significant, even if the alternatives stay tangled.

For help with the answers, turn to Nietzsche to trace the fine line between
telling and troping, informing and performing. And lessons from Enrique
Dussel, Paul Ricoeur, and the shades of Church-affiliated victims of Guatemalan death squads will remind us that bearing witness has been a sacred
responsibility throughout Christianity, which is why witnesses are martyrs
etymologically and historically. Rigoberta glosses those lessons in her story

of responsible survival. Her techniques include maintaining the secrets that keep readers from knowing her too well. One conclusion to draw is that parties to productive alliances respect cultural distances among members. Like the rhetorical figure of metonymy, alliance is a relationship of contiguity, not of metaphoric overlap. To reduce the distance between writer and readers would invite false identifications that make one of those positions redundant. Rigoberta is too smart to do that. Embattled Indians generally know that reductions are dangerous. It is the word for conquered communities.

SYMPATHY AND SURVEILLANCE

But first we might notice that Rigoberta's protests of silence are responses to anthropologist Elizabeth Burgos Debray's line of questioning. If she were not asking possibly impertinent questions, the Quiché informant would have no reason to resist. From the introduction to *Me llamo Rigoberta Menchú* (1983) (My Name Is Rigoberta Menchú), we know that the testimonial is being mediated at several levels by Burgos, who records, edits, and arranges the information. The book never presumes immediacy between the narrating "I" and the readerly "you." Nor does Rigoberta offer intimacy when she claims authorship for the interviews that remain catalogued under the interrogator's name—one reason for writing her 1998 sequel was to sign her name to it.[1] Yet many readers have preferred the illusion of immediacy, perhaps from certain (autobiographical?) habits of reading that project a real and knowable person onto the persona we are hearing, despite being told that the recorded voice is synthesized and processed, and despite the repeated reminders that our access is limited. Could our ardent interest and best intentions toward the informant construe the text as a kind of artless "confession," like the ones exacted by surveillance techniques of nineteenth-century colonizers? Maybe empathy for an informant is a good feeling that covers over a controlling disposition, what Derrida calls "an inquisitorial insistence, an order, a petition . . . To demand the narrative of the other, to extort it from him like a secretless secret."[2] The possibility should make us pause. Natives who remained incalculable, because they refused to tell secrets, obviously frustrated colonial state control.[3]

Rigoberta understood the passive aggressivity, while her sentimental readers miss the point. She frustrates unabashed demands for calculable confessions. Think of Dinesh D'Souza's tirade when Stanford University made her testimonial part of a required curriculum. Instead of scientific information about genuine Indians, stable objects of investigation, he gets a protean subject of multiple discourses in Indian disguise.[4] Those of us who dismiss his inquisitorial demand for data should worry that the demand lingers in us, in our sentimental interest and solidarity. Sympathetic readers can be as reluctant as is D'Souza to accept insincerity in a life-story; they are reluctant, as well, to question their own motives for requiring intimacy.

"What draws the reader to the novel," in Walter Benjamin's scornful observation, "is the hope of warming his shivering life with a death he reads about."[5] Now that novels seem unobliging, given the sheer difficulty of modern fiction, testimonials promise more warmth. *Testimonio* is precisely not fiction. In Latin America it is a first-person narrative that can be elicited by sympathetic intellectuals who interview illiterate or semi-literate working people. The genre is juridical and broadly political, because a speaker "testifies" against abuses suffered by a class or community. As a politicized alternative to fiction, testimonials received official literary status in Cuba after that country lost the support of Latin American liberal novelists because Castro defended the Soviet invasion of Czechoslovakia. Cuba's response was to say good riddance: there were more interesting stories being produced than the difficult experimental novels of the late modernist "Boom." There were real stories about real people in struggle.[6] In 1970, Cuba's official publishing house, Casa de las Américas, designated *testimonio,* along with poetry, novel, and essay, as a prize category in the international competitions. Rigoberta won that prize in 1983. A strong case for differentiating it as genre is John Beverley's argument that *testimonio* is poised *against* literature; its collective denunciatory tone distinguishes testimony from the personal development narrative of standard autobiography, and it tends to erase the elitist author who mediates the narrative. This allows for a "fraternal or sororal" complicity between narrator and reader; in other words, a tighter bond of intimacy than is possible in manipulative and evasive fiction.[7]

I have already argued that the projections of presence and truth are less than generous here.[8] Empathy is hardly an ethical feeling, despite the enthusiasm for identifying with the Other among some political activists, including some first-world feminists.[9] In effect, the readers' projections of intimacy allow us to shorten the stretch between writer and reader, disregarding the text's rhetorical (decidedly fictional) performance of keeping us at a politically safe distance. To close in on Rigoberta would threaten her authority and leadership.[10]

David Stoll is probably right to raise some objections. Rigoberta's data are probably partial, in both senses of that word. Perhaps her father's pre-political wrangles over land did bring him into conflict with in-laws (*Anthropology Newsletter*, April 1998). And maybe Quiché and Ixil people have a habit of fighting over land (*Active Voices*, May 14, 1998). But skeptics are wise to wonder about Stoll's intention. Is it to get knowledge or to give advice? Other scrupulous fact-finders have also quibbled with passionate accounts of atrocities in Latin America, starting with the well-known objections to Bartolomé de las Casas, accused of being no historian at all, but a fabricator of tales. "He has been called noble Apostle to the Indians, piously fanatic . . .; but few men in his time or later have considered him to be a true historian," Lewis Hanke wrote in an apologetic prologue to the *Historia de las Indias*. The ineluctable fact is that a short generation after the "discovery," Caribbean peoples were practically exterminated. Hanke concludes that legends tend to be as true in substance as they are false in detail. Stoll might have concluded the same. "If poetic truth is good enough for you," then Rigoberta's story "is all too true," he writes. But he dismisses her authority in order to enhance his own, slipping from gathering facts to offering counsel.

The very fact that I am able to call self-critical attention to our culture-bound proclivities is a sign that I have been reading Rigoberta. When I began, her forthright refusals to satisfy my interest woke me to the possibility that the interest was being cultivated in order to produce the sting of rebuff. Concerns about the text's authenticity seemed beside the point, as I began to appreciate the evident manipulations. Perhaps the informant was being more active and strategic than our essentialist notions of authenticity have allowed. The possibility triggered memories of other books that had refused intimacy, and their distancing tropes came into focus as corollaries to Rigoberta's lesson.

Why should we assume that our interest in the "Other" is reciprocated? Do we imagine that the desire is mutual, or that we are irresistible? Could we consider that sympathy is not bilateral in an asymmetrical world? This possibility of unrequited interest is one lesson to learn from the kind of textual resistance Rigoberta offers. The problems raised by presuming anything less than political inequality and cultural difference are both epistemological and ethical, and they ring familiar now that postmodern skeptics have lowered the volume on masterly discourses in order to hear some competing, even incommensurate, voices.

Masterful reading, even just as aspiration, not presumption, is what some particularist narrators try to baffle. Secrets can cordon off curious and controlling readers from the vulnerable objects of their attention. Secrecy is a safeguard to freedom, Emmanuel Levinas argues, against Hegel who ridiculed it; it is the inviolable core of human subjectivity that makes interaction a matter of choice rather than rational necessity. "Only starting from this secrecy is the pluralism of society possible."[11] Menchú will repeat, with Villaverde's fictional contraband dealer in slaves, "Not everything is meant to be said."[12] But her discretion is more subtle than his, and far less corrupt. Perhaps, as I suggested, Menchú's audible silences and her wordy refusals to talk are calculated, not to cut short our curiosity, but to incite it, so that we feel distanced.

STAGED STANDOFFS

Notice that Rigoberta's refusals remain on the page after the editing is done. The refusals say, in effect, this document is a screen, in the double sense that Henri Lefebvre uses the term: something that shows and that also covers up.[13] From the beginning, the narrator tells us very clearly that she is not going to tell: "Indians have been very careful not to disclose any details of their communities."[14] They are largely "public" secrets, known to the Quichés and kept from us in a gesture of self-preservation. "They are told that the Spaniards dishonoured our ancestors' finest sons, . . . And it is to honour these humble people that we must keep our secrets. And no-one except we Indians must know."[15] By some editorial or joint decision, the very last words of the testimonial are, "I'm still keeping secret what I think no-one should know. Not even anthropologists or intellectuals, no matter how many books they have, can find out all our secrets."[16]

Readers have noticed the inevitable interference of the ethnographer in these transcriptions. And they have been critical or disappointed at the loss of immediacy, perhaps with a resentment born of ardor that chafes at insulating frames around heartwarming stories. Most offensive to many readers is Burgos Debray's Introduction, in which she presumes to share intimacy and solidarity with Rigoberta as they share meals of black beans in Paris. Almost unremarked, however, but far more remarkable for being unanticipated, are the repeated and deliberate signs of asymmetry throughout Rigoberta's testimony. Either the informant, the scribe, or both were determined to keep the admonitions in the published text. Uncooperative gestures may be typical of ethnographic interrogations, but they seldom survive in scientific reports.[17] Here, however, scientific curiosity turns out to be impertinent, to judge from the refusals to respond. If Rigoberta had not refused audibly and repeatedly, we might mistake her resistance for passivity. This contrast between the possibility of speech and an impossibility imposed by others is what Jean-François Lyotard adapts from Aristotle in order to distinguish between a plaintiff (who can attest to a crime against her) and a victim (who is silenced by her fear or is dismissed as irrelevant).[18] Are we being warned, by Rigoberta's active refusal, that our curiosity may be an impulse to warm our own cold bodies with the fuel of violated lives? In the backhanded logic of metaleptic effects, our curiosity may be the result of Rigoberta's resistance. Before she demurs, how desirous are we? I wonder whether she staged even more questions than she was asked, just to perform more refusals. This seductive possibility doesn't enter Lyotard's legal logic.[19] Without refusing our putative interest often enough for us to notice, she could hardly have exercised the uncooperative control that turns a potentially humiliating scene of interrogation into an opportunity for self-authorization.

Nevertheless, the almost 400 pages of testimony are full of information. About herself, her community, traditional practices, the armed struggle, strategic decisions. Therefore, a reader may wonder why her final statement insists, for a last and conclusive time, that we "cannot know" her secrets.

Why is so much attention being called to our insufficiency as readers? Does it mean that the knowledge is impossible or that it is forbidden? Is she saying that we are *incapable* of knowing, or that we *ought* not to know? My line of questioning repeats the quandary that Nietzsche posed in a posthumous work about the nature of truth. His dilemma highlights one of Rigoberta's tactics.

Nietzsche considers the possible truth value of language, including philosophical language that makes claims to truth, by wondering what our general criteria for validity are. The first, he says, is the identity principle. "We are unable to affirm and to deny one and the same thing," but adds immediately, "this is a subjective empirical law, not the expression of any 'necessity' but only an inability . . . The proposition therefore contains no criterion of truth, but an imperative concerning that which should count as true."[20] Can it be that logical claims to truth—from Aristotle on—depend on a *presupposition*? Does A equals A amount merely to an ethical restriction against seeing double? Nietzsche unsettles truth if identity is a voluntaristic beginning, a fiction through which one grounds systematic philosophical thinking. If the claims of philosophy are based on fiction, what is the categorical difference between one kind of writing and another, between logic and literature? The only difference, Nietzsche says, is the degree of self-consciousness. And literature is more self-conscious than other texts which confuse tropes with truth. Language, he continues, cannot absolutely affirm anything without acknowledging that any affirmation is based on a collective lie. Finally, the difference is unstable between truth and fiction, philosophy and literature, constatives and performatives, philosophical persuasion and literary troping.

How then are we to take Rigoberta's protestations of silence as she continues to talk? Are there really many secrets that she is not divulging, in which case her restraint would count as true and real? Or is she performing a kind of rhetorical, fictional seduction in which she lets the fringe of a hidden text show in order to tease us into thinking that the fabric must be extraordinarily complicated and beautiful, even though there may not be much more than fringe to show? If her readers happen not to be anthropologists, how passionately interested does she imagine they are in her ancestral secrets? Another way of posing the Nietzschean alternatives is to ask whether she is withholding her secrets because we are *empirically* different and would understand them only imperfectly; or whether we must not know them for *ethical* reasons, because our knowledge would lead to power over her community.

Rigoberta continues to publicly perform this kind of silence, like a leitmotif. At the Political Forum of Harvard University, in April of 1994, she opened her address with some literally incomprehensible words. It was an incantation, said with a smile and with friendly eyes. Later, during the question period, a student asked her to translate these words. "No," was her polite response, "I cannot translate them." They were a formal and formulaic greeting in Quiché, she said, and they would lose their poetic quality in a different rendering. This speech act was not hostile, but it was a reminder of difference: its meaning resided in the very foreignness of words.

As in the case of Nietzsche's meditation on the nature of rhetoric in general, the choice between ethics and epistemology is undecidable. Even if her own explicit rationale is nonempirical, ethical (claiming that we should not know the secrets because of the particular power attached to the stories we tell about ourselves), Rigoberta suggests the other reason. It is the degree of our foreignness, our cultural difference that would make her secrets incomprehensible. We could never know them as she does, because we would inevitably force her secrets into our framework. "Theologians have come and observed us," for example, "and have drawn a false impression of the Indian world."[21]

Guatemalan Indians have a long history of being read that way in European languages. From the sixteenth century to the present, the Maya have been "Surviving Conquest," as a recent demographic analyst puts it. If some readers perceive a certain ahistorical inflection in Rigoberta's sense that the Spanish conquest is an event of the recent past, George Lovell might corroborate her sense of continuity in this new period of cultural genocide.

> Viewed in historical perspective, it is disconcerting to think how much the twentieth century resembles the sixteenth, for the parallels between cycles of conquest hundreds of years apart are striking. Model villages are designed to serve similar purposes as colonial congregaciones—to function as the institutional means by which one culture seeks to reshape the ways and conventions of another, to oper-

ate as authoritarian mechanisms of resettlement, indoctrination, and control.[22]

The less comprehension in/by Spanish, the better; it is the language that the enemy uses to conquer differences. For an Indian to learn Spanish can amount to passing over to the other side, to the Ladinos, which simply means "Latin" or Spanish speakers. "My father used to call them 'ladinized Indians,' . . . because they act like *ladinos,* bad *ladinos.*"[23] This kind of caution has managed to preserve Mayan cultural continuities, and the political solidarity it can activate, beyond the social scientific paradigms that have tried to account for it.[24]

DOUBLE DUTY

Not all theologians were equally insensitive. Rigoberta, after all, became a catechist devoted to the spirit of liberation theology. And she continued to believe in a God who inspires political commitment, even after Marxist comrades objected. Those objections surely underlined her determination to keep an autonomous distance from allies. Testimony itself, the kind of juridically oriented narrative that she produces, is a Christian's obligation, as Paul Ricoeur reminds us. He explains that from the moment God appeared to human beings, testimony has implied an investment of absolute value in historical, contingent events. The Old Testament prophets had prepared the connection, with their divine intuitions of God's will. But the New Testament, where eternal truth irrupts into human history, obliged even average people to bear witness and confront a defensive, punitive world. "When the test of conviction becomes the price of life, the witness changes his name; he is called a martyr . . . *Martus* in Greek means witness."[25]

The root word also grounds Enrique Dussel's project to Latin Americanize ethical philosophy by way of lessons from theology of liberation: "He who opens himself to the other, is with him, and testifies to him. And that means *martys;* he who 'testifies' to the other is a martyr. Because, before murdering the Other, totality will assassinate the one who denounced its sin against Otherness."[26] One limitation of European, basically Levinasian, ethics, he objects, is that absolute and awe-inspiring otherness leaves the philosopher paralyzed, too stunned and too cautious to do anything useful. Another limitation is that in order to face otherness, ethics turns its back to a long tradition of subject-centered ontology that has ravaged difference by reducing it to more of the same. For Levinas, in other words, to identify the self *as* the subject of history would be self-serving. But, Dussel argues, if an inhospitable first world has always had its back turned to the outside, the discovery of otherness at home is nothing less than liberating.[27] A Latin American ethics needs to be actively committed, not cautiously self-effacing. As a corollary, or rather as a precondition for activity, it needs to refocus the Levinasian asymmetry from this side of the relationship between colonial centers and colonized peripheries.

Gayatri Spivak used to quip that if the subaltern could speak, she would be something else.[28] But after lessons from historian Ranajit Guha, Spivak has appreciated the "subject-effects" of subaltern eloquence.[29] It is the eloquence of marking frontiers, limiting access, distinguishing the speaking subject from the target of speech. Acts of organized resistance also function as narrative speech. For Dussel, too, violence is the language of a "subaltern" committed philosophy. Liberation means reconstituting the alterity of the other in a fallen world where Cain has already murdered Abel,[30] a violated and violent world. "If there is no reply to domination, nothing happens; but if a reply is made, the war begins." At the end of his essay, in a climax after which words are insufficient, he repeats, "The war begins."[31]

From the comments by Ricoeur and Dussel, it would seem that a commitment to absolute imperatives requires physical self-sacrifice, that the discourse of subalternity is written in blood and in statistics of martyrdom. But, Rigoberta glosses, sacrificial responsibility can be finessed. A person engaged in rhetorical self-defense—witnessing—can slip off the mantle of martyr. In her comportment, which manifests the apparent incommensurability between vulnerable testimony and coy control, Rigoberta manages to accept the traditional Christian robe *and* to redesign it as strategic armor.

Ricoeur might have guessed at her designs, given the mediation of language. The incorrigibly compromising medium of fallible human languages derails God's truth; it translates between a truth to die for and a life that goes on. Charged with a communicative duty imposed by absolute truth, language cannot avoid humanizing, debasing, the message by interpreting it. There is no help for it. Even sacred testimony passes through the contingency of interpretation. So, Ricoeur concludes, the only possible philosophy of testimony is hermeneutics, interpretation.[32] Testimony is hermeneutical in a double sense. It gives a content to be interpreted, and it calls for an interpretation; it narrates facts, and it confesses a faith during the juridical moments that link history to eternity.

Rigoberta apparently appreciates testimony's double duty: the message of liberation pulls in one (ideal) direction, and the (earthly) medium of political persuasion pulls in another. To collapse the two is foolish, maybe disastrous. She will not mistake (ideal) demands for justice with sentimental interest from (earthly) interrogators. Offers of solidarity probably confuse doing good with feeling good. The double challenge for this Christian leader, as new and as beleaguered as Christ's first witnesses, is to serve truth in ways that make a difference in the world. Testimony to that truth and coyness about how to convey it turn out to be voices in counterpoint. If we cannot hear the complexity, perhaps our inability is simply that, as Nietzsche reminded us, rather than a sign that contradictions cannot exist.

"J'accuse" rings loudly throughout the text, between the provocative, and protective, pauses of information flow. The pauses work in two directions. Rigoberta's secrets stop avid readers in their appropriative tracks; and they whet anemic appetites by producing intrigue that can turn into collaborative political desire. If her secrets are so important, they must be interesting.

STRATEGIC LOSSES

The paradox for Rigoberta is that her politics of cultural preservation unmoor the culture she tries to preserve. Coalition politics needs Spanish as the lingua franca, in a country of 22 ethnic groups. But learning Spanish turns Indians into enemies. A formal education makes them "forget about our common heritage,"[33] her father had warned. He and other community elders know that Indian identity is a fragile cultural-linguistic construction, not an indelibly "racial" given. At Quiché weddings, brides and grooms promise to raise children as Indians. "After that they ask forgiveness from their parents and for help with bringing up their children as Indians, remembering their traditions, and throughout trouble, sadness and hunger remaining Indians." The danger, in other words, is as much assimilation as extermination. Whether Ladinos are welcoming or murderous, they bring cultural extinction. And that fear of mixing racial and linguistic categories is either the cause, or the effect, of a general prohibition against stirring up differences in Quiché ritual life: "Bread is very meaningful for the Indian, because of the fact that it was mixed with egg, flour with egg. In the past, our ancestors grew wheat. Then the Spaniards came and mixed it with egg. It was a mixture, no longer what our ancestors ate. It was White Man's food, and white men are like their bread, they are not wholesome . . . We must not mix our customs with those of the whites . . ."[34]

Rigoberta's political work depends on mixing and transgressing categories, on violating the ethnic boundaries that her secrets, paradoxically, raise in public. In the Comité de Unidad Campesina, at the United Nations, she uses the homogenizing medium of Spanish. Then she attributes her political doubts to straying. "I was very ashamed at being so confused, when so many of my village understood so much better than I. But their ideas were very pure because they had never been outside *their* community."[35] The italicized third-person possessive is one sign of her alienation. But straying instead of staying is not only unsettling. It is enabling. The dangerous supplement of Spanish that undoes Indians also makes them flexible. For the price of the destabilizing distance, Rigoberta earns a broad political vision. "Indianist to my fingertips, I defended everything to do with my ancestors. But I understood this incorrectly, because we only understand ourselves in conversation with others . . . Ladinos . . . with us, the Indians."[36]

SER AND ESTAR; "TO BE" AS AUTOBIOGRAPHICAL ESSENCE AND TESTIMONIAL TROPES

I pose the question of rhetoric in Rigoberta's telling or troping, in order to read responsibly this text, which ceaselessly calls attention to its difference from the reader and to the danger of overstepping cultural barriers. I prefer to think of her secrets as more "literary" than "real." Reading her refusal as a textual strategy gives her credit for agency. It acknowledges the gesture as intentional rather than passive; not silence but flamboyant noncompliance. Calling attention to an unknowable subtext is a profound lesson, because it is an imitable trope. Not that a reader should want to compete with Rigoberta's text, but that s/he might well want to learn from it how to engage in politics by defending differences to keep a polity open and flexible. The calculated result for sympathetic readers is, paradoxically, that Rigoberta excludes us from her circle of intimates. Any way we read her, we are either intellectually or ethically unfit for Rigoberta's secrets. Either way, it produces a particular kind of distance akin to respect. So simple a lesson and so fundamental: it is to acknowledge modestly that difference exists. This is hardly a paralyzing admission, as Sacvan Bercovitch has argued for rethinking American Studies. Recognizing our limitations is "enabling," because it has a double valence: acknowledging what we cannot know *and* what we can.[37] This defends us from harboring any illusions of complete or stable knowledge, and therefore from the desire to replace one apparently limited speaker for another more totalizing one.

The undecidability of Rigoberta's performance cannot be resolved, because on both epistemological and ethical readings she delivers a slap to interrupt her embrace. The testimonial is an invitation to a tête-à-tête, not to a heart-to-heart. This should not be disappointing. Putting heads together is precisely what members of her community do every time they plan a wedding or a military maneuver. Respect and distance describe engagements inside her own community. "The thing is that Indians have secrets and it's not always a good thing for children to know them. Or not so much that it's not a good thing but because it's not necessary . . . We respect the different levels in the community."[38] Perhaps, then, our difference from that community is one of degree. We are not so much outsiders as marginals, allies in a possible coalition rather than members. We are not excluded from her world, but kept at arm's length.

Are we still surprised by this decorum in a first-person narrative? Do we expect self-writing to be personally revealing, more intimate and confessional than coy? I register surprise because we expect autobiography, and expect it to blush with a confessional glow. This is a standard but relatively recent expectation, says Sylvia Molloy, "supported by the introspective streak found in certain autobiographical writings since the nineteenth century."[39] Rigoberta's text does not fit the genre in either its early or late forms.

Since Georges Gusdorf's "Conditions and Limits of Autobiography" (1956), and especially since James Olney's translation of it (1980), students of autobiography have had to consider its originally parochial and then imperializing nature. "It would seem that autobiography is not to be found outside of our cultural area; one would say that it expresses a concern peculiar to Western *man,* a concern that has been of good use in *his* systematic conquest of the universe and that *he* has communicated to *men* of other cultures."[40] Not surprisingly, autobiography is a relative latecomer to Western literature, associated with Humanism's focus on "the singularity of each individual life." "Throughout most of human history, the individual does not oppose himself to all others; he does not feel himself to exist outside of others, and still less against others, but very much with others in an interdependent existence that asserts its rhythms everywhere in the community." Even if the genre began with Saint Augustine, "at the moment when the Christian contribution was grafted onto classical traditions,"[41] autobiographies became really popular during the Renaissance and Reformation, when self-made men became the fashion.

Part of the charm for the reader, no doubt, is a contagious self-aggrandizement. Autobiographers are singular subjects who, ironically, spill over the page to be taken up by other liberal subjects who repeat the narrating "I." An initially metonymic relationship, when reader takes up the autobiographer, ends with imperious metaphorization, when reader takes in the other. "The autobiographical moment happens as an alignment between the two subjects involved in the process of reading in which they determine each other by mutual reflexive substitution."[42] We become the Cellini or Franklin figure who is conquering the world by dint of sheer talent and hard work. Domingo Faustino Sarmiento read his Franklin like that. "I felt that I was Franklin; And why not? I was very poor, like he was, studious like him, and trying as hard as I could to follow his footsteps, I could one day be as accomplished as he . . . making a place for myself in American letters and politics."[43] Even if texts resist the slippage of identity, insisting that the particular experience is beyond the rest of us, we are free and maybe even stimulated to make our own inimitable "I" the subject of a new autobiography. Setting up one kind of textual resistance, claims Nancy Miller, women autobiographers typically mark their difference from other women (readers) by speaking through what they consider to be more differentiated, male, personae.[44] Or, as Elaine Marks put it, women's autobiographies proclaim that "I am my own heroine."[45] Some autobiographers assume that they represent others, and that the reader is ideally among them. Think of Violette Leduc who begins, "Mon cas n'est pas unique" (1964), and of Michel Leiris (1948–1976).[46] But to assume a group persona that excludes the reader stretches the genre to a breaking point.

Perhaps the most telling rhetorical difference between testimonial and autobiography is the plural but particularist subject of testimony. Instead of one inimitable person, Rigoberta is a representative. She is not different from her community, only different from us. "The important thing is that what has happened to me has happened to many other people too."[47] This sounds like a quote from another woman's testimonial, written six years earlier by a representative of the Comité de Amas de Casa in a Bolivian mining town. Domitila Barrios begins *Si me permiten hablar* (1977) (Let Me Speak) like this: "I don't want anyone at any moment to interpret the story I'm about to tell as something that is only personal ... What happened to me could have happened to hundreds of people in my country."[48] And Claribel Alegría's testimonial montage of the martyred heroine in *No me agarran viva* (They Won't Get Me Alive) starts with this prologue: "Eugenia, exemplary model of self-denial, sacrifice and revolutionary heroism, is a typical case rather than an exception of so many Salvadoran women who have dedicated their efforts and even their lives to the struggle for their people's liberation."[49] Alegría experiments with a multiple mirror image that constructs her testimonial subject; instead of one narrator who assembles her community by extension, here a community of narrators reconstructs the life of a single revolutionary.

The testimonial "I" in these books doesn't invite us to identify with it. We are too foreign, and there is no pretense here of universal or essential human experience. That is why, at the end of a long narrative in which Rigoberta has told us so much, she reminds us that respectful limits still hold. They bind her too, as she takes care not to conflate her community with herself. Personal identity depends on, doesn't replace, the collective. The singular represents the plural as a distinguishable part of the whole, not a synecdochal stand-in. *Metonymy* describes Rigoberta's relationship; it is a lateral identification which acknowledges the possible differences among "us" as components of a centerless whole. This is where we can come in as readers, invited, in Levinas's words, to be "*with* others. All these relations are transitive. I touch an object, I see the other; but I *am* not the other."[50] In Spanish this is to be with the speaker *(estar),* rather than to be her *(ser).*

The phenomenon of a collective subject in the testimonial is not the result of personal style in the witness. It is a variation in the autobiographical pose of a colonized subject who does not equate identity with individuality. Life continues at the margins of Western discourse, as disturbance and challenge.[51] Arguably, the tradition of Latin American autobiography had anticipated Rigoberta and Domitila's identification with a cultural group outside of which the text would be misread. The tradition assumes that the autobiographer is continuous with his/her community (as in Leduc and Leiriss). Sarmiento, as Molloy points out, creates intimacy and complicity with Argentinian, ideal readers as a result of excluding others:

> The Spanish American "I" (if one dare generalize in this fashion) seems to rely more than other "I"s—to rely in a nearly ontological manner—on a sort of national recognition. Representativeness and identity are closely linked in Spanish American self-writing. Sarmiento dedicates the book (Recuerdos de provincia) that will show him as the true son of the new republic "to my compatriots only"—those who will truly understand him and give him being.[52]

Even Victoria Ocampo's privileged persona understands specialness in terms of her family's prominence in national history, that is, in a context she has in common with her readers.[53] From them, Sarmiento and Ocampo claim to have no secrets.

HALTING READERS

But for Rigoberta there are literally no ideal readers. The notion is a contradiction here. The Maya Quiché who ideally understand her are no readers at all, neither in Spanish nor in English. Their resistance to Spanish safeguards a communal life, in her father's warnings that haunt Rigoberta and us. "I remember my father telling us: 'My children, don't aspire to go to school, because schools take our customs away from us'"; "If I put you in a school, they'll make you forget your class, they'll turn you into a ladino."[54] Rigoberta resists identifying with other women differently from the way Miller's French autobiographers do. She resists us, her European(ized) readers, and claims at the same time that her individuality is irrelevant. If we read her, we enter into a peculiar kind of pact, not the "autobiographical pact" of sincerity between writer and reader that Philippe Lejeune described as the genre's enabling fiction,[55] but one in which we agree to respect Rigoberta's terms. This means agreeing to forfeit the rush of metaphoric identification.[56]

What kind of text do we have in hand? Should we think of testimonials as a sub-genre of autobiography, and take strategic coyness as a permissible departure from the familiar genre? Or does the departure constitute a generic difference? This is another moment of tension between *can* and *should*. At what political and aesthetic price do we favor one genre despite the nagging lack of fit? Does the difference boil down to an ethical imperative? Should the difference be defended as an extension of Rigoberta's own cultural self-defense? Again, the question may be undecidable outside of tactical concerns. Some readers will prefer to project themselves in familiarly heroic autobiographical terms through this apparently available text; and others will take note of its warnings against usurpation.

One feature that keeps Rigoberta distant is her peculiar Spanish, a language she studied for only three years before she testified in it. The sometimes discordant language is a reminder of difficult negotiations that make up her life and story, and a measure of the editor's respect for the informant's voice.[57] Paradoxically, in this rhetorical tug-of-war, pulling backwards from the "modernizing" Western culture to the indigenous one may be going forward. Rigoberta sometimes brings back the forgotten egalitarian assumptions of the Mayan community's Law. I am thinking specifically about her use of the *Popol Vuh*, the cosmogony and "paideia" of the Guatemalan Indians. It is not exactly an epic, according to translator Munro S. Edmonson. "Although it belongs to a heroic (or near-heroic) type of literature, it is not the story of a hero: it is (and says it is) the story of a people, and the text is bracketed by the opening and closing lines declaring and affirming that intent."[58] From the early Spanish translations of the "Book of Counsel" one would think that patriarchy was at least as fundamental to the Maya of Guatemala as it has been in the West. In fact Edmonson seems to miss his own point about the nonhierarchical and communal nature of this tradition, when he reports that "traditional Quiché life revolves around a patriarchal, patrilineal, and patrilocal family." His translation nonetheless gives a clue to the opportunities for lateral moves the spirit of the book offered Rigoberta; along with the "somber" or sacred feeling of responsibility, *Popol Vuh* describes an egalitarianism in gender that Western monotheism finds heretical. That equality was lost in older translations, which reduced the term parent to "father."[59]

Gender equality extends to communal organization, as Rigoberta tells us in her recently acquired Spanish, a hierarchical language whose insistence on gender and number concordance can barely accommodate the system she describes.

> In our community there is an elected representative, someone who is highly respected. He's not a king but someone whom the community looks up to like a father. In our village, my father and mother were the representatives. Well, then the whole community becomes the children of the woman who's elected. So, a mother, on her first day of pregnancy goes with her husband to tell these elected leaders that she's going to have a child, because the child will not only belong to them but to the whole community, and must follow as far as he can our ancestors' traditions.[60]

Evidently Rigoberta loses power from having to use a language borrowed from the oppressive Ladinos. The loss is common to colonized peoples, as María Lugones reminds us when she defines the racial and class exclusivity of existing feminist theory: "We and you do not talk the same language. When we talk to you we use your language ... We try to use it to communicate our world of experience. But since your language and your theories are inadequate in expressing our experiences, we only succeed in communicating our experience of exclusion."[61] The complaint is important, but another equally valid consequence of borrowing the politically dominant language is the transformative process of borrowing. Rigoberta's Spanish is qualitatively different from that of her teachers. And her testimony makes the peculiar nonstandard Spanish into a public medium of change that appeals to us.

The scars of translation and the liberating incongruities of code-switching give an oral quality to the text. Unlike the lonely moment of autobiographical writing, testimonies are public events. Autobiography strains to produce a personal and distinctive *style,* and testimonial strives to preserve or to renew an interpersonal *rhetoric.*[62] That rhetoric suspends the interchangeable "I" of autobiography. Instead, the author addresses a flesh-and-blood person, an interviewer, who asks questions that mark her outsider status. The narrative, therefore, sometimes shifts into a second person, the "you" who ask to be engaged. Respectful appeals can be granted. If readers acknowledge the narrator who talks to you about herself as a representative of a particular community, a discreet invitation is extended for us to identify with the narrator's project and, by extension, with her political community. The appeal produces something other than admiration for the ego-ideal that makes one yearn to be (like) the Other and to deny distinctiveness. It produces cautious complicity. Precisely because the reader cannot take the writer's place, the map of possible identifications spreads out laterally. Once the subject of testimonial is understood as the community in which each has a role to play, the reader can fill one. It is useful to examine our habit of identifying with a single subject of the narration, which repeats a Western, logocentric limitation. If we find it difficult to entertain the idea of simultaneous points of activity—several valid roles—then testimonials help to remind us that democratic politics is not a heroic venture.[63]

Consciously working in a translated, borrowed language, those who testify appreciate the arbitrary nature of signs. From their marginal position among existing discourses, they may typically adopt features of several, not because they are unaware of the contradictions between being a mother, a worker, a Catholic, a Communist, an indigenist, and a nationalist, but because they understand that none of these codes is sufficient to their revolutionary situation. Rigoberta Menchú's community, for example, adapted the story of Moses, a model of spiritual and political leadership, for a theology liberation. Enrique Dussel singles him out, too, as an active, ethical listener, silent enough to hear the Other's call; and as a human subject, particular enough to be called by name. No abstract universal subject of totalizing Greek ontology, Moses is a concrete, historical, and potentially free agent.[64] But even this deontologized difference falls short of Rigoberta's gloss, a more radical departure from Western paradigms of personal heroism. Her adjustment of his particular name to a cacophonous but promising plural is a sign that the lone figure of Moses, ideal for metaphoric identifications, misses the dynamic metonymy of collective liberation. "We compared the Moses of those days with ourselves, the Moseses of today."[65]

For Rigoberta feminism is not an independent goal but the by-product of class or ethnic struggles which some might consider inimical to women's issues. Her priorities remind the reader of Domitila Barrios's reluctant feminism. This Bolivian miner's wife resists identifying herself with gender struggles. "Our position is not like the feminists' position. We think our liberation consists primarily in our country being freed forever from the yoke of imperialism and we want a worker like us to be in power."[66] But her political practice, as a woman who should have left politics to men, was necessarily and aggressively feminist. Since the first struggle, for this woman who identifies herself primarily as a housewife, was to get out of the house, gender relations are her first target. The trick is not to identify the correct discourse (Marxism, or feminism, or nationalism, or ethnic survival) and to defend it heroically, but to combine and recombine the constellation of discourses in ways that will respond to a changeable reality. This flexibility or eclecticism doubtless explains why women's testimonials (outside Cuba) tend to be written just beyond the constraints of party lines, or any lines. "I want to emphasize that, because it seems there are people who say that they made me, their party made me. I don't owe my consciousness and my preparation to anything but the cries, the suffering, and the experiences of the people. I want to say that we have a lot to learn from the parties, but we shouldn't expect everything from them. Our development must come from our own clarity and awareness."[67]

ALLIANCES, METONYMIES

Rigoberta's community is equally reticent to serve outside agendas. Instead, it tends to be syncretic, as in the worker-peasant alliance of the CUC (Comité de Unidad Campesina), and to be selective, as for example with its adaptation of Catholicism. "In this way we adjusted the Catholic religion . . . As I said, it's just another way of expressing ourselves. It's not the only, immutable way, but one way of keeping our ancestors' lore alive."[68] Not surprisingly, the conservative nuns and priests of Acción Católica were sure this was heresy. "They say, 'You have too much trust in your elected leaders.'" Why, Rigoberta muses, do they fail to get the point? "But the village elects them *because* they trust them, don't they?" "Nevertheless" she adds, careful to keep opportunities open, some missionaries who came to the area as

opponents of communism learned a new political language: "they understood that the people weren't Communists but hungry ... And they joined
our people's struggle too." The codes are always plural. "The whole truth is
not found in the Bible, but neither is the whole truth in Marxism, ... We
have to defend ourselves against our enemy but, as Christians, we must
also defend our faith within the revolutionary process."[69] Her multiple
unorthodoxies constitute what post-structuralists might call an exercise in
decentering language, sending the apparently stable structures of Western
thought into an endless flux in which signifiers are simply destabilized, not
abandoned.

Some academic readers of testimonials have fixed only on the reality of
reference. To worry about the instability of the signifier and the need to
reinvent language as part of political struggle seems treacherous; it tends, so
the argument goes, to reinforce the system of oppression by doubting its
effects. Their response is to highlight the power of the existing order in
order to affirm the efficaciousness of struggle against it. A couple of opportunities are lost here: first, the irony that can help to wither the apparent stability of the ruling structure, and second, the testimonials' playful—in the
most serious sense of that term—distance from any pre-established coherence. That distance creates the space for what Mikhail Bakhtin (1980) called
heteroglossia, the (battle)field of discourse where revolutions are forged
from conflict, not dictated. In neo-Gramscian terms, what is lost is a strategy for establishing a socialist hegemony based on coalitions.

Ernesto Laclau and Chantal Mouffe theorize this promise in a thoughtful
post-Marxian analysis. Their critique of the essentializing habits of Marxism emphasizes political complexity and the opportunities for change.
Conceptual rigidity perpetuates repressive political language. In a fixed system, particular words (such as "the working class") can be substituted for
others (such as "the proletariat," "the people," "the masses," "the vanguard"),
or in the least case considered to be "equivalent" to others, and so describe a
very limited scope for differences and interaction.[70] Among the key words
they dislodge is the political "subject." The subject, like other signs, is available simultaneously for different contexts, including workers' groups, feminist movements, ecology, others. With a rhetorical flourish learned from
deconstruction, they contrast the unproductive habits of *metaphoric* substitution in party politics with the more promising *metonymic* or lateral moves

of coalitional politics. "[A]ll discourse of fixation becomes metaphorical: literality is, in actual fact, the first of metaphors." By contrast, "we could say that hegemony is basically metonymical: its effects always emerge from a surplus of meaning which results from an operation of displacement. (For example, a trade union or a religious organization may take on organizational functions in a community, which go beyond the traditional practices ascribed to them, and which are combated and resisted by opposing forces)."[71]

How disappointing that they smuggle back reified categories as soon as they stop talking about the industrialized West. When Laclau and Mouffe refer to the "periphery," well after the middle of the book, an aporia gapes between theoretical sophistication and political sympathies. Class and subject had withered away as stable signs, but equally "fictional" terms such as the Third World or the People remain.[72] The double standard is disturbing.[73] In fact Rigoberta's peasant organization and Domitila's Housewives Committee are as constructive of "democratic" subject positions as are the examples given above. Why are they not as valuable in theorizing a fissured political subject available for metonymic, or hegemonic politics? Certainly a trade union or a religious organization can be as humble and local as are the Latin American movements. And if the popular Catholic Church, with its theology of liberation and base communities, is brought to bear, the Latin American space seems far more promising indeed. Why, then, are its struggles imagined as unitary, as if they were a matter of replacing one masterful signifier for another? In fact, we learn from first-person testimonies that those struggles are as multiple and flexible as any in the First World, often combining feminist, class, ethnic, and national desiderata. One advantage of reading the "First" back from the "Third" world is to notice that what Laclau and Mouffe call "contradictions"[74] become glaringly visible without necessarily becoming antagonisms, just as the authors point out. No one ideological code is assumed to be sufficient for either Rigoberta or Domitila; instead they inherit a plurality of codes that intersect and produce a flexible and multiple political subject. If Laclau and Mouffe miss the point, it may be because their skepticism about narrative, which they assume to be necessarily teleological, has steered them clear of these testimonials. The result is a reifying distance from the Latin American subject, a distance that seems more patronizing than respectful.

To read women's testimonials, curiously, is to mitigate the tension between First World "self" and Third World "other." I do not mean this as a license to deny the differences, but as a suggestion that the testimonial subject may be a model for respectful, nontotalizing, politics. It is not necessary to fill the distance that testimonials safeguard with either veiled theoretical disdain or sentimental identification. Instead, that distance can be read as the condition for success of coalitional politics. It is similar to learning that respect is the condition for lasting love.

HOT PURSUIT AND COLD
REWARDS OF MEXICANNESS

6

What grew in me, or what perhaps had been
there for years, was my Mexican being,
becoming Mexican, feeling that Mexico was
inside me and that it was the same that was
in Jesusa and that it would come out by
simply opening the gate . . .

—ELENA PONIATOWSKA

"Now fuck off. Go away and let me sleep." That's how Jesusa Palancares cuts off her story and shuts out the persistent interrogator who has been asking for it. Dismissal is her final word, after more than three hundred very full pages of a life so detailed and boldly narrated that it reads like a picaresque novel. The motherless girl who was a combat soldier in the Mexican Revolution, a factory worker in the capital, a cabaret dancer, hairdresser, and laundress, becomes a narrator late in life. And just to make sure we're impressed, the portrait adds real or imaginary brushes with historical characters like Emiliano Zapata and old "Goat-Beard" Venustiano Carranza.[1] In view of the apparent effort to impress us, the unceremonious good-bye on the last line seems abrupt. But the door in the face probably doesn't surprise either writer/editor Elena Poniatowska, the immediate target of reproach, or the eavesdroppers we readers become. From the scandalously unsentimental epigraph to this 1969 testimonial novel, *Hasta no verte, Jesús mío* (Till We Meet Again, Dear Jesus), Jesusa has been rebuffing, rebuking, and otherwise putting readers off: "Miss me?" she quips rhetorically on the epigraphic page before there is any "me" to be missed; "the hell you will when I'm no use to you any longer."

Identifying the book as a testimonial novel is already a sign of tension between two genres and two narrative agents.[2] Testimonio *against* literature was John Beverley's strong distinction, as I mentioned in the previous chapter: a collective voice allegedly sounds stronger than the single persona of development narratives; and the broad historical strokes erase the marks of an elite mediator. A testimonial novel, then, would be a contradiction in terms, a text teetering between immediacy and manipulation. But it is just the kind of disturbance that Pontiatowska wisely leaves on the page, in Jesusa's controlling voice and in the writer's confessional glosses.

NOT FOR SALE

Poniatowska has worried about the ethical conundrum of socially unequal conversation. It can testify to injustice, but it also takes lives to display them like so much evidence in court or value in the marketplace. The worry can daunt any ethnographer, as it haunts literary criticism. Daphne Patai theorizes on the multiple hazards from her sensitive interviews with Brazilian women.[3] And Alejo Carpentier, as ethnomusicologist, had confronted the problem, dangerously, when he jotted down some musical notes at a *ñáñigo* ceremony; the celebrants took offense at the cultural robbery and told their white observer to put away his notebook or to expect trouble.[4] Jesusa has also been telling her guest to be careful, and Poniatowska listens enough to be anxious about robbery, and about vampirism:

> An ethical problem arises around the writing of testimonial novels. Are those who create them writers or not? Are they simply opportunists who ... plunge into the manufacture of easily consumed works that will fill the void between the elite and the illiterate in Latin American countries? ... They confiscate a reality, present it as their own, steal their informants' words, plagiarize their colloquialisms, tape their language and take possession of their very souls.[5]

Jesusa won't be easily consumed, as Poniatowska knows from the old woman's acrid defenses against verbal cannibalism. This informant is hardly the intimate sister that some readers expect from *testimonios*. Why should we expect familiarity, or imagine that only privileged intellectuals can master fiction's techniques of evasion? These assumptions have made

Jesusa lose critical ground to her editor. The question most professional readers have asked of her book is *who* the writer is. And the answer is almost always Poniatowska, even if she herself blurs the difference between narrator and writer by including Jesusa in a 1985 essay about professional authors in Mexico.[6] Does it flatter a narrator like Jesusa to be considered artless, transparent, available for easy intimacy? I do not think so; neither, evidently, did Poniatowska. Her narrator's mordant asides not only underline the denunciatory points of the story but also make a point about strategic telling. Beth Jörgensen dares to notice the obvious, in contrast to so many sentimental readers of Jesusa: "The speaking I . . . scolds, fusses, and shouts her way . . . into history."[7] If the editor had preferred to control the often indifferent, sometimes shrill tone, if the story had actually interpellated her effortlessly and intimately, readers would hardly be able to perceive political or cultural differences between narrator and her sororal other. But Poniatowska does record these differences; it is the reader who may have trouble hearing them.

Until now, privileged readers have been taking quite literally Jesusa's question about missing her when she's of no use any more. They have been shrugging off her rudeness as an untutored expression of natural reserve,[8] or of the hermetic national character that Octavio Paz described in *The Labyrinth of Solitude* (1950). Poniatowska herself characterized the reluctant informant as "hermetic," as if that were a grudging signature of Mexican authenticity. Jesusa's early refusal to talk is precisely what makes her interrogator desire the story. Like the consumers of literature she writes for, Poniatowska expected reticence and worked to overcome it. She may not have realized that her effort threatened its object, that is, Jesusa's identity. The particularity of Jesusa's expression disappears, for example, if readers are quick to understand her in the terms Paz made familiar, so quick that they explain away her reluctance before it has any effect.[9] Echoes of his classic meditation on Mexican solitude are unavoidable for educated readers of Spanish. Half a century ago, Paz set the paradoxical terms for acknowledging reticence and describing it out loud. He said something literally unspeakable about Mexicanness by speaking its mute defenses:

The Mexican, whether young or old, *criollo* or *mestizo*, general or laborer or lawyer, seems to me to be a person who shuts himself away to protect himself: his face is a mask and so is his smile. In his harsh solitude, which is both barbed and courteous, everything serves him as a defense: silence and words, politeness and disdain, irony and resignation. He is jealous of his own privacy and that of others, and he is afraid even to glance at his neighbor, because a mere glance can trigger the rage of these electrically charged spirits.[10]

Why, then, are readers not wary about probing and provoking Jesusa? Do we imagine ourselves to be immune to verbal barbs, or to be cozily inside the barbed wire that safeguards her subjectivity? If Jesusa is truly Mexican (an identity that Poniatowska banks on), and if Paz is right about the impenetrability of "Mexican masks" (which seems taken for granted in Poniatowska's choice of hermetic Jesusa as representative), should readers anticipate anything like intimacy with the protagonist? But readers (warned by Paz) have managed to insulate themselves from the occasional barbs and shocks of reading Jesusa with a gush of unprocessed sympathy. To the reciprocally dismissive "Miss me?" of her epigraph, middle-class readers have been protesting rather defensively, "Of course we will miss you, Jesusita," as they use her cult-like figure to celebrate feminism and the working class.

But Jesusa's style disturbs the terms it evokes. Her matter-of-fact gruffness makes Paz's magisterial tone ring false, too glib to be engaging. And his self-disavowing third-person report *about* Mexicans should make any reader of Jesusa's first-person story skeptical about Paz's inside information. Readers will do well to wonder where he stands. On the next page, the observer doubles himself as a participant inside a plural first person: "we believe that opening oneself up is a weakness or a betrayal"—is there not a different, sexist, betrayal here. Paz's slippery inclusion of himself in the solidary "we" of serial and solitary Mexicans excludes women, necessarily. They are biologically open to penetration, we know, and therefore literally and physiologically incapable of integrity. It is possible that Paz is being perversely critical of machismo as masquerade, when he reports that women's "inferiority is constitutional and resides in their sex, their submissiveness, which is a wound that never heals."[11] Nevertheless, he associates Mexicanness with masculinity, whatever its merit or liability, so a hardened woman like Jesusa would be Mexican only because she is unnaturally *macha*.

Solicitous feminist readers come to the unsolicited rescue. Of course she is authentically Mexican. Her very identity, *pace* Paz, rips open the masculine rigidity of his Mexico. Whether Jesusa makes unfriendly gestures because she is an authentic Mexican recluse, or because gender-specific resistance to public intercourse awaits our sisterly support for "breaking the silence,"[12] (self-)interested readers have typically overshot the barbed border of Jesusa's story with the energy of unstinting patronage. What accounts for their ardor? Is it Jesusa's intrinsic attractiveness? Or, as I am beginning to suggest, is it her continuing usefulness for our own difficult projects of feminist and culturally specific self-fashioning?

The question is so obvious, and so obviously embarrassing for Jesusa's middle-class fans, that it is just now being asked aloud. Not everyone finds her fascinating. In Spanish American literature classes throughout the hemisphere, where *Hasta no verte, Jesús mío* is regularly featured, privileged students are incautiously candid. They don't like the book, more often than not. It is heavy, even sometimes offensive reading, although working-class readers reportedly tend to be less dismissive.[13] And privately, some professional readers will confess to feeling politically incorrect boredom, indifference, irritation. "She won't get me to donate to the orphanage or to the people's struggle," was one telling response. An anecdote about a possible publication in English translation repeats the point. Almost ten years ago, a very able translation, judging from the published passages, was prepared and scheduled to come out with a trade publisher eager to cash in on the book's popularity and its promise to become required reading in women's studies courses. But publication has been delayed there and at other likely presses, perhaps indefinitely.[14] The book must have seemed disappointing to uninvested readers.

The reactions of public admiration and private irritation make me wonder which response is the more appropriate, that is, more authorially calculated. Does Jesusa want a privileged class of readers to want her, or does she want to keep them at a safe distance? And if the answer is mixed, pulling at intimacy and pushing at the bad faith of disinterested love, why would Jesusa have programmed her own partial failure to entertain those readers? Is it possible that her ingenious specificity is to share information without sharing herself? And is it equally possible that she wants neither to be the stuff of mass sales nor the beneficiary of charitable contributions?

Critics have typically treated this book as Poniatowska's production, a necessarily fictionalized and unauthentic life; they have carefully measured its truth value and found it wanting, upbraiding Poniatowska for *her* self-authorized "poetic license" and *her* artistic freedom, and implying the writer's unavoidable and almost tragic irresponsibility, because writing necessarily reduces life to lies.[15] With loud beating of breasts and laments for the inescapable unreality that conspiring writers and readers inflict on a life converted into text, critics take unlimited license to speculate about Poniatowska, to interview her, and to elicit more writing from the professional writer. No one, except for Jörgensen, has yet written about Jesusa's remarkable performance. It is her story after all. Otherwise, readers wouldn't fret about the liberties Poniatowska takes. But fretting hasn't yet brought our focus onto Jesusa; most readers have not yet stopped to notice her controlling voice in the conversion from experience to exemplum. Poor Jesusa looks like so much raw material to guilt-ridden readers tormented by their own powerful agency as they collaborate with the writer. Jesusa may be active and proud, of course; she is even respectably hermetic in her Mexicanness, but the simple woman could hardly be calculating or strategic. Or could she be? We ought to stop at this possibility, because failing to stop and to wonder is to overshoot the problem with a kind of misfired sympathy that does more character damage than could the penchant for fiction in the editor. To her credit, editor Poniatowska hears Jesusa's haughty humility and records the unfriendly apostrophes, from the epigraphic assault to the very last dismissive line. This is one indication that Poniatowska continues to be Jesusa's best reader, allowing the other woman's voice to interrupt the flow of what passes for intimacy. Those interruptions hint at an entire language of refusals. Maybe Jesusa's story is a stage for performing gaps in communication.[16]

Roland Barthes might have put his finger on those breaks as places in which to expect textual bliss, spots where diagetical meaning shows gaps, like the gaps between pieces of clothing where the skin peeks through tantalizingly. Barthes, though, would surely have noticed the difference between the flirtations that engage him and Jesusa's offputting performance. Her interruptions don't interfere with the drone of her style as much as they deflate the possible intimacy between two women talking. But his kind of interruption goads the fantasy of writerly-readerly trysts that privileged readers have learned to expect. That expectation is worth considering.

Interruptions, for Barthes, break the monotony of predictable narrative rhythms (like Jesusa's) and lead to bliss. An edge, a stop, a gasp of the text's language is an invitation to the reader to be the clandestine, perverse voyeur of other people's pleasure. Barthes takes it for granted that the text—eroticized and magical—exists to give him pleasure, that in fact he is its reason for being: "The text is a fetish object, and *this fetish desires me.*"[17] Barthes works tirelessly to reciprocate the text's incitations. His self-celebration as the active partner of the encounter might sound as frankly scandalous as the eroticized scene of reading that arouses his speculation. But the scandal falls flat for contemporary criticism, because self-empowering interpretation is taken for granted in the rather narrow current approaches to reader-response. Barthes's exuberant narcissism is fundamentally continuous with other strains of reader-response, from Georges Poulet's *pas de deux* with a seductive text that can be conquered and interiorized[18] to Wolfgang Iser's dialogic motion that readers generate with a text they engage.[19] Either way, readers are partners for texts, and the darlings of literary theory.

CLOSING IN

Jesusa's interruptions locate a boundary (away from Barthes' erotic border) where self-centered ludicism and speculation meet unwilling partners. That place is surprisingly close to another limit, where most politically and ethically committed reading stops making progress. The trouble with "commitment" is that it usually makes the same assumption about the text's availability as does reading for pleasure. Politicized readers rarely consider that they may be targets of a text instead of its comrades, that participation doesn't necessarily mean partnership. Feminist critics get into this trouble, for example, when they object to reader-response theory as male-oriented, and then repeat the theory's assumption about collaboration between reader and text. Take Patrocinio Schweickart's standard summary of response criticism. She draws an intimate parallel between the Poulet essay I referred to above (as a strong case of eroticized appropriation) and Adrienne Rich's reading of Emily Dickinson: "The reader encounters not simply a text, but a 'subjectified object': the 'heart and mind' of another woman. She comes into close contact with an interiority—a power, a creativity, a suffering, a vision—that is *not* identical with her own. The feminist interest in construing reading as an intersubjective encounter suggests an affinity with Poulet's theory."[20]

The problem, some feminists say, is that the reader in canonical literature is assumed to be male, so collaboration of female readers with the text has amounted to treachery against themselves. The result is *immasculation,* as Judith Fetterly called this male-identified training in 1978, a term that Schweickart approvingly repeats in 1986 as she develops a feminist remedy to reading (like) men: in addition to resisting male-centered works, we can "read ourselves" in women writers.[21] The solution, in other words, involves a dissolution of difference between reader and writer, a stronger chemistry even than Poulet's eroticism. "Mainstream reader-response theory" tracks a struggle for control between the text and its reader; but feminist readings are pleasantly confined between the bounds of friendly relationship and intimate merger. The male reading paradigm strains but ultimately reaffirms the frontiers of personal subjectivity, while the female paradigm (here Schweickart invokes Nancy Chodorow and Carol Gilligan) weakens exclusionary frontiers and exchanges struggle for conversation.[22]

The lines are rather neatly drawn between boys' books and girls' books in Schweickart's essay, even though she uses dissonant readings of Malcolm X's *Autobiography* as a wedge into universalizing male-centered responses, to free up some space for women. That first move is revealing. She notes that Wayne Booth reads the *Autobiography* as a standard Western paideia; he mainstreams Malcolm through elliptical quoting of a passage that, in the original, had rejected Western thought as racist. Her conclusion is that one's cultural background skews one's reading. From her cultural position, she announces, it is possible to read like a woman who identifies with all other women. The result is an alchemy worthy of Booth's transmutation of rejection into embrace: Schweickart has dismissed issues of class and color. Malcolm X, meanwhile, has become her solvent for producing feminist solidarity. Women don't read like men, and the books they write are just as different. Boys' books either ignore women or abuse them in other ways (as Virginia Woolf's persona at the British Museum found out); but girls' books attend to the intelligence and heroism of women who dare to respect themselves in a surprising variety of ways, above all as writers.

The assumption about reading and writing being friendly opportunities for uncensored connection among women had become so standard, that by

1989 Julia Swindells is compelled to offer a caution in her comments on *The Diaries of Hannah Cullwick*. "With the best of intentions," she complains, the 1984 Virago editor of these Victorian manuscripts reads liberation into a woefully constrained writing project that was one more service to a master who loved to watch Cullwick work, and loved to feel her perform all sorts of domestic duties. "The paradox that exists here," the Virago editor had claimed, "is that the drudgery that was everyday life for the maid-of-all-work also in a sense liberated her." Freedom, for this editor, is a break from the constraints of corsetted Victorian womanhood. This prompts Swindells to wonder: "Would we, by the same token, say that the black person in South Africa, or, for that matter, in contemporary Britain, manifests the paradox of freedom in not having to 'suffer' the position of the white person?"[23] Another way to pose the ethical and political error is to notice that feminist enthusiasm can underestimate the differences among us, as Drucilla Cornell underestimates them. Enthusiasm overrides the difficulties of making conversation, in the interest of making a new and better universality to replace male-centered versions. This is literally Schweickart's aspiration at the end of her essay: "Feminist reading and writing alike are grounded in the interest of producing a community of feminist readers and writers, and in the hope that ultimately this community will expand to include everyone."[24] The wish seems benign enough, even friendly, but the will to overcome difference can lead to dismissing it. If feminist reading begins with an acknowledgment of different positions (such as Wayne Booth and Malcolm X), the next step could be to develop a sensitivity to difference, rather than dream of improving on the homogeneity of a "male-centered" culture. That sensitivity would alert readers, women and men, to textual strategies not aimed at coaxing a reader's identification with an author's position, whether by "immasculation" or by gender affirmation.

The possibility that readers may be the sustained objects of aggression rarely occurs to critics, even when they track such intentions in defiant or elusive books. Alongside a feminist politics of reading (that can amount to resisting one identification only to embrace another), and a familiar reading of *testimonios* as presumably welcoming the reader as brother or sister, we also saw the good intentions of Ross Chambers's *Room for Maneuver*, which sublates the text's aggression by removing the reader's struggle. Jesusa doesn't excuse readers benignly. She targets us for the kind of chastening abuse that pious readers expect from didactic writing. The tradition of didactic reading survived in secular criticism—at least through Stanley Fish's interpretation of *Paradise Lost*. Readers are important in the poem, as its victims. Milton punishes readers who desire to know the ways of God, because true Christians should be more modest.

This is the kind of modest acknowledgment that we might revive as we learn to listen to an Other, to Jesusa for example. As in Milton's case, Jesusa may be toying with enlightened modern readers who expect to achieve a level of mastery commensurate with the amount of energy they expend. The energy is wasted on Jesusa, some disappointed readers will say. But that is probably the point of her performance. She discounts the unsolicited labor of self-defined collaborators. She says she doesn't need us. Like Milton but less grandly, she will insist that we miss the point by striving after it so actively. From the very beginning to the very end, she dodges our efforts to close in so close that we make her an extension of ourselves.

BOREDOM

Jesusa's technique is entirely different from Milton's rush of expectation and crash of meaning over deluded mortal heads. There are no long lyrical passages to distract readers from the danger, no theological bombast, no cajoling or threatening. In fact, there is very little reader-oriented address in Jesusa's book, except for the interruptions that question the value of telling anything at all, interruptions that imply a devaluation of the listener. What we get is prattle, with the result that the book bores many of us.

Now, boredom is no simple matter, only an undertheorized one, maybe because it is inauspicious for active and collaborative reader responses. Patricia Meyer Spacks recently wrote an entire book about this menacing backdrop to the frenzied literary activity of the past two centuries. "The need to refute boredom's deadening power impels the writer's productivity and the reader's engagement."[25] Walter Benjamin expected this anxious intensity and objected to it, on the grounds that novels are heat conductors for frigid and frantic modern souls. Storytelling, on the other hand, makes time for contemplation; it allows boredom to do the good work of pausing to incubate experience. Roland Barthes, too, has let boredom stop him long enough to consider its charm, in moments of hiatus after bliss exhausts the spirit and frees it from all activity, including the work of contemplation. He might have appreciated the monotone that Jesusa sustains as she tells her multifarious life. The hectic story hardly skips a beat; its interruptions don't invite engagement, let alone bliss. Jesusa lulls readers beyond taking their possible enjoyment of her, skirting moments of delight to fall straight into boredom. "Boredom," Barthes writes, "is not far from bliss; it is bliss seen from the shores of pleasure."[26]

From that far shore, exiled beyond the satisfactions that we have been trained to expect, reader-response theory recovers its chastening potential. It is the potential to notice the reader as a function of the text, not its co-producer. "Voluntarily picking up a book, we expect—indeed *demand*—to have our interest engaged," Spacks continues. And the implied contract between the writer's effort and a reader's friendly disposition is inscribed in all the "white middle-class" texts that she mentions. Working-class writing, she explains, shows no signs of boredom, which is why she excludes it from her book.[27] (Middle-class "minorities" don't figure here at all.) Boredom, as Spacks defines it, is always an unwanted response to some immediate stimulus, in the writer, in the reader. It is never a purposeful effect. That a text might mock the reading contract by repaying a reader's availability with a writer's indifference, this is the outrageous possibility raised by Jesusa's life story.

The object of her language game is to lose the match that her opponent is playing. I am suggesting this as a possibility, not insisting upon it, as a way of taking Jesusa's agency into account. My exercise is worthwhile, whether or not I am exactly right in my reading. She wins, because double-dealing would be the point of her game. The losing tactic may sound strange to middle-class readers who are bent on success, but some of us may remember a variation from sidewalk games of an urban childhood. It went like this: you challenge someone to hit you softer than you can hit back. After the opponent uses up his turn to barely brush against your shoulder, you smack him and announce, "I lose." Lyotard would have appreciated the joke, to judge from one of the glosses he wrote on Wittgenstein. That guide to language games had observed that the rules of a game (tennis, chess) are one thing, but the recommendations for winning are something else. So you can choose to lose. "I know I'm playing badly, but I don't want to play any better." All an interlocutor can say to this, according to Wittgenstein, is: "Ah then that's all right."[28] But Lyotard adds that "playing 'badly' might be a good strategy, an unprecedented one."[29] And I conclude that it amounts to playing a different game.

INCLUDE YOU OUT

If Jesusa doesn't engage us in the familiar and challenging games of piecing a text together (because unlike a modernist literary puzzle, her life is straightforward), if she leaves nothing to interpret (because the story seems transparent), and if she cancels the possibility for empathy (because her flat tone is beyond the experience of emotion), where are we? Where are we privileged readers, the darlings of flirtatiously difficult texts, of an entire industry in literary criticism that assumes our responsibility—and right— to activate a text and to coauthor it? The stunning outcome is that we are nowhere, not needed at all as necessary co-conspirators or problem solvers. The only times we do figure, by extension from the interrogator-writer, are in the dismissive asides. The book continues for a while, from one dismissal to another, the way Milton's poem continues between scoldings. But finally, Jesusa shuts us out entirely. "Now fuck off. Go away and let me sleep."

The effect is ultimately chilling, although ardent readers cool off very slowly, in a cumulative and delayed response. Not that Jesusa is coy or even subtle about refusing us access to exciting intimacy, but that we are so stubbornly sentimental when we take on literary lives, so sloppy that we confuse lip-synching a life with experiencing it, and so generally given to facile friendships in fiction. "We read fiction, in part, to widen our social circle: to make new friends effortlessly, receive their confidences and enter their worlds," is the blithe confession that begins the front page of a recent *New York Times Book Review*.[30] The possibility that effortless friendship may be unethical because it discounts the disparities between potential friends,[31] that the protagonist may be indifferent to—or even offended by—her interlocutor's presumption of competence or collaboration, this possibility dawns very slowly. One instance of what I mean showed up as a typo in the program for the October 1993 "Lifelikenesses" conference at Harvard University, where I read a first version of this essay. My title was listed as "Hot

Pursuit and Old Rewards" instead of "Cold Rewards," as if the rhythm of literary give and take were so familiar, so vital for our projects of self-fashioning, that it ignored syncopated interruptions. We are utterly unprepared to recognize demands for respect and denials of intimacy, even when aggressive apostrophes to the writer/reader layer a rich text with such controlling pressure as Jesusa's. What else but our empathetic reflexes allow us to assume that rich necessarily means gooey? Empathy sticks one person's feelings onto another; it denies the difference, Georges Poulet cheerfully admits. But Mikhail Bakhtin had cautioned against the mushiness that "introjects" the observer's emotions onto the object and cancels another's interiority. Empathy conflates the hero (or the book) with the reader, while intersubjective engagements, like love, safeguard a distance that leaves two to entangle.[32]

Jesusa has no taste for sweetness, and no trust in disinterested affection. Real love demands and delivers; it has use-value, like the love Bakhtin requires of readers who should "consummate" a hero from an enabling distance; they should provide what we might call a "Lacanian" mirror that will reflect a pleasingly coherent image from narrative fragments and limited internal perspectives. Real love is also like the care Jesusa received from the strict stepmother who taught the girl domestic skills to benefit them both. Or it might even be a feeling that Jesusa attributes to Pedro Aguilar for his insistence on marrying her. "The young officer might have loved me, or not, I don't know. I figure that if he didn't love me, since he was a soldier in the revolution, he could just have grabbed me and done what he wanted."[33] But Poniatowska's attention is different; without mutuality or any visible benefit to Jesusa, the interest is apparently self-serving. So you can save your crocodile tears when I'm no use to you, Jesusa responds. You have taken my life, for what it's worth, and I have nothing more to give.

THE REAL THING

What that life is worth is the question I want to ask. What is it worth to us, and why does Jesusa provoke a doubt about its value by producing a text that flattens an exciting life to a boring read? I don't mean to evaluate the real, lived life, which we could never presume to know, and which is probably a composite of Pontiatowska's primary informant, Josefina Bórquez, with other colorful lives that served to embroider the text. I mean the storied version that journalist Poniatowska transcribed and embellished. For all its transgressive excitement, its gender-crossing, border-crossing, double-crossing, and spiritually enhanced complexities, that life is replayed here with a tone of indifference; it is one of Jesusa's signatures, not Poniatowska's.

The point needs to be emphasized. Poniatowska had an absolute horror of boring her public, and she made real efforts to enliven the story by cutting out details here, adding others there (notably in the Zapata incidents), killing off colorless characters, and inventing replacements.[34] The sheer quantity of material about Jesusa's Temple of Spiritual Work bored the editor so much that she "wouldn't give it much emphasis. A little French logic."[35] Later, remorse set for pandering to consumers' taste. It was an instance of her general and class-based guilt complex. "I do feel that I should have fleshed out her inner life. But I'm always afraid that people will get bored, so I think I should have a lot going on."[36]

Jesusa doesn't mind boring the readers she hasn't sought out; she isn't marketing published copies of her self. Her only interest, she says, is ending it all, whether or not the story gets told. "She's going to die on me, just like she wants to,"[37] Poniatowska worried. That would have preempted the story. So while she could, intrepid Poniatowska pursued Jesusa, practically forcing questions on the old woman who would raise one objection after another to the weekly Wednesday interrogations. What was the clunky tape recorder doing in her rented room, and who would pay for the electricity? If Jesusa was going to waste her time answering useless questions, who would walk the chickens around the neighborhood (everyone knows that chickens need sunlight to lay eggs)?[38] Poniatowska dutifully let go of the tape recorder and took care of the chickens, so long as Jesusa would talk.

Why does Poniatowska insist so much? Why does she invest herself and defer to a woman who might have been one of her many maids? Jesusa would have known why, with the unsentimental clarity that irks some readers ("I'm not lovable; I don't like people.")[39] Poniatowska wanted something from her, her life, an authentic but uniquely aggressive Mexican life that had an admirable identity even as reflected on eavesdroppers and voyeurs.[40]

By the time she came to write this book, Elena Poniatowska had schooled herself in the available techniques and learned caution about easy conclusions, first as a reporter specializing in interviews with stars and statesmen, and then as an assistant to sociologist Oscar Lewis. Lewis had been in Mexico, gathering oral histories from poor people to write *The Children of Sánchez,* his controversial representation of their circular, culturally determined patterns of failure. Unrealistic when their expectations are high, self-defeating and resigned when they are not, indigenous Americans bring a palette of tragedies for his "scientific" representations (in the line of racially colored positivism) of the "culturally limiting" effects of poverty. Since the time of Aztec sacrifices, masses of indigenous hearts supposedly learned resignation. And centuries of Spanish colonial stability (ending with an independence that benefited mostly the white creoles), made passivity an almost innate feature of the Indian character.

This racialized stereotype ignores the pre-Columbian wars between Aztecs and their rebellious colonies, the almost relentless struggle against Spain, and the long years of indigenous vanguard activity during the Independence movement. Indians and mestizos are hardly resigned in Mexican history. To think of men like Guerrero, Juárez, and Zapata is also to think of their mass military and political support among indigenous people. And if observers had any lingering doubt about the explosive potential of this seeming resignation, the recent rebellion in Chiapas is instructive. An overwhelmingly indigenous population literally disarmed a government that hardly expected such consistent and intelligent resistance. Years before the rebels refused to be spoken for, Jesusa Palancares was speaking for herself and signing her style with the drone that made her editor frantic, but that stays audible through the book. The difference in their styles is a safeguard against the vanishing act of ventriloquism, against vampirism. Safeguards are important when a cosmopolitan writer is bent on getting a local life. Palancares cautioned Poniatowska, like the rebels reminded the authorities, that despite poverty and years of apparent "conforming" to fate,[41] inviolable positions were being drawn.

Poniatowska evidently learned to respect those positions, despite her training in Lewis's socially scientific expectations. After he left, she listened to a range of active compatriots. They were quite vocal in the late 1960s, making international news through the student uprisings. When the army

tried to stop them in 1968, with a massacre of 400 students, Poniatowska listened intently to Mexicans who testified in rage and disbelief. She recorded
them in *La noche de Tlatelolco* (1970),[42] for which she won Mexico's presti-
gious Xavier Villarrutia Prize for literature. Poniatowska declined the
award, and thereby refused to exonerate President Gustavo Díaz Ordaz or
neatly to end the story.[43] Instead, she continued to record testimonials.
Among the books that followed are *Fuerte es el silencio* (1980), a series of
news items about grass-roots resistance, including the student insurgence
and a hunger strike by mothers of the "disappeared"; and *Gaby Brimmer*
(1979), coauthored with the paraplegic subject of the book, which became
the basis for the movie *Gaby; Nada nadie: Las voces del temblor* (1988), which
collects responses to the 1985 earthquake; and *Compañeras de México:
Women Photograph Women* (1990, with Amy Conger).[44]

Her novels take a different, more autobiographical route toward creative
self-realization. *Lilus Kikus* (1954) portrays a girl who grows up Catholic and
grows out of those constraints. *Querido Diego, te abraza Quiela* (1978) is an
epistolary novel of imaginary love letters to Diego Rivera by Angelina
Beloff, the (historical) Russian-born painter he knew in Paris. And *Tinísima*
(1992) follows the peregrinations of Tina Modotti, an Italian photographer
who rediscovered Mexico image by image. In these, Poniatowska recreates
(herself in) Mexico through the transformative efforts of artists and outsiders who learn something about her country.

Jesusa's book promised to reconcile the factual (testimonial) writing
with fictional creativity. And the combination promised to achieve something qualitatively different from either genre: the extra-literary, nationally
grounded identity that Poniatowska craved. In one interview after another,
she explains how estranged she had always felt in and from Mexico, because
she was born in Paris to a Polish aristocrat and his beautiful Mexican
bride, spent her Catholic school days in Philadelphia, and in her home
in Mexico City only the servants spoke Spanish.[45] She grieves for lost identities and longs to be really Mexican. The quest for belonging led her
to Jesusa's door. No doubt Poniatowska repeated her sad story there, along
with some predictable flattery about Jesusa being the real thing, a model
and inspiration for national pride and for unfettered womanhood; she is
a corrective for "machista" masquerading and a local grounding for the
Europeanized intelligentsia. We don't exactly hear Poniatowska's patriotic

(and poignant) appeal in the book, but it is spelled out in an essay she wrote later:

> While she talked all sorts of images came to mind, and they all made me very happy. I felt strengthened by all those things that I never experienced myself . . . What grew in me, or what perhaps had been there for years, was my Mexican being, becoming Mexican, feeling that Mexico was inside me and that it was the same that was in Jesusa and that it would come out by simply opening the gate . . . One night, just before sleep came, after identifying myself with Jesusa for a long time and reviewing the images she showed me, one by one, I could whisper to myself: "Yes, I belong."[46]

PURLOINED PERSON

We don't hear the desire and the demand until this late meditation on writing the novel, but we can surmise them from Jesusa's sarcasm. She tells the well-dressed woman who has the time to complain that, in effect, these are your problems not mine. First of all, I'm no hearth to warm yourself at, and second, all this doesn't matter to me at all. The only Mexican here is you, she blurts out, since you're rich enough to afford a title, and privileged enough to fill up your time with worry instead of work. "I have no country," Jesusa says bitterly, "I'm like the gypsies, from nowhere. I don't feel Mexican and Mexicans are nothing to me. The only thing that matters here is . . . self-interest. If I had money I'd be Mexican, but since I'm not even as good as garbage, well, I'm nothing."[47]

Calling herself an outsider to everything, including country and kindness,[48] Jesusa says she has nothing to lose, and her information flows freely, as if nothing were being held back. She doesn't protest the occasional indiscretions of her interrogator; she doesn't block the narrative with secrets she wants to keep; instead, she dismisses everything with a "why bother?" Reading the young Guatemalan woman who won the 1992 Nobel Peace Prize provides a real contrast in strategy. Rigoberta Menchú conspicuously announces that secrets are being kept, lest readers presume to know enough to compete with her leadership and to make political decisions in her stead.

Her flamboyant suppressions (whether the secrets are important or even real) tell us that we will never know enough.

By contrast, cynical and apolitical Jesusa hides nothing, it seems. "I don't feel anything, from feeling too much."[49] What difference would hiding make anyway, since any strategic seduction would be beside the point for a woman just waiting to die in peace. Unlike Rigoberta, with her coquettish omissions, Jesusa delivers a practically seamless text, unpunctured by markers of mystery, and stopping only to dismiss the reader. Consider how differently they discuss the *nahual*, for example, from their particular corners of Mayaland. For Rigoberta, this spiritual *Doppelgänger* from the natural world is the subject of sacred and social secrecy. Small children are not told if their *nahual* is a sheep or a lion or a tree, because that knowledge could bias their development. Obviously, outsiders are even less reliable repositories for that information:

> We Indians have always hidden our identity and kept our secrets to ourselves. This is why we are discriminated against. We often find it hard to talk about ourselves because we know we must hide so much in order to preserve our Indian culture and prevent it being taken away from us. So I can only tell you very general things about the *nahual*. I can't tell you what my *nahual* is because that is one of our secrets.[50]

But Jesusa cares nothing for these pretenses of propriety. In the devalued cult she knows, secrets are used to swindle people:

> The *nagual* is a Christian in disguise so that he can rob like an animal. He's a Christian in a dog's skin and walks around on all four, on his hands and knees, but when he comes to a house to rob it, he has to get up to get what he wants. But at the moment he's discovered, he runs away howling and everybody in the house crosses himself in horror. He goes out at night when there's a full moon, to see better. Nothing more than a plain crook dressed like an animal, a dog or a coyote or a wolf. People short on spirit are very afraid of them, but not me because I have really seen them. I saw him. I was alone one morning and . . .[51]

Instead of titillation, which is what we get from Rigoberta, Jesusa puts out a full story. Her text is full of detail, even compromising detail about her own drunkenness and about her rage (like the time she got so angry with a cop, she pulled down his pants and bit into his b . . . b . . . berries),[52] about her successes and failures with work and with people. Nevertheless, Jesusa's life is impenetrable because penetration makes no sense when there are no holes to fill. The account is a ready-made, disturbingly full product that offers no engagement. It keeps us idle; there is no confusing our observation with participation. Idleness can infuriate readers more surely than the effort a difficult book demands. Like the Pampa, transmuted in a Borges story ("The Two Kings and the Two Labyrinths") into a desert that traps the refined king more surely than could any labyrinth, Jesusa's book confounds the sophisticated reader by refusing to supply conquerable challenges. It loses the reader in an arid monotone.

Here no tantalizing intimacy is withheld, nor any problem arises about indiscreet information being dangerous to the informant. Instead, Jesusa seems to give it all away with a verbal shrug: What does anything matter? Why bother telling you; what good does it do me?[53] Sounding indifferent or resigned, she repeats these rhetorical questions and so puts the value—and the purpose—of her performance into serious question. Perhaps we are not getting what we had bargained for, some intimacy or borrowed authenticity that autobiography is supposed to deliver. But if we stopped to calculate the deal, we might ask how we could possibly get what we want vicariously, through Poniatowska. The Mexicanness that Poniatowska desires is characterized by intellectuals like herself, following Octavio Paz, as unavailably "hermetic."[54] So her pursuit of intimacy already predicts her failure; it marks her as an unauthentic Mexican. Paradoxically (here and—alas!—elsewhere), desire gets in the way of satisfaction. As I said above, if Mexicans keep silent even as they speak, if they reserve themselves as they expend words, then to exact the intimate revelations of a personal account is irrational; it is to empty that account of anything worth banking on. This means that the bargain Poniatowska wants to strike with Palancares—the informant's private authenticity for the writer's hand in giving her voice—leaves Poniatowska necessarily empty-handed. If her informant is really Mexican and hermetic, little real meaning can change hands; and if she offers intimacy, it hardly has any authentic(ating) value. Perhaps purposefully tone-deaf to the paradox of information "said" without much interpersonal "saying" (to remember Levinas's distinction), one woman persevered with the other. Breaking silence is, after all, the slogan for intellectual feminists of the period. Even if Jesusa didn't want to be saved, Elena would force the rescue. And her force proved irresistible to the working woman. Maybe it was the flattery of Poniatowska's persistent interest, or the poignancy of a privileged woman's quest after Mexican meaning. In either case, or in both, Jesusa responded with a torrent of words whose very flow drowns out the interest for many readers. What intimate purchase can they have?

The uncensored revelations of this independent woman may be so eviscerated by practiced indifference that they are meant to leave us cold. Even the mysterious opening sequence about the spiritist sessions and visions, a sequence that Poniatowska must have chosen for its dramatic effect, is immediately demystified, sanitized, interpreted away. "They told me that all that white clothing was the habit in which I was supposed to appear at the hour of Judgment and that God had allowed me to contemplate myself like that and how I behaved during the three times I came to earth."[55] Jesusa has no patience for mystery or secrets. The life of the spirit, yes, but how dare we imagine this is anything mysterious, to be interpreted, possibly by us.

If Jesusa needn't bother telling us her life, and if she gains nothing by it, why indeed does she keep holding forth as if nothing were being held back? Could she be deploying an almost comical strategy of refusal that defies an insistent authority by apparently pandering to it, like the "featherbedding" technique that Zora Neale Hurston described? The strategy is familiar to everyone in Eastern Europe, I am told, through stories like *The Good Soldier Schweik*. He would infuriate his interrogators by answering with so much detail that it was impossible to tell what piece of his tedious report mattered.[56] And the game of hide-and-seek, so obvious in Rigoberta's maneuvers, is announced in voluble Schweik's very name, which (misspelled in mock-German) means "Silence." Jesusa too may be staging a performance that makes the information irrelevant, so available and public that it offers no political or personal pathos for readers. In that case, self-aggrandizing empathy would be as impossible as our imperious tendency to substitute autobiographical subjects with ourselves in a game that Paul de Man described as reciprocal replacements.[57] Some readers actually manage to ignore Rigoberta's demand for distance and to embrace her in an autobiographical reflex that identifies the reader with the writer. And we just saw that Poniatowska went on record about her identifications with Jesusa. The intimacy is not friendly, despite good intentions. It forces itself on people who insist on the political value of keeping us at a distance.

Poniatowska sometimes worried about her own morality as a player in the game of "de-facement," as we saw; she also worried about Jesusa's mortality. She need not have worried about that, because Jesusa lasted long enough to give up the whole story. For two years she participated in the "conversations" that a feminist critic like Schweikart (no pun here) imagines to take place between a woman's text and a woman reader. "Jesusa has been freed to speak by the timely intervention of Elena Poniatowska."[58] But the speaker seems less grateful than we expect her to be. Her integrity doesn't flinch before the interest she kindles or the kindness her interrogator offers in these amateur therapy-like sessions, as one woman probed and the other disclosed one intimate memory after another. But the therapeutic value of middle-class sympathy is less than nothing, Jesusa objects, because the language of pain and paralysis entirely misses who she is. "I don't know what sadness is. You're talking to me in Chinese, because I don't understand sadness. Crying is one thing, but sadness is another. It's bad, doesn't work, means nothing to anyone but yourself."[59]

Dismissed. Jesusa rejects Poniatowska's sentimental language toward the end of the book, a few pages before the door shuts in her/our face. This rejection at the end repeats the message and tone of the offputting beginning, "Miss me?" And it shows editor Poniatowska framing the book as a series of frustrated encounters, as if disencounter were the point of the book.[60] Jesusa's message is not only to save your crocodile tears after you have taken my life, but also that the life you have managed to eke out over years of diligent plunder (hours of committed reading) is undigestible for you because it needs no digesting, it is too simple to be processed or to leave nourishing traces, so it is expelled and forgotten. It is a desert, not a labyrinth. Despite the lavish adventures she serves up one after another, she holds back any flavor or meaning from disappointed and possibly chastened readers. You can take away the frenzied activity of my life, she seems to be saying, but you leave this purloined person hiding in full view, safely untranslated and inassimilable.

We empty-handed readers are then caught red-handed, singed by a frustrated desire to have our way with Jesusa. When she refuses to be our matrix for narcissistic self-duplication, the willing partner for a textual tryst, or the comrade of political commitments that would replace her agency with ours, readers confront the ethical boundaries of ventriloquism, pleasure-seeking, and political engagements. Maybe we will learn to hesitate at those limits.

BELOVED KNOWS

HOLOCAUSTS BEYOND TELLING

7

"You can't say everything."
"Disappointed? Did you desire it?"

—LYOTARD
  The Differend

Two thirds into *Beloved,* Paul D marches into Sethe's kitchen and demands her story, straight out, about killing her baby nineteen years earlier. Readers may be grateful for the bluntness that will clear up doubts after so many pages that only hint at the story. Or they may cringe at the aggression in a novel that has been coaching us in more delicate recoveries of the past, often through Paul D himself. Until now, he has been a model of sensitive reading—of Sethe's back, feet, and her story, which he puts next to his own.

Morrison stages Paul's impatience at this late point, maybe to catch data-hungry readers in an identification with the commanding partner. This is just after Stamp Paid has told Paul D everything, and more explanations are either superfluous or insufficient. So Sethe says nothing. Instead, she recoils from the world and secludes herself with Beloved. The pregnant daughter swells with a mother's life, while Sethe grows dangerously thin. Finally her youngest daughter, Denver, appeals for witnesses outside the stifling house to break the spell, so that Sethe can come back to the living and Beloved can go back to the dead.

Throughout the pages before Paul D's demand and Sethe's silence, a counterpoint has been playing between memory and forgetfulness. The need to tell motivates the novel from the beginning, in hints of decipherable information played like many-voiced music.[1] By page 163 readers already know the facts about Sethe's slavery, about the abuse she suffered from her new masters, her escape, and the infanticide that haunts her. We know the facts very soon, and in as much detail as we should require, despite the heroine's "keeping the past at bay," "beating back the past,"[2] holding the story back from the hero who is sometimes equally reluctant to remember. That is why, so late into the book, he comes to demand the story that she has never fully told.

UNANSWERABLE DEMANDS

Testimony plays against a rhythm of stagy silences in *Beloved.* Purposeful forgetfulness interrupts remembrance in staccato bursts that draw attention to the gaps inherited from more traditional genres—chronicle, personal confessions, slave narratives. The collective experience narrated in those genres had, long before Morrison's performance, signaled the silences that distinguish African American history from others. Oral and written versions fulfill the general responsibility that Walter Benjamin assigned to history, to cement present generations to the past and oblige them toward the future.[3] But telling African American history includes telling its silences. In the web of underrecorded and repressed stories, most ancestors don't even have names, whole languages and cultural worlds are practically effaced, and time, traumatized and mythologized, loses linearity in memory's effort to deal with ghastly absences.

The ghosts show up immediately in Toni Morrison's novel, like those that make trouble for the story of Africans in America, mainly through the unmoored spirit of a baby who comes back to trouble her mother, a spirit that has no resting place in African pantheism or in Christian heaven. (Jewish folk belief in unlaid ghosts would call Beloved a *dibbuk.*) Ghosts disrupt the narrative in every reluctance to remember (Sethe "tried to remember as little as was safe"[4]), in every allusion to unspeakable pain ("Silent, except for social courtesies, when they met one another they neither described nor asked about the sorrow that drove them from one place to another. The whites didn't bear speaking on. Everybody knew"), and especially in the climactic scene where Paul D commands and Sethe refuses.

> Sethe knew that the circle she was making around the room, him, the subject, would remain one. That she could never close in, pin it down for anybody who had to ask. If they didn't get it right off—she could never explain. Because the truth was simple . . . she was squatting in the garden and when she saw them coming . . . if she thought anything, it was No. No. Nono. Nonono. Simple. She just flew.[5]

The demand is already a sign of misunderstanding: either you know or intuit what it feels like to be caught as a runaway, whose barely free children are slaves again; or you do not know and refuse to imagine.[6] Rational explanations cannot evoke the feeling. It is too immediate, too simple. Paul D's demand is unanswerable because it collapses the "differend" between two kinds of knowing: the cognition of *saber* (in Spanish or French) against the familiarity of *conocer*. To ignore the abyss between empirical "knowledge" and emotional "knowing" blocks the passage from one to the other.

To force information isn't to gain intimacy. It is to extract confession with an interrogator's control. Does Paul D want a guilt-ridden, sobbing, break-down story of Sethe killing her baby instead of painstaking composure? Would a flood of Sethe's grief cover the distance between them, or would it open up their wounds? Paul D doesn't stop to ask himself that question. His demand overrides the sense of responsibility that made his love something more than desire. The demand is damaging in the technical sense that Lyotard assigns to "damage." It denies Sethe the (legal) recourse to be appropriately heard. Paul D disallows the specificity of her story by assuming that it can and should be narrated like any other.

Sethe's evasion goes unremarked by critics (and undone by Jonathan Demme's 1998 film version, where Stamp Paid's story is cut and pasted onto Sethe's lines), the way Rigoberta's secrets seemed beside the point of her ethnographic information. Neither gesture of noncompliance stops readers who process suspended information as a delay tactic to build intrigue. Who is Beloved? seems to be the relevant question. Is she a child-ghost full grown, or an orphaned slave-girl forced into early sexual service, or a figure for uncounted ancestors wrenched from normal history by the Middle Passage? There is no dearth of sleuthing, speculation, interpretation. Reticence can be a goad to curiosity, but it means more in Rigoberta's secrets and in

Beloved's circling. Menchú and Morrison dig a trench between telling and what is told, between readerly competence and our satisfaction.[7]

The appetite for empirical intrigue misses Morrison's intriguing double bind: to tell Sethe's story to those who can be therapeutic witnesses is also to rehearse the pain that can reinscribe terror and humiliation. Yet not to tell would leave Sethe, Paul D, and an entire society of slave survivors without the history that binds them, leave them unwritten like the displaced postwar blacks who were "Silent, except for social courtesies." It is Denver's broken silence, after all, that makes her mother available for healing.[8] Morrison is both bound to say and to claim she is not saying. "It was not a story to pass on," says the double-binding epilogue.[9]

"It was not a story to pass on," the ironic ending repeats, after the story has just passed on to us. Competent readers are trained to expect such ironies, along with complicitous winks in our hide-and-seek games of literary seductions and readerly conquests. Passing through *Beloved*'s impasse has the charm of an open secret, a titillation satisfied even before pleasure is withheld. Whatever the epilogue claims to conceal is showing brazenly through the erasure. The joke is on keeping things private in public. And once educated readers get the deconstructive joke that jumbles invitation with exclusion, public with private, secret with scandal, we may close the novel knowing its ploys and satisfied in that knowledge. This is how many critics have closed the book, happy with the healing performed at the end,[10] focused on "the join" between the fragments of history,[11] even assuming a reversal of intention, as if the "not" were simply erasable in this "story to pass on."[12] Only James Phelan has taken the obstacles as cues by the author to underinterpret *Beloved*.[13]

The final and equivocal instruction for handling the book is the last of Morrison's relentless double messages. The story has been gripping its readers throughout in a *fort da* rhythm that choreographs our hide-and seek game, and that Morrison would compare to the alternating satisfaction and frustration produced by African American music, the mirror of her writing. As she said in an interview with Paul Gilroy: "Music makes you hungry for more of it. It never really gives you the whole number. It slaps and it embraces, it slaps and it embraces."[14] This describes an entire rhetoric of particularism. Morrison's brilliant performance is irresistible for professional readers,[15] a plenitude which might have dissuaded me from adding one more essay to the *Beloved* industry. But the advantage of so much critical attention is that readers probably share this English-language context for my point.

The point is that particularist texts play with more than one irony. In addition to *Beloved*'s nod toward knowing readers in the epilogue, a different irony might surface if we counted less on our competence and more on the possibility of rebuffs. Then we might detour from the fast track of interpretation to stop at the roadblocks. Deconstructive ironies, after all, don't point in only one direction. Could the epilogue be telling us that while we already know what is being concealed, what we know is empty, because the meaning or the affect of the story is reserved and not transferable? Is it possible that *Beloved* follows a vitiating strategy that gives good plot but takes away the rush of titillating identification?

Perhaps it is like the strategy in Richard Rodriguez's memoirs, in which his grandmother's Spanish is too intimate to translate.[16] Morrison is already inside a more subtle negotiation for distance, squarely inside an English language that had exiled some and then eliminated others. But she produces distance with the same kind of distinction between the Saying and the Said that separates Rodriguez's Spanish message from its translatable meaning. "What Nan told her she had forgotten," Sethe remembers, "along with the language she told it in. The same language her ma'am spoke, and which would never come back. But the message—that was and had been there all along."[17] Is the strategy of *Beloved* also like the calculated coldness of Jesusa Palancares, the Mexican washwoman who had fought in the revolution and lived through the disappointments of its aftermath? At the end of two years interviews with a dauntless interrogator, Jesusa said: "Fuck off now. Go away and let me sleep." And Rigoberta, of course, has been my trainer in picking up strategies that foster desire in order to frustrate it.

Morrison is an expert at flaunting possible intimacies to withhold satisfaction; she locates and then safeguards an autonomous human core of feeling. ("She put her arms around him. The others she did not put her arms around. Never. Never.")[18] The story of slavery is public, it needs to be, but she won't have readers warming their cold bones on harrowing confessions of degradation and death. Secrets interrupt the confessional flow, Levinas wrote, in defense of the speaker's inviolable subjectivity, so that interaction becomes a free option rather than a demand.[19] Yet Sethe's stories are not secret. We know about her milk that is stolen, about Halle's maddening impotence to stop it, about Paul D's chain gang that sinks into death by mud-slide. All the broad and bloody strokes of the horrific picture are there, made tolerable by lyrical asides about love, flight, family, and by the masterful fragmentation of late modernist writing. The novel's very polish can be a cause for criticism (more informal than published), in the line of criticizing Ralph Ellison as too studied in the school of white masters to be authentically black.[20] Morrison holds nothing back, it seems, just like Jesusa. The story is given. What is taken away is the heroine's pandering to readers greedy for excitement. Her reluctance to speak stanches the flow of intimacy. We can and should know the story, but not because we demand to know it of the victims. (I remember how my mother felt violated every time someone asked her how much she suffered during World War II or compared her story with those of people who "really" suffered.) We should know because it is obvious, simple, a historical burden.

Deliberate silence is a way that victims make themselves heard, says Lyotard. "Silences, instead of a *Resultat.* These silences interrupt the chain that goes from them, the deported, and from them, the SS, to us who speak about them . . . Those silences signal the interruption of the *Selbst,* its splitting apart."[21] Critics need more stamina to endure the hush, even when they notice that *Beloved* makes readers strain against conventions of interpretation, just as Morrison's writing strains against the formulas of confessional novels and historical texts.

Morrison also pries open slave narratives that deliberately silence intimacy. "Over and over," she notes, "the writers pull the narrative up short with a phrase such as, 'but let us drop a veil over these proceedings too terrible to relate.'"[22] Cuba's slave poet Juan Francisco Manzano threw a similar shroud over the intimate parts of his autobiography ("but let's leave to silence the rest of this painful scene"), even though he had promised a full story to abolitionist Domingo del Monte.[23] That is to say, Manzano's reticence is practically defiant. He is not simply tactful lest he upset the ideal reader, which is the reason Morrison gives for reticent slave narratives in the United States. Manzano is also tactical, affirming his autonomy before the powerful reader. I am saying that their precautions (the blanks that Morrison fills in with densely psychological writing), are the spots that "pull the narrative up short" and signal the reader's limited grasp.

Is Frederick Douglass, for example, merely prudent when he refuses to tell secrets, or is he also provocative, counting on our curiosity to heighten the interest of his story and to increase the worth of the author who can resist demanding readers? Houston A. Baker, Jr. reads Douglass in the key of sentimental-romantic oratory.[24] This key makes his pauses, his syncopations, sound dissonant. Reticence may be familiar to Victorian readers, but Douglass uses the convention of delicacy to let it speak the stark language of survival. His refusals to say everything do not show (only) a concern for readers; they also show what Morrison would elsewhere call "absences so stressed, so ornate, so planned, they call attention to themselves; arrest us with intentionality and purpose."[25]

> I deeply regret the necessity that impels me to suppress any thing of importance connected with my experience in slavery. It would afford me great pleasure indeed, as well as materially add to the interest of my narrative, were I at liberty to gratify a curiosity, which I know exists in the minds of many, by an accurate statement of all the facts pertaining to my most fortunate escape. But I must deprive myself of this pleasure, and the curious of the gratification . . .

> "Trust no man!" I saw in every white man an enemy, and in almost every colored man cause for distrust. It was a most painful situation; and, to understand it, one must needs experience it, or imagine himself in similar circumstances. Let him be a fugitive slave in a strange land.[26]

Harriet Jacobs can be as dramatically decorous. In a letter to Amy Post, Jacobs agreed to tell as much as her Christian duty demanded; but before the public of the *New York Tribune,* on June 21, 1853, she drew the limit at efficacious history and refused to focus on her person: "But no, I will not tell you of my own suffering—no, it would harrow up my soul."[27]

Morrison's strategic silences stay discreet for avid readers. They prefer the fuller features of *Beloved,* especially the psychological detail that leads away from historically specific bondage toward general patterns of bonding.[28] The pre-Oedipal mother-daughter dyad gets attention; it seemed so promising a theme for feminist independence, but implodes here self-destructively. Denver's liberation from the dyad, set in the language of social relations, is also noted. And Paul D engages readers through his quest for family and fecundity that might reverse the barrenness of slavery.[29]

LESSONS AND LIMITS IN LYOTARD

Barbara Christian complains that all this focus on universal passions has left the cultural specificity of *Beloved* underdeveloped,[30] despite some efforts to make connections between Western psychoanalysis and African spirituality. The psychological approach is a tribute to the novel's affective powers. It also signals sentimental reading habits that thrive inside complicitous interpretive systems (psychoanalysis, feminism, some theories of writing history).[31] Habitually, readings slip into metaphoric identifications between particular characters and universalizing readers. No doubt *Beloved* offers the possibility for neutralizing the differend (African American particularities of history and culture) by inviting readers to extract the all-purpose core of extraordinary relationships. Otherwise, sophisticated readers would not be likely to translate historically bounded passions into a universally valid vocabulary. Would they? In a 1988 talk, Morrison said that she ushers readers into *Beloved* and guarantees safe passage. "Come on in," is what listeners heard, like the welcome of ladies at church.[32] But her care underlines the dangers that confront readers at the door. Unlike the "intimacy I was aiming for [in *Sula*], the intimacy between the reader and the page," *Beloved* begins with a jolt: "Because the *in medias res* opening that I am so committed to is here excessively demanding. It is abrupt, and should appear so. No native informant here . . . The friendly observation post I was content to build and man in *Sula* (with the stranger in the midst), or the down-home journalism of *Song of Solomon* or the calculated mistrust of the point of view in *Tar Baby* would not serve here."[33] Morrison explodes obliging approaches, even if our conventions of reading make us too stubborn to notice this.[34]

A general deadlock between professional conventions and the data they process is Lyotard's complaint. "An intellectual is someone who helps forget differends, by advocating a given genre"; "One's responsibility before thought consists, on the contrary, in detecting differends and in finding the (impossible) idiom for phrasing them. This is what a philosopher does." The exhortation motivates Lyotard's book-length response to "reasonable" revisions of Holocaust history: "The time has come to philosophize," "to bear witness to differends."[35] Witnessing, he repeats, can falter or mislead when it reduces unaccountable details to genres of discourse. The most evident trap, he says, is narrative, which neutralizes the particularity of an event into a neat chain of cause and effect. Even when stories allow codes to collide, in what Bakhtin would call dialogue or heteroglossia, Lyotard objects to the aesthetic coherence of all narrative, its fictional, historical, and theoretically proleptic varieties.[36] Most readings of *Beloved* bear out the philosopher's skepticism. They celebrate the novel's ultimate coherence and closure. Inevitably, he observes, witnesses who tell stories force them into manageable discourse.

But I would ask Lyotard how one can witness without narrating. Has *philosophy* developed the new idioms that he claims should voice the differend without damaging it? Evidently it has not; otherwise his call for those new languages would be superfluous. Neither the "abyss" between descriptive and prescriptive discourses (from Aristotle through Kant), nor the unaccountable sense of obligation in Levinas's ethics, provides this necessary idiom. In the limited reaches of our existing languages, the only expressions for witnessing remain storytelling and silence, the aphasic silence of a traumatized witness, the accusatory silence that refuses to collaborate, the fearful silence that anticipates more trouble. In fact, Bakhtin's description of novels as unorthodox experiments will help to notice that *Beloved* disrupts the generic frames that trouble Lyotard. The novel plays a counterpoint between the two kinds of witnessing he mentions: telling horrors and refusing to tell, remembering and beating back memory. Not one theme but two play in the text and echo past it. The differend is heard in the "abyss" between revealing and concealing, between the unhinged connections of cause to effect in Morrison's unreasonable story, and through the unanswerable demands to hear it.

The question is not whether to uncover the facts; they are known. It is rather the style and timing of rememory, for what purpose and at what cost. How can Sethe possibly respond to Paul D's self-defeating command? And yet response is the mechanism for any relationship, political, ethical, personal. Linking onto a discourse is necessary, says Lyotard, although the kind of link one makes is a matter of judgment.[37] Sethe's circling may dramatize her inability to link onto Paul D's confessional "phrase regimen," as if it were her psychological problem.[38] And Paul D. may imagine that Sethe's muteness is an admission of guilt, that his confrontation of the issue is proper, a matter of clearing up suspicion and asserting his incontestable right to know. But, as Lyotard points out, refusing to speak is a kind of response; it "pulls up short" the interlocutor's genre of discourse. A preference for silence produces the resistant "phrase" of the plaintiff, who could speak if speaking would serve her. That mute phrase is not the imposed silence of a victim who, by definition, has no right to speak, but the agency of one who has nothing to say to a man who speaks another language. If Sethe had submitted to Paul D's language, she would have become a victim, without a legitimate phrase regime or the possibility of establishing it.

Her cold response is an "impertinence" for the genre of confession. Paul D gets this point and he leaves, offended. Impertinence is defensive here. It is Sethe's refusal to undo the differend of her own more cautious and circumspect regime. She veers away from predictable and unsuitable linkages. The offense is Paul D's insistence on the "hegemony of one phrase regime over another, the usurpation of its authority."[39]

When readers get to the scene of his demand and her refusal, how do we react, in the sense of where do we stand? Interpretations of *Beloved* are more likely to position and to pass judgment on the characters, or to withhold judgment by advancing wise arguments about the embeddedness of ethical behavior in experience.[40] Readers seldom target themselves for moral and political scrutiny, even when a novel like *Beloved* makes circumspection a reading requirement. All the books that occupy me in these chapters require it. For example, *The Storyteller* by Mario Vargas Llosa implicates readers in the contemporary extermination campaigns in Amazonia, whether or not we attribute guilt to characters, to the author, or even to Bartolomé de las Casas who preached love for the Indians, but did so much damage to them and to their African replacements. For *Beloved*'s readers, the question is, do we second Paul D's universal and abstract condemnation of Sethe? "You got two feet, not four."[41]

The point is not how we *judge* Sethe, but how we *desire* her. Do we lust after her personal confession along with Paul D? Do we conflate love with interest? Does the fragmented but unmistakable story of her life fail to satisfy a desire to hear it told straight out, just in case we missed a measure of pathos? Morrison has covered all the bases before she drives the point home: she has strewn conspicuous traces of the story from the first page and has linked them repeatedly, so that even careless readers get the connections. Then Stamp Paid, the boatman who literally moves Sethe from one stage of life to another, tells the story plainly to Paul D, just before the collision between his imperious desire and her impertinent silence.

At this moment, after curiosity has been sated and the fragmented narrative line has straightened out, Morrison can stop the story to make us reflect on a residual lust for something else, perhaps for power over the informant. After everything is already known, Paul D demands to know. Do readers, I am asking, share his frustration and lipsync his insistence? Or do we, gradually instructed by her delicacy about saying too much, censure him for violating her clear limit? I have heard both responses; but mostly the craving for confession. Either way (lusting after the horror story, or cringing at the trespass), his/our damaging desire to know is exposed as something different from love.

The novel can train us to notice the difference. By the time Sethe finds explanations superfluous, the intimate circle of knowing readers has learned elements of the story and it has made them complicitous, prepared to intuit the terrible efficacy of her sacrifice. Morrison seduces readers into a particular American code of feeling as masterfully as Whitman had done when he confided in each reader individually. "This hour I tell things in confidence, / I might not tell everybody but I will tell you."[42] Morrison purposefully enthralls less and discriminates more than this liberal supply of demand for oneself.[43] Like Rigoberta, she counts on our imperfect readings and marks the kind of distance called respect. So simple a lesson and so fundamental: to acknowledge Rigoberta's refusal to be redeemed from difference, to remember that Morrison writes ignorance into the very demand for information. "She could never close in, pin it down for anybody who had to ask."[44]

Imperious desire marks off the distance between the heroine and her admirers, a breach where the differend survives. Through her telling refusals, Sethe circles the issue that should be self-evident. Yet the breach is easily overstepped, to judge from the many essays about *Beloved*. Perhaps stepping is easy because stopping is strange for critics. Even after Paul D is rebuffed, readers evidently assume that the refusal is temporary, something to overcome rather than the point of a story about telling limits. We expect candor and self-exposure from anything that resembles the genre of a slave narrative, or a sentimental novel, even though there may be no secrets left to tell. Sethe's impertinence blocks those expectations.

But we press onward, driven by the anxiety of losing the links. Lyotard notices that people are understandably worried about not being addressed, given the constitutive gaps between phrase regimes (empirical talk, prescriptions, evaluations, each untranslatable to the other), and given also the possibility of impertinence that refuses to answer. Heidegger had accounted for anxiety as a response to our consciousness of living towards death. But Lyotard shifts from this existential register to a philosophy of communication. For him, man is Being's ideal reader, and we are nervous because Being doesn't always speak to us; we do not necessarily exist for the other. Anxiety happens when we miss the links between phrases, feel surprise at pieces of language that don't fit our world-picture, worry that the silences won't give up their secrets with time.[45]

"You can't say everything"[46]—Disappointed? Did you desire it? Or at least did something—'language'—want it? Wanted to unfurl its full powers? A will? A "life"? A desire, a lack? These are so many teleologies of fulfillment, or melancholias for the unfulfilled.—But you [Lyotard] certainly accept that "something asks to be put into phrases"?—This does not imply that *everything* ought to or wants to be said. This implies the expectant waiting for an occurrence, for the "portentiousness," that indeed everything has not been said. The vigil. This waiting is in the phrase universe. It is the specific "tension" that every phrase regimen exerts upon the instances.[47]

When words don't come forth, they are held in abeyance *(en souffrance)*, one of Lyotard's favorite concepts. Suffer the words to come is an invitation, a password for safe passage, not a command. Part of what Lyotard wants to do is to conjure up new codes that will acknowledge the differend. Deliberate silence is not nothing; it is a sign of a discourse delayed. His strong example is Wittgenstein's famous dismissal of ethical and aesthetic issues at the end of the *Tractatus* ("What we cannot speak about we must pass over in silence").[48] Lyotard will call it a deferral, because, as a speech act, the passing over cannot help but anticipate an arrival. If there is yet no appropriate phrase in the common idioms, "it is already phrased, as feeling. The avowal has been made. The vigil for an occurrence, the anxiety and the joy of an unknown idiom, has begun."[49]

Sethe's refusal is a dramatic case of cautious deferral, the kind of case that worries Lyotard's faith in legal justice. For it is not mystery or lack of authority that holds her back; it is knowing that her words would go nowhere. To talk, one needs an appropriate idiom and an available listener. If she is silent, it is because Paul D cannot yet listen with the feeling that will make sense of her story. For the same reason Richard Wright's native son character is mute before the law:

> He knew as he stood there that he could never tell why he had killed. It was not that he did not really want to tell, . . . His crimes were known, but what he had felt before he committed them would never be known. He would have gladly admitted his guilt if he had thought that in doing so he could have also given in the same breath a sense of the deep, choking hate that had been his life, a hate that he had not wanted to have, but could not help having. How could he do that? The impulsion to try to tell was as deep as had been the urge to kill.[50]

Sethe is no longer in court, where she had already been absolved or dismissed by people who had no frame of reference for her story. How disappointing that now, as she stands before her lover, no one is listening. Sethe has been a model of "suffering" the words to come without forcing them.

By the time Paul D commands Sethe to confess, *Beloved* has staged and averted a series of dangerous temptations to tell too much, too soon. Morrison's assurance of safe passage means that dangers are being cautiously averted. The jeopardy is not merely in the mother-daughter dyad that occupies feminist readings; it is a constant condition of telling this story. Remembering is full of risks. History haunts its survivors. Nothing immediately liberating comes from reliving loss and humiliation. Sethe knows this long before Paul D finally learns to proceed with caution; she knows enough not to press him when the words stick in his throat. He "had only begun, what he was telling her was only the beginning when her fingers on his knee, soft and reassuring, stopped him. Just as well. Just as well. Saying more might push them both to a place they couldn't get back from."[51] (I am reminded of a young German scholar who wondered why we children of Jewish survivors preferred to elicit that "Just as well" from our parents, as if it were difficult for him to intuit that the hunger for memory could be spoiled by a surfeit of unbearable recollections.) Stories that strain to be told come to us in *Beloved*'s syncopated rhythm, between telling and withholding, like the traumatized memory of slavery that keeps breaking through efforts to suppress it. Another master of staccato, James Baldwin, handles the memory of contemporary pain in a similar way. He practically stutters trauma's effect:

> From afar, one may imagine that one perceives the pattern and one may. But, as one is not challenged—or more precisely menaced—by the details, the pattern may be nothing more than something one imagines oneself to remember. And, after all, what I remembered—or imagined myself to remember—of my life in America (before I left home!) was terror. And what I am trying to suggest by *what one imagines oneself to be able to remember* is that terror cannot be remembered. One blots it out. The organism—the human being—blots it out.[52]

Bits and snatches of Sethe's story, we get those right away. But the coherent linear version that impertinently curious readers (including Paul D) have been craving, that is reserved until later. After the facts have been parsimoniously dealt, listeners may gradually learn respect for hesitation and link onto the story delicately. Otherwise, they will either continue to demand their way, or dismiss the story as too much unspeakable horror.

What can be called impossible "after Auschwitz," Lyotard asks, or after slavery and lynchings? Nothing, despite the smug skepticism of revisionist "historians" who argue that there never was an extermination campaign, that it wasn't possible.[53] The argument is technically irrefutable, because no amount of empirical evidence can refute it. The victims are, by definition, gone. (Harriet Jacobs's story met with similar skepticism, by almost everyone who wasn't black and female.[54] White female readers were quicker than black men to accept Jacobs's authorship and veracity.[55]) Mere data, in other words, may not suffice to convince those who are blind to what seems excessive, impossible. It was "impossible," for example, for the blacks of Saint-Domingue to have organized a successful revolution against France. No amount of data could prove to Europeans that something so unimaginable actually happened. Michel-Rolph Trouillot literally underlines the paradox in *Silencing the Past* (1995): "*The events that shook up Saint-Domingue from 1791 to 1804 constituted a sequence for which not even the extreme political left in France or in England had a conceptual frame of reference.* They were 'unthinkable' facts in the framework of Western thought."[56]

What Lyotard objects to in Wittgenstein's exclusive concern with existing "language games" is his narrowness and impatience with what *could* be (for example, legal languages that might acknowledge a differend). Perhaps Wittgenstein's empiricist bias against the "impossible" also blunted his perception of World War II, while he served the Axis as a medical orderly. Possibility becomes a legal and a historical issue for Lyotard and for Derrida.[57] If the Holocaust cannot be proved by its victims, neither can it be disproved by skeptics. It haunts us, unspeakably, the way slavery haunts the Americas.[58] Trouillot reads both experiences as targets for history's silencing of impertinent details. Unlike Sethe's disruptive silence, or Bigger's mutenes, or Baldwin's stuttering, official history neutralizes the disruptions that repeat from one trauma to another.[59]

REPEATING HOLOCAUSTS

Adorno formulated his negative dialectics "after Auschwitz," when the world turned upside down to drag universal progress into a downward spiral. Ironically, even though Jews are supposed to be good at writing down history, there seemed to be no more European-Jewish history to write. (Oral lore, by contrast, is typically an African American art, although it will have to cede to writing in order to prosper, says Morrison among others.[60]) Jewish history had taken a similar turn from talk to writing after the Roman occupation scattered the Jews and Europe's Middle Ages reviled them, as Leo Strauss explains. Only reluctantly was "haggadic" oral lore collected in the Talmud, and despite rabbinical prohibitions against writing, esoteric teachings became texts while teachers escaped in one direction and students in another.[61] At one time, medieval Spain was a precarious home for Jews, but not quite as murderous as France and Germany. That history has been so painful and humiliating that even the written versions got lost and forgotten by Jews themselves.

Auschwitz was not sui generis, tragic as that is to say; it was a technologically advanced episode in a history of extermination campaigns. European

Jews were targeted for destruction long before. Demonic and dangerous, the only solution was a final one. When Jews lived peacefully, it was as foreigners, exotic, extraneous, and degraded by legitimate subjects who could own land, live where they chose, pursue education and military careers. Degradation was often punctuated by the violence of pogroms. The worst happened during the Crusades, between 1096 and 1146. Some of the ghastly detail is forgotten and seems impossible by now, thanks to the balm of bad memory. One specific detail bears directly on the story of parental love and racial persecution in *Beloved*. It haunts twelfth-century Hebrew chronicles and liturgical poetry (and comes back with the Nazi persecution).

Some Jewish parents actually sacrificed their children rather than let them fall into the hands of the murderers. They took knives into their own hands and cut their babies' throats. Unbelievable as that sounds to at least some historians, who seem certain that the Jewish commandment not to kill would have prevailed, mothers and fathers chose to preempt the mob. They would recite the blessing over sacrificial offerings and wait for the child to answer, "Amen." Then they commended themselves to the all-forgiving Almighty and committed suicide.

> How the outcry of the children rises!
> Trembling, they see their brothers slain.
> The mother binds her son lest he be blemished as he startles,
> The father makes a blessing before slaughtering the sacrifice.[62]

Mass suicide had been heard of in the world's history of intolerance and bondage, in the besieged fortress of Massadah and among conquered Caribbean tribes and African slaves. But the corollary of baby-killing seems too excessive to acknowledge. Maybe the disappointed murderers of the preempted pogroms shook their heads in disbelief at the "irrationality," the way the schoolteacher would shake his head at Sethe. Jewish witnesses were not there to see the response; the few who were not dead had escaped. Someone at least survived to tell the stories, often obliquely, like traumatized patients who know too much calamity to speak it. The sacrifices of children and their parents' suicides between 1096 and 1149 were transmuted into the register of *midrash* (narrative glosses on allegedly laconic passages of the Bible) about Abraham's sacrifice of his son Isaac. (*Beloved* can be read as such a gloss on the news clip about Margaret Garner and on so many slave narratives that shroud intimate lives.) Versions of the Abraham and Isaac story are the subject of Shalom Spiegel's *The Last Trial* (1954), published a few years after the Auschwitz Crusade.

Spiegel borrows his title from the Genesis text about Abraham's proof of unflinching faith in God. It recounts the ten escalating ordeals that end with the binding of Isaac. *Akeddah* means "binding" in Hebrew, not sacrifice. The inexact English translation is a Christian version of Isaac as a figure for martyred Christ. The mistranslation overwhelms the differend between Hebrew and Christian Bibles. That differend is what makes the medieval midrashim so tragic, because the Jewish *Akeddah* loses the independence that seemed worth dying for. Binding ends in sacrifice. Abraham kills Isaac.

"When Father Isaac was bound on the altar and *reduced to ashes and his sacrificial dust was cast* on to Mount Moriah, the Holy One, blessed be He, immediately brought upon him dew and revived him."[63] Of course the story cannot end in death. The anonymous writer did survive the medieval massacres, and the survivor is no apostate since he chose to write a midrash. The story continues beyond Isaac's ashes, to his sojourn in the great House of Learning in Heaven and his return as an inspired sage.

No one will miss the irony of Christian borrowings (the sacrificial death and resurrection of the son) by Jews, for whom assimilation amounted to annihilation.[64] What kind of Jewish responses were possible after the breakdown of covenants between God and the people he promised to protect? One response was to sidestep the logic of contract, of mutual obligation, cause and effect. Some Jewish legends took mystical and supernatural flight. Spirits departed from bodies, roamed the heavens, returned to teach, or in other cases to haunt mortals with unresolved stories. Similar flights are familiar to readers of *Beloved,* in the tradition of African American ghost stories that survived the Middle Passage and responded to it. What kind of response to infanticide is imaginable, I repeat, besides these supernatural and unearthly stories of returning children? This is not a rhetorical question.

Another response is portrayed in *Beloved* as despair, the unrelievable depression that ended in death for Baby Suggs. Desperate refusals of life, of God and religion, would have been difficult to write into the Jewish sources. But the novel can portray despair, as an old woman who has exhausted all efforts to make sense of life. She had grown old in slavery, bearing eight children, most of whom she couldn't remember; then she watched her son

Halle work to set her free, lost him to uncontestable cruelty, and took his wife and children into her house in Cleveland. After so much exertion, slavery reaches back to reclaim the barely escaped family, and her reckless daughter-in-law prefers to sacrifice the babies rather than return. Too tired to live and too heartsick about losses, Baby Suggs dies.

Coping with life requires diminished clarity and a short memory. And forgetting is yet another answer the novel offers to the unanswerable question of how a parent can kill her child. Sethe of the beaten-back memory remembers as little as is safe. The dam breaks of course, like the "birth-water" that breaks when Beloved shows up, and memory rushes to overtake the present. A ghostly presence will occupy the precarious void, because pain doesn't go away and coping mechanisms have ghastly side effects. The collective memories of a violent departure from Africa to a wretched landing in America, the Middle Passage and slavery, figure here in Beloved's horrific rebirth. Her talk conjures images of the slaveships, of a woman thrown overboard whose face (and Sethe's and Denver's) belongs to Beloved. "All of it is now it is always now."[65]

Beloved's readers have marked the importance of African spirit belief,[66] especially in response to the Middle Passage,[67] and they suggest analogies with Western psychoanalysis.[68] Both interpretive systems acknowledge a reality beyond empiricism, and a temporality that disrupts the present with a nagging past. Children of Africans still know, after centuries of forced forgetting, that "ancestral spirits must be nurtured and fed, or they will be angry or, at the least, sad."[69] Both systems respond actively to trauma, not simply as languages that track displacements and link trigger event with neurotic repercussions.

TRAUMA'S TRADITIONS

The connection between trauma and psychoanalysis is probably genealogical too, writes Cathy Caruth. In her reading of *Moses and Monotheism*, the old and exiled author is speculating on the parallel between delayed trauma neurosis and the Jewish history of deferment. Freud accounts for monotheism as a belated and recursive effect of an Exodus that prepared a confrontation with God. Between the exit that haunts Israel and the exile from Austria that saddens Freud (though it freed him to publish this provocation about

Moses creating the Jews), Caruth reads a rhythm of departure that both shocks the Jewish subject and enables a delayed, *nachtraglich,* and displaced response. Both psychoanalysis and traumatic history speak indirectly, as survivors of events that resist conventional storytelling. This is one theme that Caruth summarizes from her special issue on trauma for *American Imago.*[70]

Another point she makes is that trauma on a national scale occurs in many places. Jews don't have a monopoly on violent dislocations and guilt-ridden survival.[71] Testimony is the generally privileged genre of our incongruous times, Elie Wiesel says.[72] Freud's experience of antisemitism and persecution is linked to a long Jewish history of departures and repressions that gave his book a Jewish coloring. There are other colorings, each different, but each potentially linked by a need to narrate cautiously and to be heard with respect.[73]

The Middle Passage haunts African Americans as surely as the Exodus haunted Freud. The forced voyage into slavery is likely the traumatic origin of an African American sequence of spiritual displacements that transmute unbearable history into ghost stories, like the narratives of (Jewish) dislocation that psychoanalysis both theorizes and performs. And the lynchings of free blacks during Reconstruction (however historians measure it),[74] like the Crusade massacres and the Holocaust, reinscribe the limit event on imaginations already trained to expect the worst.

Freud's theory about two men named Moses was controversial (one an Egyptian who led Israel into the desert, another a rebel who deposed the Egyptian); but his corollary about two generations is standard tradition. Jewish lore has always contrasted the Egyptian-born emotionally shackled "desert generation" *(dor ha-midbar)* with the children born in a no-man's land, beyond slavery and capable of freedom. The delay, before freedom can be felt and borne, is a theme in *Beloved* too. Perhaps the years of Reconstruction amount to a liminal political space of the desert, unmarked, promising, but full of dangers. If so, Baby Suggs belongs to that first generation, too tired and disheartened to go any farther, and Sethe would also crawl into the death-bed, almost succumbing to the failures of her life. The only one who can imagine different endings is Denver, the child born outside of slavery and delivered by the hand of (Egyptian Moses) a white woman.

The analogy between Israel and Africa that Paul Gilroy and Michel R. Trouillot find promising, as I do along with Walter Benn Michaels, is no invitation to compare numbers of victims or to measure relative depths of suffering. That would beg competitions for the distinction of most sorely betrayed.[75] Experience of the unspeakable is a categorical limit of language. Whether the stopping point is "Auschwitz" or chattel-slavery, it is inassimilable for conventional history, and makes no human sense. At this full stop, the question is how life goes on without an appropriate scheme. The impasse can be acknowledged with silence, or with apparently inappropriate schemes, as I said: languages about ghosts and denials that derail people from the realm of the living. Also, a victim's testimony can disrupt what passes for normal language to force a confrontation with the limit conditions.

The possibility that psychoanalysis and African American spirituality are themselves responses to traumatic conditions lies in a question that Morrison asks of Western analysis: how can it have missed the significance of racism? "The trauma of racism is, for the racist and the victim, the severe fragmentation of the self, and has always seemed to me a cause (not a symptom) of psychosis—strangely of no interest to psychiatry."[76] One answer is that Freud's vital interest in racial fragmentation is strategically suppressed, "unspeakable" for the precariously positioned Viennese doctor (whose mother never lost her Yiddish accent). The doctor of double consciousness staked more than his science on the claim that "Jewish" pathologies were universal.[77] The trauma of racism is at the repressed core of psychoanalysis.

The traumatic origins of analysis raise questions about its "scientific" claims. In the logic of hermeneutic circles, interpretation is logically complicit with the texts chosen for it, sharing assumptions and habits for linking "phrase regimes."[78] Thus Caruth is led to speculate about the historical origins of Freud's trauma theory at a moment when a rash of Holocaust testimonies (defensively delayed) coincided with psychoanalytic caution about how to define and treat trauma. Perhaps the disorder is more historical than personal; maybe therapy needs lag-time. Memoir fever today may also signal the danger of memory loss. If aging eyewitnesses don't write now, the horror will be neutralized into history.[79]

Limit-events are incomprehensible, beyond understanding, but not beyond witnessing. The unsayable demands to be acknowledged by witnesses may have their own inklings of trauma. The word "witness" means martyr, as Paul Ricoeur reminds us, historically and etymologically.[80] Readers of slave narratives witness them second-hand and assume some of the consciousness that suffering brings. This might disrupt the traditional way of reading America's founding texts.[81] The very fact of slave testimonies shatters that color-blind frame, and these texts become what antebellum critic Theodore Parker called the truly original American literature.[82]

Holocaust testimonies can also pierce through certain assumptions, for example, that prisoners lost all sense of agency. Occasionally a survivor will tell about rebellions in the camps or on the plantations, even if the struggles failed and even if historians underline the results and quibble about details. "She saw, in other words, the unimaginable taking place right in front of her own eyes. And she came to testify to the unbelievability precisely—this bursting open of the very frame of Auschwitz."[83] "Breaking through the framework" is Shoshana Felman's figure for the dissonance of Holocaust texts. Survivors who talk (despite the risks of reliving the shock or of being misprised) and listeners who can hear the silences in stories that are dangerous to tell—both kinds of witnesses can validate and help to heal traumatized lives. This is what Morrison dramatizes between telling and teaching discretion. In this "catastrophic age," trauma has become an almost banal catch-all description for a range of disorders, both personal and collective.[84] But in its historical and collective meaning (in extermination campaigns, racial persecutions, chattel-slavery), the trauma suffered by different peoples can be the "catch-all" that holds a promise of mutual recognitions.[85]

Victims of trauma heed inner warnings about saying too much, too soon, or to someone who cannot listen.[86] The unsayable is what resists being said. This is not simply a problem. More than an inability, resistance is also a protective mechanism against retraumatization. What Freud called neurotic "latency" in trauma victims, their delayed and indirect responses, might also be unconscious discretion. The mechanism, in other words, can signal emotional health in response to historical calamity. Sethe's controlled release of information, the clues, delays, and repetitions, are not a communication disorder that some readers have imagined[87] but lines thrown to listeners who can put them together and witness her story.[88] Seen this way, the concept of trauma disturbs standard notions of illness and cure.[89] It is one thing to notice that trauma marks a narrative impasse, when clearly remembered details don't add up to a story because the recording mechanism has shut down.[90] ("In trying to tell of the wrath and the rage, / not a heart has the strength, the hand fails on the page").[91] But it is another thing to conclude that victims *should* rush past the obstacle and simply get on with life. The impasse is a warning against aggressive demands for storytelling, and a plea for patient, therapeutic, listening.

A witness to unspeakable pain can offer the reality principle, the pinch that hurts but attests to a history beyond mad dreams. A witness, therefore, does not dismiss a victim's silence, but understands that silence has been a sanctuary as well as a prison. Testimony begins there and cautiously moves outward, if someone is really listening. "The listener . . . must *listen to and hear the silence,* speaking mutely both in silence and in speech, both from behind and from within the speech. He or she must recognize, acknowledge and address that silence, even if this simply means respect—and knowing how to wait."[92] A sign of impatience can derail testimony, by hinting at an agenda driven by more curiosity than concern. So a wise interlocutor knows when to stop talking. Baby Suggs knew that, when she complained that white people never know when to stop.[93] Sethe knew it too, when she put her hand on Paul D's knee to say, in effect, that it was fine to stop his story before it got to a place from which neither of them could come back: "Just as well. Just as well." And Dr. Laub is careful to stop when he meets a patient's reticence: "I had probed the limits of her knowledge and decided to back off; to respect, that is, the silence out of which this testimony spoke . . . not to upset, not to trespass—the subtle balance . . ."[94]

Delicacy about when and how much memory to elicit respects the delay between the trigger event and effective witnessing. Enlightened assumptions that the truth will set you (who?) free are less cautious. Eleonora Lev learned caution after she took her daughter to the concentration camp: "For years you've been imagining, haven't you, that studying the technical details would help you understand, digest it, lance the inner abscess which fills with pus each time anew. Why did you imagine that?"[95] Today, therapists are acknowledging that revelations do not favor all of us equally, that universalizing demands for truth sometimes damage particular lives.

A PASSWORD TO PASS ON

Sethe understands the difference between knowing and healing, and she has been prudent all along, telling and remembering as little as she can risk. The neighbors show how risky information can be when they condemn her as too proud, rash, or crazy. Sethe's fear of telling is internal too. Without respectful interlocutors, Sethe has no distance from the past. So she becomes her own voracious reader, like the white people Baby Suggs called bad luck because they don't know when to stop.

> My greedy brain says, Oh thanks, I'd love more—so I add more. And no sooner than I do, there is no stopping . . .
>
> But her brain was not interested in the future. Loaded with the past and hungry for more, it left her no room to imagine, let alone plan . . . Other people went crazy, why couldn't she? Other people's brains stopped, turned around and went on to something new . . .[96]

But most of the time she managed to curb that appetite for life-stories, and "worked hard to remember as close to nothing as was safe."[97] It was work worth doing for a while, given the delayed rhythm between trauma and repair. Because trauma is not an inability to remember, as Sethe knows and as Freud remarked with surprise. It can be remembering too clearly, with flashbacks that resist interpretation because they are so literal.[98] Trauma patients remember the trigger event clearly; what they forget or cloud is everything else.[99]

Sethe and her mother-in-law knew enough not to remember too much, which is to say that they knew more than was safe: "Everything . . . was painful or lost. She and Baby Suggs had agreed without saying so that it was unspeakable; . . . Even with Paul D, who had shared some of it and to whom she could talk with at least a measure of calm, the hurt was always there— like a tender place in the corner of her mouth that the bit left."[100] The marks of slavery, in Paul D.'s mouth too, on Sethe's back, make memory inevitable and dangerous.

Is there no exit from the danger of memory on the one hand, and from the unsafe "haven" of guilt-ridden and ghost-bearing silence, on the other? Yes, there is, of course. Otherwise Sethe would stay locked inside her house with the ghost of her martyred baby, and Denver could not have produced the witnesses who break the spell. How is a spell broken? How does witnessing work? This is Dr. Laub's question for practitioners. His answer, we saw, is caution and respect for limits. But sometimes a word, a gesture, is indicated. If the therapist is more than merely a blank screen, it is because he or she can offer a "password." Listen for an opening in the patient's otherwise rehearsed story and then reply with an expression that says, in effect: I follow you. You make sense. I am a witness. In most therapeutic sessions, banter drowns the risky narrative. But sometimes, a detail escapes. "I seize upon it and echo it in my response . . . The patient may dismiss it or pass over it in silence; yet there are times in which it is a though a chord is struck and an internal chorus, a thousand voices are set free."[101]

The chorus outside of Sethe's house is no longer the voices of the punitive community. It is literally chanting and praying, as it does in the Greek tragedies that resonate for Morrison with "Afro-American communal structures and African religion and philosophy."[102] Finally, Sethe can safely confront the past, because witnesses acknowledge the traumatizing event and the pain beyond telling. Neighbors hear her, not to judge, but to testify. Sethe knew the difference early on. Even if she could not be a witness to herself, she can and does know how to listen to others. As she listens to Paul D, her "password" acknowledges the danger of telling.

> "I didn't plan on telling you that."
> "I didn't plan on hearing it." . . .
> "I can't take it back, but I can leave it alone," Paul D said.
> He wants to tell me, she thought. He wants me to ask him about what it was like for him . . .
> "You want to tell me about it?" she asked him.
> "I don't know. I never talked about it. Not to a soul . . ."
> "Go ahead. I can hear it."[103]

Two-thirds into the novel, just two pages before he storms into her kitchen, Paul D would get a similar cue from Sethe, and he would miss it. The cue comes when Sethe is moved by Paul's love, "love you don't have to deserve," to "go ahead and tell him what she had not told Baby Suggs, the only person she felt obliged to explain anything to." He had been coaxing her: "Go as far inside as you need to, I'll hold your ankles." And she had been shoring up the courage to go that far, "the morning she woke up next to Paul D, she . . . thought . . . of the temptation to trust and remember . . . Would it be all right? Would it be all right to go ahead and feel?"[104] Feeling is so risky; love of a slave mother for her children can seem too thick; Sethe's love for her slave husband surprises Mrs. Garner, because desire is a sign of agency, of freedom. Her surprise echoes a scene from Anselmo Suárez y Romero's abolitionist novel from Cuba, *Francisco* (1841?), in which the love between slaves is their doom because the offended mistress presumed to own their desire and to be its undisputed object. The presumption was apparently typical of slaveholders, if Gilberto Freire is right about Brazil and Eugene Genovese about the southern States of the Union. Within the culture of paternalism that bound masters to slaves, the masters evidently thought that they were, or should be, loved by their slaves. Therefore one slave's love for another, for herself, for her children, was nothing less than heroic. To follow Cornel West's praise for *Beloved,* love is still risky and liberating for African Americans.[105]

Paul D. could have freed Sethe's feelings two thirds into the telling with a nod, a smile, a password. The story might have been safely passed on to him, if he were not bent on exacting what he already knew. Unavailable for witnessing yet imperious about being told, Paul D leaves Sethe at a loss. In response to her pause he legislates, "What you did was wrong";[106] the sacrifice "didn't work, did it? Did it work?"

"It worked," she says, with a matter-of-fact defiance that sends her memory back to bondage, but refuses to neutralize the tragedy into a morality play.[107] This is not a case to be judged, but an event that unsettles any code of judgment. Tragedy is this ethical impasse. "It was absolutely the right thing to do," Morrison said in an interview, "but it's also the thing you have no right to do."[108] Unneutralized, and unredeemed by moral codes, the story remains there, in full view. Like *Shoah,* Claude Lanzmann's particularist Hebrew name for the Holocaust, the point is not to understand it, which would be obscene, but to realize that "learning" it in any reasonable way would be to forget the horror.[109] The stories stay there with a starkness that refuses to be interpreted away, open secrets that can only be admitted, not demanded, or assimilated, or painlessly passed on.

In the end, Paul D acknowledges Sethe and becomes available to her. By the last pages he has stopped asking aggressive questions. He stops respectfully and asks, before starting to bathe her, "Is it all right, Sethe, if I heat up some water?" "And count my feet?" she baits him. "He steps closer," and delivers the password, "Rub your feet."[110]

WHITE WRITING
ON DARK SUBJECTS

III

8

Si hay baile en algún Casino, / Alguno
siempre se queja, / Pues a la blanca aconse-
ja / Que no baile con negrillo; / Teniendo
aunque es amarillo, / "El negro tras de la
oreja" . . . / El que se crea preocupado / Que
se largue allá a la Habana / Que en la tierra
dominicana / No les da buen resultado.

[If there's a dance in some private club, /
Someone always complains / And advises the
white girl / Not to dance with the darkie; /
For though he's quite yellow, / He's got
"black behind the ear" . . . / Anyone who
worries about that / Can scram and go to
Havana; / Here, on Dominican soil, / It
won't do him any good.]

—JUAN ANTONIO ALIX
  (1833)

How clever and well-trained readers feel, holding *Cecilia Valdés* (1882)! Certainly more clever than Cirilo Villaverde's narrator, who cannot bring himself to say the obvious about the heroine's obscure background. Readers
have always understood it, probably flattering themselves on their literary
competence. It is clear to them that the light-skinned beauty who tries, with
some success, to pass for white, was born in Cuba, in 1812, to a *mulata* who
went mad after her white lover removed the shameful evidence of their
affair to an orphanage. We know that his cruelty abates too late for the
mother, but baby Cecilia is returned to her grandmother's house, where she
learns that any white husband is better than a black one, and to the street,

where she falls in love with Leonardo Gamboa. He is the spoiled son of a Spanish sugar planter who—horrors!—happens to be her father too. The lovers don't know that their attachment is incestuous, nor that their conflicting expectations—erotic play for him, marriage for her—will clash violently. Real deceit is the problem, not reticence. This is not Garcilaso's flaunting of insider information in order to command respect, nor Rigoberta's decorous claims to cultural secrets, nor Sethe's reluctance to tell a damaging story that everyone knows. Were it not for secrecy's perverse effects here, incest could have been avoided. Lukewarm Leonardo would have abstained had he known who was who, as he abstains with his sister Adela, described as Cecilia's double. If they "were not flesh and blood siblings," the narrator volunteers, "they would have been lovers . . ."[1]

The other woman in Leonardo's life is Isabel Ilincheta, elegant, correct, a fitting counterpart to independent and candid Cecilia. Isabel seems too good to be a standard heroine, although her combination of rational and romantic virtues was standard in the foundational fictions written elsewhere in Latin America. She is practically a hero, modeled perhaps after Villaverde's independentist wife.[2] It is Isabel who runs her father's coffee plantation (a crop that is less labor-intensive than sugar cane), and her womanly charm doesn't interfere with a markedly virile appeal. Leonardo's schizophrenic destiny of desire dooms the match; he can profess love for her and for Cecilia, the incestuous and finally narcissistic copy of himself, as well as for the ideal fiscal relationship between Isabel's coffee and his family's sugar, even boasting that many more women have room in his heart.[3] The campaigns of amorous conquest, the intrigues and jealousies, the doubts that Isabel feels about joining a smug and brutal slaveholding family, are all set on a detailed backdrop of a society that denies human rights to blacks and makes monsters of their masters.

The tragedy comes to a circular climax when Cecilia and her lover set up house together, have a baby girl, and separate once bored Leonardo feels ready to marry Isabel. Cecilia complains about the betrayal to her long-suffering mulatto admirer, a tailor's apprentice by day and a musician by night, which doubles him as a creator of an autonomous Cuban style, and hints at the mulatto tone of national style.[4] The tailor had been waiting for a chance to cut the traitor down, and his murderous race to the wedding ceremony—where Cecilia hoped the bride would die, not the groom—leaves the mistress as mad as her mother was. And it leaves her baby quite helplessly orphaned.

Long before that climax, though, the reader has been building toward it with the pleasure of interpretive control. No one but the reader, it seems, can anticipate the nefarious finale from the first pages on. Don Cándido Gamboa has been careful to keep his illicit affairs secret, to the point of sending his baby to an orphanage and controlling possible informants. "Not everything is meant to be said,"[5] he once winked to his wife, in a conversation about new slave imports after that traffic had become illegal in 1817. But everyone knew about the violations of the trade ban that England forced on Spain, just as everyone knew that rich white men were having their way with poor mulatas. When his jealous wife and legitimate daughters bring pretty Cecilia into their house, neither she nor they succeed in learning the girl's parentage. All they know is that she has an uncanny resemblance to Adela, which is probably why Leonardo finds Cecilia so alluring. But the reader knows. We know who the father is from the very beginning of this long four-part novel about Cuba during the 1830s; and we know that incest will be a figure for social dangers in a slave society, just as we sense that the plot lines of secrecy and intrigue will cross one another to tangle even the legitimate stories of family and nation. All this is obvious, as I say, and it must have been blatant to Cubans when the novel was published, between the wars of Independence, while blacks and whites distrusted each other with good reason.

Yet the educated and articulate narrator never spells out the connections between Don Cándido and Cecilia, between her lover and her/his father. For some reason, Cándido's habit of stalking and inquiring after the girl, her resemblance to Adela, and Leonardo's taste for sisters don't come together. The narrator is intrigued by these details, but doesn't put them together; he punctuates the tale with one revealing point after another, but doesn't connect the dots. Why is this so? The connections are plain and the pattern is sadly predictable in a cynical slave society where the whites acknowledge decent norms in theory while controlling indecent information. Incest—as a synecdoche for the vice of deceitful relations—was already a compelling theme in Latin American literature (think of Ecuador's *Cumandá*, Peru's

Aves sin nido), and the theme would continue. What is noteworthy in this 1882 novel is the narrator's apparent ignorance. Villaverde is calling attention to discretion that hides nothing, before unreliable narrators became standard in modern fiction. No one could be stupid enough to miss such obviously perverse social relationships, unless, of course, the narrator and his equally discreet protagonists were acting dumb for some unsaid reason.

FRAMED

To overlook the white narrator's reluctance to say the obvious is to miss the point of the narrative style. His hesitation to assimilate information permits competent readers to congratulate themselves on the good job of filling in blanks and tying up loose ends. With the text neatly knotted, readers have rested comfortably, confident of their command. But their repose would be disturbed if they admitted that they don't need it; they might confess that the book was too easy, and that the minimal effort exerted never earned the right to satisfaction. In that state of disturbed inactivity a doubt may gnaw at the hastily tied knots until the texture of a competent reading loosens and frays into a web of worries.

Who, finally, conquered whom? Did readers adeptly process unconnected information? Or was the story studiously and artfully disconnected in order to lure readers into weaving so carelessly that they were bound to feel a snag? The problem is precisely the apparent lack of problems for interpretation. The conquest is so ridiculously easy that the conquerors may find themselves at the butt of a textual joke. They feel smart for no reason at all.

Competent readers fill in a story that is purposefully laconic. It makes a spectacle of discretion to show how dangerous it is to be candid. On the very first page, where a gentleman is hiding under a broad-brimmed hat, behind the thick curtain of a carriage that stops at Cecilia's house, the narrator does not identify the obvious. About the gentleman, he says only that "all the precaution seemed superfluous, since there was not a living soul on the street."[6] The narrator might have been describing himself. The same superfluous precaution repeats in his pretense of mystery. It is transparent, practically luminous, as a backdrop for the stark information he supplies. The narrative veil hides nothing, but it does serve as a figure for the social conventions that the narrator locates around himself.

He theatricalizes the limits of communication without creating suspense, as Sethe dramatizes the danger of telling a story everyone knows in *Beloved*. If Villaverde were writing a mystery story, he would not supply all the relevant information long before we hear out the plot. Like *Beloved*, this novel hesitates and stutters at the obstacles that get in the way of knowing and telling. At points, the narrator even thematizes the trouble that positionality makes for understanding, as when he comments on the punishment of a slave by his master. "It is difficult to explain, for those who have been neither one nor the other, and impossible to understand in all its force for those who have never lived in a slave country."[7] And the epigraph of part III, chap. 6, reads, "About blacks . . . Oh! my tongue holds back / From forming the name of their misfortunes!" Each time the narrator underlines his own incompetence, he suggests ours too. And the insistence makes the incompetence of the privileged class into a thesis of the book, while it puts off—more and more mechanically—those who could tell. It suspends the story every time a character decides to white out the black marks that make up the writing here. Cecilia's grandmother, for example, is relieved when she can stop telling the girl more about her parents than was prudent, though Cecilia probably guesses more than she wants to know for sure. The novel calls her *maliciosa,* which means astutely suspicious.[8]

> Nothing more opportune could have happened than the interruption that came with the friend's visit. The old woman had said more than prudence allowed, and the young one was afraid to find out the intimate meaning of her grandmother's last words. What did she know? Why was her language so veiled? Did she have well-founded suspicions or was she just trying to intimidate her?
>
> The truth is that, during the dispute, with their consciences alarmed and with some facts at hand, both of them had advanced onto a slippery terrain previously hidden from their sight. The first to step in would have to gather an enormous harvest of pain and remorse. For her part, Grandma Josefa didn't think the moment had come to let Cecilia in on the real facts of her life.[9]

For related reasons, Don Cándido prefers not to say what he knows. He refuses to discuss either his personal past with his suspicious wife, or his political present as a contraband slave dealer.[10] In response to Doña Rosa's curiosity, her husband is discreet, with a reluctance that, throughout the book, forms the origin of intrigue and misunderstanding. Discretion and double dealing will finally explode in disaster to make a point about who tells and who listens. "Are you with me?" Cándido asks Rosa, in a scene that echoes back and forth in the book. "Not everything is meant to be said."[11] The cagy reader may be winking back, apparently wise to Cándido and to the rest of the characters who refuse to be candid with one another. Who, besides the reader, realizes so much about Cecilia's unidentified parents and about her romance with Leonardo? Who else has figured out that the men in her life are already intimately related? Hardly anyone in the novel seems to know what is going on, not the mulata nor her white lover, and certainly not the apparently benighted narrator.

But there are characters in the novel who can and do tell the story straight to those who will hear it.[12] They are the black slave informants: Dionisio, the lonely cook in the Havana house, and his wife María de Regla, the wet nurse (who stands for the jet-black mother-goddess of the waters, *Yemayá*); she is banished to the plantation because she knew too much.[13] Each time a pale protagonist (or reader) turns a deaf ear to the slaves' stories, Villaverde exposes the inability to listen as a dissembled gesture of control which keeps the text of Cecilia's life conveniently blank, that is, white. The gesture is one of those defensive denials that end by destroying the deniers. To defend the privilege that comes with whiting out her history, Cecilia and other presumptively white characters must ignore the details that make her so compromisingly colorful, so available for the final tragedy of misfired affairs. And to protect our expert reading, readers are also tempted to ignore competitors. Rather than defer too soon to the authority of black narrators, readers tend to flatter themselves as collaborators of the prudent white one who frames the novel.

Who would suspect that he is framing us too? To date no one has accused Villaverde of double-dealing, but a suspicion may wedge itself in, I already suggested, if we notice that the paradoxical interpretive problem here is that it is no problem at all. We win less than a Pyrrhic victory; we grasp at a delusion. The point of making a spectacle of the narrator's reluctance is to show how difficult it is to say anything in a society based on deceit, especially if (what is true for the narrator and his contemporary white readers) deceit is one's guarantee of privilege. Practically the only characters who do not profit from it are the black slaves. If we will listen, they would defy restrictions and tell freely.

Defiance is risky by definition. Talking freely can compound the injustices that these stories would tell. "I'm afraid of many things, of everything. Blacks have to be careful about what they say," says María de Regla.[14] Her young mistress Adela responds: "Your fear is unfounded," as if an enlightened sense of universal justice were not obscenely out of place in a slave society.[15] "But, my lady," María instructs her, "you seem to forget that a slave always stands to lose when she suspects her masters."[16]

PIERRE MENARD'S LESSON

For over a century, admiring readers of *Cecilia Valdés* have been as forgetful as Adela about the importance of positionality in the circulation of knowledge. The disconnectedness of the narrator's story line ought to have been a constant reminder, though, long before this late scene when María reminds her mistress that danger is asymmetrical. Critics don't remark on the narrator's stuttering; maybe they excuse it as a tired convention of intrigue. Instead, they have engaged the book's complex realism and enjoyed the satisfactions of piecing together spotty accounts of local customs, its psychological complexity, economic and political analyses, and its general attention to the details of history.[17] If now I can notice, with you, that the narrator's disconnectedness is conspicuous, theatrical, it is because history makes a difference in reading literature, not only in writing it.[18] Borges gave that reading lesson in his story "Pierre Menard, Author of Don Quijote," in which Cervantes's classic novel had entirely changed its meanings and allusions from the time it was first published to the time Menard rewrote parts of it, word for word, three centuries later. A little more than a century has passed since Villaverde published his enduring novel. He described it then as realistic, meaning that it was true to the characters he knew, down to their styles of dress and speech ("their hairs and warts, as the common expression goes"). As a realistic novel, it avoided the formulas of romance popularized in Latin America through *Atala* and *Paul et Virginie*.[19] Commentators have generally followed his instructions for reading the book, downplaying the romance, focusing on the sociological information so intimately detailed that it verges on self-ethnography.

The current postmodern moment is suspicious of objectivity and realism; it notices that storytelling is unavoidably partial, in both senses of limited and interested. Questions follow fast about who gives information, for what purpose, inside which interpretive frame. And it is clear that the primary source of information about the plot in *Cecilia Valdés* plays a fool. Surely this means something. It certainly means a dysfunction in the tradition of omniscient narrator, which was still viable in contemporary foundational romances such as *Cumandá* (Ecuador, 1879) and *Enriquillo* (Dominican Republic, 1882), written in countries slow to consolidate modern projects. Cuba hadn't achieved political independence or economic modernity, even at this late date. The opportunities for progress festered in an anachronistic but lucrative slave economy, and in a racist colonial administration. No wonder the white narrator is purposefully underdeveloped.

Postmoderns may be quick to notice that Villaverde's narrator is a joke on master narratives in general. Will we also notice the joke on the reader, whose early textual conquest mocks us later on, after black slaves put the story together more ably than we possibly could? Readers should be "growing wary of the hermeneutic circularity," in George Steiner's words, which assumes a text to be continuous with the reader's cultural assumptions.[20] Messages moved from one social and cultural context to another have a way of getting garbled, while interpreters are loath to acknowledge the remainder lost in asymmetrical translation (let us say in the transaction between a Cuban slave and her mistress). That remainder, though, is what Villaverde features; it is the difference between master-slave experience and white reporting, between free love and aristocratic secrecy, between Cuba's cultural autonomy and Spain's colonial accounting for it. Readers erase that remainder if they force Villaverde's multivoiced Cuban novel into conventional formulas. They don't get the point if they get it too easily; that is, if the book leaves them thinking that the only character playing the fool here is a white narrator.

CUBAN STORIES IN BLACK AND WHITE

By 1882 Villaverde must have thought that his first version of *Cecilia Valdés* (1839) sounded monotonous.[21] His early narrator has no competitors, no slave storytellers who face the facts that whites won't tell. His is discreet without sounding silly, and engaging enough to let readers *maliciar* the rest. He leaves loose ends for the female readers he addresses directly; and they surely tie things up, along with Leonardo's sisters, who immediately see themselves, their brother, and their father, in Cecilia's face.[22] The daring feature of the early novel was its celebration of interracial love: the repressive colonial regime had outlawed "unequal" marriages, though the Church would have allowed them and averted more bastard births.[23] At the story's end, Leonardo vows that nothing can keep him from his "santa mulata," neither Isabel's feelings nor earthly treasures.[24] Daring as this is, it was evidently inoffensive enough to appear in Cuba and then in Spain at the same time that Spanish censors were proscribing abolitionist novels like *Francisco* by Anselmo Suárez y Romero (finally published in 1880), and confiscating others, like *Sab* (1841) by Gertrudis Gómez de Avellaneda. The second *Cecilia Valdés* would be more probing. The title names two different novels, and Villaverde himself is two distinct authors. A lot of history intervened.

Villaverde had written the 1839 novel at the urging of Domingo del Monte, the abolitionist editor and journalist who hosted a famous *tertulia* (salon) in Havana where intellectuals read from works that del Monte himself would commission for supporters of the cause. The works might be sent to England as part of the 1838 *dossier* that del Monte was preparing for Richard Madden, the British representative to the International Tribunal of Justice that oversaw the ban on slave trading and the protection of freemen. The purpose of del Monte's circle of liberal planters and professionals was to embarrass Spain into granting abolition and other reforms, including representation in the Spanish *cortes*. Representation had been granted, briefly, before absolute rule returned in the 1830s. And it would be reinstated in 1879 as a thin formality after ten years of independence struggle convinced Spain that a measure of Cuban autonomy was the empire's best bet; but the sham soon discouraged the Cuban delegates.[25] Anselmo Suárez y Romero read from his *Francisco* in del Monte's salon. (Gómez de Avellaneda didn't; she lived in the less industrialized province of Oriente and never warmed to the English who played the opportunists in her *Sab*.) And the slave poet Juan Francisco Manzano read from his *Autobiography*, after which enough money was collected for the author to buy his freedom.[26] Until recently, Manzano's was considered the only slave narrative in Spanish, but thanks to Sonia Labrador-Rodríguez we know that others had been published before abolition, and that they continue to be hidden, or discounted, as if the tradition of a black intelligentsia were still too threatening or embarrassing for a Cuban national culture.[27]

Villaverde was neither slave nor planter. If he were, abolition would have been a clear priority. For the slave it meant freedom; and for the modern planter it meant rational reform in an increasingly mechanized sugar industry. The thirty-five-year-old writer was a self-supporting lawyer and journalist. The sixth of ten children born in 1812 (the same year as Cecilia) to a plantation doctor, Villaverde had grown up between the field and the infirmary, where bodies were wrecked and then repaired for more abuse. His parents sent him to the capital for a decent education, which he got, after presenting proof of "purity of blood" for admission to the University law school.[28] His proof was probably straightforward; but certificates could often be bought for a price, a corrupt practice that helped to "democratize" the professions in Cuba.[29] Perhaps for these and other personal historical reasons, Villaverde lost patience with reformists who thought they could negotiate Cuba's relative autonomy with the racist and corrupt empire. So he began to conspire against Spain in favor of Cuba's separation. Villaverde left del Monte to his elegant gatherings and joined Narciso López, an early advocate of armed resistance. Their conspiracy was betrayed, and Villaverde spent sixth months in jail, from late 1848 until early 1849, when he escaped to Florida and continued to New York City, where López was renewing his efforts.

Until his death in 1894, just before the definitive War of Independence, Villaverde will be a major figure in the important New York wing of Cuban revolutionary politics. History books have downplayed his leadership in the New York Junta and in spin-off organizations, and have almost forgotten his influential journalism in exile, but a closer look is bringing him into the center of that scene.[30] Political historians are more likely to remember his outspoken, unconventional wife, Emilia Casanova, memorialized by Villaverde in *Apuntes biográficos de la ilustre cubana Emilia C. de Villaverde* (1874). His reputation as a writer of fiction has evidently overwhelmed his political accomplishments, by countrymen who dismiss creativity as dreaming or entertainment. Villaverde preempts their dismissal in the 1879 Prologue to the second *Cecilia Valdés,* explaining that politics and fiction didn't mix, that he hadn't so much as read a novel in thirty years. (Is this true? Could he have avoided the ubiquitous *Uncle Tom's Cabin* during the Civil War, for example, or the slave narratives that were being published in the 1850s and 1860s? These would have played in provocative counterpoint—for the future novelist of competing voices—to Stowe's standard sentimental tone.) Lest the reader imagine that Villaverde had frivolously wasted time on the novel he was presenting, he adds that it was written in short order. His anxiety about not being taken seriously sounds familiar among Caribbean literary-leaders of the period, although at an earlier, more confident period, in already established Latin American republics, the statesman-novelist had been celebrated as a national hero. Among Villaverde's contemporaries, Puerto Rican Eugenio María de Hostos was protesting that his novel *La peregrinación de Bayoán* (1863) had been a distraction from his patriotic responsibilities (though his protest appears, ironically, in the preface to an 1873 second edition of the novel);[31] and José Martí would punish himself, in beautiful poems and other literary expressions, for losing time and emotional energy to the seductions of creative writing.[32]

Thirty years in New York is a long time. Forty, between one *Cecilia* and another, is even longer. Villaverde began those New York years as a militant separatist, an ally and secretary to Narciso López. But he was no independentist. That came much later. From the late 1840s through the 1850s, independence seemed impractical to most white Cuban dissidents, for whom the prudent alternatives were either autonomist reforms or separation from Spain with a friendly connection to the United States. (Prudence, you may remember, was the justification Cecilia's grandmother used for keeping the girl's background an explosive secret.) The political options seemed limited to reform or annexation, for one thing, because the vicarious experience of Latin American independent republics was a warning as much as an inspiration. Successful revolutions had typically led to a generation of civil wars that left the new countries poor and mortgaged to neocolonial powers. Another and even more troubling reason was that Cubans still had nightmares about the revolution in Haiti, where slaves took revenge on their masters. On an island like Cuba, with as many blacks as whites, with enough incentive for vengeance to turn a political struggle into a race war, and a disciplined military tradition among blacks and mulattos in Spanish regiments that secured the island against invasion (England managed to capture Havana in 1762), most whites were afraid of freedom.[33] The rash of uprisings in

Cuba that ended with the slave conspiracy (La Escalera) of 1844 worried the white creoles as much as it did the Spanish government. In reprisal, the colonial authorities executed many illustrious mulato artisans of Havana, whether or not they were guilty of sedition.[34] Villaverde commemorates them in the detailed guest list at the formal dance for colored people (part II, chap. 17). For the Cuba to be, stability was preferable to anarchy and bloodletting, not to mention the nuisance of lost property and privilege. Along with separation from Spain, therefore, many Cubans favored annexation to the stable, modern, and prosperous United States.

Why not? White Dominicans were making the same calculations, some in favor of the United States, others in favor of reannexation to Spain. (The pro-Spanish party won in 1861, and the opposition drove Spain out by 1865). Anything seemed better to the precarious white leadership of the Dominican Republic, recently liberated from Haiti, than the fear of a new invasion by the "Africans." Why not? There was support in the United States for expansion to Cuba, notably from Southern slave-holding states. Black and mulato insurrectionists would know why not: because Cubans couldn't trust either one self-serving empire or the other. But López was confident that the United States would give its tacit blessing to his planned invasion, and that annexed Cuba would maintain its cultural distinctiveness, its language and customs, and get ready for the next step toward complete independence. Reformist José Antonio Saco thought this was a delusion; he warned that annexation would mean the end of Cuba as it had meant the end of autonomy for Texas and California, because the United States could not tolerate cultural differences.[35] A generation later, José Martí repeated the warning about Anglo intolerance, and he dismissed the step-by-step approach to independence: "Once the United States is in Cuba, who will drive it out?"[36]

Saco had been exiled from Cuba for daring to object to the illicit slave trade. Seeking refuge in the United States, he continued to argue for Spanish reform and Cuban autonomy. Villaverde fired back a series of polemical editorials in 1852 through New York's La Verdad, an émigré newspaper published jointly by the Cuban Junta and United States expansionists, including John O'Sullivan, who coined the term "Manifest Destiny."[37] Villaverde denounced Saco's impractical abolitionism and his irresponsible rejection of the U.S. connection. Worse, he accused Saco of working in the interest of the few sugar-rich families that would profit from wage slavery in Cuba. "Mr. Saco, who appeared to dedicate himself to the cause of Cuban liberty and independence at the beginning of his political career, later turned all his attention and talents to the cause of one race of Cubans, the blacks. And today he serves the interests of one class . . . that of a few Cuban families."[38] Annexation for Villaverde was a self-preserving calculation, the only prudent move to start the process of gradual emancipation for blacks and for Cuba.

But after the mysterious betrayal in 1851 of militant Narciso López's armed expedition to Cuba—so the authorities intercepted it and López was executed—annexationists lost confidence in the host country. The United States was holding out for a diplomatic solution with Spain and actively discouraged Cuban insurgency. By 1855, it was clear that the U.S. government would support only a negotiated settlement with Spain, *and* that negotiation was an impossible solution because Spain would never sell the island. (A letter of a Spanish consul, retrieved from Havana, mocks McKinley for taking a possible deal seriously.[39]) Disappointed dissidents went home to their plantations, or to artisanal and professional careers. Only the most militant separatists, like Villaverde, stayed in New York. In 1865 they formed the Sociedad Republicana de Cuba y Puerto Rico. By then the exiles understood that their alliance with the slave states had hurt the cause. And their policy changed dramatically to uncompromising support for immediate abolition (elite Cubans on the island were still reluctant), probably because by then ending slavery was a prerequisite for joining the Union. At the same time, the New York-based leadership was responding to popular pressure to give up the separatist campaign for U.S. diplomatic support in favor of a military campaign for independentist insurrection.

Villaverde had evidently got caught in the major blind spot of his political life. As late as 1863, he was telling history with a slaveholding bias, by translating and publishing Edward Pollard's *History of the First Year of the Southern War*.[40] And Villaverde's polemic against Saco's abolitionism was notorious. Cubans still remember it with embarrassment, even Villaverde's official fans who excuse the polemic as a sign of ideologically immature times.[41] That there was more than one option at the time is obvious from Saco's impassioned antislavery campaign and from the reformist platform in general. In 1855 the New York newspaper *El Pueblo* went so far as to include slaves in the call for a separatist revolt. It took the U.S. Civil War to produce Villaverde's about-face on the importance of slavery. He turned completely around, concluding that immediate freedom for slaves was the first and most important step to Cuba's liberation. Gradually, a broad-based, multiracial revolution became the nation's only real option. And Villaverde became its most important and ardent defender.

Another blind spot of Villaverde's followed from his underestimating abolition. He had thought that annexation was at least prudent if not ideal; now he admitted that it was wrong. While white Cubans were negotiating their continued privilege under one empire or another, black and mulato countrymen were mounting a struggle for independence. Whites, including Villaverde and his stubbornly discreet narrator, tried for a long time not to acknowledge that it was the only way to win freedom for Cuba. They told themselves a wishful story about annexation bringing gradual freedom. When that made no sense, some retrieved the equally unconvincing story about autonomy and Spanish reform. Neither of these stories was realistic, but both kept white privilege at the center. Meanwhile blacks were telling a counter-story (as they would in the novel): that the United States couldn't be trusted, which agreed with Saco and other reformists, *and* that Spain was a losing proposition too, which agreed with annexationists. Because both imperial partners were bad for Cuba, independence was the only and obvious route. The only thing lost in this story was white privilege. Cubans of color argued and acted on this clarity; and the white leaders (along with Villaverde's narrator) continued to act as if they couldn't put the picture together.

By 1869, shortly after the Ten Years War (1868–1878) had begun under the leadership of mulato General Antonio Maceo and Dominican exile Máximo Gómez, Villaverde demanded that the New York Junta get behind its own decree to destroy the island's sugar wealth as part of the insurrection against Spain. He was sure that the Junta was sabotaging its own declared public policy (as sure as his reader will be that Leonardo Gamboa is playing on the mulata's loyalty to his own advantage). Villaverde accused the Junta of opportunism; and, a vehement anti-annexationist by then, he helped to found the pro-independence Sociedad de Artesanos Cubanos. Events were bringing about a story of self-determined Cuban independence, and Villaverde listened. A year after the frustrated Ten Years War had left most white Cubans exhausted and resigned, the Little War (La Guerra Chiquita, 1879–80) was launched by uncompromising black and mulatto forces. And it was denounced by whites as a prelude to race war.

By 1880 it appeared that racial fears of whites and resentments of blacks had put an end to the independence movement. That's when José Martí began an ambitious coalition among the multiracial Cuban tobacco workers in Florida and the white émigré elite in New York, in order to prepare for the final struggle, which began in 1895 and ended in 1898. Villaverde was ready to respond.[42] In fact, his 1860s radicalism was probably one of Martí's inspirations for insisting that the insurrection begin inside Cuba, so that military expeditions to the island would be welcome and useful.[43] Martí succeeded in mitigating some white anxiety by eliminating race as an organizing principle of the war: "everything that divides men, everything that separates or herds men together in categories is a sin against humanity . . . there can be no racial animosity because there are no races."[44] And other white leaders were erasing the category from their speeches, from the records of armies and hospitals. But black insurgents didn't give up the link between independence and racial liberation. And they resented rich whites who joined the movement late enough to know it would succeed and got army commissions that outranked the black leaders. Villaverde had apparently sympathized with the blacks' objections to whiting out the difference during preparations for war, to judge from the knowledge he assigns to the slaves in the second version of his novel. It is true that all the lines come from one white author, and it is possible that the dialogic tension he creates is too neatly resolved under his control. But even this skeptical reading is testimony to the skepticism and self-doubt that competent readers learn from his novel.[45]

Villaverde died in New York before the definitive war began. He could not have known, but might have suspected, that the white leadership—always afraid of black rule—was negotiating behind Martí's back for a U.S. intervention once the Cubans got control of the island. Secret dealing and sabotage by privileged whites had been the targets of Villaverde's militancy since the 1860s and into the Ten Years War. Nationalists were sure that the Junta was double-dealing: "The facts regarding these intrigues are difficult to establish," writes historian Gerald Poyo, "but the nationalists believed that during 1874 and 1875 the junta orchestrated a major effort to find a compromise with the Spanish and terminate the war."[46] (One oppositional response, from the radicalized Eastern province of Cuba, was a secret society literally called Los Hermanos del Silencio.) Double-dealing would also be the uncontrollable motor of Villaverde's tragic novel.

NOT MEANT TO BE SAID

Is Villaverde's narrator a victim of compatriots' deceit as well as of his own prudence? I think prudence is the problem, and the novel targets him as self-deluding; he hardly seems deceived by others. The narrator delays transparently, with a studied and stubborn clumsiness like that of New York leaders who refused to give up privilege. Why won't the narrator listen to the black informants that Villaverde supplies? This question may occur to some readers, at least in passing. Forcing the question is probably Villaverde's most pointed political effort in the novel. But the answer is depressingly clear, after all the double-dealing and secrecy that had been delaying independence. Whites don't listen to blacks, not even apparently well-meaning whites, like our narrator who tells tragic stories about Cuba, or like those who form separatist juntas in New York, even though blacks are the ideal informants here, as they were in Gertrudis Gómez de Avellaneda's abolitionist novel *Sab* (Cuba, 1841).

Writing before the slave insurrections of the early 1840s and the baffled cross-racial alliances that finally broke over the Guerra Chiquita in 1879, Avellaneda could portray her slave protagonist as an unproblematic hero. Sab was more than an idealized sentimental lover; he was practically the author of his own novel, a figure for the culturally shackled woman who wrote it. "Sab, c'est moi," she could have said. He is omniscient, sensitive, controlling, and then revealing in the posthumous letter that sets all the records straight. When his passion and frustration mount, when he complains to free-thinking white Teresa (who fearlessly agreed to meet him at midnight) of love's torment in a slave society that makes blacks scream for white blood, readers are poised to listen. Readers listen to incendiary Sab, afraid for their safety, perhaps, but sure that he is right.[47]

Hardly anyone listens to slaves in *Cecilia Valdés*. The evidence has piled up during the intervening forty years (between the two novels) of white control (and treachery) over black and mulatto initiative. Whites' reluctance to listen shows up in Cuba's frustrating history, and it determines Villaverde's Cuban tragedy. Hundreds of pages pass before the slaves can tell about Cecilia, secretly nursed by María de Regla, who thereby knows too much. So she is sent to the sugar cane fields, where she nurses the tortured slaves and then knows even more of Don Cándido's indelicate secrets. She is eager to talk, an ideal but unbidden informant, like her husband Dionisio who stays in Havana for a dozen lonely years before anyone can hear him.

The black informants cannot be dismissed as uncivilized or inarticulate in this novel. They speak in a superior register of Spanish that could itself be a promise of social coherence, as it had been in *Sab*.[48] Minor characters of color do keep their linguistic distance, and newcomers or social marginals who don't collaborate in standard spoken Cuban-flavored Spanish either give Villaverde the opportunity for innovative writing in local slang or stop the interaction through suicidal muteness.[49] No one, for example, damns slavery louder than the recently imported field hand, who literally swallowed his tongue rather than learn to speak like a slave. Villaverde's ideal informants are distinctly black, not light-skinned like Sab, who passed for white as easily as does Cecilia, the deluded heroine. In 1839, Sab's racially indefinite color was a promise of freedom. It had no Old-World name to confine or to control it. Not white, nor black, nor Indian, nor even mulatto, Sab was a New-World original, a Cuban whose local color could soon recognize itself as a nationality. By 1882, though, a distinctly Cuban coloring was making the whites nervous about losing the privileges that came with color coding. So color lines mattered more than the revolutionary leadership could say. Cecilia's light skin is a mirage of national color. It encourages her to pass; but it also makes the whites defensive, duplicitous, and bent on stopping her.[50] Mulatos were more dangerous than blacks, was the Crown's conclusion in its 1844 "Report on the Promotion of White Population in the Island of Cuba and Gradual Emancipation of the Slave Population." The colonial administration openly warned against the population boom among mixed races, because the offspring were notorious social climbers and imitators of whites.[51] Sab's skin had been an invitation to recognize a composite and common Cuban color, "a yellowish white with a dark tinge."[52] But Cecilia's identical and indefinite color focuses the narrator's inquisitorial eye: "To what race, then, did this girl belong? It was hard to say. Nevertheless, to a trained eye, the red lips could not hide their dark border, nor could the light on her face fail to show the shadow at the hairline. Her blood was not pure, and you might be sure that somewhere back in the third or fourth generation it was mixed with Ethiopians."[53]

Cecilia can't tell to which generation she belongs, but black Dionisio can tell a lot. He is an educated slave who knows how to read and write,[54] which was often knowing too much. The poet Manzano had already told us of being beaten when his masters caught him writing.[55] At least as credible and certainly more Cuban than his coarse slave-smuggling Spanish master, Dionisio has an "aristocratic mien, [is] well-spoken and rational."[56] And his wife, María de Regla, impresses her white listeners with "the precision and clarity of her words . . . along with her crystalline pronunciation." The problem, for a slave society that legitimates inequality through color-coded grades of intelligence, is precisely how well these slaves speak, and how informed they are. " 'That black woman knows how to talk,' said Cocco to Don Cándido as they left the (plantation) infirmary. 'You have no idea how well,' replied Don Cándido in a lowered voice. 'That is the very source of her many misfortunes.' "[57] Given the opportunity to tell, María de Regla promises the information requested about the suicidal silence of the captured field slave, and she delivers. Her preamble is reported and repeated: "I will tell my master what has happened," to show that at last we have a trustworthy teller. But other more personal information that she commands remains unrequired for a long time. Finally, at the end of part III, chap. 8, she connects the dots in what had remained a spotty story.

Adela Gamboa ushers María into the ladies' bedroom, during the family's visit to the sugar plantation, because the young mistress is determined to find out why her former nurse was exiled to the fields. She and the others get more than they ask for. As the nurse who provided Adela Gamboa and Cecilia Valdés with a mother's milk, María de Regla also knows who fathered both. This woman, who never got the chance to nurse the field slave who swallowed his tongue, now keeps the ladies of the house listening for hours about how slavery separates black families and sells them off in pieces. She is the Hegelian slave whose story-telling power over the enchanted mistresses comes from having done the work that only she was fit to do.

Although the ladies demand to be told, the intelligence is dismissed with an authoritarian gesture that dramatizes—again—the crisis of legitimacy when the authorities (and authors) resist knowing enough to be responsible. María de Regla fills pages with a long report that ties up the story lines left purposefully hanging by the narrator. She tells about having been rented out to a doctor in order to nurse a baby girl whose origins were kept scrupulously secret, about a mother driven mad and a suspiciously discreet grandmother, about a gentleman hidden behind his cloak but nevertheless familiar . . .

"Who was the gentleman on the street corner?" Adela and Carmen asked together, as if in a single voice.

"I'm not really sure, my noble ladies," stammered the old nurse. "I wouldn't dare vow that the doctor said: Don Cán . . ."

"Aha!" Carmen exclaimed. "If you're not sure who it was, that means at least you have someone in mind. What did you think his name was?"

"I don't think anything at all, mistress Carmita," María de Regla answered, much disturbed. "I wouldn't even dare to say my own name at this point . . ."

"Your fear is unfounded," Adela interceded.

"But, my lady, you seem to forget that a slave always stands to lose when she suspects her masters."

"What! How can you?!" interrupted Carmen, visibly angered . . . "You act dumb when it suits you and then you think you know more than we do."[58]

Of course she knows more. The good reader here is not like Carmen, who refuses to listen and rushes to interpret away whatever the slave could tell her. The ideal reader is like Isabel Ilincheta, who stays quiet and listens; the hard-working coffee-grower is on a visit to the Gamboa plantation as Leonardo's fiancée.

Once María frees the novel's flow of information, the reader who identifies with honest Isabel may feel an uncomfortable twinge of self-reproach in retrospect. The feeling has nothing to do with the evidently incestuous mystery plot that María lays out and that had unfolded from the very beginning of the novel. Any reader can enjoy the satisfaction of getting the point long before the punch line. The self-reproach or self-doubt would attach to an earlier refusal to hear the same information María de Regla has just authorized, just as Carmen refuses, because the information came from a questionable source. It came from the kind of man that white people, especially white women, have been taught to ignore, from María's husband Dionisio.

Much earlier (in part II, chap. 17), the lonely and bitter man, separated from his wife for twelve years, had crashed a formal dance restricted to free "colored" artisans (whose fame survives La Escalera in this commemorative chapter). At the dance, Dionisio invited Cecilia to be his partner, and she rebuffed him. Enraged, he blurted out what we partially know and she suspects: that she and Leonardo are already too intimately related to be lovers, that her nursemaid was banished to the sugar plantation so that Gamboa's secret would be safe. In short, because of this haughty and thoughtless mulata who was about to consummate her own disaster, Dionisio and his wife were leading lonely and humiliating lives.

It is not the badly guarded information that is troubling, especially not when the facts are cautiously repeated by a nonthreatening female slave in the ladies' bedroom, the conventional space for reading sentimental novels. The trouble is the refusal to know—Cecilia's, that of her admiring companions, and also perhaps that of readers. Villaverde sets the trap by keeping Dionisio anonymous for a while, just an aging, too-black man dressed in ill-fitting finery, forcing himself on the Cuban Venus. Borrowing standards of good taste—and whole pages[59]—from his society articles for *La Moda,* Villaverde's novel counts on strict conventions of etiquette that would censure the aggressive outsider for coveting the lightly bronzed object of everyone's desire. Arguably, fashion news was meant to customize a particular national style in Cuba, as it did in Juan Bautista's Alberdi's Argentine journal of the same title. Surely the invited guests—free men in fashionable professions—are worthier of her attention.

Isn't Cecilia's caution, even her disdain, understandable? Who was this easily aroused, unsolicited suitor? What possible significance could Dionisio's string of recriminations have for her? She worries about this for a little while, at least until the next dance. But then she forgets, as we do. María de Regla's story reminds the reader to worry again about why Dionisio, a good source of information and appropriate storyteller, cannot be heard. Shouldn't the setting have enabled more communication? Dances were the occasion for cross-racial contacts and romance. But there was a big difference between this *baile de etiqueta* (where free mulatto artisans emulate the aristocracy) and the *bailes de cuna* that brought Cecilia and Leonardo together and provided the main setting for *Cecilia* in 1839.[60] These were open to everyone, as functions of religious fairs (called "Babel, scandal," in the early novel).[61]

Cuban readers just after the Ten Years War might have appreciated the political potential of the dance scene, as the black man advanced and the light girl retreated, because dances in the revolutionary camps turned out to be testing grounds for a nascent democratic culture. Campaign diaries recently collected by Ada Ferrer are telling:

> Two similar incidents, one in 1876 during the first war and the other in 1895 during the final war, reveal the uses to which that language [to attack racist behaviors] could be put by the end of the independence period. One night in 1876 at a gathering in a rebel camp, a white woman rejected the overtures of an officer of color. The officer became furious, insisting that she refused him only because of his color. In anger, he then threatened her and anyone who dared to court her in the future. Twenty years and two wars later, at a dance at another rebel camp, another black officer tried to court a white woman. He asked her to dance, and when she refused the black officer again became angry and confronted the woman with an accusation similar to the one made in 1876. "You won't dance with me" he said, "because I am black." In this instance, however, the officer made no threats. Instead he gave a long speech on valor, patriotism, and equality, and he condemned her refusal as anti-patriotic. Now, to be racist was to be anti-Cuban.[62]

We won't dance with Dionisio—not Villaverde's heroine nor his readers. By the time we realize that he was a fine leading partner, the opportunity has gone. If this pessimistic novel shares with *Sab* a contrast between slaves who know how to lead and masters who don't, the difference is that Avellaneda's slaveholders seem innocently inept compared with Villaverde's disingenuous whites and almost whites. To keep that bad faith in focus, Villaverde does not confuse his authorial self with an omniscient informant, as Avellaneda had done. Her narrator and the slave protagonist shared information so equally that the colored line between them blurred enough to have Sab sign his name at the end of her book. Villaverde plays at the same game, but perversely, through his own initials on the title page (C.V.), which also begin to spell Cecilia Valdés.[63]

He is Cecilia, born in the same year, deluded like her, unwilling but obliged to divorce desire from destiny, more white than black, which, as Leonardo Gamboa remarks about his own privileged color, is very Cuban in its indefinite origins. "My mother really is a Creole, and I can't vouch for her purity of blood."[64] The confusion does not produce a new autochthonous archetype as in *Sab,* but an impossibly precarious hierarchy in which the mulata's desire to move up tragically meets her white lover's taste for slumming. Compared to Avellaneda's bold abolitionist pronouncements, the politics in *Cecilia Valdés* is insidious, because color coding has become so constitutive of Cuban culture that the lovers never unlearn it. While one of them yearns for racial privilege, the other plays on it.

Conscious of his complicity with privileged compatriots, Villaverde repeats their defensive deafness and blindness in his narrator. They refuse to hear or see the population of blacks, emboldened after the liberalizing Moret Law of 1870 and just over the brink of abolition (it finally came in 1880).[65] The whites simply decline legitimate intercourse with blacks. And Villaverde's text keeps pointing to the white narrator who draws blanks in order to preserve the color-fast fabric of slave society. In this way Cirilo Villaverde invites his white countrymen to notice that they have been reading Cuba from within the claustrophobic constraints of a colonial society. Maybe they will notice that the exits are marked by black guides.

TALK CUBAN

This novel is about impossible relationships, not because blacks and whites should not love one another—after all, they are mutually attractive and produce beautiful children—but because slavery makes it impossible. As Havana's frustrated magistrate puts it, "In a country with slaves . . . morals tend . . . towards laxity and the strangest, most monstrous and perverse ideas reign."[66] Unlike the foundational fictions of other Latin American countries, where passion together with patriotism produced model citizens, Villaverde's Cuban novel cannot make romance and convenience coincide.[67] Cuba was not quite American, nor even a country yet. It was too closely bonded with aristocratic, hierarchical Europe. We know that Gamboa Sr.

married his wife for her money and then looked elsewhere for love (she probably accepted him because he was European and unquestionably white), and that Leonardo admired Isabel for her useful virtues but lusted after sexy Cecilia. Both men undercut—or overextend—their affections because archaic privilege exceeds the individual bourgeois self. Father and son are seduced as much by the absolute power of their racial and sexual advantage as by their partners' charms. This is no modern and rational free market of feeling where unprotected desire could produce social growth,[68] but a bastion of colonial custom where erotic protectionism doesn't give local (re)production a legitimate chance.

The novel, then, poses the problem of racial exploitation whose other face is self-annihilation. The marriage contract to reproduce the family within domestic confines is as transparently fictional here as was the 1817 treaty to end the slave trade, an agreement which should have forced the development of a labor force at home. Beyond a metaphoric relationship between broken conjugal contracts and violated treaties, Havana's moralizing magistrate senses a link of cause and effect between social dissolution and slavery. The brutality allowed by new slave imports, and the unproductive privilege it fostered, he said, corroded society's most sacred values: "familial peace and harmony."[69] The family might not be quite so threatened by extramarital affairs, on which the men look with indulgence, were it not for the secrecy imposed by the conflicting code of bourgeois marriage contracts.

It is secrecy that puts Leonardo at risk of incest. He will not be guilty with Adela, because their relationship is clear. But Cecilia's parentage is an unstable secret, festering where privilege double-crosses family ties. Both the narcissism and the secrecy point to the moral contradictions of a slaveholding society that assumes it can be modern. Neither the sugar industrialists—whose irrational excesses produced slave rebellions, suicides, and English meddling—nor the inter-racial lovers can make a slave society honor bourgeois contracts.

The tragedy is caused by the contraband dealings in production and reproduction. Several centuries of lying, in a system that was evidently more flexible and porous than United States slavery and that blurred racial categories more than the elite would acknowledge. Whites and mulattos are either ignorant of their situation, or they would like to ignore it, in order to preserve even their most illusory privileges. Having exhausted every possible avoidance strategy (as the New York émigrés exhausted reform and annexation), they eventually give the knowledgeable narrators a hearing. Blacks know and tell, with admirable command, about the overlapping affairs of Cecilia's family.

But the deteriorating distinction between familial and foreign goes unattended too long, and the whites are so stubbornly blank that, after a while, their ignorance looks as forced and unsatisfying as a slave's fate. Why has the narrative been stopping its rhythm with apparently aimless hesitations and tired pretenses of misunderstanding? Villaverde's spectacularly silly narrator was probably no fool, just acting dumb as one might at a party, to get a leading partner for the next dance. Cecilia missed her chance with Dionisio, and we readers may have missed it too. But the long Cuban struggle gave time enough for the dance scene to repeat. Is it merely frivolous to note that popular musical theater version of *Cecilia Valdés* builds to a grand finale that can turn into a general rumba? Then, at last, everyone dances with everyone else, before they go home.[70]

GRAMMAR TROUBLE
FOR CORTÁZAR

9

The worlds within and without the Veil of
Color are changing, and changing rapidly,
but not at the same rate, not in the same
way; and this must produce a peculiar
wrenching of the soul.

—DU BOIS
The Souls of Black Folk

From the opening lines of "The Pursuer" (1959), Julio Cortázar's narrator is
nervous.[1] Bruno the jazz critic is respected among Parisian publishers and
academics, yet he is surprisingly out of phase from the very beginning of
his story.[2] By contrast, the saxophone-playing subject of his criticism is
disarmingly lucid. Any jazz buff would recognize the musician as a stand-in
for Charlie Parker. The biographical dates and details give him away, and
maybe even the title and our first glimpse of a self-destructive and arrogant
"Johnny Carter." But Cortázar makes sure that we get the reference by dedi-
cating the story to Parker *in memoriam.* The narrator seems awkward even
before Johnny greets him sardonically—"Faithful old buddy Bruno, regular
as bad breath."[3] Not that Bruno thinks the distasteful reception is justified;
on the contrary, he assumes no responsibility for Johnny's bad mood. Why
should he, when he, the loyal friend, had rushed to the musician's cheap
hotel room to rescue him—once again—from the childish irresponsibility
that only artists get away with. This time Johnny had forgotten his saxo-
phone under the seat of a subway car, and Bruno offered to replace it.

The rescuer's condescending concern obviously grates on the black
musician, who looks helpless, sweating and shivering after some forbidden

drug-induced high. Patronized and misprised, Johnny surely knows the self-serving motives for solicitude, and he probably dismisses the measure of Bruno's genuine concern for the man wasting his talent and his life, just as Charlie Parker was said to dismiss his own friends and fans.[4] Bruno objects to heroine, as Johnny sees it, on grounds that the drug takes him away from work. Johnny's work, after all, is necessary for Bruno's livelihood. "I'm thinking of the music being lost, the dozens of sides Johnny would be able to cut, leaving that presence, that astonishing step forward where he had it over any other musician."[5] The poor "savage monkey" of a musician is not only the object of Bruno's own, casually racist, dismissals;[6] he is also the character in the critic's authoritative biography. Johnny plays the alto sax as "only a god can play,"[7] and he continues to be the capital for Bruno's critical purchase. But Johnny is precarious capital, because—as Bruno frets toward the end—the character could publicly contradict the writer, or simply leave him behind in the wake of musical and personal mischief.

MUSICAL FRETS

Bruno has good reason to worry. To admit that the biographer doesn't really know his subject, that the critic can't quite keep time to the music, is to admit defeat in criticism and authority. Critics are supposed to know best, and Bruno can stand in for so many professional consumers of art whom Cortázar challenges in this narrative meditation on the difference between exploration and expertise. Ever since interpretation freed itself from its origins in the pious exegesis that could remain open to wonder and to awe, critics have tended to take the responsibility, and the credit, for understanding art better than the artist. Don't ask a writer to interpret his own work has been the common caution, as if writers and musicians were inspired but not very smart people. Even in the improvisational styles of today's critical riffs, where striking the right note is less interesting than playing on variations, and where "correct" interpretation fragments and multiplies into a range of competing takes, critics continue to assume that they know the score. To be fair, Bruno does know a lot; he understands Johnny and his music far better than the musician wants to acknowledge. But Johnny's refusal to acknowledge Bruno's expertise is the sticking point; his resistance claims an impasse, in order to control Bruno's mastery. The question, as I said in Chapter 1, is not what "insiders" can know as opposed to "outsiders"; it is how those positions are being constructed as incommensurate or conflictive.

Bruno, in fact, has two good reasons to fret about his position. One is his doubt about whether anyone can know someone else. The other is knowing himself to be a target of Johnny's hostility. The jazzmen of the 1940s and early 1950s were notorious for psychologically harassing anyone who couldn't keep up with them, meaning other musicians as well as a public still avid for the musical Uncle Toms who played the sensual sounds of "hot" music.[8] Louis Armstrong was probably the most visible target, and his characteristic courtesy to other jazzmen cracked with the boppers: "they want to carve everyone else because they're full of malice, and all they want to do is show you up," he complained. "So you get all them weird chords which don't mean nothing . . . and you got no melody to remember and no beat to dance to."[9] Sometimes literally turning its back on the audience, "cool" jazz refused to pander. Instead of tortured and passionate melodious songs, cool "bebop" delivered an oblique sense of melody, a deliberate exploration of unsuspected harmonies and rhythms. Bruno fancies himself a "hipster" on the inside of innovation, but he can feel the chill of being left out (*"And furthermore, cool doesn't mean, even by accident ever, what you've written,"* Johnny would accuse him.[10]) So Bruno worries about a possible professional shaming.

> [To be honest, what does his life matter to me? The only thing that bothers me is that if he continues to let himself go on living as he has been, a style I'm not capable of following (let's say I don't want to follow it), he'll end up by making lies out of the conclusions I've reached in my book. He might let it drop somewhere that my statements are wrong, that his music's something else.][11]

That "something else" haunts Bruno, when he's with Johnny. Brooding about getting it all wrong (Johnny, his music, his biography), Bruno knows the pain of writing it anyway. He also knows, and tells us early on, that his pathetic insufficiency is its own paradoxical license to narrate. Because he admits his shortcomings, Bruno can become strangely trustworthy as a critic of what continues to elude him. (By extension, this paradox permits the reader to comment on this elusive story by Cortázar, on his pursuits and accomplishments.)

> Soy un crítico de *jazz* lo bastante sensible como para comprender mis limitaciones, y me doy cuenta de que lo que estoy pensando está por debajo del plano donde el pobre Johnny trata de avanzar con sus frases truncadas, sus suspiros, sus súbitas rabias y sus llantos. A él le importa un bledo que yo lo crea genial, y nunca se ha envanecido de que su música esté mucho más allá de la que tocan sus compañeros. Pienso melancólicamente que él está al principio de su saxo mientras yo vivo obligado a conformarme con el final. El es la boca y yo la oreja, por no decir que él es la boca y yo . . .

> [I'm sensitive enough a jazz critic when it comes to understanding my limitations, and I realize that what I'm thinking is on a lower level than where poor Johnny is trying to move forward with his decapitated sentences, his sighs, his impatient angers and his tears. He doesn't give a damn that I think he's a genius, and he has never boasted that his music is much farther out than what his contemporaries are playing. It drags me to think that he's at the beginning of his sax-work, and I'm going along and have to stick it out to the end. He's the mouth and I'm the ear, so as not to say he's the mouth and I'm the . . .][12]

Self-awareness, though, does not mean that Bruno is resigned to the aesthetic and intellectual asymmetry. The limitations he confesses, together with Johnny's relentlessly searching talk, evidently make the critic anxious. The very next thing Johnny says, in fact, sounds like a reproach: "Bruno, maybe someday you'll be able to write . . . Not for me, understand, what the hell does it matter to me."[13] Bruno feels diminished in Johnny's presence, both because he has trouble following the musician's verbal improvisations and because he may be serving as Johnny's instrument to be played on and with. "[A]fter the wonder of it's gone you get an irritation, and for me at least it feels as though Johnny's been pulling my leg."[14] In either case, Bruno can't wait to leave the hotel room, so that Johnny's troubling text can safely unravel into commonplaces. "I smile the best I can, understanding fuzzily that he's right, but what he suspects and the hunch I have about what he suspects is going to be deleted as soon as I'm out in the street and have got back into my every day life."[15]

The layered relationship that Cortázar portrays in this initial scene would be admirable enough: Bruno's vexed reverence for the "childish" genius who makes the mature critic feel stupid; Johnny's reluctant respect for the interpreter who gets more things right than is safe to say, and who listens well enough to keep Johnny talking. (In fact, experimental jazz was indebted to European, even academic, influences.)[16] But the story is admirable beyond the probing dialogue and reflexion, just beyond, in the subtly disquieting narrative passages that frame the encounter. From the first lines, while the narrator still casts himself as blameless and forebearing, before acknowledging any uneasiness at the level of story, his plight is *felt* in the grammar.

PURSUING A PERFECT PRESENT

To be precise, Bruno's nervousness comes out in his obsessive recourse to the present perfect tense. The very term "present perfect" is oxymoronic, unstable, dislocating, with one foot in the past and the other in the present. Its function is logically pivotal, a point of departure from one component tense to the other. But Bruno's compound tense doesn't resolve itself into either the past or the present; instead it stays deadlocked and dizzying in its continuous contradiction. Fourteen present perfect verbs cluster on the first full page of text. ("Dédée me ha llamado . . . yo he ido . . . Me ha bastado . . . he encontrado . . . ha dicho . . . he sacado . . . no he querido . . . he preguntado . . . se ha levantado y ha apagado . . . nos hemos reconocido . . . ha sacado . . . he sentido . . . ha dicho . . . Me ha alegrado.")

Dissonant, almost shrill with repetition, the present perfect becomes a structural feature of Bruno's writing. It is as if the writing refused to fit into time, the conventional grammatical time that opposes past to present in neat, mutually exclusive categories. The present perfect scrambles categories. It straddles between excess and inadequacy, too much time and too little. Does a present perfect action spill over from past to present, an exorbitance and difference carried in a single composite tense? Or does the action fit nowhere, already exiled from the past and not quite making it into the present? The specific problem for Bruno is that Johnny is unstable, elusive as the subject of a definitive biography. He is still alive and willful, too present and palpable to be the manageable material of an informative story. Alive, he is not really perfect, a term which I take here in the grammatical sense of finished, past. Only at the end of Bruno's long struggle in the disturbing present perfect of Johnny's life, after 63 closely written pages, does the biographer finally put a full stop to his work in simple, perfect, grammar. Johnny dies, Bruno reports with some relief and no less bad faith, "as he really is, a poor sonofabitch with barely mediocre intelligence . . ."[17] And the story achieves the finality of a simple past tense that can be superseded by the repose and plenitude of a perfectly simple present.

> Todo esto coincidió con la aparición de la segunda edición de mi libro, pero por suerte tuve tiempo de incorporar una nota necrológica redactada a toda máquina, y una fotografía del entierro donde se veía a muchos *jazzmen* famosos. En esa forma la biografía quedó, por decirlo así, completa. Quizá no esté bien que yo diga esto, pero como es natural me sitúo en un plano meramente estético. Ya hablan de una nueva traducción, creo que al sueco o al noruego. Mi mujer está encantada con la noticia.

> [All this happened at the same time that the second edition of my book was published, but luckily I had time to incorporate an obituary note composed under full steam, along with a newsphoto of the funeral in which many famous jazzmen were identifiable. In that format the biography remained, so to speak, intact and finished. Perhaps it's not right that I say this, but naturally I was speaking from a merely aesthetic point of view. They're already talking of a new translation, into Swedish or Norwegian, I think. My wife is delighted at the news.][18]

Presumably the verbs were always simple in the biography, even in the first edition, but now there are comforting grounds for simplicity. Real death, mercifully for Bruno, has stabilized the virtual loss that biography effects into loss, pure and simple. The very genre that presumes to preserve a life defaces it, as Paul de Man argued so poignantly, because biography petrifies living movement into a monument, spirit into letter.[19] Here an unstable present perfect tense hardens into a solidly perfect past. Until that final page, though, Johnny's vitality has been outstripping Bruno's best biographical efforts to control it. The biographer would reduce the complexity of his subject's relationships to an orderly arrangement of information. The violence of that project is clear. It collapses the obliging and ensnaring discourse of *sociability* into the unencumbered, antiseptic, language of *knowledge,* to use Emmanuel Levinas's terms.[20] In the place of a social subject who makes claims on his interlocutors, Bruno prefers the unfettered objective hero, a cluster of data available for bloodless exchanges among music mavens.

But the biographer is not able to package the narrative interlude we are reading now, the story that comes between the official editions of Johnny's life. Bruno's writing in "The Pursuer" doesn't cooperate with marketing demands. As if to call attention to his performance in an anxious present perfect tense, the narrative voice pauses after a first page. The writing is, in fact, so apparently clumsy that Paul Blackburn's overly graceful translation smoothes out the redundant awkwardness. The English version presumes to correct Cortázar's purposefully unpleasant Spanish with the predictable elegance of variety that good taste dictates. For example, the first two Spanish verbs, which set the dissonant tone and timing for Bruno's nervous style, are fixed in the translation into easily chronologized past perfect conjugations: "Dedée had called me . . . and I'd gone." Johnny, we know, reviles conventional "good taste"; and perhaps surprisingly, respectable Bruno seems incapable of practicing it.

The attention-getting pause after that first narrative page is a short dialogue about timing, the very feature that has presented a problem. Bruno begins with a conventional comment about how long the friends had not seen one another. That triggers Johnny's objection to Bruno's penchant for putting everything into orderly, linear time. The irony, of course, is that the page we have just seen, but that Johnny has not, can hardly keep things in order. And Bruno's messy compound tense continues to frame the dialogue in uneasy timing. "'We haven't seen one another for a while,' I [*have*] said to Johnny. 'It's been a month at least.' 'You got nothin' to do but tell time,' he [*has*] answered in a bad mood. 'The first, the two the three, the twenty one. You, you put a number on everything.'"[21]

Johnny's objection is to counting, to marking time in foreseeable sequences. Were his emphasis on time, understood differently, it would point to his own obsession as well. "Johnny . . . kept on referring to time, a subject which is a preoccupation of his ever since I've known him. I've seen very few men as occupied as he is with everything having to do with time."[22] Johnny talked about it. Louis Armstrong didn't; but Ralph Ellison's Invisible Man noticed that even his inoffensive style of jazz made trouble for our sense of timing:

> Perhaps I like Louis Armstrong because he's made poetry out of being invisible. I think it must be because he's unaware that he *is* invisible. And my own grasp of invisibility aids me to understand his music . . . Invisibility, let me explain, gives one a slightly different sense of time, you're never quite on the beat. Sometimes you're ahead and sometimes behind. Instead of the swift and imperceptible flowing of time, you are aware of its nodes, those points where time stands still or from which it leaps ahead. And you slip into the breaks and look around. That's what you hear vaguely in Louis's music.[23]

No wonder Bruno worried about a possible shaming. It could take so many forms, including Ellison's double-take on Armstrong: too subtle to let everyone keep time, but too naive to know it.

Among the rare obsessive talkers about time is the narrator himself. Johnny noted as much, but too impatiently, perhaps because he is not reading the text before us. In it Bruno's discordant performance in the present perfect is unmistakably doubled. While it seems to comment coolly on the confusing temporality of the jazz musician, the narrator's timing is in fact contaminated by Johnny's own experiments with music. This slippage between musical timing and verbal tenses works in both directions, particularly when Johnny's drive to get beyond convention finds textual representation in oxymoronic verbs. Consider the way he forces the present progressive or the simple past to perform in the future. "I am playing this tomorrow, . . . I already played this tomorrow, it's horrible, Miles, I already played this tomorrow."[24] And Bruno himself will play an extended variation, when he takes a break from the present perfect and narrates the recent past (or the present?) in a long future tense improvisation.[25]

By making his agonists share a preoccupation with time, Cortázar is clearly deconstructing the difference between Bruno's intellectual work and Johnny's artistic genius. Bruno should logically be talking about artistic challenges; instead he performs them. And Johnny should be pursuing his speculations through performances, musical rather than verbal; yet he talks here more than he plays. Like Charlie Parker's critics—who acknowledge his superior intelligence and technical appreciation for his own work—Bruno is careful to let Johnny talk, always quoting rather than reporting his textual riffs.[26] This slippery difference between art and critique has at times, of course, been taken to be a more stable opposition. It was, for instance, fundamental to a fascist aesthetics that distinguished between two types of writers: the pedantic *Schriftsteller* and the inspired *Dichter*. Cortázar unhinges the opposition with his own variegated virtuosity, combining inspiration and intellection for a continual challenge to his own critics. Readers usually learn to follow his experimental writing, but more slowly.

COUNTERPOINT

Cortázar's accomplishment in "The Pursuer" both depends on, and overrides, a naive reading that would simply oppose Bruno to Johnny. To appreciate the deconstructive turn here is also to acknowledge that it overcomes a polarized pretext, a simple reading that pits Bruno's caution against Johnny's pursuit. He "was no victim, not persecuted as everyone thought, as I'd even insisted upon in my biography of him . . . Johnny pursues and is not pursued."[27] Only this disingenuous interpretation could mistake Johnny as the sole vehicle of the story's almost mad metaphysical desire to beat down the doors of arbitrary limits. Only willful simplicity could demote Bruno to the prosaic condensation of everything Johnny resists. It would be wrong to draw a stark contrast between the castrating conventionality of Bruno's timing and the liberating trespasses of Johnny's music.

One conclusion, logically, would be that Cortázar is celebrating extralinguistic and nonintellectual communication. This is not the only story in which he uses nonliterary arts to compensate for the limitations of his medium. (See "Apocalypse in Solentiname," in which viewing his own slides of naive Nicaraguan paintings shocks the narrator into finally seeing Somoza's official terror; "Return Trip Tango," where the recursive rhythm of urban music provides the logic of human disencounters; and "Graffiti," where an academic painter wakes up to political repression through an amorous dialogue of public drawings.)[28] The examples come readily to mind, and Cortázar's borrowings from the visual and performing arts are already the topic of important studies.[29] But the obvious fact is that

Cortázar's own pursuit takes place through the apparently disdained medium of literature. In other words, a simple reading that would diminish the value of Bruno's probing literary styles in order to exalt the spontaneity of experimental music would miss the charm of this story, as "The Pursuer" manages to accomplish those winning experiments through writing. Even Johnny's putative superiority is, after all, an effect of his own evasive words and of Bruno's tortuous, tense-troubled, responses. Bruno's haunted memory "insists and insists on Johnny's words, his stories."[30]

This irony—about outperforming writing through writing—might make a nice point in a deconstructive reading, a generalizable or abstract point that could follow from the personalized ironies about Bruno's unstable difference from Johnny. And if we cared to circle back to insist on the virtual collapse of differences between the cautious *Schriftsteller* critic and the daring *Dichter* musician, we could develop the point about Johnny's capacity for intellectual speculation being more than equal to Bruno's. Johnny does more than merely quote lines from Dylan Thomas; he glosses them. "O make me a mask," the line that frames the story from Cortázar's epigraph to the coda on Johnny's words,[31] is an opportunity for the jazzman to extrapolate on the general arbitrariness of signs. His own life, for example, could not possibly be contained in Bruno's biography; it is not even in the musical record.[32] And his face, for an even more intimate example, could not possibly be an adequate representation. It is, rather, a mask that makes recognition both possible and impossible; it is someone else, to be caught by surprise as he stares from the glass, threatening to pass for and replace the person looking in.[33] Tirelessly driven, Johnny develops the mystery by wondering about words as such, the way they stick to things and overcome them with the connecting slime that passes for meaning.[34]

> Imagínate que te estás viendo a ti mismo; eso tan sólo basta para quedarse frío durante media hora. Realmente ese tipo no soy yo . . . lo agarré de sorpresa, de refilón y supe que no era yo . . . No son las palabras, son lo que está en las palabras, esa especie de cola de pegar, esa baba. Y la baba viene y te tapa, y te convence de que el del espejo eres tú.

> [Imagine that you're looking at yourself; that alone is enough to freeze you up for half an hour. In reality, this guy's not me . . . I took it by

surprise, obliquely, and I knew it wasn't me . . . No, not words, but what's in the words, a kind of glue, that slime. And the slime comes and covers you and convinces you that that's you in the mirror.][35]

Johnny's speculations range in apparent disorder, disorder itself being one theme in his obsession with "elastic" time. Even more than an obsession, more than simply a problem to harass him the way it does Bruno, the variability of time for Johnny is an invitation to study and to speculate. "I [have] read some things about all that, Bruno. It's weird, and really awfully complicated . . . (sic) I think the music helps, you know. Not to understand, because the truth is I don't understand anything."[36] His own reflections sound distinctly Bergsonian, about the variable *durée* of experience. Sometimes, Johnny muses, a suitcase, like a song, will hold more and sometimes less. At times it is packed so full that the contents seem limitless. "The best is when you realize you can put a whole store full of suits and shoes in there, in that suitcase, hundreds and hundreds of suits, like I get into the music when I'm blowing sometimes. Music, and what I'm thinking about when I ride the metro."[37] With this breathless transition, the speculation about elasticity continues with the subway as a vehicle for musical compression: the minute-long ride from one stop to another is so crammed with lovingly detailed reveries that the trip seems impossibly concise.[38] "Bruno, if I could only live all the time like in those moments, or like when I'm playing and the time changes then too . . ."[39] Timing was always Charlie Parker's musical frontier, too. "Charlie Parker's idea of rhythm involves breaking time up. It might be said that it is based on half beats. No other soloist attaches so much importance to short notes (eighth notes in quick tempos, sixteenths in slow)," writes André Hodeir, early enough for Cortázar to have read it.

Hodeir's *Hommes et problèmes du jazz* was published in the same place and year as Bruno's biography (Paris, 1954) to become a standard work for other jazz historians. At about the same time, jazz pianist Jay McShann was saying that Parker "played everything offbeat. He had it in his head long before he could put it together."[40] And none of his contemporaries ever caught up to him in pursuit of polyrhythms, the very pulse of the new music.[41] As the period's giant of jazz (along with Gillespie), Parker pioneered a variety of styles that evolved into the opposing "hot" and "cool" trends that lesser musicians would choose between.[42] They appropriated pieces of Parker, mostly his experiments with melody and harmony. But no one had his talent for timing, not even his most admiring students like the pianist Hampton Hawes. "It was Bird's conception that . . . made me realize how important meter and time is in jazz . . . I began experimenting, taking liberties with time, or letting a couple of beats go by to make the beat stand out, not just play on top of it all the time."[43]

A reading of deconstructed oppositions would be the counterpoint to our artist's critical acuity. And Bruno the critic has in fact been showing himself to be an unconventional artist. We have already heard him play with the dissonant "chord tensions" (one of Charlie Parker's performative signatures) of an unstable tense. Now we might add that Bruno is also given to the kind of cramming, overpacking, and overloading so characteristic of bebop and of Johnny's particular speculations about music and time. Bruno makes sure that we get the connection when he comments about another hanger-on whose language is "contaminated"[44] by jazz: "When the marquesa started yakking you wondered if Dizzy's style hadn't glued up her diction, it was such an interminable series of variations in the most unexpected registers . . ."[45] Bruno stretches and pads his own story, especially through the long middle section, where linear writing breaks down under the weight of worry. Telling asides erupt through spaces that are visually represented as parentheses for words that won't fit, but won't go away. In those unpredicted spaces, extra-diegetic writing plays with and against Bruno's simpler themes. Ready to breach the line of continuity (like the way Johnny crouches, "in ambush")[46] are pieces of dangerously supplemental information, Bruno's reflexive musings, and his wonder at what he admits to misinterpreting. He squeezes words into his paragraphs as bebop musicians squeeze the notes of a melody. They squeeze so hard that the new music threatens to explode the familiar line; melody is not entirely overwhelmed, but it is continually commented, challenged, critically caressed.[47] And Bruno sees his own project ready to burst from the pressure of overwriting ("I swear I don't know how to write all this"),[48] he confesses in one parenthetical riff.

In trespassing from music to manuscript Cortázar may have borrowed the particular use of parentheses from André Hodier, who notes that Parker played "in parentheses." That is, he suggested as much music as he actually played: "his phrase frequently includes notes that are not played but merely *suggested* . . . Thus, anyone who writes down a Parker chorus is obliged to include, *in parentheses* (my emphasis), notes that have hardly been played at all."[49] Hodeir's own page then visibly breaks up in parenthetical asides, as if consciously imitating the master. Maybe Cortázar was imitating in turn, taking cues for improvisation from jazz criticism for his own stunning variations. Usually his variations are doubled solos (between Bruno's non-stop narrative and his preoccupied parentheses), but at least one inspired adaptation sets competitive voices in counterpoint. Regular print alternates with italics as they mount in crescendo during a debate about Bruno's book, between an ever more anxious biographer and his progressively angrier hero:

> —Faltan cosas, Bruno—dice Johnny— . . .
> —Las que te habrás olvidado de decirme—contesté—bastante picado. Este mono salvaje es capaz de . . . (habrá que hablar con Delaunay, sería lamentable que una declaración imprudente malograra un sano esfuerzo crítico que . . . *Por ejemplo, el vestido rojo de Lan*—está diciendo Johnny—. Y en todo caso aprovechar las novedades de esta noche para incorporarlas a una nueva edición; no estaría mal. *Tenía como un olor a perro*—está diciendo Johnny—. Y es lo único que vale en ese disco. Sí, escuchar atentamente y proceder con rapidez, porque en manos de otras gentes estos posibles desmentidos podrían tener consecuencias lamentables. *Y la urna del medio, la más grande, llena de un polvo casi azul*—está diciendo Johnny—*y tan parecida a una polvera que tenía mi hermana.* Mientras no pase de las alucinaciones, lo peor sería que desmintiera las ideas de fondo, el sistema estético que tantos elogios . . . *Y además el* cool *no es ni por casualidad lo que has escrito*—está diciendo Johnny. Atención.)

> ["There're things missing, Bruno," Johnny says . . .
> "The things that you've forgotten to tell me," I answer, reasonably annoyed. This uncivilized monkey is capable of . . . (I would have to speak with Delaunay, it would be regrettable if an imprudent statement about a sane, forceful criticism that . . . *For example Lan's red dress,* Johnny is saying. And in any case take advantage of the enlightening details from this evening to put into a new edition; that wouldn't be bad. *It stank like an old washrag,* Johnny's saying. And that's the

only worthwhile thing on the record. Yes, listen closely and proceed rapidly, because in other people's hands any possible contradiction might have terrible consequences. *And the urn in the middle, full of dust that's almost blue,* Johnny is saying, *and very much like a compact my sister had once.* As long as he didn't go beyond hallucinations, the worst that could happen would be that he might contradict the basic ideas, the aesthetic system so many people have praised . . . *And furthermore, cool doesn't mean, even by accident ever, what you've written,* Johnny is saying. Attention.)][50]

One result of all this overwriting is a very long short story. The tale seems compact—a conversation in Johnny's hotel room, a get-together at the marquesa's place, a drink and more talk just before Johnny dies—but the telling stretches beyond the length of more conventional stories. Cortázar almost always writes them within 20 pages. More than doubling that span by adding variations, speculations, reveries, and repetitions is the kind of experimental performance that brings the writing close to bebop.

The analogy between modern music and modern writing is redundantly clear. Even so, Cortázar takes few risks relying on his readers' interpretive skill. He informs us, outright, that Johnny's jazz is part of a general postwar culture exploding with artistic experiments. (Toni Morrison would make the same explicit connection between her improvisations and the African American culture of jazz that took over after the war.)[51] "This is not the place to be a jazz critic," says Bruno, "and anyone who's interested can read my book on Johnny and the new post-war style, but I can say that forty-eight—let's say until fifty—was like an explosion in music . . ."[52] The image of exploding standard forms, the following reference to an ever greater and more avid public, and the timing in the late 1940s and early 1950s are unmistakable allusions to the Latin American literary "Boom" that Cortázar helped to detonate. So is the geographical displacement of American jazz to Paris, the same haven that attracted the most influential new Spanish American novelists: Carlos Fuentes, Mario Vargas Llosa, and Cortázar himself among others. A late and supremely self-ironizing wave of modernist experiments, Boom writing distinguished itself from the kind of expository prose that Bruno's biography stands for. The genre of biography in Cortázar's Argentina, had been extolled by the great nation-builder, Domingo F.

Sarmiento. For him and for generations of practical and productive disciples, biography was the most effective guide to personal and political development.[53] And Bruno's book about the bebop artist who "turned the page"[54] on music history might well have fit the mold of celebrating exemplary men in a mimetic effort to become one of them.

Cortázar is presumably offering a critique of this self-improving genre by replacing biography with a story that tracks the troubled afterthoughts about the very possibility of writing a life. Like Johnny, Cortázar can publicly shame his critics, by defending experimentation over the biographical developmentalism that stays beyond the scene of writing, like some guilty pretext for the drama. Some of his readers were trying to tidy up Cortázar's unpredictable moves into a story of development, which means that they (and Bruno the biographer) were missing the magic of art.[55] Art resides in the pursuit of nonchronological play, which, ironically, can make artistic history. Conceivably, "The Pursuer" means to leave Cortázar's critics in the dust raised by his own superior flair for speculative interpretation, and by his endless pursuit of forms that describe desire without controlling it.

COUNTERDEPENDENCE

I don't deny the possibility of Cortázar's self-promotion or self-defense, and I certainly won't discard the deconstructive reading already suggested. But I do want to argue a different point here. It sidesteps immediate self interest and gets beyond the kind of deconstruction that heaps glaring ironies onto inconsistent oppositions in order to level the feeble differences between Bruno's positivism and Johnny's performance. The story, I make bold to point out, is not merely about the ultimate naiveté of binary oppositions. It is also—and most powerfully—about a refusal to overcome them. The agonists resist the leveling effect and remain in murderous tension with one another. Johnny refuses to be contained in Bruno's smug prose. And Bruno strains to be free of Johnny, of the self-doubts and the complexity he inflicts. In other words, the "naive" interpretation that a familiar version of deconstruction would override survives the sophisticated assault, in a more responsible deconstructive practice. This survival is most palpable in the diegetic passages and at the level of grammar. Whereas a standard deconstructive reading (more de Manian than Derridean) would focus on Bruno's bebop style, on the futility of keeping oppositional categories clear, the "agonistic" emphasis I prefer to give this story keeps an eye on the energy invested in safeguarding the oppositions. The differences between the agonists are not essential, not organic. But their very fragility, their almost arbitrary constructedness, makes the characters whose identity depends on them nervous enough to insist on distinctions.

The fact that Bruno and Johnny overlap is no happy liberation from the tensions of difference; instead, it is a threat to what gives each character his specificity, his life. ("[M]aybe I'm a little afraid of Johnny, this angel who's like my brother, this brother who's like my angel").[56] To override that respectful distance between self and other, a distance that provides the ground for dynamic social relationships, is to risk reducing sociability to solipsism. Closing up distances and coming perilously close to the other threatens to overtake him or her in a gesture of ontological appropriation that Levinas calls "totality."[57] Both Bruno and Johnny threaten one another in this way.

Bruno cannot help but perfect his living subject into an inanimate object of discourse. That is the cost of writing a life. Mikhail Bakhtin too benignly called that process "consummation," in an early philosophical essay titled "Author and Hero in Aesthetic Activity." It is an especially suggestive piece in connection with Bruno's relationship to Johnny.[58] Consummation, for Bakhtin, describes the process whereby an author contextualizes and completes his hero from a necessarily exterior vantage point. Thus critics, Bruno protests after feeling especially stupid, are more necessary than they sometimes realize, "because the creators . . . are incapable of extrapolating the dialectical consequences of their work, of postulating the fundamentals and the transcendency of what they're writing down or improvising."[59] To hear this almost funny, hollow and impersonal academic jargon, after Johnny has just complained about being left out of Bruno's biography, is to get Johnny's point. Bruno has had to fictionalize his friend, to flatten and substitute him, in order to celebrate him. This describes the culpability of completing a character. And Bakhtin is explicit, at points, about the violence inherent in the process, although the thrust of his sometimes rambling essay is to define a properly ethical engagement: authors must respect their heroes' qualified autonomy even as they help to confer it. A violent surplus is produced by establishing pleasing contours for a hero that do not jibe with his inner sense of self. That is, to confer coherence on a character is, necessarily, to finish him.

> Artistic vision presents us with the *whole* hero, measured in full and added up in every detail; there must be no secrets for us in the hero with respect to meaning; our faith and hope must be silent. From the very outset, we must experience all of him, deal with the whole of him: in respect to meaning, he must be dead for us, formally dead.
>
> In this sense, we could say that death is the form of the aesthetic consummation of an individual.[60]

Cortázar's fans may remember his own repeated explorations of the murderous price authors pay for congealing incoherent lives into perfected fictions. In fact much, if not most, of Cortázar's writing is driven by his sense of the danger posed by fixing and finishing. He will resist perfection, characteristically, by deforming his grammar, with "shifty" pronouns as well as oxymoronic verbs.[61] Perhaps the most dramatic example of the danger is, predictably, a story that succumbs to it. "We Love Glenda So Much" (1981) is practically a parable about deadly perfectibility. The story ends once Glenda's fans conspire to kill her in order to polish the movie-star image that stabilizes their devotion. The very last lines draw an unmistakable parallel with another necessary sacrifice to cultish heroism. "We loved Glenda so much that we would offer her one last inviolable perfection. On the untouchable heights to which we had raised her in exaltation, we would save her from the fall, her faithful could go on adoring her without any decrease; one does not come down from a cross alive."[62] Sacrifice and deification can also describe Bakhtin's dynamic between hero and author. But his efforts run directly into the irrational possibility that the hero can be redeemed by the author's finishing work. Love runs the risk of fixing and killing the beloved; but it also promises to raise him or her to another, more perfect plane.

> It is only love (as an active approach to another human being) that unites an inner life (a *subiectum*'s own object-directedness in living his life) as experienced from outside with the value of the body as experienced from outside and, in so doing, constitutes a unitary and unique human being as an aesthetic phenomenon. The enrichment in

this case is formal, transfigurative in character—it transposes the recipient of the gift to a new plane of existence. And what is transposed to a new plane, moreover, is not the material, not an object, but a *subiectum*—the hero. It is only in relation to the hero that aesthetic obligation (the aesthetic "ought") as well as aesthetic love and the gift bestowed by such love are possible.[63]

Some pages earlier, Bakhtin had spelled out the fundamentally Christian and paradoxical nature of this consummating and redemptive love. In that passage, Bakhtin might have capitalized the word "Author" because he casts himself as one possible creation. The mystery of redeeming a life through death can be read here as one result of Christ's synthetic embrace of traditions, a synthesis that allows for slippages from one plane to another.

In Christ we find a synthesis of unique depth, the synthesis of *ethical solipsism* (man's infinite severity toward himself . . .) with *ethical-aesthetic kindness* toward the other. For the first time, there appeared an infinitely deepened *I-for-myself* . . . one of boundless kindness toward the other . . . [Thanks to Christ,] God is no longer defined essentially as the voice of my conscience . . . God is now the heavenly father who is *over me* and can be merciful to me and justify me where I, from within myself, cannot be merciful to myself and cannot justify myself . . . What I must be for the other, God is for me. What the other surmounts and repudiates within himself as an unworthy given, I accept in him and that with loving mercy as the other's cherished flesh.[64]

To become "the other's cherished flesh" is a phrase passionate enough to send chills through readers of "Glenda," where passion achieves its sacrificial meaning and the heroine's fans (short for fanatics) become living shrines to her memory. By the time he writes this story, Cortázar is himself a venerated superstar, or a venerable monument as vulnerable to his carping critics as Glenda was to her fans. "As always, why don't you live in your country, why was *Blow-Up* so different from your story, don't you think writers should be committed? And . . . chez Saint Peter there'll be no difference, don't you think that down below you used to write too hermetically for regular people to understand?"[65] "Glenda," therefore, may be a cautionary tale about loving the beloved to death. But such a reading would diminish the meaning of love, shrink it into a simple cannibalistic appropriation. Glenda's fanatics could not possibly have loved her, Cortázar was probably saying, not in the generous and tolerant sense that Bakhtin gave the word. No one among the "faithful" could have justified Glenda in her imperfections, forgiven her for that which she could not forgive herself. Therefore, no one could have consummated the character with the pleasing coherence achieved only outside one's own intolerant "ethical [or aesthetic] solipsism."

Bakhtin's idea of redemptive love is obviously an answer to the ritual cannibalism of Glenda's celebrants. In the least case, their cannibalism digests the tension between interiority and exteriority that makes writing possible. The expression of their love means the end of Glenda, as a character and as a narrative. Even an autobiographer, Bakhtin observes, needs to define a tension between author and hero in order to write of himself. And beyond the aesthetic need to keep them apart, there is an ethical imperative for the author to maintain, or regain, a respectful distance from his hero: the distance allows the hero's fullness to come into focus.[66] "What's hard is to circle about him and not lose your distance," Bruno reminds himself, "like a good satellite, like a good critic."[67] Despite, however, Bakhtin's own cautions about overtaking or being overtaken by the Other, despite repeated warnings against an empathy that offers cheap rushes of feeling and shirks the labor required for consummation,[68] his essay seems so steeped in the paradox of redemption through death that even his reflexive and careful kind of loving nudges the argument toward the foot of a cross. An author's loving justification hardly allows for struggle; it is more likely to stop the hero, to substitute his development for an external and more pleasingly coherent perspective.

Maybe approaching the cross is inevitable. Writing, even or especially writing with love, tends to flesh out characters, to finish them off and then to finish narrating. Therefore, to read from the ending, at the point of closure, is almost inevitably to read the violence loosed on life when it is stabilized as a story. But more specific and interesting observations are to be made before the inevitable endings, during the engagement between author and hero, sometimes, that is, between characters cast in those roles. The particular process of consummation, rather than its mere fact, gives a narrative its specificity. And Bakhtin himself would later sharpen his critical focus on the almost open-ended dynamic he called dialogism, so characteristic of modernity, rather than on the consummate promise of salvation as the end of writing. Consider how different are Glenda's fans from Johnny's biographer. Their refusal to engage her is a brutal narrative shortcut, a dime-store deification, while Bruno's vulnerability to Johnny keeps the hero, their conversations, and therefore the narrative alive for many, many pages. The temptation to crucify Johnny is there for Bruno too, but it is openly and self-critically there. So, besides being an unavoidable trap, temptation is also a goad for more writing: "Basically we're a bunch of egotists," Bruno admits in this rehearsal of Glenda's demise; "under the pretext of watching out for Johnny what we're doing is protecting our idea of him, . . . to reflect the brilliance from the statue we've erected among us all and defend it till the last gasp."[69] Later on, Bruno will even imagine spectators looking at him looking at Johnny, as if Bruno were "climbing up on the altar to tug Christ down from his cross."[70] The first to reproach him was Johnny himself, and to the extent that they struggle against one another, author and hero survive the violence. The story flows between them, through the fissures of Bruno fictional but still functional authority. Compared to Glenda's fans and to privileged narrators who stay in business by being willfully stupid (like the one who keeps missing the connections in *Cecilia Valdés* and like Bartleby's boss in Melville's story), Bruno seems almost defenseless.

Yet he menaces Johnny by the very fact of taking his life down, of getting it right. And Johnny reciprocates by dismissing Bruno's capacity to understand him. He practically demands that Bruno leave biographical logic alone and, like himself, pursue the inarticulable energy behind art, even in the uncooperative medium of writing. "Bruno, maybe someday you'll be able to write. . . ."[71] Each makes unsatisfiable demands on the other; yet each resists those demands and remains himself. It is the resistance that safeguards their vexed, but dynamic, sociability. The agonists depend on one another in their differences, and they know it. Bruno needs the unfettered genius as the featured subject of an academic career and the goad to his own probing performance, while Johnny needs Bruno's sensible attentions in order to survive. He also needs the critic's trained ear to elicit more music and more talk. "You ought to have been happy I put on that act with you," Johnny tells him a few days after the scene in the hotel room. "I don't do that with anybody, believe me. It just shows how much I appreciate you. We have to go someplace soon where we can talk."[72]

But Johnny usually prefers not to admit his dependency, and his attitude suggests the bad faith of a man who declines any real engagement with another. "I understand nothing," he protests. Johnny fears that any text would betray him, that any meaning assigned to him would be a falsification. "Right away you translate it into your filthy language . . ."[73] The filth, the slime that makes language work also makes Bruno's book "like a mirror," as falsifying and substitutive as a mirror. Bruno apparently gets it wrong even when he modestly writes that Johnny's real biography is in the records. The point is that his biography cannot be written, because Johnny's life is driven by inarticulable desire. "And if I myself didn't know how to blow it like it should be, blow what I really am . . . you dig, they can't ask you for miracles, Bruno."[74] But Bruno tries to content himself with less than miracles, as he translates Johnny's objection to being left out of his own biography with a literary critical commonplace: "Basically, the only thing he said was that no one can know anything about anyone, big deal. That's the basic assumption of any biography, then it takes off, what the hell."[75]

Of course his dismissal of the problem doesn't make it go away. Right before Johnny dies, and just as the biography was going into its second edition, Bruno indulges in self-criticism in his thoughts about rewriting. "To be honest within the limits permitted by the profession, I wondered whether it would not be necessary to show the personality of my subject in another light." But another light might promote a "literary infection," Bruno's colleagues worry, which could weaken the points about Johnny's music, "at least as all of us understood it."[76] Whether the infection is *of* literature (Bruno's biography), or *by* literature (Johnny's poetic version of finally ineffable experience) seems purposefully ambiguous. In any case, Bruno closes—prophylactically—the cover of his book against any possible disease. It is a characteristically self-preserving move.

For all of his repeated admissions of intellectual and spiritual inferiority, Bruno usually braces himself against Johnny. To be in Johnny's company is to lose composure, to become a misfit in time. The parallels with Johnny's experiments (present perfects, future for the past, and the parenthetical riffs) are problems for Bruno the character, as opposed to opportunities for

Cortázar the writer. Bruno's problem would perhaps not be so profound if his *resentiment* were not so obviously driven by jealousy along with self-defensiveness. Less guilty of provocative bad faith than Johnny's conversation, Bruno's private writing seems brutally self-reflective. "I envy Johnny, that Johnny on the other side, even though nobody knows exactly what that is, the other side . . . I envy Johnny and at the same time I get sore as hell watching him destroy himself, misusing his gifts . . ."[77] And the solution for problem-solving Bruno is to finish Johnny, to make him perfect and stable in a finite past. "[M]aybe basically I want Johnny to wind up all at once like a nova that explodes into a thousand pieces and turns astronomers into idiots for a whole week, and then one can go off to sleep and tomorrow is another day."[78] Thirty pages later the murderous wish recurs: "Sure, there are moments when I wish he were already dead" (p. 210). Then Bruno undercuts the wish by worrying if release is even possible.

> Sí, hay momentos en que quisiera que ya estuviese muerto . . . Pero cómo resignarse a que Johnny se muera llevándose lo que no quiere decirme esta noche, que desde la muerte siga cazando, siga salido (yo ya no sé cómo escribir todo esto) aunque me valga la paz, la cátedra, esa autoridad que dan las tesis incontrovertidas y los entierros bien capitaneados. (p. 302)

> [Yes, at times I wish he were dead already . . . But how can we resign ourselves to the fact that Johnny would die carrying with him what he doesn't want to tell me tonight, that from death he'd continue hunting, would continue flipping out (I swear I don't know how to write all this) though his death would mean peace to me, prestige, the status bestowed upon one by incontrovertible theses and efficiently arranged funerals.] (p. 210)

TENSE RELIEF

But relief and repose finally do come. The last sentences, over Johnny's consummately finite body, rescue Bruno from the mire of deconstructive contaminations and tangled tenses. Whatever subtle complications may haunt the biographer after his hero's death, the writing shows symptoms of release. Bruno has straightened out his verbs; he has disaggregated past from present, disengaged himself from the present perfection that Johnny pursued. Finally, Bruno frees himself from Johnny, after "sticking it out to the end" (p. 167; p. 256). He releases his grip on the unmanageable genius who has dragged him through relentlessly self-reflexive writing. Now tension abates. The energizing if tortuous present perfect tense slackens and breaks down into either a haltingly simple past or a comfortingly stable present. And the supplementary parenthetical riffs are dropped from the text, now hellbent on setting itself straight.

Only now, in the deadly timing of his verbs and in the cause-and-effect continuity of the necrological notes, does Bruno show some bad faith. He shows it clearly in the mildly embarrassed reflection that follows his relief at Johnny's death. More than relieved, Bruno actually seems happy about the lucky timing of Johnny's funeral, because it produced pictures for the improved biography. The book "remained, so to speak, intact and finished. Perhaps it's not right that I say this," Bruno interjects almost contritely, "but naturally I was speaking from a merely aesthetic point of view" (p. 220; p. 313). Merely aesthetic is what Johnny's life becomes for Bruno, after the finishing touches that fix the hero in a satisfying story. Therefore, the embarrassed aside is hardly exculpating. Although Bruno manages to play a kind of happy note in the last paragraph, he knows that the note is drowning out much richer music. He holds that easy note long enough to stop everything else, as if to say that counterpuntal melodies no longer matter, as if dissonance were now merely cacophony, a problem to be solved. Again, it is Bruno's grammar that plays so convincingly. Whatever information we may or may not get about Bruno's will to survive, that will is *felt* through his newly orthodox verbal conjugations. Willfully simple, Bruno evokes here the purposefully deaf, self-serving narrators of *Cecilia Valdés* and of "Bartleby"; they defend their privilege by defending against understanding. All Bruno wants to know, as he gets on with his life, is what fits into the disaggregated, perfectly simple past and present tenses that end Johnny's story. The hero died, and the book is finished.

ABOUT FACE:
THE TALKER TURNS
TOWARD PERU

10

If one listens patiently to the many
and various self-accusations of the
melancholiac, one cannot in the end avoid
the impression that often the most violent
of them are hardly at all applicable to the
patient himself, but that with insignificant
modifications they do fit someone else,
some person whom the patient loves,
has loved or ought to love.

—SIGMUND FREUD
   "Mourning and Melancholia"

The first sentence of *El hablador* (1987) gives a start, a shock, a double take, as the narrator misses a step to gasp with surprise. Facing him is the very thing he had escaped. "I came to Firenze to forget Peru and the Peruvians for a while, and behold, the damned country forced itself upon me this morning in the most unexpected way."[1] The first movement of the story is an about-face. Long before the narrator identifies himself as a writer named Mario Vargas Llosa, even before the text spells out any identity or attributes, any subjectivity, background, or future for the speaker, he responds to Peru in this syncopated moment of choosing to leave and being taken aback. His double take is an involuntary reflex that will trigger reflection. Hailed by an authority that can stop him short and call him home, the call begins to constitute Vargas Llosa as a character.

HALT

This is the way Louis Althusser understood the subject of an ideology, as one who responds to authority when, for example, a policeman yells "Hey you" to someone running. The runner can respond by accepting the interpellation of the law and stopping dead.[2] And, more to the point here, the narrator's halt is like the commanding moment in Emannuel Levinas's ethics, when the subject is born from the labor of facing an unknowable but inescapable Other who demands recognition.[3] Transfixed and helpless in their derivative identity and in their humbling mortality, Levinas's subject and Vargas Llosa's character practically shudder at the awe-ful impact of a human face that issues divine demands. The novel that follows is about the face, which is inscrutable on ethical, not on epistemological, grounds. After the stunning first sentence stops the narrator in his escapist tracks, the paragraph explains why, fixed on photos from Peru:

> I had visited Dante's restored house, the little Church of San Martino del Véscovo, and the lane where, so legend has it, he first saw Beatrice, when, in the little Via Santa Margherita, a window display *stopped me short (me paró en seco):* bows, arrows, a carved oar, a pot with a geometric design, a mannequin bundled into a wild cotton cushma. But it was three or four photographs that *suddenly (de golpe)* brought back to me the flavor of the Peruvian jungle. The wide rivers, the enormous trees, the fragile canoes, the frail huts raised up on pilings, and the knots of men and women, naked to the waist and daubed with paint, *looking at me unblinkingly (contemplándome fijamente)* from the glossy prints.
>
> Naturally, I went in. With a strange shiver and the presentiment that I was doing something foolish, that I was *putting myself at risk (arriesgándome)* out of mere curiosity.[4]

The commanding images draw Vargas Llosa, turn him toward Peru, and threaten nothing less than his freedom to be far away, a subject-centered freedom that Levinas would have recognized as ethically suspect.[5] Curiously, though, the riveting presence of Peru is only a trace here, instead of the flesh and blood that would command a Levinasian engagement, face to face. The eyes in the pictures glare from already absent faces, flattened into

235

two photographic dimensions to show Indians caught by the eye of modern technology. The contrast between the passivity of pictures and their active effect on the narrator, "staring at me," is not only a symptom of what Lacan might have called paranoia about things that know more than people.[6] It is also a symptom of the novel's general indecision about Indians, in a country where they are either its deepest soul or its most stubborn obstacle to national development.

Besides providing a double start for this story, the scene of impossible flight may also call to mind another Peruvian writer who had stopped in Italy years before, and had been just as dramatically pulled homeward. Perhaps himself standing for so many New World subjects digging for European roots, he turned up more contrasts than confirmations, and confirmed instead his Americanist calling. Yet the reflexive traveler seems an unlikely secret sharer for a narrator named after the increasingly conservative Mario Vargas Llosa.[7] That other errant American in Italy was José Carlos Mariátegui, chief ideologue in the 1920s for the variant of Marxism that has, until now, marked left-wing Peruvian politics.[8]

> In Italy I felt the fragility of the lie that makes us a spiritual annex of Rome [Mariátegui mused]. I understood how alien we Spanish-Americans were at that banquet. I perceived simply and precisely how artificial and arbitrary was the flimsy myth of our kinship with Rome ... Like him, [Waldo Frank] I didn't feel American except in Europe; on the streets of Europe I encountered that American country which I had left and where I had lived almost in absence, as a stranger. Europe revealed how much I belonged to a primitive and chaotic world, and at the same time it imposed on me the responsibility for an American project.[9]

Visions of a primitive world compel Vargas Llosa's narrator too, but more theatrically than in Mariátegui's nonfictional memoirs. The pictures in the window are practically protagonists who hail the speaker and dictate his mission. Whereas Mariátegui turns inward to find his own American self during the famous disencounter with Italy, Vargas Llosa stages a sharp turn around, toward the American Other. The jolt of recognition is dramatic, probably to capture the disaffected narrator, and perhaps to capture readers who may have imagined themselves equally free from home. If Mariátegui had located an internally divided Peruvian self, between modernized occidental and traditional native, Vargas Llosa doesn't presume to contain the contradictory sides.

His reluctance to construct a Peruvian whole big enough to contain its contradictions may be based on rigid notions of difference between Indian traditions and modern projects. Or it may be an ethical caution against containment and control of the incommensurate cultures in a multifarious nation. On the one hand, Vargas Llosa could be absolving himself from the moral obligation of inclusiveness and tolerance, a likely stance given his impatient prescriptions for neutralizing and nationalizing Indian cultures.[10] But on the other hand, more promisingly, the refusal could be read against his politics, as a defense of difference. *El hablador* may not be an argument for the survival of parallel and simultaneous story lines; but the novel *is* a sustained performance of simultaneity. Primitive Peru is, admittedly, outside of the narrator named Vargas Llosa. But it holds him, along with us, hostage in its gaze.

The moment of recognition is gripping, and it announces the recursive shape of the entire novel, which circles around the sticking point of Peru's claim on our attention, and returns obsessively to the confrontation in Florence. To repeat the danger and to predict calamities inside the novel as well as out, we should note that the grip may be paralyzing and non-negotiable in ways that portend unethical responses to entrapment.[11] The dilemma underlines a certain peril in the Levinasian moment of ethical engagement, a peril that comes into focus once the moment of confrontation drags on into the messiness of narrative development. The problem is that unstinting attention to the Other cannot remain static and unblinking; what may follow is either an identification with otherness so complete that it denies one's self, or a self-preserving dismissal of the agonist. Absolute alterity makes one or the other kind of aggression practically inevitable. It leaves no room, philosopher Enrique Dussel worries, for the social dynamism that Latin America desperately needs;[12] that is, for the political pragmatism of "lesser evils" that Lyotard defends.

Vargas Llosa would experiment with both ways out of the Levinasian hold. Through a selfless storyteller, he wrote that any interference with the Other is murder: " 'That these cultures must be respected,' he said . . . 'And the only way to respect them is not to go near them. Not touch them.' "[13] But more consistently, he has argued—as a sorry but single-minded spokesperson—for necessary interference and incorporation: "It is tragic to destroy what is still living, still a driving cultural possibility, but I am afraid we shall have to make a choice . . . [W]here there is such an economic and social gap, modernization is possible only with the sacrifice of the Indian cultures."[14] Nevertheless, El hablador, at least, keeps the alternatives in tension and fixes the dilemma into static, unnerving, irresolution. The rhythm of this novel is almost lyrical in its reluctance to move beyond the gripping moment, into the unethical disorder of historical time.

TURN

The visions that rush at the halted narrator soon conjure up memories of talk, as if to move him from confrontation to engagement (or at least into a narrative flow).[15] The memories are of a Jewish friend who had studied anthropology in Lima and had become fascinated with the fragile existence of the Amazonian Machiguengas. That was before the misfit friend—called Mascarita, for the birthmark that covered half his face—disappeared from the capital, maybe to settle in Israel. His non-Jewish mother and his refugee father had produced the divided or doubled identity of their son, grotesquely masked in the two-tone face, so that Saúl Zuratas fit nowhere in Peru. The splintered life and the line of escape are apparently modeled after the novelist Isaac Goldemberg. Like Mascarita, Goldemberg moved from his mother's native province to his father's Jewish community in Lima, and from there to Israel and to New York, where he published The Fragmented Life of Don Jacobo Lerner (1979).[16]

The character Zuratas had abandoned anthropology early on, because he came to believe ethnography itself was killing Indians. His professor seems incredulous:

"Saúl is starting to have doubts about research and fieldwork. Ethical doubts . . . [H]e has taken it into his head, can you believe it, that the work we're doing is immoral . . . He's convinced that we're attacking them, doing violence to their culture . . . That with our tape recorders and ball-point pens we're the worm that works its way into the fruit and rots it . . ." Saúl Zuratas had flabbergasted everyone, proclaiming that the consequences of the ethnologists' work were similar to those of the activities of the rubber tappers, the timber cutters, the army recruiters, and other mestizos and whites who were decimating the tribes. "He maintained that we've taken up where the colonial missionaries left off. That we, in the name of science, like they in the name of evangelization, are the spearhead of the effort to wipe out the Indians."[17]

In a novel structure similar to that of *Aunt Julia and the Script Writer* (1977),[18] in which chapters from young Mario's autobiographical romance alternated with suggestively similar scenes in radio soap operas, *El hablador* switches back and forth from one kind of narration to another, from a history of the Hispanic intelligentsia in Lima to an evocation of repetitive Amazonian lore. The style of the evocation, it should be said, is a cause for concern in a novel that seems to respect culturally specific languages, because the indigenous speech is familiar from Quechua-inflected Spanish, with its trailing gerunds *(diciendo, hablando)* at the end of sentences, for example.[19] The Andean sounds are so improbable in the jungle that the effect is to suggest the writer's indifference to Indians.

Unlike *Aunt Julia,* however, the story lines of the ethnographic novel do not implode into the hilarious jumble of the radio-style romance, in which real life takes leads from fiction, and high art aspires to the charm of kitsch. Instead, the slips from one side to the other in *El hablador* feel like raids or contaminations. One story line overtakes the other, tragically. The overlaps are aggressions, not ironies; and differences vanish because they are overridden, not because they are misprised. Alternating chapters move from the narrator's memories of Saúl's activities in Lima's mass media, to chapters in the *hablador*'s voice, which are recitations of creation myths and cultural history of a people described as the dispersed and precarious Machiguengas. The tribe barely holds together through the act of ritual telling. That is why the American missionaries are so monstrous in the end, with their translated vernacular Bibles that drain the lore from language. By the time Bible fragments filter into the jungle stories (adapted from the translations of Padre Joaquín Barriales), they sound like a prelude to doom.

The narrative slips might have suggested flexibility, the creative indefinition of frontiers that animates *Aunt Julia.* If one culture is not entirely immune to another, it may not be allergic, either. Millennial traditions can be adaptive, as activists for cultural survival argue. But here, the Machiguenga names that the narrator drops in his own story[20] amount to decoration rather than to a dynamic cultural disturbance. And on the other side, the unbidden biblicized tales of Tasurinchi-Jehová, his triple form, an expulsion, and a future-annihilating wind[21] profoundly disturb listeners for whom time itself should work differently. "For the Machiguengas," the narrator explains unambiguously, as if to forestall any more interpretation, "history marches neither forward nor backward: it goes around and around in circles, repeats itself."[22] So their response is to leave, to further disperse deeper into the precarious jungle.[23] A small number of the tribe had survived natural disasters (thanks to their modest expectations of nature and to inflexible standards for themselves), and some had escaped the forced labor of lumber and rubber barons, but the remnant is finally overpowered by translators: "Those apostolic linguists of yours [Saúl protests to Mario] are the worst of all. They work their way into the tribes to destroy them from within . . . The others steal their vital space and exploit them or push them farther into the interior. At worst, they kill them physically. Your linguists are more refined. They want to kill them in another way. Translating the Bible into Machiguenga! How about that!"[24]

The accusation, and by extension the whole novel as a debate-driven drama about the future of Indians in the Americas, forecasts the revolutionary climate that the jungle eventually incubated long after Mario the narrator and his friend disputed the country's future between 1953 and 1956.[25] In 1963, when Saúl was reported in Israel (news that makes Mario intone a prayer to Tasurinchi for his friend's safety from border conflicts),[26] student rebellions were flaring in Peru.[27] During the same 1963, long before the Sendero Luminoso launched its guerrilla in 1980,[28] some Cuba-inspired intellectuals were trying to trigger rebellions in focal points throughout the countryside. One early *foco* was in the jungle town of Puerto Maldonado, where an unlikely combatant and victim was a personal friend of Mario's. It was Javier Heraud, the well-known poet who was hardly more than a boy and who had recently been in Paris, making the rounds of cafés and bookstores with Vargas Llosa. Still stunned and grieving, he delivered a eulogy that was an indictment of a desperate country. "That Javier Heraud should decide to take up arms and become a guerrilla only indicates that Peru has arrived at a breaking point. No one was further from violence than he, by temperament and conviction."[29] The memory returns in the novel, when the narrator mentions his frustrating 1981 trip to Puerto Maldonado. The whole production team of his television series, "The Tower of Babel," goes there to recreate the battle and to commemorate Heraud, although their malfunctioning equipment "screwed up" the effort.[30] The martyred poet is the subject of another novel contemporaneous with *El hablador:* Aida Balta's 1987 *El legado de Caín,* which names Heraud among the country's irrecoverable losses to violence.

Heraud's move from the capital to the tribal interior may find a tribute in Vargas Llosa's portrayal of Saúl's desertion of the academy for the people it studies. But the fictional friend is a different kind of rebel. Saúl's specific rage targets cultural imperialism. As background to the armed struggle at Puerto Maldonado, an ideological battle was waged among nationalist ethnographers. One side drew upon the self-reflexive and engaged ethnology of José María Arguedas (1911–1969), whose Andean boyhood and cultural ties were giving social science a local cast. His enormous contributions to ethnology are sometimes overshadowed by Arguedas the novelist, wrote Angel Rama in a eulogy for the tormented bi-cultural man who finally committed suicide.[31] It was that novelist, with his flair for ethnology, who surely inspired Vargas Llosa as he doubled himself, irreconcilably, in the homonymic narrator of personal histories and in the nameless *hablador.*[32] Arguedas is the only Peruvian writer about whom Vargas Llosa repeatedly writes and teaches.[33]

During the 1960s and 1970s, local ethnologists were taking positions for and against interference from foreigners, including North American anthropologists who tended to idealize "native" cultures.[34] The standard line of thought, and of government programs from the 1930s to the 1960s, had favored a dynamic *mestizaje* that amounted to progress toward national integration, and objected to pristine indigenous cultures.[35] But progressive anthropologists in Vargas Llosa's generation, according to Enrique Mayer, accepted the Americans' respect for Andean continuity as welcome relief from the establishment's renewed denigration of Indians. It was conservative Peruvians such as Vargas Llosa, and his conservationist alter-ego Zuratas, who used anthropological romanticism to defend static and extreme distinctions between tradition and modernity; they were counterpoising "deep Peru" (doomed as backward and Indian) to "official Peru" (the modern and whitened future), and thereby getting the country into deep trouble, Mayer says.

Critics are right to say that Zuratas is driven by the same abstract language of cultural incommensurability that defines Vargas Llosa's dichotomous and inflexible politics. But the novel's indigenist hero is not simply a sentimental double for its writer. Saúl is also the novel's vehicle for lingering in "deep Peru" for as many pages as are devoted to the official country. Whatever rush toward modernity may be moving the plot and pushing Vargas Llosa's political pronouncements, whatever evacuation confronts us from the first page of picture-book Indians, the novel *performs* a parity of attention between tradition and modernity. It detains the rush for as long as we read. In fact, the "deep" and "official" lines will cross, in the crossover hero himself and in narrative threads that weave from one context to another. The borrowings bring back the Peruvian tradition of dialectical anthropology, even though the novel will frame the dynamism as contamination rather than adaptability. However Zuratas is framed, whether as the conservative's alter-ego or as a self-defeating dreamer, his indigenous world holds us throughout the novel. Through Saúl, Vargas Llosa seems reluctant to let it go, not just guilty of it.

While debates about "American" anthropology simmered during the 1960s, another North American interest in Peru was more explosive. The Summer Institute of Linguistics (SIL) outraged traditionalists who, like Saúl, railed against the "apostolic linguists." SIL had been founded in the early 1950s by evangelical Protestants from Oklahoma known as the Wycliffe Bible Translators (named for the fourteenth-century English translator) who shared McCarthy's anticommunist mission. From the beginning, SIL counted on support from USAID and the CIA to establish bases throughout the underdeveloped world.[36] Its declared purpose was to study indigenous languages; in fact SIL also established bilingual schools, vaccination campaigns, and introduced isolated peoples to an expanding market economy and state institutions, all of which pleased local governments. But SIL's most devout purpose, as everyone knew, was conversion. Indigenous languages mattered because they were potential vehicles for the Bible. The enterprise elicited conspiracy theories left and right. From these David Stoll culls some complicated details:

Wycliffe has fielded linguistic missionaries in more than 300 languages, supported by air and radio networks and sponsored by governments. Although it has started [in 1982] to lose government contracts . . . in the mid-1970s Wycliffe was an official arm of the governments of Mexico, Guatemala, Honduras, Panama, Surinam, Colombia, Ecuador, Peru, Bolivia and Brazil. Unless all the mission orders of the Roman Catholic Church were counted as one, no other transnational organization surpassed Wycliffe's influence among Indians. None matched its command of Indian languages and loyalties, its logistical system and official connections. Nor did any collide so spectacularly with Indian civil rights organizing and Latin American nationalism. The ties binding together this interior empire, to native people and to governments, started to snap.[37]

Local pressure strained SIL's delicate legitimacy, as the missionaries of God's truth kept telling strategic lies about their linguistic interests. "Then governments started to decide that SIL might be a useful sacrifice." They warned Washington that SIL's influence had limits, as a way of conceding to Indian and indigenist oppositions while maintaining control. In Peru, SIL's days seemed numbered until it was reprieved in 1976; Brazil issued an embargo against SIL in 1977, while Colombia threatened expulsion. And Mexico revoked its contract in 1979, followed by Panama in 1981; that same year Ecuador ordered it to leave within the year. "Each government faced the same, disquieting phenomenon: increasingly visible, militant Indian organizing. Indigenous nationalism was on the ascent, a trend to which, like a number of other brokers, SIL had contributed in largely unintended ways. Promotion of literacy, the trade language and inter-group contacts helped members of scattered local communities identify themselves as ethnic wholes."[38]

Accused of everything—from fronting for U.S. imperialism and misleading potentially Catholic souls, to fomenting Communist conspiracies—the linguists are the main concern of chapter IV in *El hablador*.[39] It is not that Catholic evangelists (so visible in *La casa verde* [1965]) were more benign, explains Saúl, but that they had fortunately become too isolated and impoverished to do much harm. By contrast, the Bible-belt evangelists had the resources to conquer peoples who had resisted everyone else, from the Incas to the colonizers and the capitalists.[40]

Vargas Llosa personalizes the history of the Summer Institute with accounts of his own visits (beginning in 1958) to an Amazonian camp, which are condensed from his writer's notes on *La casa verde*.[41] Despite warnings from the Hispanophile historian Raúl Porras Barrenechea about the nefarious influence of the meddling gringos, the narrator accompanied anthropologist José Matos Mar on an expedition organized for Juan Comas, a Mexican colleague. In his fictional persona, Matos is the mentor of an increasingly unwilling Saúl Zuratas, whose reluctance prefigures the general "third world" skepticism about ethnography's interests and interferences, as Edward Said describes it.[42] (Today's self-critical anthropology is one response.) Conversely, some missionaries respond to the moral dilemmas of saving souls by damning native religious identities with tolerance (or at least forbearance) of "specific, limited, cultures." Their mission can be preventive rather than acquisitive; it can be the obligation to bear witness in order to obstruct authoritarian power. "Not being able to speak for others, however, does not mean we have no obligation toward them."[43]

Other observers take liberties to speak. And one who spoke up for the Summer Institute's meddling was Mario Vargas Llosa. In 1976, seven years after the Soviet invasion of Czechoslovakia showed that Cuba was in dutiful step with the aggression, Vargas Llosa had long since abandoned socialist ideals. As he moved to ever more conservative positions, he found SIL in need of support. The novelist was grateful to the translators; their literal agility had helped him to write *La casa verde*. They were adept not only at moving from one language to another, but also at getting from one place to another inside the apparently impassable greenery. Vargas Llosa did his research among the forest dwellers with the help of the polyglots' airplanes.[44] Other outsiders had benefited too, he recalls, echoing Saúl's (and David Stoll's) list of ethically suspect allies: ethnologists, missionaries, teachers, and soldiers.[45] But Vargas Llosa still offered them his political support. In a public letter of April 25, 1976, he urged the Peruvian government to renew SIL's contract with the country. The linguists should be shielded from the suspicious indigenists, he declared. The government evidently agreed, thinking that if SIL were to leave, the institutions it had initiated could be overtaken by more dangerous groups, such as Communists and Indian organizers. The letter was published in the major papers of Lima and co-signed by 65 notable citizens, later seconded by 66 others. None of

these was a linguist, Stoll reports; and the few participating education offi-
cials, indigenists, and anti-Marxist academics hardly offset the number of
retired military leaders.[46]

But a dozen years later, and despite the echo of thanks to the linguists on
the back page of acknowledgments in *El hablador,* despite his alleged support for scientific investigation beyond "nativism,"[47] the dilemma about the
rights of translation had apparently revisited the troubled novelist. The return of the repressed is written into every aggressive photo that accosts his
narrator in Florence. During the interim between *La casa verde* and *El
hablador,* the world had turned, and anxieties once directed at the jungle
were now fixed on the Andes. From 1985 to 1987, while Vargas Llosa was
writing *El hablador,* Peru's political seams were splitting more dangerously
along the Andean mountain range than in the Amazonian basin. And the
Indians who now seemed most at risk, or themselves risky, were no longer
the tribesmen of the lowlands but the peasants of the Altiplano. Once the
Sendero Luminoso loosed confusion on the Andes, outside observers had
trouble distinguishing "revolutionary" terrorism from "official" military
abuses. Nor was it clear where the doubly imperiled indigenous communities stood politically. At that point it seemed safer to worry about Indians in
the jungle.

Displacement is a mechanism that Freud named to describe problems so
gravely threatening to the subject that they are routinely substituted by
peripheral signs. When an experience is too painful to remember and too
intense to forget, memory may replace that event with a related but inoffensive element. The process is metonymic, a sliding from the essential part of
that experience to "something in the neighborhood."[48] And in the general
neighborhood of the country, the most urgent problem was no longer in
Amazonia. Vargas Llosa's soul-searching and sympathy during the 1980s
might well have been displaced from the dangerous highlands onto the forgotten front in the jungle. How sobering, and sad, that a defensive mechanism like displacement finds no safe terrain in Peru, but only more or less
urgently troubled territory. In this self-conscious novel (or self-interpretive
in ways that preempt criticism), the text glosses or rationalizes the difference.
Saúl argues that Andean culture has been contaminated since the conquest,
and the faster it can be fully absorbed into the Peruvian nation the better for
the already marginalized Indians; but Amazonia is still unconquered and

independent. Absorption there, Saúl says, would bring only cultural death and ecological disaster.[49]

In the quiescent jungle, the novel's peace-loving Machiguengas are at first reticent to change, but then they become institutionalized in translation camps.[50] They had raised little resistance to the culturally annihilating good will of the foreign linguists, little resistance except for the hostile vagrancy of the storyteller. It is his aggressive anxiety that most distinguished him from the others, and it becomes the last piece of the novel's puzzle over the *hablador*'s identity.[51] During Mario's second visit to the missionaries' camp, where he is preparing a television special, rumors about a skittish and obscure ritual talker are far more fascinating to him than the "athletic" and well-scrubbed hosts who were translating the Machiguengas into transparency. Readers, of course, have been hearing the *hablador*'s ritualized narrative for several chapters, and don't doubt his existence. What is more, his identity had, for a long while, been coming into focus as the red-headed, blotchy-faced, mixed-breed Jew, a millennial martyr to Christianity's forced conversions. He used to be Saúl Zuratas.

Is it Saúl whom Mario anxiously anticipates as he looks through the fifty photos in Florence? After fixing on scenes of scarce, scattered, natives bent over their recent and meager crops, crouched among brilliant plumes for weaving crowns, and poised behind bow and arrow near a jungle river, Mario spots him "at first glance" *(a primer golpe de vista)*. A silhouette standing in profile and talking animatedly inside a circle of cross-legged, "hypnotically concentrated" Indians. What doubt can there be now? Mario has seen the real thing: "Un hablador."[52] The first chapter ends with this two-word gasp of recognition. The very next words, in evident apposition on a second reading, are "Saúl Zuratas." They begin chapter II, as well as the novel's pendular rhythm between the city and the *selva*.

TURN AROUND

For a while, though, the rhythm is detained. The narrative delays its exploration of exotic folklore, and it stays the flights of political reflection. It invites, or commands, readers to withstand, for a bit longer, the Amazonian gaze that accosts and commands the narrator and his readers, perhaps to his peril and to ours. It will take an effort of submission to another's will to stay here, because an unwillingness to stop may be the most flagrant symptom of our spiritually diminished modernity, as Stanley Cavell puts it. He calls attention to this dehumanizing loss of attention span in a classic essay on *King Lear*, "The Avoidance of Love." Relentless movement toward problems to be solved, toward anticipated developments and conclusions, all this dynamism rushes beyond presentness and its insoluble mysteries to impoverish modern art forms of music, theater, and narrative.[53] Vargas Llosa's missionaries of monotheism and modernity are named Schneil, by the way, and mentioned by name in Saúl's diatribe.[54] The name obviously seems a corruption of the German "quick," a heavy-handed image of modernizing assimilation and acceleration. In fact, Snell was the name of the real missionaries who translated and then published manageable condensations of Machiguenga lore.[55] Vargas Llosa took an orthographic liberty with the name, but history is already uncanny. Being quick and efficient, the translators have little capacity for the presentness that myth makes palpable, in the recursive recitation of lore. Without that capacity, the most binding human relationships come undone, Cavell complains. Even love can be avoided.

Vargas Llosa's first pages call for a temporary halt to modernity, a pause in the acquisitive and problem-solving movement through time to stare hypnotically into the mystery of lost presence. And the following pages, until the very last one, keep up the recursive rhythm that holds Florence in focus. Everything there, from the picture gallery to the mosquitos, returns the reader to Peru.[56] Arrested from the first page by photographs, in his exercise of a modern prerogative called escape, the narrator doubles back with surprise at seeing an object he had escaped transformed into the subject before him. Vargas Llosa had left Peru behind only to finds the country confronting him, defiantly, across the distance. To take a lead from the ironic "behold" in the opening line, it is almost like God confronting Jonah after the reluctant prophet tried to take a different route. Or, to follow up on the feeling of double-take, Peru may be more like that unrelenting cat in classic cartoons who is poised, ready to pounce, in the very room to which a desperate mouse had just escaped.

Face to face with the cat's demanding ubiquity, in response to its hunger and to the time-space bending enigma of its always being there before one arrives, a mouse is compelled to respond. And the responses to danger, to unsatisfiable demands, to the incommensurable differences between the cat and himself, constitute the mouse as a subject (like the vulnerable narrator who becomes a persona by stopping at Peru's call). Without the confrontation, what would either character be in the cartoon? A deconstructive reading could point to the constitutive overlaps between the agonists: the same turf, understanding conflict, the same desire for victory and survival. Without sharing so much there could be no cat and mouse conflict. On another, psychological, reading, the mutual imbrication of antagonists might have a developmental dimension, since the mouse has become what he is through a series of near cat-astrophes. And because there is no escaping what he is, the catastrophic fantasies accompany the mouse as a structural necessity of his character; a cat appears because the mouse practically conjures him in order to feel normally neurotic.

On one reading, and on the other, we should note that the constructions and imbrications are mutual. They are reflexive, in the sense that reciprocal verbs are reflexive; we see one another, for example. Whether the subjects of the story are called antagonists or, more benignly, interlocutors, an assumption of both deconstruction and of a particular psychological reading is a fundamental parity between the partners. Some years ago, deconstruction's ironizing project promised to democratize the polarized terms that structuralism had deployed almost inevitably in hierarchical relationships. It was liberating to see beyond the confining oppositions between male and female, black and white, self and Other, to see both into the mire of mutually dependent constructions, and into the corollary of destabilizing traces constitutive of meaning itself. This fundamental skepticism about the possibility of true meaning had a profound philosophical and even moral appeal. By denouncing the arrogance of knowing anything absolutely, it made an appeal to carefulness and circumspection.

The problem of course, for any democratic use of these insights, is that political difference is at risk, if difference seems universally constitutive of any terms and if all tensions relax into partnerships. If troubling barriers seem less important than the fissures that make barriers collapse, from what position does one make demands? The sticking point of an argument can get stuck in the rubble of collapsed categories. A more politically creative style of deconstruction might move from the cracks in one "language game" into another game, through political confrontation, to legal adjustment.

Acknowledging difference then would not be the final word, but a first step towards enabling ethical negotiations.

AND AROUND

Dynamic and meritorious, maybe even feasible, this unstuck (Wittgensteinian?) twist on deconstruction may be a promising lead for pursuing some readings and some politics.[57] But it has almost nothing to do with the opening lines of *El hablador*. There, relationship is not reflexive, in the reciprocal sense of mutually affective verbs and character constructions. Instead, one character is reflective, in both senses of the word: the narrator thinks hard about the Other he would have preferred to ignore, and he is made visible in the Other's light. Instead of partnership between the narrator and Peru, there is astonishment before an already existing, ubiquitously demanding agonist.

Rather than reciprocity, the opening lines offer an initiating asymmetry. What is staged is not a deconstructive struggle for meaning, nor a conspiracy to make meaning stable, but something close to a Levinasian face-to-face. It is a confrontation with an inscrutable face whose godlike stare frames the yet formless "hostage" in a demand for recognition. The very fact that the Other (country, cat, God) is there before us in time and space locks us into responsibility: "Diachrony is the refusal of conjunction, the non-totalizable, and in this sense, infinite. But . . . this commands me and ordains me to the other, to the first one on the scene, and makes me approach him, makes me his neighbor . . . It provokes this responsibility against my will, that is, by substituting me for the other as a hostage . . . it is the very fact of finding oneself while losing oneself."[58]

Hostage first, and persona as a consequence; the Other first, as a precondition for the response that constitutes a subject. The self as a byproduct; persona as response-able. With this dramatic reversal of subject-centered ontologies, Emmanuel Levinas wants to trap traditional philosophy in its ethical shortcomings. Like Vargas Llosa's narrator halted before Amazonian images, Levinas detains readers in front of a difference that doesn't go away. Since Socrates, he says, fundamentally developmentalist and aggressive Western ontology has welcomed difference as a challenge to be overcome and incorporated into the self. Difference has been an opportunity to quest for greater and deeper dimensions of one's own humanity.

> This primacy of the same was Socrates's teaching: to receive nothing of the Other but what is in me, as though from all eternity I was in possession of what comes to me from the outside—to receive nothing, or to be free. Freedom does not resemble the capricious spontaneity of free will; its ultimate meaning lies in this permanence in the same, which is reason. Cognition is the deployment of this identity; it is freedom. That reason in the last analysis would be the manifestation of a freedom, neutralizing the other and encompassing him, can come as no surprise once it was laid down that sovereign reason knows only itself, that nothing other limits it. The neutralization of the other who becomes a theme or an object—appearing, that is, taking its place in the light—is precisely his reduction to the same.[59]

"Philosophy is egology."[60] This is a stone that Levinas hurls against voracious reason. The uncharacteristic staccato rhythm is surely meant to shock us with lucid simplicity. Likewise, the issues related to respect for Otherness, and responsiveness as initiating behavior, are glaringly simple. Anyone who cares to get the point will do so in the first few pages of his two long books and his many essays. But readers who are driven to follow more intellectually complicated and therefore self-flattering routes manage to avoid the obvious, as Cavell and Stanley Fish remind us.[61] Readers do not necessarily stop at the signs of difference that command respect, so Levinas engages us there, for a long time. Like Vargas Llosa's circular novel, like the mythic time that preserves the Machiguengas, a dizzy reader finds that Levinas's text "marches neither forward nor backward: it goes around and around, repeats itself."[62]

Readers who stop to listen may gain a different kind of sensibility, a capacity for wonder at infinity. The switch might spoil the imperializing appetite for philosophical knowledge ("To know amounts to grasping *being* out of nothing or reducing it to nothing, removing from it its alterity"[63]), and leave room for an infinite, unsatisfiable, desire for the Other. Then social science would cede to sociability, and instrumentality to love. Saúl Zuratas made that move when he turned from anthropology to the people it presumes to study. "Surely more emotional than rational," Saúl's fascination with the Machiguengas is "an act of love rather than intellectual curiosity or the taste for adventure that seemed to lurk in the choice of career made by so many of his fellow students in the Department of Ethnology."[64] This possibility of disinterested identification is the liberating commitment that Enrique Dussel holds out for Latin America as a step beyond Levinasian awe of the absolutely Other.[65]

The "being," whose difference Levinas is loath to reduce, dissents profoundly from its Heideggerian homonym, which was written with a capital letter and pointed beyond people to a general, almost other-worldly, horizon between life and death. No less awe-inspiring for Levinas, is the "being" that resides in a particular human face, which is the ultimate horizon of our devotion and obligation. His transcendent ethics is rigorously grounded in worldly relationships; nothing is more holy, or more commanding, than a human being.

TURNING AWAY

This is one disturbing reason to remember the silhouette standing inside the enraptured circle of the Peruvian picture. It is the man's posture that is disturbing, vis-à-vis (but not face to face with) the camera. The photographer catches him sideways, looking at his listeners or at the jungle, in an obviously stolen shot. Probably warned by the traducing missionaries that the *hablador* would refuse to cooperate, as so many South American Indians refuse to be photographed and turn away from camera-toting tourists, the professional resorts to sharpshooting. And he produces gorgeous pictures, worthy of his best work with fashion models and furnishings for magazines like *Vogue* and *Uomo*. It is surely not the quality of the photos that earns him his fictional name of Malfatti. The pictures are well done, but malfeasance has produced them. Evidence of stealth is, as I said, one disturbing feature of the photo. ("How did that Malfatti get them to allow him to . . . How did he manage to . . .?").[66] Another worry is the very fact that the subject refuses to show his face.

The talker turns away from modernizers and missionaries. He makes no demand on the camera's eye, and none on the viewer from the Florentine gallery. The man who denies his face, thereby refuses to face either viewer or reader as a subject. He won't talk to outsiders because talking, he knows better than anyone else, works the social magic of acknowledging and legitimating one's interlocutors. The *hablador* is practically an allegorical figure for what Levinas calls the Saying. Saying is a sonorous appeal to the Other, more gripping than dynamic. The talker knows he can preserve an entire vulnerable society by continuing to talk. That is what makes us human, after all, as Wittgenstein would remind philosophers who were losing their way in technical languages and forgetting the commonality of words and their social contexts. The translatable "content" of what the talker says is not the main point of it.

The point is to appreciate the enabling enchantment of address. That is why the title character of the novel is the "talker," in Mrs. Schneil's tentative term, or "speaker," in Edwin Schneil's variation.[67] The word is something of a neologism that seems neutralized by the common "storyteller" of the English translation. Nevertheless, it may be wonderfully apt as a reminder of an obsolescent tradition, a premodern narrative practice that Walter Benjamin embraced in an essay called "The Storyteller." It is a tradition of sparse and suggestive tales told to groups, in contrast to modern novels that are written and read in private.[68] The distinction between storyteller and narrator is by now hard maintain in English, and even harder to hear in the existing Spanish words *narrador,* or *cuentero,* or *cuentista.* So Vargas Llosa forced a new use for *hablador.* He borrowed it from a colloquial expression in Spanish that characterizes unusual loquacity; but here, out of context, and used to name an anonymous, ceremonial locutor, *hablador* calls attention to its foreignness in European uses. *Escuchadores* is the equally uncommon, even clumsy, counterpart for those who hear the talk. *Oyente* would have been the standard Spanish word; it is as unremarkable as its English translation, "listener."[69] Vargas Llosa's use of these slightly strained terms had fixed attention on the socializing activity of talking and listening. He had emphasized the contact, as opposed to the content, the process, rather than what was being processed.

Given the arresting first sentence of the novel, in which Peru itself came out to confront the narrator, the cold shoulder from its most fascinating talker feels like an indictment. Startled into book-length reflections on the tragic heroism of indigenous cultures (reflections exhaustively interpreted and thematized in a novel that seems to make criticism superfluous), the narrator knows that he was the first to turn his back. Vargas Llosa, after all, is a runaway who had forfeited his chance for subjecthood (even in the Hegelian, pre-Levinasian, sense of being recognized by the Other) when he averted his eyes from the Amazon that his fellow student was bringing home. The narrator stared a bit then; but only later, when the jungle caught up with him, did he stare uncomfortably, unable to look away.

TOWARD JERUSALEM

Some years earlier, the novelist Mario Vargas Llosa publicly reminisced about another shock brought on by photographs, and about his helplessness in the face of unanswerable demands. The occasion was his acceptance speech of the Human Rights Award from the Congreso Judío Latinoamericano in 1977. At a time when dictatorship was the norm for the continent, his long address in Lima featured a roster of totalitarian abuses elsewhere, mostly by misguided socialist regimes abroad and, by extension, their misguided supporters at home. His theme of culturally and technologically advanced civilization that can develop devastating policies of homogenization and control begins, as one may imagine for this occasion, with the national socialism of Germany. Specifically, it begins with a personal memory. Two years before the speech, Vargas Llosa was in Jerusalem, where he was enjoying the city's rose-colored light and his distance from Peru. He was there not to think about persecution, or even to feel connected with the millennial culture that surrounded him, but to relax and to write *Aunt Julia and the Scriptwriter*. During the mornings that autumn, he would write in an apartment that looked out on the Tower of David, the Jaffa Gate, and hills on the horizon just beyond the Dead Sea.

> The vision was beautiful beyond reality and, in my case, it contributed every morning to accenting my sensation of being apart from the world. The story which I was trying to write had as its theme precisely the shifting of reality into unreality by means of melodrama. Since the story took place in Lima, thousands of miles from where I was, it

required a real effort to disconnect from my immediate surroundings. In that state of somnambulism, my friend found me, the friend who came every afternoon to show me around the city.[70]

That particular afternoon, the escort didn't take Vargas Llosa to the markets, or to streets that seemed like stage-sets for the *Arabian Nights;* he drove past Temple excavations, the orthodox quarters of Meah Shearim (the Hundred Gates), and the rest of the magical city. That afternoon, the writer remembers, "*the return to reality was brutal.* My friend took me to Yad Vashem, the memorial consecrated to the Holocaust, which rises on one of the pine-covered hills that circle Jerusalem."[71]

What was it, exactly, about the memorial, that startled him? It certainly was not the modern building, or the isolated setting, or even the knowledge that six million Jews were exterminated by the Nazis. Everybody knew that. The historical data about mass graves, advanced biological experiments on practically dead meat, artifacts hewn from human skin, teeth, and bones, these came into brutal focus through the pictures on the wall. "There, in front of the photos," Vargas Llosa was also facing Nazi horror and the world's complicity. (Holocaust images can be so disturbing, concluded John Frohmayer when he was chairman of the National Endowment of the Arts, that the general public should be protected from seeing them.)[72] But the novelist forces the confrontation in the 1977 human rights speech. Selected pictures frame the published text (on pages 6 and 16); a final image makes an undeniable demand on the viewer.

There is in Yad Vashem a photograph which, I am sure, everyone has seen at one time or another . . . It was taken after the destruction of the Warsaw Ghetto. The picture is of a little Jewish boy, only a few years old, stuffed into a cap too big for him and a coat that looks old, with his hands in the air. A German soldier, wearing a helmet and boots, is aiming at the boy with a short-barrelled rifle, and looking toward the photographer with that blank look they call martial. The soldier looks neither proud nor ashamed of his trophy. His face shows only tranquil indifference to the scene he is acting. In the boy's expression, on the other hand—in the sadness of his eyes, the constriction of his face distorted by fear, and the squeezed shoulders of a body that wants to disappear—there is a dizzying clarity about what that moment means.[73]

One scene of confronting photos and another cannot be a fortuitous parallel. The liberating distance from home that he hoped to enjoy in Jerusalem and in Florence, the haunting history memorialized in Yad Vashem and the picture gallery, the structurally sibling novels about narrative and historical contamination between modern reality and lines of escape—this cluster of coincidence suggests a corollary cluster of observations.

THROUGH DIASPORA

Half-Jewish Saúl becomes a figure for the Machiguengas for reasons beyond a general affinity between one marginalized group and another. He is more than a metaphor for the minority culture condemned to extinction by majoritarian redemption campaigns. For one thing, both nomadic tribes cling to, and are sustained by, ritually repeated narratives that amount to the Law. Diasporic Jews know, in a folk refrain, that "Torah is the best *skhorah* (merchandise)," because learning is one thing that cannot be confiscated. And oral—post-biblical—"Torah" is traditionally as important as is Scripture itself. For another thing, the Jew as *hablador* evokes a shared history of persecution. Had it kept the memory of horrible connections, the figure would have been a metonymy. The world that had stood by in disingenuous disbelief while extermination camps reduced Jews to smoke is the same world that stands by again, while Amazonian Indians are translated and traduced, and jungle is processed into slum.

To recover the metonymy turned metaphor is not to minimize the differences of fate and possible futures between one remnant of a people and another. But we might note that just as Peru's Indians have been demoted and displaced since the Spanish conquest, Jews were pushed out of Spain in the internal wars of the Reconquest. And like the Machiguenga misfits who are being squeezed deeper into the Amazon, perhaps to be squeezed out of conservative Peru, European Jews were at a loss to find a place almost anywhere in the Americas. During World War II, ships full of refugees were refused at American ports and sent back to German authorities. Even after the war, the Americas kept immigration quotas for survivors so inhospitably low that some waited for years in displaced persons' camps. Others managed to buy visas from the corrupt bureaucracies of Bolivia and Paraguay, while Ecuador and the Dominican Republic were officially hospitable to small numbers of refugees. Brazil took in larger numbers, but only later, after having barred "Semites" before and throughout the Nazi extermination.[74] Sometimes, without ever reaching their official destinations, the cosmopolites wandered off to centers of westernized economy and culture or remained stuck on the more active coastlands.

Mario banters about the last Peruvian indigenist being his friend, the Jew. But Saúl knows that he is a natural:

"Well, a Jew is better prepared than most people to defend the rights of minority cultures," he retorted. "And, after all, as my old man says, the problem of the Boras, of the Shapras, of the Piros, has been our problem for three thousand years."

Is that what he said? Could one at least infer something of the sort from what he was saying? I'm not sure. Perhaps this is pure invention on my part after the event. Saúl didn't practice his religion, or even believe in it. I often heard him say that the only reason he went to the synagogue was so as not to disappoint Don Salomón. On the other hand, some such association, whether superficial or profound, must have existed. Wasn't Saúl's stubborn defense of the life led by those Stone Age Peruvians explained, at least in part, by the stories he'd heard at home, at school, in the synagogue, through his inevitable contacts with other members of the community, stories of persecution and of dispersion, of attempts by more powerful cultures to stamp out Jewish faith, language, customs, which, at the cost of great sacrifice, the Jewish people had resisted, preserving their identity?[75]

Before I had read, or even known about, the Jewish Congress speech, before I could guess at any autobiographical link between photographs at Yad Vashem and Vargas Llosa's haunting book about Peru, I might have imagined that the novel was picking up a narrative design where Julio Cortázar had left it off, a design in which pictures of reality put a stop to artistic escape. In "Apocalypse in Solentiname," the last scene shows Cortázar back in Paris after a trip to Nicaragua. The slides he developed failed to show the fanciful primitive paintings by Nicaraguan peasants that had filled his camera frame; instead, the pictures played back the horrors of military repression that he had refused to see. Likewise, photos would force Vargas Llosa to look at an endangered people. The possibility of literary borrowing exists, no doubt. But when I had the opportunity to talk to Vargas Llosa about his novel, that suggestion seemed uninviting. Instead, I asked what had motivated his pairing of the Mosaic cult with the Machiguenga. Almost an idle query, it was meant to go elsewhere, perhaps into the pairing structure of the novel as an experiment in politically tolerant imaginings, despite the narrator's postsocialist skepticism about a future mosaic of Peruvian cultures.[76]

As for my question about the connection between Jews and Indians, the very leitmotifs of the novel give the obvious answers: the parallel marginalizations of Jews and Indians, the dangers of assimilation, their continuing survival thanks to a collective narrative (although the novel does not play this up. The point would, of course, have helped Vargas Llosa to spell out why he seems as taken with "the people of the Book" as with the Machiguengas). The narrator explains Saúl this way: "I believe that his identification with this small, marginal, nomadic community had—as his father conjectured—something to do with the fact that he was Jewish, a member of another community which had also been a wandering, marginal one throughout its history, a pariah among the world's societies, like the Machiguengas in Peru, grafted onto them, yet not assimilated and never entirely accepted."[77]

But the answer I got from Vargas Llosa was neither about obvious parallels nor about overlaps. It was, rather, the polar extremes of their difference, he said, that attracted him. The two peoples revive the kinds of social and geographic differences whose coordination was the heroic project of nineteenth-century national consolidation, a project inherited from colonial times.[78] Together, Indians and Jews represented Peru at its limits, like the geo-historical limits of dusty Piura in the north and the steamy jungle on the south side of the Andes that *La casa verde* barely braces together.[79] Primitive and poor Amazonian Indians and generally rich cosmopolitan Jews were at opposite ends of the country's population, he explained. And the novel was an effort to talk about Peru in the most inclusive and capacious way possible, from a focus on its demographic extremities.[80] Surprised by what I took to be an about-face from the intimacy of the vulnerable bedfellows I found in the book, and perhaps personally reluctant to pursue a line that cast Jews, once again, as extraneous to national constructions, the conversation hobbled onto other issues. Only now do I begin to appreciate Vargas Llosa's narrative reach. It went purposefully beyond mainstream Peru toward an idealized nation, whether one that opts for continuing the homogenizing Conquest that pursued Indians after it had finished with the Jews, or one that is obliged to halt its narrow drive for consolidation and open up into a capacious embrace.

TALK CHRISTIAN

Vargas Llosa, the political persona, evidently holds on to the culturally coherent focus. The hold is notorious in a 1983 document commissioned by Peru's President Balaúnde Terry. Appointed to lead an investigation into the death of eight reporters and photographers who were murdered in the Andean town of Uchuraccay, Vargas Llosa wrote up the collective report. His authoritative voice there gives the tone as well to an equally notorious journalistic version of the report called "Inquest in the Andes"[81] ("Historia de una matanza" in Spanish), which was published in the *New York Times.* The article itself, along with other details of Vargas Llosa's comportment, was an issue in a subsequent investigation. A skeptical provincial judge, Hermenegildo Ventura Huayhua, appointed to the case in November of 1984, grilled the urbane defendant about allegations of official cover-up for military malfeasance and governmental complicity.[82]

In the *Times* article, Vargas Llosa recalled early speculations that blamed the Sendero Luminoso for this latest act of terrorism, in keeping with other acts they had perpetrated against Indians, police, tourists, and now reporters; these were speculations that the newspapers were dying to develop. But the evidence that the Commission gathered, of ritual mutilations and the victims' distinctive burial positions, indicted the "innocent" Indians themselves. Skeptics wondered, because although the residents of Uchuraccay were known to take reprisals against guerrilla terrorism, and were therefore capable of collective violence, their action had always been a response to clear abuse. Moreover, the peasants were clearly outgunned on both sides, by the military and by the guerrillas. And since the signs of violence against the newspapermen differed from the Sendero's typical traces, suspicion fell upon the notoriously aggressive and insecure armed forces. The army was new to the area, sent to replace the openly abusive police, and it was just as new to the rigors of legitimate authority. Suspicious too was the fact that each of the Indians who testified in the case turned up dead soon after the

Commission had absolved the authorities. Later reports, and the incriminating photographs that Vargas Llosa managed not to face, confirmed that neither the killings nor the burials showed any signs of Andean ritual. Instead, bodies were found in pairs, wrapped in plastic and buried in lowlands to promote decomposition, the way North American soldiers buried the Viet Cong.[83]

The Commission's report had speculated about various motives and scenarios. Oddly, it affirmed them all. Maybe the Indian residents had decided to keep all white men away from their community, imagining that Sendero's encroachments were no different in kind from others; maybe they were especially incensed or terrified by the photographers, who didn't bother to hide from their subjects (it was much harder to hide on the Altiplano than in Amazonia). Vargas Llosa even takes seriously a careless quip by General Roberto Clemente Noel, military commander of the counterinsurgency, who said that the Indians probably couldn't tell a camera from a gun.[84] In any case, the Indians' alleged failure to distinguish between professionals and delinquents, and the Spanish speakers' failure to fully understand their Quechua informants (though two of the victims also spoke Quechua), bring Vargas Llosa to the conclusion that incomprehension is deadly and dead-ended. The Indians will simply have to become real Peruvians, to "talk Christian" in Spain's enduring jargon of the Reconquest, because the difference is paid too dearly in white and mestizo blood. Indians will finally have to assimilate into a modern state built upon Western principles of democratic responsibility.

The conjectures about ritual murders would later take on more fabulous proportions, in the 1993 novel *Lituma en los Andes,* in which the benighted but lovable army lieutenant takes almost four hundred pages to figure out why his host village has been safe from the Sendero.[85] The implicit absolution of the army is one measure of the distance between this novel and *El hablador,* in which memories of "civilized" savagery by militia men and mercenaries against Indian leaders revived the horrors detailed in *La casa verde.*[86] On his way out of the mining town, now a ghost town without metal or men, Lituma can hardly control his nausea. He has finally solved the mystery of missing bodies, sacrifices to a decaying culture of drunken homosexuality and ritualized cannibalism that appeases pre-Incan gods.[87] In the novel, homosexuality is a figure for cannibalism, as if one invasion of the flesh opens irreversibly onto the other. Vargas Llosa's willful version of Andean practices is no doubt a metaphor to capture a country turned against itself, but his poetic freedom takes dangerous liberties.[88] They recall his Commission report, both its allegations of Indian barbarism and its vindication of the army.

Homosexuality evidently disturbs Vargas Llosa the novelist.[89] It disturbs the journalist too, as when he fretted about the "Rainbow Crusade" in a piece that chronicles the Gay Rights March on Washington on April 25, 1993. He notes that the democratizing effects of gay activism are now irreversible in the United States, where sexual politics has practically eclipsed other concerns. But the price of legitimacy for that "perverse" population of apparently normal citizens who thronged to the capital and represented far greater numbers, could be, he warned, the desexualization of sex. Without some secrecy, without the titillation of almost unspeakable urges or the discreet dangers that whet desire, sex threatens to stop being fun, at least for Vargas Llosa. "Gays and lesbians might come to discover at the end of their efforts to be recognized and considered 'normal' that, once the transgressive character of their sexual choice has disappeared, it has lost, if not all, then a good part of its reason for being. Totally 'normalized' sex ceases to be sex."[90]

Similar objections to banal homosexuality in the United States had been raised by Reinaldo Arenas, in the book he finished before ending his own AIDS-ridden life.[91] But why should Vargas Llosa be ruffled, and even defensive, about the democratizing "perversities" that the "Rainbow Crusade" chose to flaunt? In the article, he stays carefully uncontaminated by Arenas's sympathies. Careful to write himself into the company of his wife during the march, and cautious in his conversations with activists, Vargas Llosa seems to safeguard against any possible implication of self-interest in the homoerotic debates between ludicism and legitimacy. Hardly at stake here are the violent intimacies that Vargas Llosa's fictional men visit on their women in one novel after another, including *Lituma*. In the heterosexual love story of its subplot, the prostitute-heroine is "saved" from a scene of mock abuse when her naive hero shoots the client who was paying her to plead for her life between desperate screams. Hardly in danger from the demands of the march, I am saying, are Vargas Llosa's titillating representations of remunerated abuse, or the almost ritualized rape we get in *The War of the End of the World*, or the range of heterosexual tussles that evidently excite his fiction and fantasy. Vargas Llosa's discomfort at the Gay Rights March, therefore, seems unfounded on the alleged grounds that it secularizes sex, if heterosexuality remains, as Foucault said of the Victorians, discreetly underrepresented in political arenas. (More obviously threatening is the notorious incident of Lorena Gallo Bobbitt who castrated an abusive husband.)[92] The uneasiness, perhaps, hovers around homoeroticism itself, not around a loss of intimacy but a loss of shame.

The shame of sexual perversity in *Lituma* is, as I said, an irreversible step toward the ultimate perversion, as physical contact translates into a more perverse "communion": the baneful banquet of blood and flesh from sacrificial bodies. "'Everyone had communion and, although it disgusted me, I did too,' said the worker, stumbling over himself, 'That's what's screwing me up. The mouthfuls I swallowed.'"[93] The cult's bar-tending and prostituting priests are Dionisio and Adriana, declensions of their Greek namesakes, as the town named Naccos is a corruption of Naxos,[94] and perhaps a hint of Soccos, site of a massacre by the police in 1983.[95] The explicit analogies between one primitive cult and another call to mind Garcilaso de la Vega's comparison between the heathen pre-histories of Europe and Peru. We should not be surprised, he says, by the spottiness or by the fabulous quality of founding Incan fictions. Are not the first murmurs of Old World civilization equally faint, and their fables just as laughable?[96] In both the Greek and the pre-Incan cases, barbarous practices of cannibalism and promiscuity were what civilization had wisely conquered. The problem in *Lituma* is that heathen remnants still function. The detective story ends with the frustration of having learned too much, namely, that horror outstrips any hope of overcoming it. "I regret having been so stubborn about finding out what happened to them. Better to have stayed suspicious."[97] Knowing is dangerous for the detective himself, in Lituma's epistemological trap. His is a tale of self-preservation. How different this is from the epistemological problem that plagues *El hablador*. There, knowledge threatens to neutralize difference, to cannibalize the "primitive" Other into the insatiable sameness of modernity. The danger is ethical in nature, about the ravages we modernizers wreak on others; while for Lituma, in stark contrast, worry is self-centered in a world not modernized enough.

The unhappy hero descends toward the coast and hopes not to remain haunted. The novel groans at a political impasse, but the greater effect is a sigh of fatigue. Peru's predicament is inherited, perhaps insoluble. It is not merely that the Europeans never finished the job of consolidating the country. It is also that the Incas failed in their preparatory work. Barbarism stubbornly persisted in "many regions never conquered by the Incas, and is still today found in many places conquered by the Spaniards," grumbled Garcilaso.[98] In gory detail, he quotes the mestizo Jesuit Blas Valera, who encounters cannibalism mostly in the unconquered jungle, far away from Incan practices; but his care to distance the taste for human blood from the highland of Peru removes it suspiciously as far as Mexico, where it was a staple of urban life and possibly an influence on other urbane Indians. "They performed these sacrifices of men and women, lads and children by opening their breasts while they were still alive and plucking out their hearts and lungs. The idol that had bidden the sacrifice was then sprinkled with still-warm blood."[99] By the time Lituma abandons the mountains that gobble up men in avalanches, mud slides, and demonic lusts (by the time Vargas Llosa himself leaves Peru), the authorities have to admit that they cannot gauge, or even stomach, the degree of unfinished business.

GUILTY CHOICES

The self-conscious narrator of *El hablador* feels far less victimized than does Lituma. The Vargas Llosa who doubled back from Florence to Peru suggested lingering complicities with an ethnic disappearing act. His country's campaigns to "reduce Indians" to civilization (in Garcilaso's language), through a history that runs from Manco Cápac's Incan foundations to Lituma's farce, pause and lose their way amid the jungle talk. Here, Vargas Llosa's writing takes a step back from the journalistic problem-solving of "Inquest in the Andes," where it was requiring that misfits be made to fit, and takes a step down from the Andes to the Amazon. From there, stretching our view to the limits of Peru's peripheral vision, the probing fiction of *El hablador* deliberately stages a coincidence between peoples that are the country's polar opposites, as if they mattered most as indices of the country's humanity. But the impulse of solidarity, in this fantasy about Jews and Indians, is also a sure index of their shared danger as paralyzed civilizations. We the bystanders share the guilt of passive association with their oppressors, of unresponsiveness, and nonacknowledgment, in Cavell's term.

In the speech framed by Yad Vashem, Vargas Llosa says that Jerusalem's Holocaust memorial tells the story of "Good, educated, gentle citizens of an ancient country who one day turned into wild animals, lunging at defenseless victims, or letting others do the dirty work for them, while the surprised and stupid world stared complicitously. And that is Yad Vashem's terrible accusation; it is directed against not one, but all, countries."[100] Vargas Llosa's novel, a decade after the speech, would writhe in the guilt-ridden hyperconsciousness of collusion. Novels can make these admissions with impunity, cynics may be saying. Fiction's reckless lucidity and breast-beating histrionics can act out a self-criticism that doesn't demand redress. If the novel turns out to have a tragic shape, it may make us suffer; but it lets us off in the end, exhausted with grief, and relieved to have finished.

The essay is a different form, at least in the case of Vargas Llosa's essays about the Indian question, from the "Inquest" to his 1990 presidential campaign and its aftermath. His essays take sides. The status of Indians in Peru has been perhaps *the* most burning question since independence, since the Spanish conquest, in fact. It began when Quechua chroniclers contested Spanish authorities, and it continued with the rash of seventeenth- and eighteenth-century uprisings that delayed cautious creoles from proclaiming independence. From the nineteenth century on, liberal programs in law and literature have striven to incorporate Indians, programs that produced novels like Narciso Aréstegui's *El Padre Horán* (1848), Clorinda Matto de Turner's *Aves sin nido* (1889), José María Arguedas's classic *Los ríos profundos* (1957), culminating in the indigenized Marxism of Mariátegui's slogan "Peruanicemos al Perú," the title of a posthumous collection.[101] Like the 1983 report on the "Inquest in the Andes," Vargas Llosa's post-election essay, "Questions of Conquest: What Columbus Wrought, and What He Did Not,"[102] takes sides to affirm the value of a coherent country. The essay became Chapter 2 of *A Writer's Reality* (1991),[103] without the first page that had marked it as an occasional piece.

The occasion was his response to a press conference held in Madrid by "a shadowy group calling itself the Association of Indian Cultures" that was preparing acts of sabotage in Spain and throughout Latin America to protest the planned celebrations of Columbus' quincentennial conquest.[104] The threats made at that conference were, for Vargas Llosa, fixed in the past, misguided as "means of achieving justice, or self-determination." To him they were obviously inspired by the same kind of fanaticism that was making Peruvian terrorists blow up their country along a Shining Path. In fact, the media blitz from Madrid continued mostly through the media, in demonstrations and in spectacular "sabotage" of the Columbus celebrations. Nevertheless, and despite what he considers to be self-defeating efforts at self-determination, Vargas Llosa impugns his own Hispanized culture when he asks: "Why have the postcolonial republics of the Americas—republics that might have been expected to have deeper and broader notions of liberty, equality, and fraternity—failed so miserably to improve the lives of their Indian citizens? Even as I write, not only the Amazonian rain forests but the small tribes who have managed for so long to survive there are being barbarously exterminated in the name of progress."[105] He gives no answers that could lead to reversals of the failure, or to relief from guilt. "We, the westernized Latin Americans, have persevered in the worst habits of our forebears," he continues. "We must remember that in countries like Chile and Argentina, it was during the Republic, not during the colony, that the native cultures were systematically exterminated."[106] But it is useless, concludes Vargas Llosa, to speculate about whether the conquest was a good thing or bad. What is significant is simply that the conquest happened, which is to say, in the narrative logic of things past, that it was historically necessary.

What are we to do now? This is a different kind of question from the one about redress of past sins. By pointing nowhere, this essay erases the politics of indigenous rights, including efforts to achieve autonomy, a politics that would break up Vargas Llosa's imagined community of Peru. This putative "nowhere" in fact marks a dynamic "somewhere" in which non-Western strains of culture and politics have a distinguished national history, from the indigenous chroniclers of conquest through to the Indian organizations spurred by SIL's meddling. So the question of amends is silenced, along with the possibility of lessons to be learned from historical blunders. The argument skips, with no apparent textual motivation, to present programs. There is nothing to be done, Vargas Llosa concludes, but sorrowfully to choose modernization, as if Indian traditions were incapable of adaptation. Referring to the anguish scripted into *El hablador*, he admits, "It is tragic to destroy what is still living, still a driving cultural possibility, even if it is archaic; but I am afraid we shall have to make a choice." That is, to sacrifice the Indian cultures,[107] since they interfere with modernity's fight against hunger and need. The line of argument has now made two skips: first by eliding any consequence to the question about the West's failures regarding Indians; and now moving from choices that Indians face to choosing for them. Of course, Vargas Llosa had already noted that leaders of Latin American republics inherited reprehensible traits from their forebears.

Choice is the pivotal concept on which his essay turns. It is the apparently non-ideological axis on which the individual can turn. But in Peru the words "choice," "individuality," and "freedom" are part of an abstract and inflexibly "ideological" vocabulary that paralyzes political debate, because the abstraction doesn't acknowledge dissent, as critics of Vargas Llosa have complained.[108] Abstraction allies with repression to prevent dialogue, just as the self-interpretive passages in *El hablador* act to preclude more interpretation. In both genres, Vargas Llosa tries to fix the delicate anthropological balance between observer and participant into the noncontested collusion between witness and judge, a move that had raised suspicions about his Uchuraccay report. The collapse of ethics into pragmatics confuses authoritarian means with allegedly liberal (free market) ends, according to William Rowe.[109] What gets lost in the crush, Mirko Lauer points out, is liberalism as a form of politics that defends individual freedom.[110] Vargas Llosa exercises his own freedom by making authoritative choices for others. He tends to speak for them in general. Even in the Commission's report, witnesses in Uchuraccay lose their voices to mediating "experts" who truncate sentences and translate the peasants away.[111]

Indian words won't fit into the "official" nation, Vargas Llosa laments. "Perhaps there is no realistic way to integrate our societies other than by asking the Indians to pay that price."[112] Personal freedom is at the heart of Western culture, and it was the magic charm that allowed a handful of willful Spaniards to topple Amerindian empires, according to Vargas Llosa. Hosts of disciplined and suicidally obedient soldiers were at a loss for what to do, after the Inca was taken hostage. Overlooking the forty years of resistance under four successive Incas,[113] Vargas Llosa alleges that rather than run, or fight, or decide on any move at all, the Indians allowed themselves to be slaughtered. Personal initiative, voluntary and self-determining capacities in the face of the unexpected, these characterize Western, or modern, subjects. Freedom is not only a liberating slogan from the French Revolution on; it is also the voluntarism of the conquest's most crass and criminal agents. Still, Vargas Llosa celebrates it as the West's greatest contribution to static and hierarchical cultures. "The first culture to interrogate and question itself, the first to break up the masses into individual beings who with time gradually gained the right to think and act for themselves, was to become, thanks to that unknown exercise, *freedom,* the most powerful civilization in our world."[114]

Could the skips in his argument be symptoms of bad faith? Do they recall his unacknowledged nervousness about homoeroticism? The doubt follows in the wake of inexplicable contradictions. On the one hand, if Western voluntarism was devastating to Indians, both because they were unaccustomed to making choices and because the Spaniards insisted on choosing for them, what justifies making more sorrowful choices for others? And on the other hand, if the essay's point is to show the enabling virtues of freedom and self-determination, why do Indian initiatives seem so pointless when they write history, or take over bilingual schools and establish autonomous institutions? In the absence of answers, Vargas Llosa sees no dearth of solutions.

The contradiction here is not just personal or Peruvian. It is practically constitutive of modern cultures. In the language of political philosophy, it is the disparity between (Lockean) liberty and (Rousseauvian) rights to free access. To a great degree, the difference between them is what motivates modern history, its conflicts and negotiations. Emmanuel Levinas refuses to get caught up in the action. He would agree that freedom is at the core of Western culture; that is why he targets it for attack in his argument about philosophy having bulldozed alterity into sameness. Freedom, for Levinas, is not simply *available* for abuses, not merely given to skipping from negotiation to conquest; it is the very *vehicle* of abuse and recklessness. The same caution that focuses the dilemma in Vargas Llosa's novel now haunts the discussion of his essay. "Freedom, [Levinas had said] has its ultimate meaning in this permanence in the same, which is reason . . . That reason in the last analysis would be the manifestation of a freedom, neutralizing the other and encompassing him, can come as no surprise once it was laid down that sovereign reason knows only itself, that nothing other limits it."[115]

The ravages of subject-centered freedom, the raids on difference led by a tautological reason that presumes, potentially, to comprehend, literally to contain, everything, these are the dangers that *El hablador* exposes in Peru's drive towards modernity. Vargas Llosa's programmatic pronouncements take sides, as I said; but the unconnected dots in "Questions of Conquest" link up to show the scars of an ethical wound that had worried the narrator of his novel. Vargas Llosa's critics don't hesitate to connect those dots.[116]

HALTING AND HAUNTED

The most trenchant critic of them all, however, may be the one who narrates *El hablador;* more precisely, he is the writer who doubled himself through the novel: as the troubled tourist in Italy and as the traditional talker of the alternating chapters. Saúl asked Mario why thinking about the *habladores* gave him goose-bumps. " 'They're a tangible proof that storytelling can be something more than mere entertainment,' it occurred to me to say to him. 'Something primordial, something that the very existence of a people may depend on.' "[117] Both narrators turned their backs on Peru: one with weariness, the other with purpose. Both know the power of narrative, even if the essayist Vargas Llosa makes bitter jokes about the connection between literature and political life after the 1990 election defeat. Is this why a possibly self-serving novelist sometimes holds back from the modernity that loosens the social grip of stories, while the essayist rushes forward to modernize? The Latin American habit of mixing fiction and reality, he banters, is one reason "why we are so impractical and inept in political matters."[118] And both storytellers know that presuming to understand the Other willfully ignores the mystery of his Saying; it razes difference and replaces it with the same. "Learn the aboriginal languages! What a swindle! What for? To make the Amazonian Indians into good Westerners, good modern men, good capitalists, good Christians of the Reformed Church? Not even that. Just to wipe out their culture, their gods, their institutions off the map and corrupt even their dreams."[119]

Vargas Llosa's novel displays the flair for self-criticism that the essay's claim dignifies Western culture. Bartolomé de las Casas is his best example of "those nonconformists"[120] who turned their backs on adventure in order to face Indians. We know, although Vargas Llosa doesn't say, that blind spots obstructed Las Casas's view; even the successful evangelizations and the liberalizing laws that he championed were, in the spirit of *El hablador*'s radical indictment of encroachment, travesties against the Indians. His most laudable work was probably not programmatic or problem-solving; it was the published stories of death and devastation, so overwhelming that many Spanish readers simply dismiss Las Casas as a madman or a liar. No doubt he exaggerated some things and misremembered others. But the glaring truth is that only one generation after the Discovery, so few Indians were left in the Caribbean that, to save the remnant, a man like Las Casas would promote African slavery only to rue it later. His "fiction" confronts the facts of conquest, even though his policies negotiated with conquerors. Las Casas was one inspiration for Andrés Bello, when the dean of nineteenth-century education advised young historians to train themselves on the personal narratives and fictionalized accounts of Latin America's past. They were truer in spirit than the professional histories.[121]

The spirit of Las Casas's stories implicates his readers. No wonder some Spaniards tried to discredit him. Their entire country is the targeted reader in the question of conquest and its aftermath. It almost doesn't matter if Las Casas himself is vindicated or condemned, because the text survives as an indictment of general complicity. Instead of judging his text, readers are invited to judge themselves. Vargas Llosa's novel survives his essays in the way that Las Casas' history survives pedantry. *El hablador* can bring some critics to decry the author's fatalism about Amazonian cultures, so apparently doomed from the first page of the novel.[122] And some can call him cynical, alleging that the novel repeats his patronizing lament over cultures that refuse to be redeemed from primitivism and poverty, that it dismisses Indians' "utopian" efforts to plot a self-determined future.[123] One could say of Mario Vargas Llosa what Angel Rama commented about José María Arguedas as ethnologist: the novelist has sometimes been overshadowed by the politician. Whether unsympathetic critics complain about fatalism or about aggressive dismissal, they read the novel like formalists, from its tragic ending backward toward a general meaning.[124] Bakhtin, of course, cautioned against reading novels reductively and retrospectively, because the "genre" defies fixed forms; to fix on a novel's closure is to lose sight of its experimental risks and specificity. It reduces wonder to legible signs and flattens difference into sameness.

The reduction allows us to turn away from the book, like the disingenuous readers of Las Casas who prefer to quibble about numbers of Indians massacred and dates of devastations than to get the glaring point. And the point of Vargas Llosa's Amazonian novel is our general complicity with the cultural extermination campaigns. Our uncontainable modernity expands in concentric circles, turning peripheries into reflections of the center. *El hablador* doesn't simply dissolve into a classical tragedy and catharsis. Detained for many pages, readers rehearse the narrator's turn toward Peru once the country takes him hostage and refuses to let go. At the end of the novel, Mario knows that the country occupies him. Through the friend who defends particular traditions against homogenizing modernity, a vision of Peru "opens my heart more forcefully than fear or love has ever done."[125] The very last words admit that all lines of escape would be futile. "But tonight I know that wherever I might wander—on the ocher stone bridges over the Arno, . . . I will still hear, close by, unceasing, crackling, immemorial, that Machiguenga storyteller."[126]

We have heard that voice too, and perhaps because cultural *convivencia* was never really an option for the modern West,[127] readers remain caught inside the doubled Spanish-Machiguenga narrative. In Vargas Llosa's "Questions of Conquest" too, Peru is "an artificial gathering of men from different languages, customs, and traditions whose only common denominator was having been condemned by history to live together without knowing or loving each other."[128] He repeats the complaint after the Sendero's Abimael Guzmán leader, is captured in September of 1992: unlike other Latin American countries, where *mestizaje* and middle-class mobility helped to heal historical wounds, Peru stays schizophrenic.[129]

El hablador performs the doubling act without diagnosing it as schizophrenia. The duality is a source of both concern and of hope. It can lead to dismissing indigenous otherness as inassimilable and inessential to the Peruvian body politic. Yet as the narrator confronts the Other, the endless but intimate stand-off also holds out a hope. It is the possibility of recognition—on a reading from this geographic remove—even if the promise is betrayed by the man called Vargas Llosa.

The fact is that the confrontation he stages generates an unresolved tale that stops to look, learns to listen, and dares to love. It loves selflessly, through a narrator whose face is the color of an open wound. The novel stares, uncomprehendingly perhaps, but respectfully, at the Other. A voyeur like Malfatti ends badly here; mediated by his camera and motivated by self-interest, he is literally a victim of jungle fever. Along with him, all of us selfish visitors are contaminated by the contact. But after the reading ends, the novel may survive, hauntingly, like the talker who will accost Vargas Llosa beyond the very last line: ". . . I will still hear, close by, unceasing, crackling, immemorial, that Machiguenga storyteller."[130] Or, like the little Jewish boy—lost in his cap and very present in his lucidity—pictures and sounds from the novel may survive to haunt a range of readers.

What do we do with a hostage imagination? This is the question that Dussel demands of Levinas. Perhaps we will plan our escape to magical cities. And maybe we'll stop there, at museums erected to the boy's memory. It may even be possible that we will pause for a while, in our translations of living areas like Amazonia into empty, available, space for more of the same modernity. Can we also imagine some creative responses to jungle talk? They would go beyond the paralyzing awe that grips Vargas Llosa the narrator, and they would break out of the brittle redundancy that dooms the Other talker. Real responses would also stop short of the cultural conquest demanded by Vargas Llosa the politician. Creativity can come after the speechlessness of first confrontations and before the murderous monolingualism of final solutions. It can come inside experiments like *El hablador,* where the novelist Vargas Llosa has been engaging us, patiently, in the slippery space that moves back and forth from one permeable language to another.

NOTES / ACKNOWLEDGMENTS / INDEX

NOTES

ADVERTENCIA/WARNING

1. Particularism is a word I borrow from historians to name cultural embedded-ness in experience and circumstance. It was also a favorite term for New Critics, but for them it denoted inimitable originality available for universal appreciation.

2. See, for example, Richard A. Lanham's useful *Handlist of Rhetorical Terms,* 2nd ed. (Berkeley: University of California Press, 1991); Amelie Rorty, *Essays on Aristotle's Rhetoric* (Berkeley: University of California Press, 1996).

3. Toni Morrison, "Unspeakable Things Unspoken: The Afro-American Presence in American Literature," in *Michigan Quarterly Review,* 28, 1 (1989): 1–34.

4. This is the gambit that Sacvan Bercovitch theorizes in "Games of Chess: A Model of Literary and Cultural Studies," in *Centuries' Ends, Narrative Means,* ed. Robert Newman (Stanford: Stanford University Press, 1996), pp. 15–57.

5. See Henry Louis Gates, Jr. on "signifying" in *The Signifying Monkey: A Theory of Afro-American Literary Criticism* (New York: Oxford University Press, 1988), and Stanley Fish on Milton's victimization of readers in *Surprised by Sin: The Reader in 'Paradise Lost'* (New York: St. Martin's Press, 1967).

6. "Strategies of containment" is a term from Fredric Jameson's *The Political Unconscious: Narrative as a Socially Symbolic Act* (Ithaca: Cornell University Press, 1981), where it refers to neutralizations of political energy. Here I use it to name defenses of political difference.

1. A RHETORIC OF PARTICULARISM

1. "Hablemos el mismo idioma" from Estefan's very successful CD *Mi tierra;* music and lyrics by Gloria Estefan and Emilio Estefan Jr. (Foreign Imported Productions and Publications, 1993).

2. Catherine Clément, *Syncope: The Philosophy of Rapture,* foreword by Verena Andermatt Conley, trans. Sally O'Driscoll and Deirdre M. Mahoney (Minneapolis: University of Minnesota Press, 1994), pp. x, 4.

3. For an excellent review of the sociological literature, see Juan Flores, "Pan-Latino/Trans-Latino: Puerto Ricans in the 'New Nueva York,'" in *Centro* (Journal of the Center for Puerto Rican Studies), 8, 1/2 (1996): 171–186.

4. Etienne Balibar, "Racism as Universalism," in *Masses, Classes, and Ideas,* trans. James Swenson (New York: Routledge, 1994), pp. 191–204. See also Marc Shell's excellent *Children of the Earth: Literature, Politics, and Nationhood* (New York: Oxford University Press, 1993).

5. See Seyla Benhabib, *Situating the Self: Gender, Community and Postmodernism in Contemporary Ethics* (New York: Routledge, 1992), pp. 3, 5. See also Richard Rorty, *Objectivity, Relativism, and Truth* (New York: Cambridge University Press, 1991), esp. p. 13.

6. Mari J. Matsuda, "Voices of America: Accent, Antidiscrimination Law, and a Jurisprudence for the Last Reconstruction," *Yale Law Journal,* 100, 5 (1991): 1329–1407.

7. Theodor W. Adorno, *Negative Dialektic* (Frankfurt: Suhrkamp, 1966), p. 172. The greedy subject is Freud's formulation. See also Diana Fuss, *Identity Papers* (New York: Routledge, 1996).

8. Jessica Benjamin, "The Shadow of the Other (Subject): Intersubjectivity and Feminist Theory" *Constellations,* 1, 2 (1994): 245.

9. For example, Richard Rorty dismisses "culture politics" on the grounds, paradoxically, that it is dismissive of real political engagement. See his Massey Lectures at Harvard University, March, 1997. See also Naomi Schor, *Bad Objects: Essays Popular and Unpopular* (Durham: Duke University Press, 1995), p. xiv, warning of "the perils of particularism and the dangers of separatism that are beginning to show through."

Nevertheless, in "French Feminism is a Universalism," *differences,* 7 (1995): 16–47, Naomi Schor defends American particularist politics. She ends by citing Derrida's exhortation in *The Other Heading,* trans. Pascale-Ann Branet and Michael B. Naas (Bloomington: Indiana University Press, 1992) to respect the universality of law, without relinquishing one's right to difference.

10. Emmanuel Levinas, *Totality and Infinity: An Essay on Exteriority,* trans. Alphonso Lingis (Pittsburgh: Duquesne University Press, 1969), pp. 57–58: "The real must not only be determined in its historical objectivity, but also from interior intentions, from the secrecy that interrupts the continuity of historical time. Only starting from this secrecy is the pluralism of society possible."

Jean-François Lyotard, "The Other's Rights" in *On Human Rights: The Oxford Amnesty Lectures 1993,* eds. Stephen Shute and Susan Hurley (New York: Harper Collins, 1993), pp. 136–147. To share dialogue with *you* requires a moment of silence, "and that silence is good. It does not undermine the right to speak. It teaches the value of that right," p. 142.

11. See Neil Gotanda, "A Critique of 'Our Constitution Is Color-Blind'" *Stanford Law Review*, 44, 1 (1991): 1–68. Citing Robert Paul Wolff, Gotanda defends racial-cultural diversity as a positive good in the polity. He also quotes Justice Brennan, whose decision in *Metro Broadcasting v. FCC* draws from *Regents of University of California v. Bakke:* "Just as a 'diverse student body' contributing to a 'robust exchange of ideas' is a 'constitutionally permissible goal' on which a race-concious university admissions program may be predicated, the diversity of views and information on the airwaves serves important First Amendment values. The benefits of such diversity are not limited to the members of minority groups . . . ; rather, the benefits redound to all members of the viewing and listening audience" (p. 57).

12. Ernesto Laclau, "Universalism, Particularism and the Question of Identity," in *The Identity in Question,* ed. John Rajchman (New York: Routledge, 1995), pp. 93–108, quote from p. 107. Judith Butler cautiously agrees that universality can be a site of translation. See Seyla Benhabib, Judith Butler, Drucilla Cornell, Nancy Fraser, *Feminist Contentions: A Philosophical Exchange* (New York: Routledge, 1995), p. 130.

See also Butler's "Sovereign Performatives in the Contemporary Scene of Utterance," forthcoming in *Critical Inquiry,* where she argues for the efficacy of "performative contradictions," a term Habermas had used to discredit Foucault's critique of reason via reason. See Jürgen Habermas, *The Philosophical Discourse of Modernity,* trans. Frederick Lawrence (Cambridge: MIT Press, 1987).

Homi K. Bhabha also makes translation the site of the movable nature of modernity in general. See *The Location of Culture* (New York: Routledge, 1994); especially pp. 32 and 242.

13. This is a commonplace of political philosophy, one that Mari Matsuda develops in "Voices of America." See also John Rawls, "Justice as Fairness: Political Not Metaphysical," *Philosophy and Public Affairs,* 14 (1985): 223–251. "[L]iberalism as a political doctrine supposes that there are many conflicting and incommensurable conceptions of the good, each compatible with the full rationality of human persons," p. 248; and Robert Dahl, *Dilemmas of Pluralist Democracy: Autonomy Versus Control* (New Haven: Yale University Press, 1982); Milton Fisk, "Introduction: The Problem of Justice" in Fisk, *Key Concepts in Critical Theory: Justice* (Atlantic Highlands, NJ: Humanities Press, 1993), pp. 1–8. "There has to be at least a conflict based on an actual lack of homogeneity for what is distinctive about justice to become relevant," p. 1. See also Benhabib, *Situating the Self,* p. 2.

14. Walter Benjamin, *Illuminations,* ed. Hannah Arendt, trans. Harry Zohn (New York: Schocken, 1969). He disdains historicism for cultivating empathy (p. 256).

See Hannah Arendt, *On Revolution* (New York: The Viking Press, 1963), pp. 69–90. Compassion is irrelevant for worldly affairs (p. 81), and speaking for (weak) others may be a pretext for lust for power (p. 84).

See also M. M. Bakhtin, *Art and Answerability: Early Philosophical Essays*, ed. Michael Holquist and Vadim Liapunov (Austin: University of Texas Press, 1990), pp. 64, 81 and 88; and Emmanuel Levinas throughout *Totality and Infinity* and *Otherwise Than Being*, trans. Alphonso Lingis (Dordrecht: Kluwer, 1981). For a proceduralist critique of grounding politics in positive feeling, see, for example, Robert Dahl, *Dilemmas of Pluralist Democracy: Autonomy vs. Control* (New Haven: Yale University Press, 1982), esp. pp. 138–164.

15. See Sacvan Bercovitch, "Games of Chess: A Model of Literary and Cultural Studies," in *Centuries' Ends, Narrative Means*, ed. Robert Newman (Stanford: Stanford University Press, 1996), pp. 15–57.

16. See Frederick Cooper and Ann Laura Stoler, "Introduction" to *Tensions of Empire: Colonial Cultures in a Bourgeois World* (Berkeley: University of California Press, 1996).

17. They might include urban musical innovations made to leave the competition behind. See Tricia Rose, "A Style Nobody Can Deal With," in *Microphone Fiends: Youth Music and Youth Culture*, ed. Andrew Ross and Tricia Rose (New York: Routledge, 1994), pp. 71–88. Excerpted from Tricia Rose, *Black Noise: Rap Music and Black Culture in Contemporary America* (Middletown: Wesleyan Press, 1994).

18. See James Clifford and George E. Marcus's collection, *Writing Culture: The Poetics and Politics of Ethnography* (Berkeley: University of California Press, 1986). Clifford's comments on Richard Price's *First-Time: The Historical Vision of an Afro-American People* (1983) are especially pertinent; see p. 7. On this issue see also Edward Said, "Representing the Colonized," in *Critical Inquiry*, 15, 2 (1989): 220.

19. Nancy Fraser reports about U.S. teen-age mothers who reject the goals of urban clinics but use the resources. See *Unruly Practices: Power, Discourse and Gender in Contemporary Social Theory* (Minneapolis: University of Minnesota Press, 1989).

20. James C. Scott, *Domination and the Arts of Resistance: The Hidden Transcript* (New Haven: Yale University Press, 1990). See also Scott, *The Moral Economy of the Peasant: Rebellion and subsistence in Southeast Asia* (New Haven: Yale University Press, 1976); and Scott, *Weapons of the Weak: Everyday Forms of Peasant Resistance* (New Haven: Yale University Press, 1985). My criticism coincides with Sherry B. Ortner's general objection: see her "Resistance and the Problem of Ethnographic Refusal," in *Comparative Studies in Society and History*, 37, 1 (1995): 173–193.

21. Walter Benjamin, "Theses on the Philosophy of History," in *Illuminations*. See the useful summary of Benjamin's debt to Baudelaire in Habermas, *The Philosophical Discourse of Modernity*, esp. pp. 1–21.

22. See Ann Stoler's critique of Guha as romanticizing peasant history and neglecting the colonial archives. See her forthcoming *Ethnography in the Colonial Archives: Movements on the Historic Turn* (Princeton: Princeton University Press).

23. Ranajit Guha, "The Prose of Counter-Insurgency," in Ranajit Guha and Gayatri Chakravorty Spivak, *Selected Subaltern Studies,* foreword by Edward W. Said (Oxford: Oxford University Press, 1988), pp. 45–84, and his now classic *Elementary Aspects of Peasant Insurgency in Colonial India* (Delhi: Oxford University Press, 1983).

24. This is the theme of the two lead articles in *AHR,* 99, 5 (1994): Gyan Prakash, in "Subaltern Studies as Postcolonial Criticism," pp. 1475–1490; and Florencia E. Mallon, "The Promise and Dilemma of Subaltern Studies: Perspectives from Latin American History," pp. 1491–1515.

25. Ludwig Wittgenstein, *Philosophical Investigations,* p. 66; see also p. 340.

26. Ibid., pp. 81, 131.

27. Ibid., p. 106.

28. Ibid., p. 67.

29. Ibid., p. 84.

30. Unwilling to free philosophy from the responsibility they assign to it, Habermas and Lyotard, for all their differences, take issue with Wittgenstein's "positivism." See Habermas, *The Philososphical Discourse of Modernity,* p. 198, and Lyotard, in *The Differend: Phrases in Dispute,* p. 76, n.122, where he calls Wittgenstein's exclusive attention to "use," "anthropological empiricism."

31. This is, in effect, what Seyla Benhabib asks of pragmatists too; see her "Feminism and Postmodernism: An Uneasy Alliance," in Seyla Benhabib, Judith Butler, Drucilla Cornell, Nancy Fraser, *Feminist Contentions: A Philosophical Exchange* (New York: Routledge, 1995), pp. 17–34. In the same book Nancy Fraser asks how a particular change can be good or bad in the absence of normative language. See her "Pragmatism, Feminism, and the Linguistic Turn," pp. 157–171. See also Ernesto Laclau, "Universalism, Particularism and the Question of Identity," in *The Identity In Question,* ed. John Rajchman (New York: Routledge, 1995), pp. 93–108.

32. See Stanley E. Fish, *Doing What Comes Naturally: Change, Rhetoric, and the Practice of Theory in Literary and Legal Studies* (Durham: Duke University Press, 1989), p. 71.

33. Stanley E. Fish, *Is There a Text in This Class?: The Authority of Interpretive Communities* (Cambridge, Mass.: Harvard University Press, 1980), p. 321.

34. Lyotard, *The Differend,* p. xiii, n. 202. See also the controversy over Robert Putnam's idea of "social capital." William A. Galston, "Won't You Be My Neighbor?" in *The American Prospect,* 26 (1996): 16–18. A critical response follows, by Alejandro Portes and Patricia Landolt, "The Downside of Social Capital," pp. 18–21. It develops the differential effects of community bonding, given the unequal resources available to communities.

35. For a magisterial review of the century's philosophical debates, see Hilary

Putnam, "A Half Century of Philosophy, Viewed from Within," in *Daedalus,* 126, 1 (1997): 175–208.

36. Stanley Cavell, *Must We Mean What We Say?* (Cambridge: Cambridge University Press, 1976), pp. 181, 236. In a similar vein Jessica Benjamin's therapy for poststructural identity problems is simply to admit that intention and agency are functions of identity options in normally complex people. See Jessica Benjamin, "The Shadow of the Other (Subject)," p. 235.

37. Gérard Genette, *Figures of Literary Discourse,* trans. Alan Sheridan (New York, Columbia University Press, 1982), pp. 183–202. For a contemporary and dilated exercise in digressions see Nicholson Baker's *The Mezzanine* (New York: Vintage, 1990), and Ross Chambers's loving analysis, "Meditation and the Escalator Principle," in *Modern Fiction Studies,* 40, 4 (1994): 765–806.

38. Chambers, "Meditation," p. 773. In *The Mezzanine* and in Barthes's *The Pleasure of the Text,* "the reader is a flaneur of texts," a mediator without leaving home.

39. See Tobin Siebers, *The Ethics of Criticism* (Ithaca: Cornell University Press, 1988) for an almost shrill rejection of contemporary criticism, from New Criticism to Post-structuralism. See also Wayne Booth, *The Company We Keep: An Ethics of Fiction* (Berkeley: University of California Press, 1988).

40. Without entering the debate on whether or not experience is a reliable "ground" for theorizing, I would say that conditioning through experience is inescapable. Tania Modleski, for example, rejects Jonathan Culler's and Peggy Kamuf's suspicions of experience, and especially Culler's pretense of imagining how a woman reads. See Modleski, "Feminism and the Power of Interpretation: Some Critical Readings." Teresa de Lauretis, "Eccentric Subjects: Feminist Theory and Historical Consciousness," in *Feminist Studies,* 16, 1 (1990): 115–150; p. 133. For another view see Diana Fuss, "Reading Like a Feminist," *Differences,* 1, 3 (1989): 77–92.

41. Peggy Phelan mistrusts visibility as appropriable in *Unmarked* (New York: Routledge, 1994), esp. pp. 6–7: "There is real power in remaining unmarked; and there are serious limitations to visual representation as a political goal. Visibility is a trap . . ."

42. In a pioneering essay, Reed Way Dasenbrock argues that, "the meaningfulness of multicultural works is in large measure a function of their unintelligibility." See his "Intelligibility and Meaningfulness in Multicultural Literature in English," in *Proceedings of the Modern Language Association,* 102, 1 (1987): 10–19. Quoted in Marta Sánchez, "Hispanic- and Anglo-American Discourse in Edward Rivera's *Family Installments,*" in *American Literary History,* 1, 4 (1989): 853–871.

43. Richard Rodriguez, *Hunger of Memory, the Education of Richard Rodriguez* (New York: Bantam Books, 1983), p. 31.

44. Michel Foucault gives a strong formulation in *The Archaeology of Knowledge,* trans. A. M. Sheridan Smith (New York: Pantheon, 1972). In *A Theory of Justice* (Cambridge, Mass.: Harvard University Press, 1971), John Rawls derives his sense of justice as fairness in from the fictional device of "original position," the socially unmarked "veil of ignorance."

45. Reed Way Dasenbrock presumes this equalization in "Intelligibility and Meaningfulness." Foreign words or unfamiliar uses signal cultural differences, "and that difference must be respected," p. 18. Yet the differences are read as invitations to work at extracting meaning, to assimilate oneself into the other's culture, just as the other has had to work at negotiating mainstream English. For a critique of easy analogies, see José David Saldívar, "The Limits of Cultural Studies," in *American Literary History,* 2, 2 (1990): 251–66.

46. Peter J. Rabinowitz, *Before Reading: Narrative Conventions and the Politics of Interpretation* (Ithaca: Cornell University Press, 1987). He reviews the generally accepted notion of authorial audience: not all readers are ideal, but they are all "deformed" in ways he would have known and shared, being "members of the same cultural community." See pp. 22, 26, 28.

47. For an earlier and very astute exploration of this inscribed difference, see Marta Sánchez, "Hispanic and Anglo-American Discourse."

48. In George Steiner's pithy indictment, "Like murderous Cordelia, children know that silence can destroy another human being. Or like Kafka they remember that several have survived the songs of the Sirens, but none their silence." *After Babel: Aspects of Language and Translation* (London: Oxford University Press, 1975), p. 35.

49. Recognition of literary figures depends on knowing what to expect. See Genette, *Figures of Literary Discourse,* p. 54. See also Peter J. Rabinowitz, *Before Reading* p. 27.

50. Oswald de Andrade, "Manifesto Antropófago" of 1928. "Cannibalist Manifesto," trans. Leslie Bary, *Latin American Literary Review,* 19, 38 (1991): 35–47.

51. Walter Benjamin, *Illuminations,* p. 100.

52. bell hooks, "Eating the Other," refered by Coco Fusco in *English Is Broken Here: Notes on Cultural Fusion in the Americas* (New York: The New Press, 1995), p. 70, n.11.

53. Melanie Klein's work on infantile subject formation hypothesizes a process of "introjecting" "good objects" and "projecting" the bad ones. "Some Theoretical Conclusions Regarding the Emotional Life of the Infant," in M. Klein, P. Heimann, S. Isaacs, and J. Rivera, *Developments in Psycho-Analysis* (London: Hogarth Press, 1952), esp. p. 200.

54. Despite Walter Benjamin's dismissal of a reader's response, he attributes to the aura a capacity to respond to a lover's gaze. "Experience of the aura thus rests on

the transposition of a response common in human relationships to the relationship between the inanimate or natural object and man." See "On Some Motifs in Baudelaire," in *Illuminations,* p. 188.

55. Roland Barthes, *The Pleasure of the Text* (New York: Noonday Press, 1975), p. 27.

56. Ibid., pp. 6, 11–12.

57. Georges Poulet, "Criticism and the Experience of Interiority," in *The Structuralist Controversy: The Language of Criticism and the Science of Man,* ed. Richard A. Macksey and Eugenio Donato (Baltimore: Johns Hopkins University Press, 1972), pp. 56–72. Reprinted in *Reader-Response Criticism: From Formalism to Post-Structuralism,* ed. Jane Tompkins (Baltimore: Johns Hopkins University Press, 1980), pp. 41–49.

58. See, as a representative piece, Wolfgang Iser, "The Reading Process: A Phenomenological Approach," in Tompkins, *Reader-Response Criticism,* pp. 50–69. For a study of the operations readers perform and the "spurs" that texts provide for interaction with the reader, see Iser, *The Act of Reading: A Theory of Aesthetic Response* (Baltimore: Johns Hopkins University Press, 1978). In *The Implied Reader: Patters of Communication in Prose Fiction from Bunyan to Beckett* (Baltimore: Johns Hopkins University Press, 1974), Iser offers readings of representative novels based on their requirement of active readerly participation. See also his "Narrative Strategies as Means of Communication," in *Interpretation of Narrative,* ed. Mario J. Valdés and Owen J. Miller (Toronto: University of Toronto Press, 1979), pp. 100–117. It focuses on the particular shape of readings as imposed by the author's regulation of the process.

59. In the "Discussion" (see Macksey and Donato, *The Structuralist Controversy,* pp. 73–88) that follows Poulet's paper, he responds that unlike reading, conversation "becomes instead, quite the contrary, a sort of battle, a radical opposition, an insistence on *differentiation.* The act of reading, as I conceive it, is . . . above all an acceding, even an adherence, provisionally at least, and without reserve," p. 73.

60. Poulet, "Criticism and the Experience of Interiority," p. 56.

61. That unreflective, universalizing love can produce perverse confusions between pets and partners is provocatively argued in Marc Shell's "The Family Pet, or The Human and the Animal," *Children of the Earth: Literature, Politics, and Nationhood* (New York: Oxford University Press, 1993), pp. 148–175.

62. Ibid., p. 57.

63. Ibid., pp. 60, 61, 62, 72.

64. James Phelan claims this view is unresponsive to rhetoric and to the possibility that certain elements of a text may be recalcitrant to interpretation: see "Toward a

Rhetorical Reader-Response Criticism: The Difficult, the Stubborn, and the Ending of *Beloved*," in *Modern Fiction Studies*, 39, 3/4 (1993): 709–728, esp. pp. 712, 714.

65. Ross Chambers, *Room for Maneuver: Reading (the) Oppositional (in) Narrative* (Chicago: University of Chicago Press), p. 26.

66. Ibid., p. 24: "I find myself in a triangulated relationship . . . both that of *tiers exclu*—the excluded third party—and that of *tertius gaudens*, the third who enjoys or profits."

67. Ibid., p. 12. The first stage towards "influencing the desires and views of readers" is an identification between powerful narratee and privileged reader. But in a second stage, because readers are allegedly excluded from the hostility, the bipolar opposition is stretched into a triangle where readers take the upper vantage point.

68. Stanley E. Fish, *Surprised by Sin: The Reader in Paradise Lost* (Berkeley: University of California Press, 1967), pp. 4, 20.

69. Toni Morrison, *Playing in the Dark: Whiteness and the Literary Imagination* (Cambridge, Mass.: Harvard University Press, 1992), and her "Unspeakable Things Unspoken: The Afro-American Presence in American Literature," in *Michigan Quarterly Review*, 28, 1 (1989): 1–34: "Perhaps some of these writers, although under current house arrest, have much more to say than has been realized. Perhaps some were not so much transcending politics, or escaping blackness, as they were transforming it into intelligible, accessible, yet artistic modes of discourse."

70. "What is important in all of this," Morrison spells out, "is that the critic not be engaged in laying claim on behalf of the text to his or her own dominance and power." Morrison, "Unspeakable Things Unspoken," p. 10.

71. René Girard, *Deceit, Desire and the Novel: Self and Other in Literary Structure* (Baltimore: Johns Hopkins University Press, 1965).

72. Genette, *Figures of Literary Discourse*, pp. 45–60.

73. Ludwig Wittgenstein, *Philosophical Investigations*, p. 198.

74. Thomas Kuhn, *The Structure of Scientific Revolutions*, (Chicago: University of Chicago Press, 1962), p. 113.

75. Mikhail Bakhtin probably has some leads on this in his "discourse typologies"; see *Speech Genres*. His discussion of "reaccentuation" is suggestive for theorizing this kind of constitutive resistance.

76. Zora Neale Hurston, *Mules and Men* (Westport, Conn.: Negro University Press, 1969), p. 18.

77. Robert W. White "Strategies of Adaptation," in *Coping and Adaptation*, ed. George V. Coelho, David A. Hamburg, and John E. Adams (New York: Basic Books, 1974), pp. 47–68. "The mechanisms of defense . . . have a legitimate place among strategies of adaptation" (pp. 64–65).

78. For Edward Said, in "Representing the Colonized: Anthropology's Interlocutors," *Critical Inquiry,* 15, 2 (1989): 205–225, divulging the mechanisms tends to vitiate them. This is his criticism of James C. Scott's otherwise admirable *Weapons of the Weak: Everyday Forms of Peasant Resistance* (New Haven: Yale University Press, 1985).

79. This, she says, was typical of her hometown in general and, one can say, of her own evasive autobiography. See Robert Hemenway, "Introduction" to Zora Neale Hurston, *Dust Tracks on a Road: An Autobiography* (Urbana: University of Illinois Press, 1984, first pub. 1942). "The conventions of autobiography create the expectation that Zora will explain how she came to her position of prominence . . . Hurston's reaction to this convention is to avoid offering such an explanation of personal success, substituting instead an interpretation of black cultural life meant to deflect attention away from herself," pp. xviii–xix.

80. Henry Louis Gates, Jr. "'Authenticity,' or the Lesson of Little Tree." *New York Times Book Review,* 11 November, 1991; 1, 26–30; quote from p. 30.

81. See Coco Fusco, who refers also to bell hooks and Richard Fung, in *English Is Broken Here: Notes on Cultural Fusion in the Americas* (New York: The New Press, 1995), pp. 65–77.

82. Henry Louis Gates, Jr., *The Signifying Monkey: Towards a Theory of Afro-American Literary Criticism* (New York: Oxford University Press, 1988), p. 52.

83. Gloria Anzaldúa, *Borderlands/La Frontera: The New Mestiza* (San Francisco: Spinsters/Aunt Lute, 1987), p. 3 and throughout. See also the volume she edited, *Making Face, Making Soul: Haciendo Caras. Creative and Critical Perspectives by Feminists of Color* (San Franciso: Aunt Lute Books, 1990).

84. *The Slave's Narrative,* eds. Charles T. Davis and Henry Louis Gates, Jr. (New York: Oxford University Press, 1985). The editors take Douglass's lead when they write that the genre "could no longer exist after slavery was abolished." See Introduction, p. xxii.

85. Hurston, *Mules and Men,* p. 17.

86. Harriet Jacobs (pen name Linda Brent), *Incidents in the Life of a Slave Girl* (New York: Harcourt Brace, 1973), p. 54.

87. One reason may have been the retaliation he feared; another may have been the literary control that comes with self-authorship. See Sylvia Molloy, "From Serf to Self: The Autobiography of Juan Francisco Manzano," in *At Face Value: Autobiographical Writing in Spanish America* (New York: Cambridge University Press, 1991), pp. 36–54.

88. Typically, Manzano locates a threshold and stops: "but let's leave to silence the rest of this painful scene." Quoted in Susan Willis in her "Crushed Geraniums: Juan Francisco Manzano and the Language of Slavery," in *The Slave's Narrative,*

Charles T. Davis and Henry Louis Gates, Jr., eds. pp. 199–224; quote from p. 208. The silence that "occurs more than once and always at an extreme moment of torture," can be read as an exercise of writerly control rather than as literary convention.

89. I borrow the term loosely from Antonio Gramsci, for whom the war of position is a process of ideological disarticulation (of bourgeois hegemony) and rearticulation (of a workers' hegemonic bloc). See his *Selections from the Prison Notebooks*, ed. and trans. Quintin Hoare and Geoffrey Nowell Smith (New York: International Publishers, 1971), pp. 238–239. See also Chantal Mouffe, "Hegemony and Ideology in Gramsci," in *Gramsci & Marxist Theory*, ed. Chantal Mouffe (London: Routledge & Kegan Paul, 1979), pp. 168–204.

90. Jacques Derrida, "Violence and Metaphysics: An Essay on the Thought of Emmanuel Levinas," in *Writing and Difference*, trans. Alan Bass (Chicago: University of Chicago Press, 1978), pp. 79–153. Derrida's remarks on Levinas underline that war of positionality: "One would attempt in vain . . . to forget the words 'inside,' 'outside,' 'exterior,' 'interior,' etc. . . . for one would never come across a language without the rupture of space," p. 113.

91. See, for example, Fernando Coronil, "Mastery by Signs, Signs of Mastery," a review essay in *Plantation Society*, 2, 2 (1986): 201–207; and José Piedra, "The Game of Critical Arrival," in *Diacritics*, 19 (1989): 34–61; and Myra Jehlen, "Why Did the Europeans Cross the Ocean? A Seventeenth-Century Riddle," in *Cultures of American Imperialism*, ed. Amy Kaplan and Donald Pease (Durham: Duke University Press, 1993), pp. 41–59. Consider also Gayatri Spivak's general indictment of "the ferocious standardizing benevolence of most U.S. and Western European human-scientific radicalism (recognition by assimilation)," in "Can the Subaltern Speak?" in Cary Nelson and Lawrence Grossberg, *Marxism and the Interpretation of Culture* (Bloomington: University of Illinois Press, 1988), p. 294. See also Simon Gikandi, *Writing in Limbo: Modernism and Caribbean Literature* (Ithaca: Cornell University Press, 1992), on Eurocentric assumptions about the Conquest.

92. Tzvetan Todorov, *The Morals of History*, trans. Alyson Waters (Minneapolis: University of Minnesota Press, 1995), pp. 34–46; quote from p. 41.

93. For the collusion between the apparently opposite projects of universalizing (saming) and subordination of the "other" (othering) see Naomi Schor, "This Essentialism Which Is Not One: Coming to Grips with Irigaray," in *Differences*, 1, 3 (1989): 38–58. "If othering involves attributing to the objectified other a difference that serves to legitimate her oppression, saming denies the objectified other the right to her difference, submitting the other to the laws of phallic specularity. If othering assumes that the other is knowable, saming precludes any knowledge of the other in her otherness," p. 45.

94. "Strategic essentialism" is Gayatri Spivak's term, although Robert Scholes suggests that John Locke came upon it some time ago. Scholes, "Reading Like a Man," in *Men in Feminism,* eds. Alice Jardine and Paul Smith (New York: Methuen, 1987), pp. 204–218, esp. p. 208. For Spivak's formulation, see "Subaltern Studies: Deconstructing Historiography," in *In Other Words* (London: Methuen, 1987), pp. 197–221. See also her interview with Ellen Rooney in the special issue of *Differences* devoted to *The Essential Difference Another Look at Essentialism,* 1, 2 (1989). "In a Word Interview," pp. 124–156; quote from pp. 128–129. In the same issue, Diana Fuss, "Reading Like a Feminist," pp. 77–92, anticipates some of Spivak's concerns.

95. Werner Sollors, *Beyond Ethnicity: Consent and Descent in American Culture* (Oxford: Oxford University Press, 1986). See his reference to Fredrik Barth, p. 28.

96. Mary C. Waters, *Ethnic Options: Choosing Identities in America* (Berkeley: University of California Press, 1990).

97. Françoise Lionnet sees it revived by Maya Angelou, for example. See Lionnet's *Autobiographical Voices: Race, Gender, Self-Portraiture* (Ithaca: Cornell University Press, 1989), p. 18.

98. See "Introduction," in *Puerto Rican Jam: Rethinking Colonialism and Nationalism,* ed. Frances Negrón-Muntaner and Ramón Grosfoguel (Minneapolis: University of Minnesota Press, 1979). "Although it has been mistaken for docility, it is instead an active, low intensity strategy to obtain the maximum benefits of a situation with the minimum blood spilled," ms. p. 29.

99. Emmanuel Levinas, *Le Temps et l'Autre* (Paris: Presses universitaires de France, 1983); quote from p. 78.

100. See D. W. Winnicott, "The Use of an Object and Relating through Identifications," in *Playing and Reality* (London: Tavistock, 1971). See also Jessica Benjamin, "The Shadow of the Other (Subject)," pp. 237–238.

101. To be fair to Spivak, her first targets were Foucault and Deleuze, who romanticized the "other" and smuggled back the humanist notions of a coherent subject identity. The simplified third-world or working-class subject is then available for representation. For Spivak, "the intellectual's solution is not to abstain from representation" but to notice that what the subaltern cannot say he or she will do: "elaborations of insurgency stand in the place of 'the utterance.'" Fernando Coronil has also reframed the point in "Listening to the Subaltern: The Poetics of Neocolonial States," *Poetics Today,* 15, 4 (1994): 643–658.

102. Spivak, "Can the Subaltern Speak?" p. 287.

103. The problem, she says, with "our efforts to give the subaltern a voice in history" (p. 296) has been the ways we essentialize that experience. "There is no space from which the sexed subaltern subject can speak," p. 307.

104. See Gayatri Chakravorty Spivak, "Subaltern Studies: Deconstructing Historiography," in Ranajit Guha and Gayatri Chakravorty Spivak, *Selected Subaltern Studies,* foreword by Edward W. Said (Oxford: Oxford University Press, 1988), pp. 12–13.

105. Donna Haraway, "A Manifesto for Cyborgs: Science, Technology and Socialist Feminism in the 1980s," in *Coming to Terms: Feminism, Theory and Politics,* ed. Elizabeth Weed (New York: Routledge, 1989), p. 173.

106. Silence "explains a great deal through the very stress of not explaining, we must assign some meaning to it that we may understand what the silence is intended to say." Sor Juana Inés de la Cruz, *A Woman of Genius: The Intellectual Autobiography of Sor Juana Inés de la Cruz,* trans. Margaret Sayers Peden (Limerock, CT: Limerock Press, 1982), pp. 18–20.

107. Adrienne Rich, "Women and Honor: Some Notes on Lying (1975)," in *On Lies, Secrets, and Silence: Selected Prose 1966–1978* (New York: Norton, 1979), p. 185.

108. This is true also for color-blind liberals like Richard Rorty, who defines pride in one's country as the ground for real, as opposed to cultural, politics.

109. See Slavoj Zizek, *The Sublime Object of Ideology,* (London: Verso, 1989); "the real subject matter of the dream (the unconscious desire) articulates itself in the dream-work, in the elaboration of its 'latent content,'" p. 13.

110. Wittgenstein, *Philosophical Investigations,* pp. 99–100.

111. This seems different from the playful love that moves María Lugones's "schizophrenic" trips between culturally differentiated worlds. See María Lugones, "Playfulness, World-Travelling, and Loving Perception," in *Hypatia,* 2, 2 (1987): 3–19.

112. Drucilla Cornell, "What Is Ethical Feminism?" in Seyla Benhabib, Judith Butler, Drucilla Cornell, Nancy Fraser, *Feminist Contentions: A Philosophical Exchange,* quote from p. 97.

113. Paul de Man, "Autobiography as De-facement," in *The Rhetoric of Romanticism* (New York: Columbia University Press, 1984) pp. 67–82.

114. Marianne Constable, *The Law of the Other: The Mixed Jury and Changing Conceptions of Citizenship, Law and Knowledge* (Chicago: University of Chicago Press, 1994), p. 146.

115. Spivak assumes, on the other hand, that coalitions are always organized by the elite participants. See "Can the Subaltern Speak?", pp. 288–289.

116. Hannah Arendt, *On Revolution* (New York: The Viking Press, 1963). She calls reliance on compassion a "misplaced emphasis on the heart as the source of political virtue," p. 92.

117. Brian Swann and Arnold Krupat, *I Tell You Now, Autobiographical Essays by Native American Writers* (Lincoln: University of Nebraska Press, 1987), p. ix.

118. Barbara Smith, "Toward a Black Feminist Criticism," in *But Some of Us Are Brave: Black Women's Studies,* ed. Gloria T. Hull, Patricia Bell Scott, and Barbara Smith (New York: The Feminist Press, 1982), pp. 157–175. "So many of the women who will read this have not yet noticed us missing either from their reading matter, their politics, or their lives," p. 158.

119. Toni Morrison, *Beloved* (New York: New American Library, 1988), p. 53.

120. Shoshana Felman, Dori Laub, and Cathy Caruth develop the startling idea that repression can be a "normal" coping mechanism, and that breaking the silence can invite disaster. See Shoshana Felman and Dori Laub, *Testimony . . .* and Cathy Caruth, ed. special issue of *American Imago,* 49, 2 (1992).

121. Eleonora Lev, "Don't Take Your Daughter to the Extermination Camp," *Tikkun,* 2, 1 (1988): 44–60.

122. See Georgia Warnke, *Gadamer: Hermeneutics, Tradition and Reason* (Stanford: Stanford University Press, 1987).

123. Hans-Georg Gadamer, *Philosophical Hermeneutics,* trans. and ed. David E. Linge (Berkeley: University of California Press, 1977), p. 19.

124. Ibid., p. 25.

125. Ibid., pp. 24, 20.

126. Genette, *Figures of Literary Discourse,* p. 12.

127. Hans Georg Gadamer, *Philosophical Hermeneutics,* p. 22.

128. Ibid., p. 25.

129. Emmanuel Levinas, *Totality and Infinity: An Essay on Exteriority,* trans. Alphonso Lingis (The Hague: M. Nijhoff Publishers, 1979), p. 40.

130. Steven Mailloux, *Rhetorical Power* (Ithaca: Cornell University Press, 1989), p. 133, insists that criticism should move from Theory (with its presumptions of pattern and predictability) to a history of differential readings as soon as possible.

131. See David E. Linge's Introduction to Hans-Georg Gadamer, *Philosophical Hermeneutics,* p. xlii.

132. Georgia Warnke, *Gadamer: Hermeneutics, Tradition and Reason,* pp. 107–108.

133. In Gramscian political philosophy heterogeneity of positions and interests is taken for granted, so that justice is a response to conflict; it exceeds existing codes. See Milton Fisk, *Key Concepts in Critical Theory: Justice* (Atlantic Highlands, NJ: Humanities Press, 1993), pp. 1–8.

134. Jean-François Lyotard, *The Differend: Phrases in Dispute,* trans. Georges Van Den Abbeele (Minneapolis: University of Minnesota Press, 1992), p. 9. Since cognitive proof is the "phrase regimen" of law, plaintiffs can become victims of the courts: for example, they cannot *prove* that the death-camps existed.

On the usefulness of Kantian Judgment see also John Rawls, "Justice as Fairness: Political Not Metaphysical," in Fisk, *Key Concepts in Critical Theory: Justice*, pp. 48–67, esp. p. 53.

135. Marianne Constable, *The Law of the Other*.

136. Jean-François Lyotard, "The Other's Rights," in *On Human Rights: The Oxford Amnesty Lectures 1993*, ed. Stephen Shute and Susan Hurley (New York: Harper Collins, 1993), pp. 136–147.

137. This is what Levinas calls "the light in which existents become intelligible." See *Totality and Infinity: An Essay on Exteriority*, p. 42.

138. Ibid., Derrida, *Writing and Difference*, p. 135. Levinas opposes Heidegger by privileging the existent over Being, ethics over freedom (*Totality and Infinity*, p. 45).

139. Theodor W. Adorno, *Negative Dialectics*, trans. E. B. Ashton (New York: Continuum, 1983). See, for example: "What we differentiate will appear divergent, dissonant, negative for just as long as the structure of our consciousness obliges it to strive for unity: as long as its demand for totality will be its measure for whatever is not identical with it," pp. 5–6.

140. Michel Foucault, *Discipline and Punish*, trans. Alan Sheridan (New York: Pantheon Books, 1977), pp. 27–28: "[P]ower and knowledge directly imply one another, . . . there is no power relation without the correlative constitution of a field of knowledge, nor any knowledge that does not presuppose and constitute at the same time power relations." See also Steven Mailloux, *Rhetorical Power*, p. 143.

141. Emmanuel Levinas, *Ethics and Infinity: Conversations with Philippe Nemo*, trans. Richard A. Cohen (Pittsburgh: Duquesne University Press, 1985), pp. 60–61.

142. Levinas, *Totality and Infinity: An Essay on Exteriority*, p. 47.

143. Ibid., p. 43.

144. Quoted in Jacques Derrida, "Violence and Metaphysics: An Essay on the Thought of Emmanuel Levinas," in *Writing and Difference*, trans. Alan Bass pp. 79–153; quote from p. 91.

145. Levinas, *Totality and Infinity: An Essay on Exteriority*, p. 40.

146. Hilary Putnam, in a lecture of April 24, 1997, pointed out the contrast between Levinas and moral perfectionists like Buber and Rosenzweig. His rejection of history and narrative in general does not allow for moral education.

147. Derrida had a similar concern. He asked how can difference be absolute? Doesn't the Other assume a point of comparison with the self, and an inescapable negativity at that? See Jacques Derrida, "Violence and Metaphysics," pp. 110, 117: "Speech is doubtless the first defeat of violence, but paradoxically, violence did not exist before the possibility of speech. The philosopher (man) *must* speak and write within this war of light . . ." See also p. 99: "Levinas is very close to Hegel, much

closer than he admits." Later in the essay, Levinas's parallels with Kierkegaard and Husserl are developed.

148. Levinas, *Totality and Infinity,* p. 295.

149. Derrida, "Violence and Metaphysics," p. 113: "This text of the glance is *also* the text of speech. Therefore it can be called Face."

150. For Derrida, the contradiction (or paradox) derives from the "nonviolent urgency" of Levinas's ethics. "The very elocution of nonviolent metaphysics is its first disavowal." See Derrida, "Violence and Metaphysics," p. 147.

151. Homi Bhabha, *The Location of Culture,* p. 31.

152. Hannah Arendt, *On Revolution,* p. 81.

153. Levinas, *Ethics and Infinity,* p. 99.

154. See Derrida's comparison with Husserl, whose ethics begin precisely from the assumption of mutual alterity; *Violence and Metaphysics,* pp. 128–133.

155. Levinas, *Ethics and Infinity,* p. 88.

156. This sounds like Peter J. Rabinowitz on "'Betraying the Sender': The Rhetoric and Ethics of Fragile Texts," *Narrative,* 2, 3 (1994): 254–267, where he worries that his reading of Nella Larsen's *Passing* may have "tampered with a finely wrought text in such a way as to damage it," p. 202. He understood the book's secret (that it was about lesbianism passing for hetersexuals), and divulged it.

157. Enrique Dussel makes a similar objection, from his position as a Latin American philosopher of liberation (see Chapter 10 above, "About Face").

158. Hannah Arendt said this before, on Billy Budd, in *On Revolution,* p. 81.

159. I am apparently siding with Kant against Schopenhauer, according to my friend Robert Gooding Williams, in their debate about the basis of ethics.

160. Steven Mailloux, *Rhetorical Power,* p. 49.

161. Doris Sommer, *Foundational Fictions: The National Romances of Latin America* (Berkeley: University of California Press, 1991).

162. Rabinowitz, *Before Reading: Narrative Conventions and the Politics of Interpretation,* p. 19: "As Michael Riffaterre's criticism of Jakobson makes abundantly clear, readers need to ignore or play down many textual features when they read lyric poetry; they need to *ignore* even more in longer works like novels."

163. Steven Mailloux, p. 43, on Stanley Fish, in *Rhetorical Power.*

2. FREELY AND EQUALLY YOURS, WALT WHITMAN

1. Mikhail Bakhtin makes this objection part of his polemic against a personalist, centralizing, and totalizing aesthetic that he evidently associated with Stalinism. See *The Dialogic Imagination: Four Essays* (Austin: University of Texas Press, 1981).

2. Walt Whitman, "Song of Myself," in *The Portable Whitman,* ed. Mark Van Doren (Middlesex, Eng.: Penguin Books, 1981), p. 1.

3. I thank Wai Chee Dimock and José Quiroga for reminding me that Whitman doesn't always have (or even want) to have his way with readers.

4. Emmanuel Levinas, *Otherwise Than Being, or Beyond Essence,* trans. Alphonso Lingis (Dordrecht: Kluwer Academic Publishers, 1991).

5. Levinas called this being out of phase with one's essence "otherwise" than being, and credits it with making relationships possible. Levinas, *Otherwise Than Being,* pp. 9–10.

6. Quentin Anderson, *The Imperial Self: An Essay in American Literary and Cultural History* (New York: Knopf, 1972), and C.L.R. James, "Whitman and Melville" in *The C. L. R. James Reader,* ed. Anna Grimshaw (London: Blackwell, 1992).

7. Philip Fisher, "Democratic Social Space: Whitman, Melville, and the Promise of American Transparency," in *The New American Studies: Essays from Representations,* ed. Philip Fisher (Berkeley: University of California Press, 1991), p. 110. "Emerson, Thoreau, Whitman, and Stevens have always been charged with a vaporous quest for the All that in its indefiniteness stands back from the thick description of realism," p. 110.

8. For this inspired phrase and idea, see Rael Mayerowitz, *Transferring to America: Jewish Interpretations of American Dreams* (Albany: SUNY Press, 1995).

9. Wai Chee Dimock, "Whitman, Syntax, and Political Theory," in Betsy Erkkila and Jay Grossman, eds., *Breaking Bounds: Whitman & American Cultural Studies* (New York: Oxford University Press, 1996), pp. 62–79.

10. Fisher, "Democratic Social Space: Whitman, Melville, and the Promise of American Transparency," p. 72. For a critique see Michael Warner, "Whitman Drunk," in Betsy Erkkila and Jay Grossman, eds., *Breaking Bounds,* pp. 30–43.

11. Roberto Schwarz, "Nacional por subtraçao," *Folha de Sao Paulo,* June 7, 1986, trans. Linda Briggs, "Brazilian Culture: Nationalism by Elimination," *New Left Review,* 167 (1988). Included in *Misplaced Ideas,* ed. John Gledson (London: Verso, 1992), pp. 1–18.

12. Michael Fabre, "Walt Whitman and the Rebel Poets: A Note on Whitman's Reputation Among Radical Writers During the Depression," *Walt Whitman Review,* 12 (1966), p. 88.

13. Ezra Pound, "A Pact," in *Walt Whitman: The Measure of His Song,* ed. Jim Perlman, Ed Folsom, and Dan Campion (Minneapolis: The Holy Cow Press, 1981), p. 29. "I come to you as a grown child / Who has had a pig-headed father;" But Michel Fabre concluded that Pound's 1913 "truce with Walt Whitman' was not to be taken seriously," p. 91. See Charles B. Willard's comments on this point in his *Whitman's American Fame* (Providence: Brown University Press, 1950), p. 205. See also Gay Wilson Allen, *Walt Whitman, Man, Poet and Legend* (Carbondale, Ill.: Southern Illinois University Press, 1961), p. 136.

14. A useful anthology of responses is *Walt Whitman & the World,* ed. Gay Wilson Allen and Ed Folsom (Iowa City: University of Iowa Press, 1995).

15. Letter of April 22, 1996. See also Jorge Salessi and José Quiroga, "Errata sobre la erótica, or the Elision of Whitman's Body," in *Breaking Bounds,* ed. Betsy Erkkila and Jay Grossman, pp. 123–132.

16. Arnaldo Cruz Malavé, letter to me, dated 8–26–96.

17. Herman Melville called it the "red year of Forty-eight" in *Clarel.* See Sacvan Bercovitch, *The Office of the Scarlet Letter* (Baltimore: Johns Hopkins University Press, 1991), p. 74. It was the year of Polk's unexpected defeat of "Chartist agitation in England, the First Paris Commune, *The Communist Manifesto,* and widespread revolt in France, Austria, Germany, Belgium, Prussia, Poland, Bohemia, Rumania, Denmark, Ireland, Italy, Czechoslovakia, and Hungary," p. 75.

18. Sacvan Bercovitch, *The Office of the Scarlet Letter:* "Hawthorne's celebrated evasiveness comes with a stern imperative. Penitence, he would urge us, has more substance than the absolutism of either/or," p. 16.

19. "1855 Preface," in *The Portable Walt Whitman,* p. 24.

20. Mark Van Doren's "Introduction," in *The Portable Whitman,* p. xxiv.

21. Walt Whitman, "Preface" to *As a Strong Bird on Pinions Free and Other Poems* (1872). In *Complete Writings of Walt Whitman,* ed. Richard M. Bucke, Thomas B. Harned, and Horace L. Traubel (New York: Putnam, 1902), vol. 5, pp. 185–192. Quoted in *Whitman, the Poet,* ed. John C. Broderick (Belmont, CA: Wadsworth, 1964), p. 9.

22. "Song of Myself," in *The Portable Whitman,* 47, p. 91.

23. "Democratic Vistas," in *The Portable Whitman,* p. 322. My emphasis.

24. See J. Roland Pennock, *Democratic Political Theory* (Princeton: Princeton University Press, 1979). For a succinct, but less satisfying, discussion of the double tradition, see Alan Wolfe, "The Predicament of Liberal Democracy," in *The Limits of Legitimacy* (New York: The Free Press, 1977), pp. 1–10.

25. John Rawls, "Justice as Fairness: Political Not Metaphysical," in Milton Fisk, *Key Concepts in Critical Theory: Justice* (Atlantic Highlands, NJ: Humanities Press, 1993), p. 50.

26. "Through 1848 he was an outspoken advocate of revolution, denouncing all forms of oppression abroad, 'modern' as well as 'feudal', and going so far as to defend the French Republican Reign of Terror: . . . After 1849, however, when similar issues of injustice were raised in America itself—along with similar threats of revenge, . . . he steadily 'recoiled' ."

27. "Democratic Vistas," in *The Portable Whitman,* p. 320.

28. "1855 Preface," in *The Portable Whitman,* p. 9.

29. "Song of Myself," in *The Portable Whitman,* 4, p. 35; 25, p. 60.

30. Hannah Arendt, *On Revolution* (New York: The Viking Press, 1963), p. 168.

31. Waldo Frank, *Our America* (New York: Boni and Liverright, 1919), p. 46. Frank went to Cuba (with Hart Crane) and then figured prominently in the early 1860s in campaigns for solidarity with the people of Cuba, as a "bridge." See Van Gosse's *Where the Boys Are* (London/New York: Verso, 1993).

32. "Song of Myself" in *The Portable Whitman*, 14, p. 44. My emphasis.

33. Ibid., 40, p. 80.

34. Lewis Hyde, "A Draft of Whitman," *The Gift: Imagination and the Erotic Life of Property* (New York: Vintage, 1983), pp. 161–215.

35. "Song of Myself," in *The Portable Whitman*, 41, p. 81.

36. "1855 Preface," in *The Portable Whitman*, p. 15.

37. "Democratic Vistas," in *The Portable Whitman*, p. 339.

38. Mauricio González de la Garza, *Walt Whitman: Racista, imperialista, anti-Mexicano.* (Mexico: Colección Málaga, 1971), p. 176.

39. Allen Kaufman, *Capitalism, Slavery, and Republican Values* (Austin: University of Texas Press, 1983).

40. "Democratic Vistas," in *The Portable Whitman*, pp. 317, 324.

41. José Enrique Rodó, *Ariel* (1900), trans. F. J. Stimson (Boston, Houghton Mifflin, 1922), pp. 120–121.

42. "Democratic Vistas," in *The Portable Whitman*, p. 369.

43. Carlos Manuel de Céspedes, representing the newly formed revolutionary government in his first (1869) message to President Johnson. Cited in Gerald E. Poyo, *"With All, and for the Good of All": The Emergence of Popular Nationalism in the Cuban Communities of the United States, 1848–1898* (Durham: Duke University Press, 1989), p. 26. "Indeed, during 1870 Céspedes expressed reservations about the diplomatic strategy that he himself had entrusted to the junta. In a letter to José Manuel Mestre he suggested that the United States' only interest was to acquire Cuba without complications," p. 45.

44. Fisher "Democratic Social Space: Whitman, Melville, and the Promise of American Transparency," p. 84. *"Discourse on the Origins of Inequality,* the essay that could be called the constitution for the international politics of sentimentality in the century and a half following Rousseau. Whitman's straightforward summary traps the heart of the elaborate theory worked out by Rousseau . . ."

45. Arendt, *On Revolution,* p. 70. Arendt quotes Sièyes, "one of the least sentimental and most sober figures of the Revolution."

46. Ibid., pp. 123–124.

47. "Song of Myself," in *The Portable Whitman*, 19, p. 51.

48. Jorge Luis Borges, "Note on Walt Whitman," in *Other Inquisitions*, trans. Ruth L. C. Simms (University of Texas Press, 1964), p. 70.

49. "Song of Myself," in *The Portable Whitman*, 21, p. 53; 7, p. 49; 33, p. 71; 40, p. 81.

50. See Enrico Mario Santí, "The Accidental Tourist: Walt Whitman in Latin America," in Gustavo Pérez Firmat, ed., *Do the Americas Have a Literature?* (Durham: Duke University Press, 1989). Uruguay's Alvaro Armando Vasseur translated from an Italian Whitman that was published as early as 1881 (6 years before Martí's essay); see his preface to the sixth edition of *Poemas, Walt Whitman* (Buenos Aires, 1950). Although Borges knew English very well, he apparently discovered Whitman in Geneva, in a German translation by Johannes Schlaf. See Borges's "Autobiographical Essay" (1970). The French connection to Latin America was developed at length by Fernando Alegría.

51. Gerard Manley Hopkins, in a letter to Robert Bridges, Oct. 18, 1882, from *Walt Whitman: The Measure of His Song*, p. 13.

52. Roland Barthes's term for stylistic utopia, a "universal language" which would not cultivate individual style but anticipate a homogeneous social state. *Writing Degree Zero and Elements of Semiology*, trans. Annette Lavers and Colin Smith (Boston: Beacon Press, 1967), especially p. 87.

53. "Song of Myself," in *The Portable Whitman*, 6, p. 36.

54. John Irwin, *American Hieroglyphics: The Symbol of the Egyptian Hieroglyphics in the American Renaissance* (New Haven: Yale University Press: 1980), pp. 37–39.

55. Ibid., p. 40.

56. Gilles Deleuze and Félix Guattari, *On the Line*, trans. John Johnston, *Semiotext(e), Inc* (New York: Columbia University, 1983), esp. pp. 9, 43, 48.

57. *The New American Studies: Essays from Representations*, ed. Philip Fisher. See Fisher's section on "Jefferson's Map," pp. 72–77.

58. José Martí, "Walt Whitman," 1887, published in *El Partido Liberal*, Mexico, and *La Nación*, Buenos Aires. The English version used in this text is from *Martí on the U.S.A.*, trans. Luis Baralt (Carbondale, Ill.: Southern Illinois University Press, 1966), pp. 3–16. The Spanish version is José Martí, *En los Estados Unidos*, ed. and foreword by Andrés Sorel (Madrid: Alianza Editorial, 1968), pp. 247–262.

59. Martí, *Martí on the U.S.A.*, trans. Baralt, pp. 13–14.

60. The relationship between literature and ideology is evidently at issue as I ask how his poetry might affect readers and therefore effect historical change. The question echoes Louis Althusser's understanding of ideology as "the representation of the subject's *Imaginary* relationship to his or her *Real* conditions of existence." Louis Althusser, "Ideology and the Ideological State Apparatuses," in *Lenin and Philosophy* (London: New Left Book, 1971), p. 162.

61. I published the original as "Supplying Demand: Walt Whitman as the Liberal Self," in *Reinventing the Americas*, ed. Gari LaGuardia and Bell Chevigny (New York: Cambridge University Press, 1985), pp. 68–91. A shorter version is "Whitman: The

Bard of Both Americas," in *Approaches to Teaching Whitman's Leaves of Grass,* ed. Donald D. Kummings (New York: Modern Language Association, 1990), pp. 159–67.

62. Mauricio González de la Garza, *Walt Whitman: Racista, imperialista, anti-Mexicano* pp. 182–183. See also p. 193: "Not that we join in what seems to us the unreasonable cry of 'annexing the whole of Mexico'—for we believe that such superlative doctrine is likely to defeat *all,* because it grasps too much and may thus get none" (December 2, 1847).

63. See Jorge Luis Borges, "La nadería de la personalidad," in *Inquisiciones* (Buenos Aires, 1925).

64. See Santí's last section in "The Accidental Tourist: Walt Whitman in Latin America."

65. Pablo Neruda, *Obras completas,* ed. Jorge Sanueza (Buenos Aires: Editorial Losada, 1962), vol. II, pp. 8, 12.

66. See Donald Pease, "Blake, Crane, Whitman, and Modernism: A Poetics of Pure Possibility," *PMLA,* 96 (1981), pp. 64–84, esp. p. 81.

67. Michel Fabre, "Walt Whitman and the Rebel Poets: A Note on Whitman's Reputation Among Radical Writers During the Depression," pp. 89–90.

68. Ibid., p. 91.

69. Tulio Halperín Donghi, *The Contemporary History of Latin America,* ed. and trans. John Charles Chasteen (Durham: Duke University Press, 1993), p. 273.

70. Published in *El Nacional,* Caracas, November 27, 1947. It provoked President González to bring official charges against Neruda.

71. Neruda, *Obras Completas,* pp. 11–14.

72. For an outline of internal struggles in Chile, see Paul W. Drake, *Socialism and Populism in Chile, 1932–52* (Urbana: University of Illinois Press, 1978).

73. Elizabeth Garrels, *Mariátegui y la Argentina: Un caso de lentes ajenos* (Gaithersburg, MD: Hispamérica, 1982), pp. 35–36.

74. Roberto Fernández Retamar, *Calibán: Apuntes sobre la cultura en nuestra América,* 2d ed. (Mexico: Diógenes, 1974), p. 55.

75. Pablo Neruda, "Comienzo por invocar a Walt Whitman," *Incitación al nixonicidio y alabanza de la revolución chilena* (Mexico: Ediciones Grijalbo, 1973), p. 12. English translation is mine.

76. Fernando Alegría, *Walt Whitman en Hispanoamérica* (Mexico: Fondo de Cultura Económica, 1954). A concise English summary of the book appears as the introduction to *Walt Whitman & the World,* ed. Gay Wilson Allen and Ed Folsom (Iowa City: University of Iowa Press, 1995).

77. Enrico Mario Santí's, "The Accidental Tourist: Walt Whitman in Latin America": "the repressed elements, internal polemics and open misunderstandings that make up its significance—a story that Doris Sommer, in a recent essay on

Whitman, has rightly called 'The Contest for a Legitimate American Poetry.' This essay departs from Sommer's by insisting on the significance of the bibliographical details of such a story. With it, however, I share a concern for the role played in it by the Imaginary . . .," pp. 3–4.

78. Perhaps César Vallejo is Whitman's most worthy heir. This is the opinion of Jean Franco, see *César Vallejo: the Dialectics of Poetry and Silence* (Cambridge, Eng.: Cambridge University Press, 1976) and *Reinventing the Americas*, ed. Gari LaGuardia and Bell Chevigny.

79. C. B. McPherson, *The Life and Times of Liberal Democracy* (London: Oxford University Press, 1977). In the first two pages of the "Introduction" he makes clear that the definitive biography can now be written because the subject has long been dead.

80. Santí, "The Accidental Tourist: Walt Whitman in Latin America," p. 7, citing Paz.

81. Barbara Herrnstein Smith, "Licensing the Unspeakable," *On the Margins of Discourse* (Chicago: University of Chicago Press, 1978), pp. 107–124. The "possible utterance" refers to the capacity of poetry to call into existence, through the agency of repetition, that which cannot yet be represented. For my purposes, this suggests that poetry may be the appropriate medium for ideological production, since it can formulate rather than merely imitate.

82. See Gordon Brotherston's "Introduction" to Rodó's *Ariel* (Cambridge, Eng.: Cambridge University Press, 1967), p. 14. "He [Rodó] certainly had second thoughts about Whitman because next to the phrase (incorporated into *Ariel*) about 'Excelsior,' originally he wrote: 'Tiene en Walt Whitman el acento de los evangelistas! . . . Inmensa expansión de amor.'"

83. Santí, "The Accidental Tourist: Walt Whitman in Latin America," pp. 9–10.

84. "Song of Myself," in *The Portable Whitman*, 28, p. 62.

85. Ibid., 22, p. 54; 24, p. 57.

86. Eve Kosofsky Sedgwick, *Between Men: English Literature and Male Homosocial Desire* (New York: Columbia University Press, 1985), pp. 206–208.

87. Reinaldo Arenas, *Antes que anochezca* (Barcelona: Tusquests, 1992).

88. D. H. Lawrence, "Whitman" (Essay, 1921), in *Walt Whitman: The Measure of His Song*, ed. Perlman et al., pp. 43–51.

89. Luce Irigaray, "Questions to Emmanuel Levinas on the Divinity of Love," in *Re-Reading Levinas*, ed. Robert Bernasconi and Simon Chritchley (Bloomington: Indiana University Press, 1991), pp. 109–118. Levinas abandons the pleasure of caressing the feminine, which is "left without her own specific face. On this point, his philosophy falls radically short of ethics," p. 113.

90. Philip Fisher assumes, as does Whitman, that this is the equal deal. See "Democratic Social Space: Whitman, Melville, and the Promise of American Transparency," p. 77.

91. "Preface," in *The Portable Whitman*, p. 14. My emphasis.

92. "Song of Myself," in *The Portable Whitman*, 48, p. 94.

93. George Thomson, *Aeschylus and Athens: A Study in the Social Origins of Drama* (London: Lawrence and Wishart, 1941) especially the chapter "Exogamy," pp. 21–34.

94. His identification of America with himself is the primary way in which Whitman negotiates the erotic and social tensions between the individual as part of the collective and as an independent personality. The danger of his limitless love is that it will become aggressive. Lacan (like Norman O. Brown) draws a connection between Freud's understanding of love as union and Sartre's notion of love as the drive for possession. That drive is motivated by a paranoid and aggressive worry that follows necessarily from the mirror stage. But once the little boy stops identifying directly with his father as a rival and begins to understand the category "father" as a linguistic sign or social space he will be able to fill, the aggressivity of the Oedipal complex can be normalized, and the child fully enters society.

But Whitman doesn't risk normalization. That is, his American subject is born through cloning, an apotheosis of self-reliance. The strategy finesses any need for legitimating founding fathers.

95. "Song of Myself," in *The Portable Whitman*, 47, p. 92.

3. MOSAIC AND MESTIZO

1. [The penis resembles the tongue in its positioning and shape and in its ability to expand and contract, and in being in the middle of things, and in the way it works; for in the same way that the movement of the penis begets corporal children, the tongue produces spiritual offspring, and the kiss is common to both, initiating the movement from one to the other.] León Hebreo, *Diálogos de Amor, traducción Inca Garcilaso de la Vega* (Buenos Aires: Austral, 1947) p. 112. References throughout are to this edition. The original is *Traduzión del Yndio de los tres Diálogos de Amor de León Hebreo hecha de Italiano en Español por Garcilasso Ynga de la Vega* (Madrid: Casa de Pedro Madrigal, 1590).

2. Luisa Martel de los Ríos was only four years older than the ten-year-old mestizo son of Captain Garcilaso. She apparently deserved her hammer-like name too, according to biographer John Grier Varner, *El Inca: The Life and Times of Garcilaso de la Vega* (Austin: University of Texas Press, 1968) p. 110.

3. Rolena Adorno, "El indio ladino en el Perú colonial," in M. León-Portilla,

M. Gutiérrez-Estévez, G. H. Gossen, and J. Klor de Alva, eds., *De palabra y obra en el Nuevo Mundo,* vol. 1, *Imágenes interétnicas* (Mexico: Siglo Veintiuno, 1992), p. 391.

4. Roberto González-Echevarría, *Myth and Archive: A Theory of Latin American Narrative* (New York: Cambridge University Press, 1990), p. 124.

5. Inca Garcilaso de la Vega, *Los comentarios reales de los Incas/The Royal Commentaries of the Incas* (Lisbon: Pedro Crasbeeck, 1609), pt. 1, bk. 9, chap. 31.

6. Ibid., pt. 2, bk. 8, chap. 17.

7. José Antonio Mazzotti, "The Lightning Bolt Yields to the Rainbow: Indigenous History and Colonial Semiosis in the *Royal Commentaries* el Inca Garcilaso de la Vega," Modern Language Quarterly, 57, 2 (1996): 197–211.

8. Inca Garcilaso de la Vega, *La Florida del Inca* (Lisbon: Pedro Crasbeek, 1605), dedication.

9. In the "Proemio al lector" (Preface to the Reader) he explains: "My intention is not to contradict them, but to supply a commentary and gloss." *First Part of the Royal Commentaries of the Yncas, by the Ynca Garcilaso de la Vega,* ed. and trans. Clements R. Markham (New York: Burt Franklin, 1869–1871), p. vi.

Cabeza de Vaca also published his *Comentarios* in 1555 (combined his report of North America to trek in South America.) See Cabeza de Vaca's *Adventures in the Unknown Interior of America,* trans. and ed. Cyclone Covey (New York: Collier, 1961) p. 15. "His account of his South American adventures, which is three times longer than that of his North American journey, was bound with the second edition of the latter in 1555 under the title *Comentarios.*"

10. Originally from the *Book of Samuel* ch. 25, v. 25.

11. Another translation might have seemed redundant, only six years after Carlos Montesa had published his Spanish translation in Zaragoza (1584). But Garcilaso may have been unaware of the work, despite the meticulously documented and time-consuming process of Inquisitorial approval and public licensing that publishing involved. Yet the likely editorial redundance is only one reason for readers to ponder Garcilaso's choice. Another was the nature of the dialogues; they were difficult and apparently quite foreign to Garcilaso's indigenist interests.

12. *Leone Ebreo (Giuda Abarbanel) Dialoghi d'amore, traduzione ebraica di Menachem Dorman,* trans. Menachem Dorman (Jerusalem: Bialik Institute, 1983), p. 17.

13. Carl Gebhardt, "León Hebreo: Su vida y su obra," *Revista de Occidente,* 12 (1934): 233–273. See also [Dorman], *Leone Ebreo (Giuda Abarbanel) Dialoghi d'amore,* p. 19.

14. [Dorman], *Leone Ebreo (Giuda Abarbanel) Dialoghi d'amore,* p. 20.

15. Ibid., p. 15; 86–88.

16. Ibid., p. 125.

17. Salomon Gaon, *The Influence of the Catholic Theologian Alfonso Tostado on the Pentateuch Commentary of Isaac Abravanel* (Hoboken, N.J.: Ktav, 1993), p. 3.

18. Cecil Roth, "Introduction," in *Leone Ebreo, The Philosophy of Love,* trans. F. Friedeberg-Seeley and Jean H. Barnes (London: Soncino, 1937), p. ix–xv.

19. [Dorman], *Leone Ebreo (Giuda Abarbanel) Dialoghi d'amore,* p. 46.

20. Ibid., quotation from pp. 40–41. My translation from the Hebrew.

21. Roth, "Introduction," p. x. See also Gebhardt, "León Hebreo: Su vida y su obra," pp. 243–244.

22. Gebhardt's more detailed version speculates that father and son reunited in Italy, because there is a document of 1560 recording a meeting in Salonica between Yehuda's grandson (and namesake), who was trying to get his grandfather's *Harmonia Coeli* published, and the neo-Christian doctor Amatus Lusitanus (Juan Rodrigo de Castel-Branco). The ms. was written at the request of Pico della Mirandola, and Amatus had read it often. The young Abravanel seems to have died soon afterwards in an epidemic. Gebhardt, "León Hebreo: Su vida y su obra," pp. 246–247.

23. The Dominican friar Gregorio García was convinced of the continuity, as was Fray Diego Durán. But Father Acosta rejected the theory vehemently and categorically, which is a sure sign, as Rolena Adorno points out, of its lasting and far-flung grip on the popular mind. Rolena Adorno, "El sujeto colonial y la construcción de la alteridad," *Revista de crítica literaria latinoamericana,* 14 (1988): 55–68.

24. Francisco López de Gómara, *Historia general de las Indias y vida de Hernán Cortés* (Caracas: Biblioteca Ayacucho, 1979), p. 8.

25. Antony A. Van Beysterveldt, "Nueva interpretación de los *Comentarios reales* de Garcilaso El Inca," *Cuadernos Hispanoamericanos,* 230 (1969): 353–390. Page (362) cites the *Comentarios,* part II, p. 227. This was a common complaint of the period, Beysterveldt adds. A. A. Sicroff cites an anonymous refutation of 1581 in *Les Controverses des statuts de la pureté de sang en Espagne du XVe au XVII siècle* (Paris, 1960), p. 148.: " . . .ya no se tiene en España por tanta infamia ni afrenta auer sido blasphemo, ladron, salteador de caminos, adultero, sacrileo (. . .) como descender de linaje de Judíos."

26. OC refers to *Obras Completas,* or complete works of El Inca Garcilaso de la Vega, ed. Carmelo Sáenz de Santa María (Madrid: Biblioteca de autores españoles, 1960), vol. 132–135, p. 14.

27. María Ramírez Ribes, *Un amor por el diálogo: El Inca Garcilaso de la Vega* (Caracas: Monte Avila, 1992), p. 49. In 1525 the Inquisition condemns *alumbrados* and there ensues a general "ruptura en relación con la apertura humanista y cristiana que el Estado español había llevado en el inicio de la Conquista."

28. Roth, "Introduction," p. x. See also Gebhardt, "León Hebreo: Su vida y su obra," p. 267. Yehuda and his entire household were exempt from all tribute. Gebhardt adds the contextual information about the Viceroy rebuffing local anti-Semitic pressure to expel the Jews from Naples.

29. Gaon, *The Influence of the Catholic Theologian Alfonso Tostado on the Pentateuch Commentary of Isaac Abravanel*, pp. 18–19.

30. Borrowings are clear, but marked by some anxious disavowals. See Amos Funkenstein, "Jewish History among Thorns," presented at the October 1994 Conference on Jewish Concepts of History at Harvard University, p. 11.

31. León Hebreo, *Diálogos de amor, traducción Inca Garcilaso de la Vega* p. 320.

32. Gebhardt, "León Hebreo: Su vida y su obra," p. 271.

33. [Dorman], *Leone Ebreo (Giuda Abarbanel) Dialoghi d'amore*, p. 128.

34. *Diálogos de amor, traducción Inca Garcilaso de la Vega*, p. 292.

35. Ibid., pp. 153, 156, 158, 173.

36. Enrique Pupo Walker, *Historia, creación y profecía en los textos del Inca Garcilaso de la Vega* (Madrid: José Porrúa Turanzas, 1982).

37. José Durand, "El Inca Garcilaso, historiador apasionado," *Cuadernos americanos*, 60 (1950): p. 161.

38. Aurelio Miró Quesada, *El Inca Garcilaso y otros estudios garcilasistas* (Madrid: Cultura Hispánica, 1971), p. 121.

39. Susana Jákfalvi-Leiva, *Traducción, escritura y violencia colonizadora: Un estudio de la obra del Inca Garcilaso* (Syracuse: N.Y.: Maxwell School of Citizenship and Public Affairs, 1984), p. 14.

40. Sabine MacCormack, *Religion in the Andes: Vision and Imagination in Early Colonial Peru* (Princeton: Princeton University Press, 1991), p. 332.

41. Margarita Zamora, *Language, Authority, and Indigenous History in the Comentarios Reales de los Incas* (Cambridge: Cambridge University Press, 1988), pp. 58–60.

42. Moshe Idel suggested a background to this focus on technique over content: after 1270 there was an intense hermeneutical period in Castile. "Concepts of Dream in 13th Century Spanish Kabbalah," a paper Idel delivered at a Symposium on the Spanish-Jewish Cultural Interaction, Harvard University, Dec. 3, 1995.

43. Dorman devotes a long section of his Introduction to the inconclusive speculations about the *Dialogues'* original language, which I summarize here:

In 1871, F. Delitzsch didn't doubt that the 1535 Italian was original, given the popular everyday language of the dialogues, but he felt that the style suggested a non-native speaker of Tuscan, thus agreeing with Benedetto Varchi (Florence, 1503–65) that the style marks the work (Dorman, 87).

The famed humanist Claudio Tolomei (1492–1555) had wondered about the original language, comparing Hebreo's unfortunate style to the admirable clarity of

Caesar and Cicero. The dialogues would have been even greater, wrote Tolomei, "if they were translated to Tuscan in a clear and clean manner" (Dorman, 88).

Carlos Montesa, who did the 1584 Spanish translation, thought that the original was in Latin (Dorman, 89); and Emanuel (Ben Yitzhak) Aboab agrees: "it was written in Latin, even though by now it is translated to almost all the languages of Europe" (Dorman, 303). See also his *Nomología o Discursos legales, compuestos por el virtuoso Haham Rabi Emanuel Aboab de buena memoria estampados a costa y despeza de Manuel Avuhav. sus herederos, en el año de la creación 5389 [1629]*. He was born in 1555 in Oporto, Portugal, and spent time in Italy near the Abravanels (Dorman, 90).

Marcelino Menéndez y Pelayo (1891) was sure that Hebreo wrote in Spanish, because of the many Hispanisms in the first Italian publication. I. Sonne (1928) agreed, pointing out that Abravanel never broke ties with Jews, and stayed mostly in Italian cities that had a large Jewish population. So Sonne reasons that the original must have been in either Spanish or Hebrew (Dorman, 92). Disagreement comes from Carlo Dionisotti (1959), who read of the third Dialogue in manuscript. He finds it written in a Tuscan too modern to have been original and reasons that Hebreo did not write in Italian, but probably in Hebrew (Dorman, 93). In that case, someone translated the book from Hebrew to Latin, the form found by publisher Mariano Lenzo of Sienna (Dorman, 94). Carl Gebhardt (1929) preferred the Spanish theory: no one denies the Spanish turns of phrase in the Italian. Spanish was not only his mother tongue, but also influenced the Italian of Naples, still in the Spanish orbit (Gebhardt, 258; Dorman, 94).

In any case, we *do not know* which language was in fact the original. Critics insist on their own preference, and the competition attests to the book's importance (Dorman, 95).

44. "Cerca del año de mil cuatrocientos ochenta y cuatro, uno más o menos, un piloto natural de la villa de Huelva, en el Condado de Niebla, llamado Alonso Sánchez de Huelva, tenía un navío pequeño . . . Fueron a parar a casa del famoso Cristóbal Colón, genovés, porque supieron que era gran piloto y cosmógrafo y que hacía cartas de mareas, el cual los recibió con mucho amor y les hizo todo regalo por saber cosas acaecidas en tan extraño y largo naufragio como el que decían haber padecido. Y como llegaron tan descaecidos del trabajo pasado, por mucho que Cristóbal Colón les regaló, no pudieron volver en sí y murieron todos en su casa, . . ." *Comentarios Reales,* parte 1, libro 1, capítulo 3.

The translation is from Inca Garcilaso de la Vega, *Royal Commentaries of the Incas and General History of Peru, Part One,* trans. Harold V. Livermore (Austin: University of Texas Press, 1966). Indicated pages are noted parenthetically in the text, here and throughout.

An earlier translation, with exhaustive comparative notes was prepared by Clements R. Markham, Ynca Garcilasso de la Vega, *First Part of the Royal Commentaries of the Yncas.*

45. For a most provocative speculation on how the Queen succumbed, in a love-hate dilemma, to a man marked as a Jew and poised for deportation anyway, see the masterful novel about discovery and conquest by Alejo Carpentier, *El arpa y la sombra* (Mexico: Siglo Veintiuno, 1979). For example, "En las noches de su intimidad, *Columba*—así la llamaba yo cuando estábamos a solas—me prometía tres carabelas, diez carabelas, cincuenta carabelas, cien carabelas, todas las carabelas que quisiera: pero, en cuanto amanecía se esfumaban las carabelas, y quedaba yo solo, andando con las luces del alba . . . ," p. 91.

46. *Royal Commentaries of the Incas,* trans. Livermore, p. 14.

47. Ibid.

48. Carpentier, *El arpa y la sombra,* p. 93.

49. *First Part of the Royal Commentaries of the Yncas,* trans. Markham, n. 6 on p. 24.

50. Garcilaso de la Vega, *Los comentarios reales de los Incas/The Royal Commentaries of the Incas,* see the part titled "Caution Prior to the Narration."

51. See Julio Ortega, "The Discourse of Abundance," trans. Nicolás Wey Gómez, *American Literary History,* 4 (Fall, 1992): p. 374. After identifying a Peruvian fruit called *ussun* Garcilaso writes, "I mention this to avoid confusion between it and the Spanish plum," and Ortega glosses: "With this, he indicates the need to preserve differences and avoid referential vagueness . . . One can see that the discourse of abundance, here practiced in full, has substituted previous discourses, turning resemblance into eloquent difference."

52. Garcilaso de la Vega, *Los comentarios reales de los Incas / The Royal Commentaries of the Incas,* pp. 1–3.

53. Roberto González-Echevarría, for example; see *Myth and Archive: A Theory of Latin American Narrative,* p. 44. But José Antonio Mazzotti has reminded me that this evaluation is based on late and stylistically adjusted re-editions, rather than on Garcilaso's first versions.

54. Garcilaso de la Vega, *Los comentarios reales de los Incas/The Royal Commentaries of the Incas,* pt. 1, bk. 2, chap. 17; pt. 1, bk. 4, chap. 17 and pt. 1, bk. 5, chap. 21.

55. Ibid., pt. 1, bk.1, chap. 4 and pt. 1, bk. 8, chap. 11.

56. Ibid., pt. 1, bk. 2, chap. 3.

57. See Beysterveldt, "Nueva interpretación de los 'Comentarios reales' de Garcilaso El Inca," p. 364. Even when Lope García de Castro, the judge who denied Garcilaso his inheritance, later seemed more favorable, Garcilaso decided to stay in his quiet corner and practice his strategy of evasiveness.

58. Emmanuel Levinas, *Otherwise than Being: Or, Beyond Essence,* trans. Alphonso Lingis (Dordrecht: Kluwer Academic Publishers, 1974), p. 7.

59. Here are a few of many instances: The Incan cult of the Sun, his consort the Moon, and of Pachacámac the Maker of all things, is called idolatry (Garcilaso 1609: pt. 1; bk. 1; chap. 15), then called religion (or, as a compromise "vana religión" [ibid.: pt. 1; bk. 4; chap. 1]), and again idolatry (or less categorically, "el culto divino de su idolatría" [ibid.: pt. 1; bk. 4; chap. 1]). Although the Moon is the Mother of all Incas, they never adored her as a goddess (ibid.: pt. 1; bk. 2; chap. 1). Is there an implied, and barbed, comparison here with Marialotry, since the Incas only venerated their Mother instead of worshiping her? On one page, the "virgins of the Sun (Son?)" are naively devoted to a pagan cult; on the next, they are translated into Christianized "nuns" (their aged superiors are abbesses), before the section ends with a reference, again, to wives of the sun (ibid.: pt. 1; bk. 4; chap. 1). And the summer solstice festival of *Raimi* is as impressive and solemn as Easter (ibid.: pt. 1; bk. 6; chap. 20). After detailing the ritual sacrifice of lambs (more evocative of Deuteronomy or Numbers than of the New Testament), he fuses the comparison into a qualified substitution: the Incas celebrated "their Easter" by publicly roasting and distributing the meat (ibid.: pt. 1; bk. 6; chap. 22).

60. Mazzotti, "Una coralidad mestiza: Subtexto andino y discurso sincrético en los *Comentarios reales* del Inca Garcilaso de la Vega," p. 123.

61. Garcilaso de la Vega, *Los comentarios reales de los Incas/The Royal Commentaries of the Incas,* pt. 1; bk. 6; chap. 22.

62. Ibid., pt. 1; bk. 9; chap. 23.

63. Ibid., pt. 1; bk. 5; chap. 29.

64. Ibid., pt. 1; bk. 6; chap. 9.

65. Ibid., pt. 1; bk. 1; chap. 15.

66. *Royal Commentaries of the Incas, and General History of Peru, Part One by El Inca Garcilaso de la Vega,* trans. Livermore, p. 41.

67. Garcilaso de la Vega, *Los comentarios reales de los Incas/The Royal Commentaries of the Incas,* pt. 1; bk. 9; chap. 15.

68. Ibid., pt. 1; bk. 9; chap. 39.

69. Ibid., pt. 1; bk. 4; chap. 8.

70. Ibid., pt. 1; bk. 6; chap. 3.

71. Ibid., pt. 1; bk. 9; chap. 12.

72. "Francisco de Carvajal, Gonzalo Pizarro's ruthless field marshal, liked to refer to those who changed allegiance during the civil war as *tejedores* (weavers) because they went back and forth. The weave of Garcilaso's *Comentarios* is so complex because his father was a weaver of sorts, . . ." González-Echevarría, *Myth and Archive,* 75.

73. Guamán Poma's *Nueva Corónica* was first published in 1936, almost four centuries after it was written. The publication opened an entire field in Andean studies, which tended to contrast the mestizo with the Indian. For recent examples of this tendency, see Nathan Wachtel, "Pensamiento salvaje y aculturación: el espacio y el tiempo en Felipe Guamán Poma de Ayala y el Inca Garcilaso de la Vega," *Sociedad e ideología: Ensayos de historia y antropología andinas* (Lima: IEP, 1973), and Patricia Seed, "Failing to Marvel: Atahualpa's Encounter with the Letter," *Latin American Research Review* 26 (1991): 1–24. See also Adorno, "El indio ladino en el Perú colonial," pp. 369–395.

74. Ricardo Rojas, "Prólogo," in Garcilaso de la Vega, *Comentarios reales de los Incas*, ed. Angel Rosenblat (Buenos Aires: Emecé, 1943), pp. 19–20.

75. Garcilaso de la Vega, *Los comentarios reales de los Incas / The Royal Commentaries of the Incas*, pt. 1; bk. 8; chap. 24.

76. Hebreo, *Diálogos de amor, traducción Inca Garcilaso de la Vega*, pp. 235–236.

77. Ibid., pp. 38–39.

78. Garcilaso de la Vega, *Los comentarios reales de los Incas / The Royal Commentaries of the Incas*, pt. 1; bk. 4; chap. 14.

79. This is a departure from the celebrations of synthesis in an earlier generation of readers. Paradigmatic is Raúl Porras Barrenechea (first published in 1945), *Los cronistas del Perú (1528–1650) y otros ensayos* (Lima: Banco de Crédito del Perú, 1986): "En él [Garcilaso] se funden las dos razas antagónicas de la conquista, unidas ya en el abrazo fecundo del mestizaje, pero se sueldan, además indestructiblemente, y despojadas de odios y prejuicios, las dos culturas, hoscas y disímiles," p. 391.

80. See also Antonio Cornejo Polar, "Cinco respuestas en torno a Garcilaso," *Literaturas andinas*, 6 (1989): p. 20.

81. Garcilaso de la Vega, *Los comentarios reales de los Incas / The Royal Commentaries of the Incas*, pt. 1; bk. 9; chap. 15; chaps. 14 and 23.

82. Walter Mignolo has developed these observations, for example in *Writing without Words: Alternative Literacies in Mesoamerica and the Andes*, eds. Elizabeth Hill Boone and Walter D. Mignolo (Durham: Duke University Press, 1994), pp. 292–313.

83. Gebhardt, "León Hebreo: Su vida y su obra," p. 270.

84. Hebreo, *Diálogos de amor, traducción Inca Garcilaso de la Vega*, p. 235.

85. [Dorman], *Leone Ebreo (Giuda Abarbanel) Dialoghi d'amore*, p. 123.

86. See Susana Jákfalvi-Leiva, "Errancia y (de)centralización linguística en la cultura andina," *Discurso Literario*, 4 (1987): 357–365.

87. Hebreo, *Diálogos de amor, traducción Inca Garcilaso de la Vega*, pp. 25, 23.

88. See Francisco Márquez Villanueva, "'Nascer e morir como bestias': Criptojudaísmo y criptoaverroísmo," in *Los judaizantes en Europa y la literatura castellana*

del Siglo de Oro, ed. Fernando Díaz Esteban (Madrid: Letrúmero, 1994), pp. 273–293. He points out that Aristotelian rationalism was common in Jewish communities, at a popular level as well as among the intelligentsia, through the Middle Ages and certainly at the time of expulsion. Averroism, the Hispano-oriental version of worldly rationalism, was polemical for insisting there was no after-life. Juan Ruiz, Arcipreste de Hita, used the Averroist concept of the centrality of sex as the poetic focus of his *Libro de buen amor.* (1343; Valencia: Castalia, 1960), p. 276.

89. Hebreo, *Diálogos de amor, traducción Inca Garcilaso de la Vega,* p. 84.

90. "If, after the innumerable 'irrefutable' refutations which logical thought sets against it, skepticism has the gall to return (and it always returns as philosophy's illegitimate child), it is because in the contradiction which logic sees in it the 'at the same time' of the contradictories is missing, because a secret diachrony commands this ambiguous or enigmatic way of speaking, and because in general signification signifies beyond synchrony, beyond essence." Levinas, *Otherwise than Being: Or, Beyond Essence,* p. 7.

91. Hebreo, *Diálogos de amor, traducción Inca Garcilaso de la Vega,* p. 112.

92. *Sefer Yezirah* is a medieval text of contested first publication date. Most recent edition is *Sefer Yezirah,* trans. Aryeh Kaplan (York, Maine: S. Weiser, 1990), vol. 1, p. 4.

93. Hebreo, *Diálogos de amor, traducción Inca Garcilaso de la Vega,* p. 189.

94. See Emmanuel Levinas *Otherwise than Being,* p. 5; "Saying is not a game. Antecedent to the verbal signs it conjugates, to the linguistic systems and the semantic glimmerings, a foreword preceding languages, it is the proximity of one to the other, the commitment of an approach, the one for the other, the very signifyingness of signification."

4. CORTEZ IN THE COURTS

1. Susan Berk-Seligson, *The Bilingual Courtroom: Court Interpreters in the Judicial Process* (Chicago: The University of Chicago Press, 1990), p. 1.

2. 111 Supreme Court 1859. The broad definition of habeas corpus followed a 1963 decision, *Townsend v. Sain,* written by Chief Justice Earl Warren. The substantial statistic represents cases heard from July 1976 to May 1991. See Linda Greenhouse, "High Court Votes to Further Limit the Appeals of State Inmates," *New York Times,* May 5, 1992, front page and B10, column 2. See also the reference in 60 US Law Week 4339, 1992; and in *American Law Reports* 2d, 540 vol. 89, a publication by lawyers about constitutionally important cases.

3. Justice White, who wrote the recent decision, reasoned that "It is hardly a good use of scarce judicial resources to duplicate fact finding in Federal court merely because a petitioner has negligently failed to take advantage of opportunities

in state-court proceedings." See Greenhouse, "High Court Votes to Further Limit the Appeals," B10, column 4.

4. Consider, for example, *Hernández vs. New York* [111 Supreme Court 1859 (1991)], in which Judge Anthony Kennedy wrote the decision that exonerated the court from charges of racism, raised because there were no Hispanics in the jury. The two Hispanic jurors had been disqualified because they would be hearing the testimony live, while the others would refer to the transcripts.

5. Américo Paredes explains that the shooting took place in Karnes County, Texas. But since that transliterates into "Carnes," or "meats," the names soon adjusted to "El Carmen." See Paredes, *"With His Pistol in His Hand": A Border Ballad and Its Hero* (Austin: University of Texas Press, 1958), p. 210.

6. Ibid., p. 57. Quote is from the *San Antonio Express,* June 25, 1901, p. 1.

7. Paredes, *"With His Pistol in His Hand,"* pp. 100–102. The respective papers are the *Beeville Picayune,* August 7, 1913, p. 1. and the Beeville *Bee,* August 15, 1913, p. 4.

8. Paredes, *"With His Pistol in His Hand,"* p. 88.

9. On women in this genre see María Herrera-Sobek, *The Mexican Corrido: A Feminist Analysis* (Bloomington: Indiana University Press, 1990).

10. *Espuma y flor de corridos mexicanos,* ed., Andrés Henestrosa (Mexico City: Porrúa, 1977), p. 10. "El corrido es el vehículo del que el pueblo se vale no sólo para expresarse: es también su órgano periodístico. Y esto de un modo natural, pues por ahí empiezan las literaturas, todas por la épica . . . Un corrido se hace de un día para otro, igual que una gacetilla de periódico, pues, como está dicho, tiene un fin informativo, es medio de propagar noticias."

11. *Canciones, Cantares, y Corridos Mexicanos,* ed. Higinio Vázquez Santa Ana (Mexico: Ediciones León Sánchez, n.d). Although no year is indicated, the corridos date the book after 1924, the year given in the "Corrido de Vargas Vila," p. 253. Clearly, it was published between then and 1926, when Harvard acquired the book. Most of the corridos in it have precise dates.

12. *Canciones,* ed. Vázquez Santa Ana, p. 240.

13. See Robert Rosenbaum, *Mexicano Resistance in the South West* (Austin: University of Texas Press, 1981), p. 49, where he refers to a point by Américo Paredes, *"With His Pistol in His Hand,"* p. 125.

14. *Canciones,* ed. Vázquez Santa Ana, p. 173. Also quoted in Paredes, *"With His Pistol in His Hand,"* p. 151. English translation is mine.

15. Paredes's book transcribes several variants. And even James Nicolopulos's book on Texas-Mexican singer Lydia Mendoza, *Lydia Mendoza: A Family Autobiography* (Houston: Arte Público Press, 1993), includes three different renditions. The first version was recorded by the Hermanas Mendoza, Lydia and Juanita, in 1967; the next, by "Los Trovadores Regionales" (Pedro Rocha and Lupe Martínez), is from

1929; and finally, Salomé Gutiérrez, composer, singer and record producer, "Felt compelled to write down his own version . . . (of the eight-year imprisonment) because he felt that the transcriptions and translations that he had seen in the pamphlet to Folkloric 9004 and Paredes's books did not tell the whole story or told it inaccurately" (ms. p. 605.)

16. José Limón reports this in "The Return of the Mexican Ballad: Américo Paredes and His Anthropological Text as Persuasive Political Performance," in SCCR Working Paper No. 16 (Stanford, Ca.: Stanford Center for Chicano Research, 1986), p. 29. See also José Limón, "Américo Paredes: A Man From the Border," *Revista Chicano-Riqueña,* 8 (1980): 1–5.

17. Frank Javier García Berumen, *The Chicano/Hispanic Image in American Film* (New York: Vantage Press, 1995), p. 199.

18. Paredes, *"With His Pistol in His Hand,",* p. 154. "En el condado de Carnes / miren lo que ha sucedido, / murió el Cherife Mayor / quedando Román herido. / . . . / Se anduvieron informando / como media hora después, / supieron que el malhechor / era Gregorio Cortez."

19. Renato Rosaldo, "Politics, Patriarchs, and Laughter," in *The Nature and Context of Minority Discourse,* ed. Abdul R. JanMohamed and David Lloyd (New York: Oxford University Press, 1990), pp. 124–145.

20. Gayatri Chakravorty Spivak, "Poststructuralism, Marginality, Postcoloniality and Value," in *Literary Theory Today,* ed. Peter Collier and Helga Geyer Ryan (Ithaca: Cornell University Press, 1990), p. 236.

21. Berk-Seligson, *The Bilingual Courtroom: Court Interpreters in the Judicial Process,* pp. 60–61.

22. See, for example, Jacques Derrida, "Signature, Event, Context," in *A Derrida Reader: Between the Blinds,* ed. Peggy Kamut (New York: Columbia University Press, 1991).

23. Frank Javier García Berumen, *The Chicano/Hispanic Image in American Film,* pp. 199–202.

24. Rosa Linda Fregoso, *The Bronze Screen: Chicana and Chicano Film Culture* (Minneapolis: University of Minnesota Press, 1993), p. 70.

25. Ibid., pp. 70–71.

26. Ibid., p. 77, quotes historian Tatcho Mindiola.

27. Ibid., p. 78.

28. Frank Javier García Berumen, *The Chicano/Hispanic Image in American Film,* quotes from *The Los Angeles Times, The Village Voice, Playboy.*

29. Jean-François Lyotard, *The Differend: Phrases in Dispute,* trans. George Van Den Abbeele (Minneapolis: University of Minnesota Press, 1992), pp. 77–79.

30. Ramón Saldívar, "Border Subjects and Transnational Sites: Américo Pare-

des's *The Hammon and the Beans and Other Stories,*" in *Subjects and Citizens,* eds. Michael Moon and Cathy Davidson (Durham: Duke University Press, 1995), p. 385.

31. David J. Wever, *Myth and History of the Hispanic Southwest* (Albuquerque: University of New Mexico Press, 1988), pp. 106, 141–148.

32. Mauricio González de la Garza, *Walt Whitman: Racista, imperialista, anti-mexicano* (Mexico: Colección Málaga, 1971). In another piece, Whitman asks rhetorically, "Who believes that the Whites and Blacks can ever amalgamate in America? Or who wishes it to happen? . . . Besides, is not America for Whites: and is not better so?" Whitman, *I Sit and Look Out,* eds. Emory Holloway and Vernolian Schwarz (New York: Columbia University Press, 1932).

33. Among critics concerned with related issues, see Tobin Siebers, *The Ethics of Criticism* (Ithaca: Cornell University Press, 1988).

34. Time is not homogeneous, though the Social Democrats believed it was and therefore considered progress to be inevitable. This made them lazy, and able to fit into fascist programs. Homi Bhabha, *The Location of Culture* (New York: Routledge, 1994), p. 95, identifies Benjamin's notion of homogeneous empty time as that of nationalist discourse. But he gives Benjamin credit for the critique in "Translator Translated: W. J. T. Mitchell talks with Homi Bhabha," *Artform,* 7 (March 1995): 110.

35. Homi Bhabha, "Race, Time and the Revision of Modernity," *Oxford Literary Review,* 13 (1991): 204–205.

36. The reference is to Fernando Ortiz, *Contrapunteo cubano del tabaco y azúcar* (originally Havana, 1941) Since then, the metaphor of counterpoint has been standard in discussions of cultural conflict and conflictual creativity in Latin America. There is a new translation with an introduction by Fernando Coronil (Durham: Duke University Press, 1995).

37. *María* (1867) is the classic novel by Jorge Isaacs. It is the most widely read, pirated, and imitated novel of nineteenth-century Latin America. Required reading in Colombian high schools, it is also on standard syllabi in many other countries.

38. Waldo Frank titled his book about the entire hemisphere *Our America* (New York: Boni and Liveright, 1919). Translated in references as *Nuestra América,* it was, for example, an inspiration and model for José Carlos Mariátegui, the major theorist of a particularized, Peruvian Marxism. "En Waldo Frank, como en todo gran intérprete de la historia, la intuición y el método colaboran . . . Unamuno modificaría probablemente su juicio sobre el marxismo si estudiase el espíritu—no la letra—marxista en escritores como el autor de *Nuestra América* . . . Diré de que modo Waldo Frank es para mí un hermano mayor." *El Alma matinal y otras estaciones del hombre de hoy* (Lima: Amauta, 1972), pp. 197; 192. Mariátegui's piece is from 1929.

39. In "Do 'Latinos' Exist?" *Contemporary Sociology* 23 (May 1994): 354–356. Jorge I. Domínguez reports this observation from two books under review: Rodolfo O. de la Garza et al, *Latino Voices: Mexican, Puerto Rican, and Cuban Perspectives on American Politics* (Boulder: Westview Press, 1992) and Rodney E. Hero, *Latinos and the U.S. Political System: Two-Tiered Pluralism* (Philadelphia: Temple University Press, 1992). "Very large majorities of Mexicans, Puerto Ricans, and Cubans identify themselves by their national origins, not as 'Latinos' or Hispanics." Domínguez, "Do 'Latinos' Exist?", p. 354.

40. Luis Rafael Sánchez, "La Guagua Aérea: The Air Bus" translated by Diana Vélez in *The Village Voice*, Jan. 24, 1984.

41. Tato Laviera, *AmeRícan* (Houston: Arte Público Press, 1985).

42. See Juan Flores, *Divided Borders: Essays on Puerto Rican Identity* (Houston: Arte Público Press, 1993).

43. José de Diego, "No," in Iris Zavala and Rafael Rodríguez, *Intellectual Roots of Independence* (New York and London: Monthly Review Press, 1980), pp. 131–133.

44. The name an Italian immigrant gives to this country in Deborah Lubar's one-woman show, *A Story's a Story.* Performed at Thornes, Northampton, MA, April 19–20, 1996. Reviewed by Chris Rohmann, "Of Miracles and La Merica," *The Valley Advocate*, April 18, 1996, p. 4.

45. I owe this to anthropologist and historian Michel Rolph Trouillot.

46. Rubén Ríos Avila, "La raza cómica: Identidad y cuerpo en Pedreira y Palés," in *La Torre*, 27–28 (julio–diciembre 1993): 559–576.

47. See Chapter 1, note 5.

48. The most obvious reference here is to Domingo Faustino Sarmiento, *Facundo: Civilización y barbarie,* first published in 1845 and subsequently a standard work for the continent.

49. The slogan comes from Juan Bautista Alberdi's *Bases*, 1851, the basis for Argentina's post-civil war constitution and an inspiration for many other legislators throughout Spanish America.

50. Inca Garcilasso de la Vega, *Royal Commentaries of the Incas and General History of Peru, Part One,* trans. Harold V. Livermore (Austin: Texas University Press, 1966; originally, 1609 and 1616), bk. 4 chap. 14, pp. 216–217. These "public women" lived in the fields, in poor cabins, each by herself. They were not allowed to enter the towns so as not to communicate with other women. They were called *pampairuna*, a word that indicates their dwelling-place and trade, composed of *pampa*, "open place" or "field," (it has both meanings), and *runa*, which in the singular means "person," man or woman and in the plural "people." Putting the two words together, if *pampairuna* means "people who live in the field, because of their wretched trade";

if the sense of "marketplace" is taken, it means "a person or woman of the market-place," implying that as the place is public and receives all those who go to it, so do they. In short it means "public woman."

5. NO SECRETS FOR RIGOBERTA

1. Alice Brittin and Kenya Dworkin, "Rigoberta Menchú: 'Los indígenas no nos quedamos como bichos aislados, inmunes, desde hace 500 años. No. Nosotros hemos sido protagonistas de la historia.'" *Nuevo Texto Crítico,* 6 (1993): 214. Rigoberta Menchú's new book is *Crossing Borders,* trans. Ann Wright (London: Verso, 1998). Worldwide rights by Giunti Gruppo Editoriale. "The moral rights of the author and the translator have been asserted." (This note by the publisher appears along with the ordinary publication data.)

2. Jacques Derrida, "Living on: Border Lines" in *Deconstruction and Criticism,* eds. J. Derrida, P. de Man, J. Hillis Miller, H. Bloom, and G. Hartman (London: Routledge & Kegan Paul, 1979), p. 87.

3. Homi Bhabha, *The Location of Culture* (New York: Routledge, 1994), p. 99.

4. Dinesh D'Souza, *Illiberal Education* (New York: Free Press, 1991), pp. 71–73.

5. Walter Benjamin, *Illuminations,* ed. Hannah Arendt, trans. Harry Zohn (New York: Schocken, 1969), p. 101.

6. Testimonio has been the object of sustained critical attention, and some debate. For collections of essays, see the special issue of *Latin American Perspectives, Voices of the Voiceless in Testimonial Literature,* ed. Georg Gugelburger, 70 (Summer 1991) and 71 (Fall 1991); René Jara and Hernán Vidal, eds., *Testimonio y literatura* (Minneapolis: Institute for the Study of Ideologies and Literature, 1986); John Beverley and Hugo Achúgar, eds., *La voz del otro: Testimonio, subalternidad y verdad narrativa* (Lima: Latinoamérica Editores, 1992); Sherna Gluck and Daphne Patai, *Women's Words: The Feminist Practice of Oral History* (New York: Routledge, 1991), and *The Real Thing,* ed. Georg Gugelburger (Durham: Duke University Press, 1997).

7. John Beverley, *Against Literature* (Minneapolis: University of Minnesota Press, 1993), p. 77, and chaps. 4 and 5.

8. Doris Sommer, "Rigoberta's Secrets," *Latin American Perspectives,* 18 (1991): 32–50.

9. See Chapters 1 and 6.

10. David Stoll, among many others, questions her claims to leadership in view of indigenous informants who do not authorize Rigoberta. See John Beverley's reference in *The Real Thing,* n. 15. Her legitimacy is not at issue for me. Rather, it is her rhetorical defense of decision-making among Indians. This implies making alliances with others, so that readers will be obliged to make judgments in order to

participate. But this is different from our presuming to replace local leadership. The difference is Rigoberta's rhetorical lesson.

11. Emmanuel Levinas, *Ethics and Infinity: Conversations with Philippe Nemo*, trans. Richard A. Cohen (Pittsburgh: Duquesne University Press, 1985), pp. 75–81; 78–79.

12. Cirilo Villaverde, *Cecilia Valdés* (Caracas: Biblioteca Ayacucho, 1981), p. 112.

13. Henri Lefebvre, "Toward a Leftist Cultural Politics Remarks Occasioned by the Centenary of Marx's Death," pp. 75–88 in *Marxism and the Interpretation of Culture*, eds. Cary Nelson and Lawrence Grossberg, trans. David Reifman (Urbana: University of Illinois Press, 1988); quote from p. 78.

14. Rigoberta Menchú, *I, Rigoberta Menchú, an Indian Woman in Guatemala*, ed. Elizabeth Burgos Debray, trans. Ann Wright (London: Verso, 1984), p. 9; see also *Me llamo Rigoberta Menchú*, ed. Elizabeth Burgos Debray (Havana: Casa de las Américas, 1983), p. 42. Page references are to the translation, followed by references to the original.

15. Menchú, *I, Rigoberta*, p. 13; p. 50. See also pp. 17, 20, 59, 67, 69, 84, 125, 170, 188; pp. 55, 60, 118, 131, 133, 155, 212, 275, and 299.

16. Ibid., p. 247; p. 377.

17. See, for example, Vincent Crapanzano, "Life Histories," *American Anthropologist*, 86 (1984): 953–960.

18. Jean-François Lyotard, *The Differend: Phrases in Dispute*, trans. Georges Van Den Abbeele (Minneapolis: University of Minnesota Press, 1992), n. 14: "Not to speak is part of the ability to speak, since ability is a possibility and a possibility implies something and its opposite . . . To be able not to speak is not the same as not to be able to speak. The latter is a deprivation, the former a negation. (Aristotle, *De Interpretatione* 21 b 12–17; *Metaphysics* IV 1022 b 22ff.)."

19. Lyotard, *The Differend*, #26. "Silence can indicate my incompetence to hear, the lack of any event or relevant information to recount, the unworthiness of the witness, or a combination of these."

20. Quoted in Paul de Man, *Allegories of Reading* (New Haven: Yale University Press, 1979), pp. 119–120.

21. Menchú, *I, Rigoberta*, p. 9; translation adjusted; p. 42.

22. W. George Lovell, "Surviving Conquest: The Maya of Guatemala in Historical Perspective," in *Latin American Research Review*, 23 (1988): 25–57; p. 47. See also Beatriz Manz, *Refugees of a Hidden War: The Aftermath of Counterinsurgency in Guatemala* (Albany: SUNY series in Anthropological Studies of Contemporary Issues, 1988).

23. Menchú, *I, Rigoberta*, p. 24; p. 66.

24. See June Nash's important contribution, "The Reassertion of Indigenous Identity: Mayan Responses to State Intervention in Chiapas," in *Latin American Research Review,* 30 (1995): 7–41; p. 9: "The rebellion attests to the extraordinary durability of distinctive cultures in Middle America. Anthropologists have attributed this persistence variously . . . Protagonists on both sides of this older [essentialist vs. constructionist] debate have shown that the persistence of distinct beliefs and practices among indigenous populations of the Americas arises from internal resources and from pressures exerted by the dominant group. Current debates are taking into account the combined force of antagonistic but interpenetrating relationships between *indígenas* and *ladinos* as they generate and sustain ethnic diversity . . . By looking inward at 'narrative strategies for resisting terror' (Warren, *The Violence Within: Cultural and Political Opposition in Divided Nations* [Boulder: Westview, 1993]), evoking dialogue between ancient and present traditions, and assessing the economic opportunities that condition their survival, researchers are constructing a theory that recognizes both the structural imperatives of the colonial and postcolonial systems encapsulating indigenous peoples and their own search for a base from which to defend themselves and generate collective action."

25. Paul Ricoeur, "The Hermeneutics of Testimony," pp. 119–154 in *Essays on Biblical Interpretation,* ed. Lewis S. Mudge (Philadelphia: Fortress Press, 1980), p. 134, 129.

26. Enrique Dussel and Daniel E. Guillot, *Liberación latinoamericana y Emmanuel Levinas* (Buenos Aires: Editorial Bonum, 1975), p. 29.

27. Ibid., pp. 8–9, 38.

28. Gayatri Chakravorty Spivak, *The Post-Colonial Critic: Interviews, Strategies, Dialogues,* ed. Sarah Harasym (New York: Routledge, 1990), p. 158.

29. Gayatri Chakravorty Spivak, "Introduction," pp. 3–35 in Ranajit Guha and Gayatri Chakravorty Spivak, *Selected Subaltern Studies,* foreword by Edward W. Said (Oxford: Oxford U. Press, 1988), p. 12.

30. Dussel and Guillot, *Liberación latinoamericana y Emmanuel Levinas,* p. 27

31. Ibid., pp. 18, 43.

32. Ricoeur, Paul, "The Hermeneutics of Testimony," pp. 143, 142.

33. Menchú, *I, Rigoberta,* p. 89; p. 162.

34. Ibid., p. 67 (translation altered), p. 71; pp. 131, 137.

35. Ibid., p. 121; p. 207.

36. Ibid., p. 166 (translation adjusted); p. 269.

37. Sacvan Bercovitch, *The Rites of Assent: Transformations in the Symbolic Construction of America* (New York: Routledge, 1993), p. 5.

38. Menchú, *I, Rigoberta,* p. 84; 1983, p. 155.

39. Sylvia Molloy, *At Face Value: Autobiographical Writing in Spanish America* (New York: Cambridge University Press, 1991), p. 3.

40. George Gusdorf, "Conditions and Limits of Autobiography," pp. 28–48 in *Autobiography: Essays Theoretical and Critical*, ed. and trans. James Olney (Princeton: Princeton University Press, 1980), p. 29; my italics to show his complicity in the exclusion.

41. Ibid, p. 29.

42. Paul de Man, "Autobiography as De-facement," in *Modern Language Notes*, 94 (1979): 921.

43. Domingo Faustino Sarmiento, *Recuerdos de provincia* (Barcelona: Ramón Sopena, 1931), p. 161; my translation.

44. Nancy Miller, "Authorized Versions," in *The French Review* 61, 3 (1988): 405–413.

45. Elaine Marks, "'I am my own heroine': Some Thoughts about Women and Autobiography in France," pp. 1–10 in *Teaching About Women in the Foreign Languages: French, Spanish, German, Russian*, ed. Sidonie Cassirer. Prepared for the Commission on the Status of Women of the MLA (Old Westbury: The Feminist Press, 1975), p. 1.

46. Violette Leduc, *La bâtarde* (Paris: Gallimard, 1964) and Michel Leiris, *La règle du jeu* (Paris: Gallimard, 1948–1976).

47. Menchú, *I, Rigoberta*, p. 1; p. 30.

48. Domitila Barrios de Chungara, *"Si me permiten hablar . . .": Testimonio de Domitila, una mujer de las minas de Bolivia*, ed. Moema Viezzer (Mexico: Siglo Veintiuno, 1977); *Let Me Speak!*, ed. Moema Viezzer, trans. Victoria Ortiz (New York: Monthly Review Press, 1978); quote from p. 15.

49. Claribel Alegría and D. J. Flakoll, *No me agarran viva: La mujer salvadoreña en lucha* (Mexico: Serie Popular Era, 1983); p. 9, my translation.

50. Emmanuel Levinas, *Ethics and Infinity*, p. 58.

51. This relative autonomy in the margins may be waning. As Gusdorf ("Conditions and Limits of Autobiography," p. 29) points out, the very fact that a first-person singular is marshalled to narrate a plural history is a symptom of Western penetration. "When Gandhi tells his own story, he is using Western means to defend the East . . ." At the same time, though, testimonials represent a "return of the repressed"—see Roger Rosenblatt, "Black Autobiography: Life as the Death Weapon," pp. 166–175 in *Autobiography: Essays Theoretical and Critical*, ed. James Olney, in both traditional and Westernizing discourses. What has been generally "repressed" in standard autobiographical writing is the degree to which the singular "I" depends on a complicated pronominal system. It nurtures an illusion of singularity, assuming it can stand *in* for others whereas testimonies stand *up* among them.

52. Sylvia Molloy, *At Face Value: Autobiographical Writing in Spanish America*, p. 151.

53. Ibid., p. 166.

54. Menchú, *I, Rigoberta*, pp. 169, 190; pp. 274, 301.

55. Philippe Lejeune, *L'Autobiographie en France* (Paris: Armand Colin, 1971); "Le pacte autobiographique," in *Poétique*, 14 (1973): 137–162; esp. 160–162; and *Le pacte autobiographique* (Paris: Seuil, 1975).

56. Nevertheless, and despite the interesting variations that this testimonial presents, it and others are undeniably autobiographical. Aren't they? They are life histories narrated in a first-person voice that stress development and continuity. In fact, the full title of Rigoberta's book is *Me llamo Rigoberta Menchú y así me nació la conciencia*. A regular nonfictional Bildungsroman! I say this to register a doubt about the genre itself, as well as to convey my impression that generic labels are meaningful here. I can simultaneously try to frame testimonials inside the perhaps more general category of autobiography *and* emphasize its departure. I should confess that I chose particular books to raise this issue; they fit somewhere at the seam of testimonials themselves, related, as it were, metonymically, but not as typical or substitutable exemplars of the heroic genre. When women in Latin America enter politics as an extension of the domestic realm and narrate their life stories to journalists or anthropologists (who have sought out these sometimes illiterate informants as representatives of particular historical struggles), we need not assign the results to the familiar category of autobiography, or even to the heroic testimonial norm of male informants.

57. Recent experiments in coauthored ethnography with bicultural informants develop this feature. See, for example, Bernard H. Russel and Jesús Salinas Pedraza, *Native Ethnography: A Mexican Indian Describes His Culture* (Newbury Park, Calif: Sage, 1989), and Martin Diskin's review, "Anthropological Fieldwork in Mesoamerica," in *Latin American Research Review* (1994): 163–175. Minor language errors keep stopping our reading of Rigoberta, while the flavor of translation consistently distracts us toward a foreign code. Thus the figural assumptions embedded in Spanish seem to be lost on her. In Spanish, as in many Western languages, the word "earth" is regularly metaphorized as woman; that is, woman is a substitute for the Land, which is the prize of struggle between men as well as their material for (re)production. On the other hand, man is metonymized as her husband; his agency and power are extended through the figure. From this follows a scheme of associations including the passive and irrational female contrasted to the active, reasoning male. This opposition has generated a populist rhetoric in Spanish America that functions left, right, and center of the political spectrum. The most bitter enemies will agree that the People's goal is to preserve or re-possess the beloved Land from a Usurper. See Doris Sommer, *One Master for Another: Populism as Patriarchal Rhetoric in Dominican Novels* (Lanham: University Press of America, 1983). Rigoberta would surely

sympathize, but first she would know who the people are and how they relate to the land; her gender lines are quite different: "The earth gives food and the woman gives life. Because of this closeness the woman must keep this respect for the earth as a secret of her own. The relationship between the mother and the earth is like the relationship between husband and wife. There is a constant dialogue between the earth and the woman. This feeling is born in women because of the responsibilities they have, which men do not have . . ." (Menchú, *I, Rigoberta,* p. 220; p. 342).

58. Edmonson, Munro S., "Introduction" to *The Book of Counsel: The Popol Vuh of the Quiché Maya of Guatemala* (New Orleans: Tulane University Press, 1971), pp. xiv, xv–xvi.

59. This merging of the female into the male may have been caused by the Spanish language itself, in which the plural of "father" means parents, "padres." Or it may be a more general habit in the West since the first version of human creation, "male and female he created them," gave way to the myth of Adam's original loneliness which made him help to engender Eve. Edmonson's translation of the Quiché cosmogony provides the term "engenderers," male and female, to replace the "fathers" of earlier translators. " . . . it was told, / By the Former / And Shaper, / The Mother / and Father / Of Life / And Mankind / . . . Children of the Mother of Light / Sons of the Father of Light, . . ." (Edmonson, *The Book of Counsel,* p. 8). With insistent repetition, the females precede the males; "They produced daughters; / They produced sons" (ibid., p. 24).

60. Menchú, *I, Rigoberta,* p. 7; p. 39.

61. María Lugones and Elizabeth Spelman, "Have We Got a Theory for You! Feminist Theory, Cultural Imperialism and the Demand for 'The Woman's Voice,'" in *Women's Studies International Forum,* 6 (1983): 573–581.

62. See Fredric Jameson, "Criticism in History," pp. 31–50 in *Weapons of Criticism: Marxism in America and the Literary Tradition* (Palo Alto: Ramparts Press, 1976).

63. See Ernesto Laclau, and Chantal Mouffe, *Hegemony and Socialist Strategy: Towards a Radical Democratic Politics* (London: Verso, 1985).

64. Dussel, *Liberación latinoamericana y Emmanuel Levinas,* pp. 21, 24.

65. Menchú, *I, Rigoberta,* p. 131; my emphasis.

66. Domitila Barrios de Chungara, *"Si me permiten hablar . . . ,"* p. 41.

67. Ibid., pp. 36, 163.

68. Menchú, *I, Rigoberta,* p. 81; translation altered; p. 150.

69. Ibid., pp. 9, 134, 246; pp. 142, 255, 376.

70. "We, thus, see that the logic of equivalence is a logic of the simplification of political space, while the logic of difference is a logic of its expansion and increasing complexity"; see Laclau and Mouffe, *Hegemony and Socialist Strategy,* p. 130.

71. Ibid., pp. 11, 141.

72. "It would appear that an important differential characteristic may be established between advanced industrial societies and the periphery of the capitalist world: in the former, the proliferation of points of antagonism permits the multiplication of democratic struggles, but these struggles, given their diversity, do not tend to constitute a 'people,' that is, to enter into equivalence with one another and to divide the political space into two antagonistic fields. On the contrary, in the countries of the Third World, imperialist exploitation and the predominance of brutal and centralized forms of domination tend from the beginning to endow the popular struggle with a centre, with a single and clearly defined enemy. Here the division of the political space into two fields is more reduced."

73. On p. 148, n.40 of ibid., Laclau retracts one point from his 1980 article, "Populist Rupture and Discourse," *Screen Education,* 34 (1980): 87–93, about contradiction necessarily leading to antagonism. But he still defends his more controversial and uncritical support of populism in this book.

74. Ibid., p. 124.

6. HOT PURSUIT AND COLD REWARDS

1. Later on, Poniatowska will admit that the scenes with Zapata are of her own invention, inspired by Jesusa's admiration for Zapata alone among the heroes of the Mexican Revolution. See María Inés Lagos-Pope, "El testimonio creativo de *Hasta no verte, Jesús mío,*" in *Revista Iberoamericana* 150 (1990): 250.

2. Beth E. Jörgensen's discussion is particularly useful. See her chapter, "Creative Confusion," in *The Writing of Elena Poniatowska* (Austin: Texas University Press, 1994), p. 53. Her reading coincides with several of the points I developed here independently.

3. Daphne Patai, in *Women's Words: Feminist Practice of Oral History.* ed. Sherna Berger Gluck and Daphne Patai (New York: Routledge, 1991).

4. See Amy Fass Emery, *The Anthropological Imagination in Latin America* (Columbia: University of Missouri Press, 1996). She quotes from Carpentier's "El recuerdo de Amadeo Roldan:" "Si no quieren que se forme una tragedia, guárdense la libreta y el lápiz . . . Aquí nadie tiene que venir a *sacar* danzones . . . Esto no es cosa de choteo . . . Nadie los ha llamado aquí . . ." (p. 33).

5. Poniatowska, "Literatura testimonial" (1984). Quoted in Jörgensen, *The Writing of Elena Poniatowska,* pp. 60–61. See also Judith Stacy, "Can There Be a Feminist Ethnography?" in ed. Gluck and Patai, *Women's Words: Feminist Practice of Oral History,* pp. 111–120; and Daphne Patai, "U.S. Academics and Third World Women: Is Ethical Research Possible?" in ibid., pp. 137–153.

6. See her 1985 Essay on La Onda, in Jörgensen, *The Writing of Elena Poniatowska*, p. 52.

7. Ibid., p. 36.

8. The expectation is prepared by standard feminist assumptions about women being trained to control expressions of desire. Poniatowska herself is one example: "in the effort to hide personal preoccupations, her own intimacy is a constant feature of her creative work." See Lagos-Pope, p. 249 (my translation).

9. Julia A. Kushigian, "Transgresión de la autobiografía y el Bildungsroman en *Hasta no verte, Jesús mío*," in *Revista Iberoamericana* 140 (1987): 667–677. She quotes Paz (p. 668) as if Jesusa had posed for his Mexican portraits: "Como todos los ídolos, es dueña de fuerzas magnéticas, cuya eficacia y poder crecen a medida que el foco emisor es más pasivo y secreto. Analogía cósmica: la mujer no busca, atrae." See Paz, *Laberinto de la soledad* (México: Fondo de Cultura Económica, 1979), p. 33.

10. Octavio Paz, *The Labyrinth of Solitude: Life and Thought in Mexico*, trans. Lysander Kemp (New York: Grove Press, 1961), p. 29. "Viejo o adolescente, criollo o mestizo, general, obrero o licenciado, el mexicano se me aparece como un ser que se encierra y se preserva: máscara el rostro y máscara la sonrisa. Plantado en su arisca soledad, espinoso y cortés a un tiempo, todo le sirve para defenderse: el silencio y la palabra, la cortesía y el desprecio, la ironía y la resignación. Tan celoso de su intimidad como de la ajena, ni siquiera se atreve a rozar con los ojos al vecino: una mirada puede desencadenar la cólera de esas almas cargadas de electricidad." Paz, *Laberinto*, p. 26.

11. Paz, *The Labyrinth of Solitude*, p. 30.

12. See Lisa Davis, "An Invitation to Understanding among Poor Women of the Americas: *The Color Purple* and *Hasta no verte, Jesús mío*," in ed. Gari Laguardia and Bell Gale Chevigny, *Reinventing the Americas: Comparative Studies of Literature of the United States and Spanish America* (Cambridge, Eng.: Cambridge University Press, 1986), pp. 224–41; and Bell Gale Chevigny, "The Transformation of Privilege in the Work of Elena Poniatowska," in *Latin American Literary Review* 13 (1985): 53, where a parallel is made between Jesusa and her antithesis Angelina Beloff (from *Querido Diego*), "sharing with her only a will to survive and a need to break silence, to assert herself . . ."

Nina M. Scott, in "The Fragmented Narrative Voice of Elena Poniatowska," *Discurso*, 8 (1990): 412, notes that in Poniatowska's "desire to identify with Mexico's *intrahistoria* as well as to affirm her own self . . . there is also a perceptibly feminist desire to give voice and visibility to women marginalized and silenced."

13. María Herrera-Sobek made this observation.

14. Information from Scott Mahler about University of California Press.

15. See, for example, Lucille Kerr, "Gestures of Authorship: Lying to Tell the Truth in Elena Poniatowska's *Hasta no verte, Jesús mío*," in *Reclaiming the Author: Figures and Fictions from Spanish America* (Durham: Duke University Press, 1992), p. 47. The hybrid genre novella-testimonial "seems to testify to the truth of what it tells through the language of literature, a good many questions may be raised about how such a text may become accepted (or not) as truthful, and about how the figure of the author associated with it may come to exercise any authority at all." See also Nina M. Scott, "The Fragmented Narrative Voice of Elena Poniatowska," p. 414: "As fine a text as Poniatowska has produced, the ambiguity between fact and fiction still undermines the effectiveness of Jesusa's testimonial."

16. See *Languages of the Unsayable: The Play of Negativity in Literature ad Literary Theory*, ed. Sanford Budick and Wolfgang Iser (New York: Columbia University Press, 1989).

17. Roland Barthes, *The Pleasure of the Text*, trans. Richard Miller (New York: Hill & Wang, 1990), p. 27.

18. Georges Poulet, "Criticism and the Experience of Interiority," in *The Structuralist Controversy: The Language of Criticism and the Science of Man*, ed. Richard A. Macksey and Eugenio Donato (Baltimore: The Johns Hopkins University Press, 1972), pp. 56–72.

19. See, for example, Wolfgang Iser, "The Reading Process: A Phenomenological Approach," in *Reader-Response Criticism: From Formalism to Post-Structuralism*, ed. Jane Tomkins (Baltimore: The Johns Hopkins University Press, 1980), pp. 50–69. Also, for a study of the operations readers perform and the opportunities that texts provide for interaction with the reader, *The Act of Reading: A Theory of Aesthetic Response* (Baltimore: Johns Hopkins University Press, 1978). In *The Implied Reader: Patters of Communication in Prose Fiction from Bunyan to Beckett* (Baltimore: Johns Hopkins University Press, 1974), Iser offers readings of representative novels based on their requirement of active readerly participation. Especially pertinent is "Narrative Strategies as Means of Communication," in ed. Mario J. Valdés and Owen J. Miller, *Interpretation of Narrative* (Toronto: University of Toronto Press, 1978), pp. 100–117. It focuses on the particular shape of readings as imposed by the author's regulation of the process.

20. Patrocinio P. Schweickart, "Reading Ourselves: Toward a Feminist Theory of Reading," in ed. Elizabeth A. Flynn and Patrocinio P. Schweickart, *Gender and Reading: Essays on Readers, Texts, and Contexts* (Baltimore: Johns Hopkins University Press, 1986), p. 52.

21. Judith Fetterly, *The Resisting Reader: A Feminist Approach to American Fiction* (Bloomington: Indiana University Press, 1978), and Schweickart, *Gender and Reading*, p. 41.

22. Schweickart, *Gender and Reading*, pp. 54, 52–53.

23. Julia Swindells, "Liberating the Subject? Autobiography and Women's History, A Reading of *The Diaries of Hannah Cullwick*," in *Interpreting Women's Lives: Feminist Theory and Personal Narratives*, ed. The Personal Narratives Group (Bloomington: Indiana University Press, 1989).

24. Schweickart, *Gender and Reading*, p. 56.

25. Patricia Meyer Spacks, *Boredom: The Literary History of a State of Mind* (Chicago: University of Chicago Press, 1995), p. 1.

26. Barthes, *The Pleasure of the Text*, p. 25.

27. Spacks, *Boredom: The Literary History of a State of Mind*, p. 6–7.

28. Wittgenstein quoted in Jean-François Lyotard, *The Differend* (Minneapolis: University of Minnesota Press, 1992), p. 137.

29. Ibid.

30. Alison Lurie, "Love Has Its Consequences: Three Novellas about Women Who Haven't Come Such a Long Way," *The New York Times Book Review*, August 8, 1993, p. 1.

31. Emmanuel Levinas, *Totality and Infinity: An Essay on Exteriority*, trans. Alphonso Lingis (Pittsburgh: Duquesne University Press, 1969).

32. Mikhail Bakhtin, *Art and Answerability: Early Philosophical Essays*, trans. Vadim Liapunov (Austin: University of Texas Press 1990), pp. 81–82: "Sympathetic co-experiencing, 'akin to love,' is no longer pure co-experiencing, or an empathizing of oneself into an object or into a hero . . . And it is true that the feeling of love penetrates, as it were, into an object and alters its whole aspect for us. Nevertheless, this penetrating is entirely different in character from 'introjecting' or empathizing another experience into an object as *its own* inner state, as we do, for example, in the case of empathizing joy into a happily smiling man or inner serenity into a motionless and calm sea, etc. These empathized or 'introjected' experiences vivify an *external* object from within by creating an inner life that gives meaning to its exterior, whereas love permeates, as it were, *both* its outer *and* its empathized inner life; that is, it colors and transforms for us the *full* object, the object as already alive, already consisting of a body and a soul . . . Coexperiencing in this form does not in the least strive toward the ultimate point of totally coinciding, merging with the coexperienced life, because such merging would be equivalent to a falling away of the coefficient of sympathy, of love, and, consequently, of the form they produced as well."

33. Poniatowska, *Hasta no verte, Jesús mío*, p. 82: "Me quedría el muchacho oficial o no me quedría, no sé. Entiendo yo que si él no me hubiera querido, como era militar y andaba en la revolución, pues me arrebata y me lleva y ya . . ." At the nadir of sentimentality, she describes their "intimacy": "Yo nunca me quité los pantalones, nomás me los bajaba cuando él me ocupaba, pero que dijera yo, me voy a acostar

como en mi casa . . . eso no. Mi marido no era hombre que lo estuviera apapachando a uno, nada de eso. Era hombre muy serio . . . El tenía con qué y lo hacía y ya," p. 85.

34. Magdalena García Pinto, "Elena Poniatowska" in *Women Writers of Latin America: Intimate Histories,* trans. Trudy Blach and Magdalena García Pinto (Austin: University of Texas Press, 1991), p. 75: "But now it seems to me that there are some things that could have been deleted and others that could have been worked on more, things about her inner life, not so many anecdotes or adventures . . . There are people who think it's like a picaresque novel . . ."

35. Ibid., p. 175.

36. García Pinto, asks, "how someone from your social background . . . should have gotten interested in the fate of Mexico's lowest classes . . ." Ibid., p. 176.

37. Kerr, in "Gestures of Authorship: Lying to Tell the Truth in Elena Poniatowska's *Hasta no verte, Jesús mío,*" p. 185, n. 13, quotes from Jesusa Palancares about terrorizing the interrogator by threatening to die before finishing the whole story: "Y se me va a morir, como ella lo desea; por eso, cada miércoles se me cierra el corazón de pensar que no podría estar," p. 9.

38. Chevigny, in "The Transformation of Privilege in the Work of Elena Poniatowska," p. 54: "Jesusa did not want to be interviewed, however, and Poniatowska for some time visited Jesusa once a week in what appears a tacit understanding of an equalizing ritual. Jesusa would set her to the task of taking her thirteen hens, a little leash tied to a leg of each, out into the sun . . . Although Poniatowska has said she made up details, her deference to Jesusa is patent in everything she says about her."

39. Poniatowska, *Hasta no verte, Jesús mío,* p. 273: "Yo no soy querendona, no me gusta la gente."

40. Jesusa's uniqueness is clear from an interview with Lorraine Roses, "Entrevista con Elena Poniatowska," *Plaza,* 5–6 (1981–82): pp. 60–61. "I see her as unique. In the first place, she's not at all like other Mexican women because she's no self-denying little Mexican mother; she's not mild, but fundamentally rebellious . . . Her pride is enormous."

41. Poniatowska, *Hasta no verte, Jesús mío,* p. 135: "Bendito sea Dios porque he sufrido tanto. Seguro que yo nací para eso . . . Pero me conformaba."

42. *Massacre in Mexico,* trans. Helen R. Lane (Lincoln: University of Missouri Press, 1992).

43. Chevigny, "The Transformation of Privilege in the Work of Elena Poniatowska," p. 50

44. University of Washington Press, 1990.

45. García Pinto, "Elena Poniatowska," in *Women Writers of Latin America: Inti-*

mate Histories, p. 163: "All the Pontiatowskis were French-Polish. One, for example was one of Napoleon's marshals. They had been expelled from Poland precisely because the last one was Stanislaus Augustus, the last king of Poland," p. 163. "I was born in Paris"; was sent to "convent school in Philadelphia [where] We got special treatment because we were considered princesses, because of my father's family name," p. 164. "We came [to Mexico] on a refugee boat . . . in 1942 or at the very beginning of 1943," p. 165; she spoke only French, was sent to British school in Mexico; "But I learned Spanish from the servants very quickly. From that time on I have always had very sympathetic feelings for housemaids, or whatever you want to call them. That explains why I like Jesusa Palancares . . . so much," p. 166.

46. Elena Poniatowska, "*Hasta no verte, Jesús mío:* Jesusa Palancares," *Vuelta* 24 (1978): 7–9.

47. Poniatowska, *Hasta no verte, Jesús mío,* p. 218.

48. See Kerr, "Jesusa's opinions and actions situate her as ever at odds with, and sometimes openly critical of, the major institutions and political or popular myths of Mexican culture (the family, the military, the church, the Mexican revolution and its heroes)," in "Gestures of Autorship: Lying to Tell the Truth in Elena Poniatowska's *Hasta no verte, Jesús mío,*" p. 57.

49. "De tanto que siento ya no siento," Poniatowska, *Hasta no verte, Jesús mío,* p. 256.

50. Rigoberta Menchú, *Me llamo Rigoberta Menchú* (Havana: Casa de las Américas, 1983), p. 20.

51. Poniatowska, *Hasta no verte, Jesús mío,* p. 120.

52. "Le bajé los pantalones, que me agacho y que me le cuelgo del racimo. Daba unos gritos! Al final lo aventé después de darle una buena retorcida." Poniatowska, *Hasta no verte, Jesús mío,* p. 209.

53. Palancares complains of the idle questions women asked her after her husband died in battle. "¿Qué me gano con decirles? No me gano nada. No con que les cuente yo mi vida, se me van a quitar las dolencias. Yo no cuento nada." Poniatowska, *Hasta no verte, Jesús mío,* p. 97.

54. "Elena Poniatowska," in *Women Writers of Latin America: Intimate Histories,* p. 169.

55. Poniatowska, *Hasta no verte, Jesús mío,* p. 11.

56. According to Kim Sheppele, the variable spelling of Schweig and Schweik is part of the point of Czech mongrelization of several languages.

57. Paul de Man, "Autobiography as De-Facement," *Modern Language Notes,* 94 (1979): 919–930. "Autobiography, then, is not a genre or a mode, but a figure of reading or of understanding that occurs, to some degree, in all texts. The autobio-

graphical moment happens as an alignment between the two subjects involved in the process of reading in which they determine each other by *mutual reflexive substitution* . . . in a text in which the author declares himself the subject of his own understanding, but this merely makes explicit the wider claim to authorship. " My emphasis, p. 921.

Julia A. Kushigian finds the movement to be a source of unproblematic affirmation. See "Transgresión de la autobiografía y el Bildungsroman en *Hasta no verte, Jesús mío.*" She quotes de Man about "substitutive exchange that constitutes the subject," but concludes: "En determinado momento el intercambio entre ambas mujeres domina; así se transforma en sujeto independiente, libre de cualquier oposición que pudiera impedir la sustitución y la inevitable fusión de los dos mismos sujetos," p. 668.

58. Lisa Davis, "An Invitation to Understanding among Poor Women of the Americas," in *Reinventing the Americas,* ed. Laguardia and Chevigny, pp. 224–241; p. 225: "much as Alice Walker has served Celie and the other characters of *The Color Purple* as 'author and medium' " (n. 9).

59. Poniatowska, *Hasta no verte, Jesús mío.* Jesusa claims that even her father's death at the hands of Zapatistas didn't make her sad: "A mí no me dió tristeza porque no lo vi. Como ya me había casado y no andaba con la gente de mi papá, la cosa hasta ahí quedó. No supe más de él, hasta que pasaron los años y en el Defe encontré a un joven espírita que le dió poderes a la facultad para que fuera a levantar su espíritu entre los abrojos," p. 89.

60. García Pinto, "Elena Poniatowska." After Poniatowska offered her a copy, Jesusa complained that the book was not a testimonial: "she told me, 'You don't understand anything . . .' She wanted more episodes about the Obra Espiritual, and was angry that [Poniatowska] didn't detail the meetings and people; that I made people up and killed others off," pp. 166–167. See Poniatowska's second thoughts on pp. 175–176. García Pinto: "So Jesusa is an excellent reader and critic."

Poniatowska: "Yes . . . It is a novel . . . but a lot of it is a testimony based on a reality she didn't recognize as hers . . . I should have used her name . . . though I'm not an anthropologist or a sociologist, would reflect a certain reality that she couldn't acknowledge . . . . It was a complete rejection." Is Poniatowska presuming to put her in a culture of poverty system, to make the struggles inevitably lost?

Susana Beatriz Cella underlines the asymmetry of their relationship, but for some reason concludes that the struggle between narrator and editor has had a happy outcome, the book itself. Is the end felicitous for us or for the narrator? The asymmetrical relationship would seem to impose the question. See "Autobiografía e historia de vida en *Hasta no verte, Jesús mío* de Elena Poniatowska," *Literatura Mexicana,* 2 (1991): 149–156.

7. *BELOVED* KNOWS HOLOCAUSTS BEYOND TELLING

1. In an interview with Paul Gilroy, Morrison described Afro-American music as the parallel to the strategies of her art, the mirror "that gives me the necessary clarity": "Music makes you hungry for more of it. It never really gives you the whole number. It slaps and it embraces, it slaps and it embraces." Paul Gilroy, "Living Memory," an interview with Toni Morrison in *City Limits* (London), 31 March–7 April 1988. Quoted in Elaine Jordan, "Not My People; Toni Morrison and Identity," in *Black Women's Writing*, ed. Gina Wisker (New York: St. Martin's Press, 1993), p. 116. See also "Interview with Toni Morrison" in *Présence Africaine*, 145 (1988): p. 148. Quoted in Eusebio L. Rodrigues, "The Telling of *Beloved*," *The Journal of Narrative Technique*, 21 (1991): 153–169. Rodrigues observes that "The structural ordering of this 'aural' novel is not spatial but musical," p. 154.

2. Toni Morrison, *Beloved* (New York: Pantheon, 1988), pp. 43, 73.

3. Benjamin, "Theses on the Philosophy of History," in *Illuminations*, ed. Hannah Arendt, trans. Harry Zohn (New York: Schocken, 1969).

4. Morrison, *Beloved*, p. 6.

5. Ibid., pp. 53, 163.

6. Satya P. Mohanty mentions this, almost as a digression. "The Epistemic Status of Cultural Identity: On *Beloved* and the Postcolonial Condition," *Cultural Critique* (1993): 41–80; p. 56.

7. See also James W. C. Perrington, *The Fugitive Blacksmith* (1849), especially the "Great Moral Conflict" chapter, in which the Reverend narrates his decision to keep his personal history to himself, in effect, to lie to the authorities.

8. Jessica Benjamin emphasizes that autonomy is still essentially relational, dependent on the recognition of an Other in *The Bonds of Love: Psychoanalysis, Feminist, and the Problem of Domination* (New York: Pantheon, 1988).

Marianne Hirsch, among others, writes specifically about Sethe, that her subjectivity, her personhood, needs to be developed through connections and speech. See her *The Mother-Daughter Plot: Narrative, Psychoanalysis, Feminism* (Bloomington: Indiana University Press, 1989), p. 7.

Valerie Smith's reading, which I found after writing this chapter, is closest to my own. See "'Circling the Subject,' History and Narrative in *Beloved*," in *Toni Morrison: Critical Perspectives Past and Present*, ed. Henry Louis Gates, Jr. and K.A. Appiah (New York: Amistad, 1993), pp. 342–355.

9. Morrison, *Beloved*.

10. Marianne DeKoven, "Male Signature, Female Aesthetic: The Gender Politics of Experimental Writing," in *Breaking the Sequence: Women's Experimental Fiction*, ed. Ellen G. Friedman and Miriam Fuchs (Princeton: Princeton University Press, 1989), pp. 72–81; Emily Miller Budick, "Absence, Loss, and the Space of History in

Toni Morrison's *Beloved*," *Arizona Quarterly,* 48, 2 (1992): 117–138; Richard Todd, "Toni Morrison and Canonicity: Acceptance or Appropriation," in *Rewriting the Dream: Reflections on the Changing American Literary Canon,* ed. W. M. Verhoeven (Amsterdam: Rodopi, 1992), pp. 433–459.

11. Homi Bhabha, *The Location of Culture* (New York: Routledge, 1994): "Although Morrison insistently repeats at the close of *Beloved,* 'This is not a story to pass on,' she does this in order to engrave the event in the deepest resources of our amnesia, of our unconsciousness . . . is also to affirm a profound desire for social solidarity: 'I am looking for the join . . . I want to join . . . I want to join,'" p. 18.

12. Karla F. C. Holloway, "*Beloved:* A Spiritual," *Callaloo,* 13 (1990): 516–525. "Morrison revisions 'Pass on,' inverting it to mean go on through . . . continue . . . tell. She privileges the consequences of the sustained echo and in this way forces the sounds of these words (orature) to contradict the appearance of the visual (literate) text. Morrison has 'passed on' this story in defiance of those who would diminish the experience she voices back into presence," p. 517; and see Barbara Hill Rigney, "'A Story to Pass On': Ghosts and the Significance of History in Toni Morrison's *Beloved,*" in *Haunting the House of Fiction,* ed. Lynette Carpenter and Wendy Kolmar (Knoxville: University of Tennessee, 1991).

13. James Phelan, "Toward a Rhetorical Reader-Response Criticism: The Difficult, the Stubborn, and the Ending of *Beloved,*" *Modern Fiction Studies,* 39 (1993): 709–728.

14. Gilroy, "Living Memory," Toni Morrison interview, *City Limits,* p. 10.

15. More than one essay focuses on the dead end of the pre-Oedipal dyad between mother and child that seemed to promise feminist liberation from paternalist law (Elizabeth Hirsch, "The Personal Turn: Of Senior Feminists, Silence, and the Pastness of the Present," *Contemporary Literature,* 36, 4 (1995): 708–717; Marianne deKoven, "Utopia Limited: Post-Sixties and Postmodern American Fiction," *Modern Fiction Studies,* 41, 1 (1995): 75–97; Jean Wyatt, "Giving Body to the Word: The Maternal Symbolic in Toni Morrison's *Beloved,*" *PMLA,* 108, 3 (1993): 474–488; and Jennifer Fitzgerald, "Selfhood and Community: Psychoanalysis and Discourse in *Beloved,*" *Modern Fiction Studies,* 39 (1993): 669–687). Others feature Morrison's use of oral history and African American spirituality to complicate conventional genres of slave narratives. (Hazel Carby, Barbara Christian, Sherley Anne Williams: "Afro-Americans, having survived by word of mouth—and made of that process a high art—remain at the mercy of literature and writing; often these have betrayed us," in *Dessa Rose* (London: Macmillan, 1987), p. 5. Carolyn A. Mitchell, "'I Love to Tell the Story': Biblical Revisions in *Beloved,*" *Religion and Literature,* 23 (1991): 27–42. Some track the course of historical trauma and collective healing; and still

others concentrate on Morrison's "musical" or "modernist" techniques, especially in Eusebio Rodrigues, "The Telling of *Beloved.*"

16. Rodriguez, *Hunger of Memory* (New York: Bantam, 1983). "This message of intimacy could never be translated because it was not *in* the words she had used but passed *through* them," p. 31.

17. Morrison, *Beloved,* p. 62.

18. Ibid., p. 62.

19. Emmanuel Levinas, *Totality and Infinity: An Essay on Exteriority,* trans. Alphonso Lingis (Pittsburgh: Duquesne University Press, 1969), pp. 57–58.

20. See, for example, Brent Staples, review of *The Collected Essays of Ralph Ellison,* ed. John F. Callahan, (New York: Modern Library, 1996), *New York Times Book Review,* May 12, 1996 pp. 6–7. " . . .[A]n essay entitled 'The World and the Jug,' Ellison's response to an attack in the early 1960s by the New York intellectual Irving Howe. Howe had called Ellison a phony for not following the line set down by Richard Wright in the novel *Native Son* . . . He despised 'concreteness' in writing and was fond of complicated rhythms and ideas. The style worked well in fiction. But his speeches and essays suffered for it . . ."

21. Jean François Lyotard, *The Differend: Phrases in Dispute,* trans. Georges Van Den Abeele (Minneapolis: University of Minnesota Press, 1988), p. 160.

22. Toni Morrison, "Site of Memory," in *Inventing the Truth: The Art and Craft of Memoir,* ed. William Zinser (Boston: Houghton-Mifflin, 1987), pp. 109–110.

23. Sylvia Molloy, *At Face Value: Autobiographical Writing in Spanish America* (New York: Cambridge University Press, 1991).

24. Houston A. Baker, Jr., "Autobiographical Acts and the Voice of the Southern Slave," in *The Slave's Narrative,* ed. Charles T. Davis and Henry Louis Gates, Jr. (New York: Oxford University Press, 1985), pp. 242–261; quote from p. 251.

25. Toni Morrison, "Unspeakable Things Unspoken: The Afro-American Presence in American Literature," *Michigan Quarterly Review,* 28 (1989): 1–34. Quote from p. 11.

26. Douglass, "Narrative of the Life of Frederick Douglas," in Davis and Gates, eds., *The Slave's Narrative,* pp. 315, 320.

27. Jean Fagan Yellin, "Text and Contexts of Harriet Jacob's *Incidents in the Life of a Slave Girl. Written by Herself,*" in *The Slave's Narrative,* pp. 262–282; quote from p. 262. Letter to Amy Post: "I have tried for the last two years to conquer . . . [my stubborn pride] and I feel that God has helped me, or I never would consent to give my past to anyone, for I would not do it without giving the whole truth. If it could help save another from my fate, it would be selfish and unchristian in me to keep it back," p. 267. See also Anna S. Kaufman, "*Incidents in the Life of a Slave Girl:* The Name Says

It All" (ms. December, 1996), in which both "incidents" and "girl" underline Jacobs's appeal to white women.

28. Mae G. Henderson, "Toni Morrison's *Beloved:* Re-Membering the Body as Historical Text," in *Comparative American Identities: Race, Sex, and Nationality in the Modern Text.* ed. Hortense J. Spillers (Baltimore: Johns Hopkins UP, 1991), pp. 62–86.

29. For the final blocking of *Beloved*'s interference with the living, see Helen Moglen, "Redeeming History: Toni Morrison's *Beloved,*" *Cultural Critique,* 24 (1993): 17–40: "she must remain always on the edge of evocation. As the novel teaches us so powerfully, the elusive erotics of connectedness necessarily underlies, as it potentially disrupts, the socially structured erotics of desire," p. 37. See also Wyatt, "Giving Body to the Word," p. 481, and Hirsch, *The Mother Daughter Plot: Narrative, Psychoanalysis, Feminism.*

30. Barbara Christian, "Fixing Methodologies: *Beloved,*" in *Cultural Critique,* 24 (1993): 5–15.

31. Moglen ("Redeeming History: Toni Morrison's *Beloved,*" p. 19) makes the point about our fears and fragmentation contaminating the very theories that should dispel fear and promote wholeness. But I wonder if part of the universalist's anxiety doesn't come from assuming that we can and should be "whole" in the sense of undifferentiated sexually, racially, culturally. Theorists like Fanon and Bhabha, whom she mentions alongside radical feminists, evidently assume that we live in a fragmented world in which emotionally healthy people are particularly positioned.

32. Karla F. C. Holloway seems carefree as she assumes an insider's position in African America and submits to Morrison's care. "*Beloved:* A Spiritual," p. 518.

33. Morrison, "Unspeakable Things Unspoken," pp. 32–33.

34. See Barbara Christian, "Layered Rhythms: Virginia Woolf and Toni Morrison," in *Virginia Woolf: Emerging Perspectives,* ed. Mark Hussey and Vara Neverow (New York: Pace University Press, 1994), pp. 164–177; and Todd, "Toni Morrison and Canonicity."

35. Lyotard, *The Differend,* pp. 202, xiii, 22.

36. Ibid., p. 202. "Narrative is perhaps the genre of discourse within which the heterogeneity of phrase regimens, and even the heterogeneity of genres of discourse, have the easiest time passing unnoticed. On the one hand, narrative recounts a differend or differends and imposes an end on it or them . . . On the other hand, the unleashing of the now is domesticated by the recurrence of the before/after," p. 219.

37. Ibid., p. 136.

38. Jean Wyatt, "Giving Body to the Word: The Maternal Symbolic in Toni Morrison's *Beloved.*" "When Sethe tries to explain her attempt to kill herself and her children to prevent their reenslavement, she finds speech blocked," p. 476.

39. Lyotard, *The Differend.* "From one phrase regimen (descriptive, cognitive, prescriptive, evaluative, interrogative . . .) to another, a linkage cannot have pertinence. It is not pertinent to link onto *Open the door* with *You have formulated a prescription,* or with *What a beautiful door!* This impertinence may be opportune, though, within a genre of discourse. A genre of discourse determines what is at stake in linking phrases: to persuade, to convince, to vanquish, to make laugh, to make cry, etc. . . . ," p. 147. "A genre of discourse exerts a seduction upon a phrase universe. It inclines the instances presented by this phrase toward certain linkings . . . ," p. 148; p. 149.

40. Satya P. Mohanty, "The Epistemic Status of Cultural Identity: On *Beloved* and the Postcolonial Condition," *Cultural Critique,* 24 (1993): 41–80. Mohanty agrees with Dominick La Capra's critique of "objective" history of the Holocaust. "What is entailed by our acknowledgment is the need to pay attention to the way our social locations facilitate or inhibit knowledge by predisposing us to register and interpret information in certain ways," pp. 73–74.

41. Satya Mohanty suggests that we do judge her abstractly, at first, before we realize that abstractions are damaging. Paul D is censured, and later scenes show him to be chastened. Readers presumably follow. See also Carol E. Schmudde, "Knowing When to Stop: A Reading of Toni Morrison's Beloved," *College Language Association Journal,* 37 (1993): 121–135. "Judging Sethe's action in all its stark extremity is in fact the crux of *Beloved.* Like a Greek tragedy . . . ," p. 123.

42. Walt Whitman, "Song of Myself," in *The Portable Whitman,* ed. Mark Van Doren (Middlesex, Eng.: Penguin Books, 1981), p. 19.

43. Morrison is not stamping out (pun?) endless series of Americans in her own image and likeness; she is suggesting that we can love even those who are not intimates, those whom we cannot fully comprehend.

44. Morrison, *Beloved,* p. 163.

45. Lyotard, *The Differend,* p. 75.

46. Descombes (1977) in ibid., p. 134.

47. Ibid.

48. Ludwig Wittgenstein, *Tractatus Logico-Philosophicus* (New York: Routledge & Kegan Paul, 1981), p. 7.

49. Lyotard, *The Differend,* p. 135.

50. Richard Wright, *Native Son* (New York: Harper, 1940), p. 277.

51. Morrison, *Beloved,* p. 72.

52. James Baldwin, framed quote in exhibition "Equal Rights & Justice: Reflections on Rights" at The Center for African American History and Culture, Arts and Industries Building, Smithsonian Institution, Sept. 22, 1995 to March 3, 1996.

53. See Dominick La Capra, *Representing the Holocaust: History, Theory, Trauma*

(Ithaca: Cornell University Press, 1994), for a review of the first important debate, between revisionist historian Ernst Nolte and the response by Jürgen Habermas. See also, *The Holocaust and History: The Known, the Unknown, the Disputed, and the Reexamined,* ed. Michael Berenbaum and Abraham J. Peck. Published in Association with the United States Holocaust Memorial Museum (Bloomington: Indiana University Press, 1998).

54. Jean Fagin Yellin writes that Jacobs's text is the only slave narrative that takes as its subject the sexual exploitation of female slaves, directly addressing the complication of racial oppression by sexual abuse. See her "Texts and Contexts of Harriet Jacobs' *Incidents in the Life of a Slave Girl: Written by Herself,*" in Davis and Gates, *The Slave's Narrative,* p. 277. The novel was well received on publication, but in the twentieth century it has been the subject of much controversy regarding its authenticity. Mary Helen Washington refers to John Blassingame's criticism, in his *Slave Testimony* (1972): Jacobs's book was "too melodramatic to be authentic." (Washington, ed., *Invented Lives: Narratives of Black Women, 1860–1960* (London, Virago, 1989), p. 7.) Hazel Carby argues that this dismissal stems from a refusal to accept a text that deviates "from the conventions of male authored texts." It has only been since the 1980s, through the research of these critics and particularly that of Jean Fagin Yellin, that Jacobs's text has been fully authenticated.

55. Narrow and racist as is Willa Cather's *Saphira and the Slave Girl,* however much it mitigates slavery, the novel is obviously grounded in the autobiographical *Incidents.*

56. Michel-Rolph Trouillot, *Silencing the Past: Power and the Production of History* (Boston: Beacon Press, 1995), p. 82.

57. Jacques Derrida takes up the issue of possibility in *The Other Heading: Reflections on Today's Europe,* trans. Pascale-Anne Brault and Michael B. Naas (Bloomington: Indiana University Press, 1992). "When a responsibility is exercised in the order of the possible, it simply follows a direction and elaborates a program. It makes of ethics and polities a technology. No longer of the order of practical reason or decision, it begins to be irresponsible . . . European cultural identity, like identity or identification in general, if it must be equal *to itself and to the other,* up to the measure of its own immeasurable difference 'with itself,' belongs, therefore *must* belong, to this *experience and experiment of the impossible,*" p. 45.

58. See Walter Benn Michaels, "'You Who Never Was There': Slavery and the New Historicism, Deconstruction and the Holocaust," *Narrative,* 4 (1996): 1–16.

59. Trouillot, *Silencing the Past,* pp. 96–97. "The literature on slavery in the Americas and on the Holocaust suggests that there may be structural similarities in global silences or, at the very least, that erasure and banalization are not unique to the Haitian Revolution."

60. Toni Morrison, "Rootedness: The Ancestor as Foundation," in *Black Women Writers 1950–1980,* ed. Mari Evans (New York: Anchor-Doubleday, 1984), pp. 339–345. See also Sherley Anne Williams: "Afro-Americans, having survived by word of mouth—and made of that process a high art—remain at the mercy of literature and writing; often these have betrayed us," in *Dessa Rose* (London: Macmillan, 1987), p. 5.

61. Leo Strauss, *Persecution and the Art of Writing* (Westport, CT: Greenwood Press, 1952), pp. 49–50, about Maimonides writing down oral esoteric tradition in *Guide for the Perplexed:* "Only the necessity of saving the law can have caused him to break the law."

62. Shalom Spiegel, *The Last Trial: On the Legends and Lore of the Command to Abraham to Offer Isaac as a Sacrifice: The Akedah,* trans. and intr. Judah Goldin (New York: Behrman House, 1954), p. 21.

63. Ibid., p. 33.

64. Eddy M. Zemach shows a similar response among survivors of the Holocaust, for whom assimilation now would amount to finishing the extermination campaign that Hitler began. See his "Custodians," in *Jewish Identity,* ed. David Theo Goldberg and Michael Krausz (Philadelphia: Temple University Press, 1993), pp. 19–129.

65. Morrison, *Beloved,* p. 210.

66. Karla F. C. Holloway, "*Beloved:* A Spiritual"; Eusebio L. Rodrigues, "The Telling of *Beloved*"; Barbara Christian, "Fixing Methodologies: *Beloved*"; Iyunolu Osagie, "Is Morrison Also Among the Prophets?: 'Psychoanalytic' Strategies in *Beloved,*" *African American Review,* 28 (1994): 423–440.

67. The novel is dedicated to the anonymous captured black Africans who "never even made it into slavery, those who died either in Africa or on slave ships." Walter Clemons, "The Ghosts of 'Sixty Million and More,'" *Newsweek,* 28 Sept. 1987, p. 75.

68. Iyunolu Osagie, "Is Morrison Also Among the Prophets?" "Utilizing both Western and African interpretations of the psyche," p. 423. "Yes, Morrison can be counted among the prophets of psychoanalysis . . . the two forms of psychoanalysis should not be conflated . . . Psychic trauma in the African world usually stems from immediate historical, social, and political environment, and is responded to in various ways," p. 424.

69. Christian, "Fixing Methodologies: *Beloved,*" p. 9.

70. See Cathy Caruth, "Introduction" to special number of *American Imago,* 49, 2 (1992): 9. See also *Trauma: Explorations in Memory,* ed. Cathy Caruth (Baltimore: Johns Hopkins University Press, 1995) "Psychoanalysis is no longer simply a statement about others, but is itself a complex act, and statement *of* survival. . . . Psychoanalytic theory . . . occasionally speaks its obscurest thoughts out of an intense and

not fully assimilated confrontation with death. And . . . [Freud] speaks, enigmatically, out of the crisis of his own survival: 'Freud's peculiar strength was to say what could not be said, or at least to attempt to say it, thus refusing to be silent in the face of the unsayable,'" p. 9. Psychoanalytic theory and trauma would indeed meet, in this perspective, on the grounds of this impossible saying.

71. See Allen Rosenbaum, ed., *Is the Holocaust Unique?: Perspectives on Comparative Genocide* (Boulder: Westview Press, 1996). For an intelligent review of the controversial book, see Jonathan Mahler, "The Killing Field," in the Arts and Letters section of the *Forward,* June 7, 1996, p. 9: "The essays . . . address such diverse tragedies as the Atlantic slave trade, the massacre of Armenians by the Turks and Stalin's decision to impose famine on the Ukraininans in the 1930s."

72. Shoshana and Dori Faub, eds., *Testimony, Crises of Witnessing in Literature, Psychoanalysis, and History* (New York: Routledge, 1991), pp. 5–6.

73. See, for example *Diaspora, A Journal of Transnational Studies* (Oxford University Press), and a spate of new books: *The Penguin Atlas of Diasporas,* ed. Gerard Chaliand and Jean-Pierre Rageau (New York: Viking Penguin, 1995); *The Oxford Book of Exile,* ed. John Simpson (Oxford University Press, 1995); Matthew Frye Jacobson, *Special Sorrows: The Diasporic Imagination of Irish, Polish, and Jewish Immigrants in the United States* (Cambridge, Mass.: Harvard University Press, 1995).

74. Historian Eric Foner quibbles with Morrison about the degree of persecution during Reconstruction, apparently unmoved by the "objective" degree or by the novel's focus on psychological violence. "Nothing that Morrison relates is 'untrue,' but she offers the reader no hint of the remarkable achievements of blacks in the *public* world in these years." He concedes that the period was particularly violent in Kentucky, near *Beloved*'s setting in Cincinnati, but not typical. See "The Canon and American History," *Michigan Quarterly Review,* 28 (1989): 48–49.

75. See, for example, Stanley Crouch's dismissive assumption that the novel "seems to have been written in order to enter American slavery into the big-time martyr ratings contest." In "Aunt Medea: *Beloved* by Toni Morrison," *The New Republic,* October 19, 1987, pp. 38–43. See also Paul Gilroy's response to Crouch's "acid polemic": "What would be the consequences if the book had tried to set the Holocaust of European Jews in a provocative relationship with the modern history of racial slavery and terror in the western hemisphere? . . . from [these histories] we might learn something valuable about the way that modernity operates, about the scope and status of rational human conduct, about the claims of science, and perhaps most importantly about the ideologies of humanism with which these brutal histories can be shown to have been complicit." Paul Gilroy, *The Black Atlantic: Modernity and Double Consciousness,* (Cambridge, Mass.: Harvard University Press, 1993), p. 217.

76. Morrison, "Unspeakable Things Unspoken: The Afro-American Presence in American Literature," p. 16.

77. See Sander Gilman's chapter on Freud in *Jewish Self-Hatred: Anti-Semitism and the Hidden Language of the Jews* (Baltimore: John Hopkins University Press, 1984).

78. See a critique of epistemological foundationalism, by Quine, Rorty, who suggest that we naturalize epistemology, which means that our questions are shaped by the practices and protocols of justification in the various sciences. Richard Rorty, *Philosophy and the Mirror of Nature* (Princeton: Princeton University Press, 1979); W. V. O. Quine, "Epistemology Naturalized," *Naturalizing Epistemology,* ed. Hilary Kornblith (Cambridge: MIT Press, 1985), pp. 15–29.

79. Michaels, "You Who Never Was There,' " p. 8.

80. Ricoeur, Paul, "The Hermeneutics of Testimony," in *Essays on Biblical Interpretation,* ed. Lewis S. Mudge (Philadelphia: Fortress Press, 1980), pp. 119–154.

81. Toni Morrison, "Unspeakable Things Unspoken: The Afro-American Presence in American Literature." On disruption, see Maggie Sale, "Critiques from Within: Antebellum Projects of Resistance," in *Subjects and Citizens,* ed. Michael Moon and Cathy Davidson (Pittsburgh: Duke University Press, 1995), pp. 145–168.

82. Theodore Parker, *The American Scholar,* ed. George Willis Cooke (Boston: American Unitarian Association, 1907), p. 44: "There is one portion of our permanent literature, if literature it may be called, which is wholly independent and original . . . So we have one series of literary productions that could be written by none but Americans, and only here; I mean the lives of the Fugitive slaves. But as these are not the work of men of superior culture they hardly help to pay the scholar's debt. Yet all the original romance of Americans is in them, not in the white man's novel." Quoted in Russ Castronovo, "Radical Configurations of History in the Era of American Slavery," in *Subjects and Citizens,* p. 169.

83. Shoshana Felman and Dori Laub, eds., *Testimony, Crises of Witnessing in Literature, Psychoanalysis, and History* p. 62.

84. Cathy Caruth and Deborah Esch, eds., *Critical Encounters: Reference and Responsibility in Deconstructive Writing* (New Brunswick: Rutgers University Press, 1994), p. 1.

85. Cathy Caruth, "Introduction," in *American Imago,* 49, 2 (1992): 10.

86. "The act of telling might itself become severely traumatizing, if the price of speaking is *re-living;* not relief, but further retraumatization. Poets and writers who have broken their silence may have indeed paid with their life for that deed (Celan, Améry, Borowski, Levi, Bettelheim). Moreover: if one talks about the trauma without being truly heard or truly listened to, the telling might itself be lived as a return

of the trauma—a *re-experiencing of the event itself.* Primo Levi narrates a recurring nightmare in Auschwitz" (Felman and Laub, *Testimony,* p. 67).

87. Jean Wyatt argues that Sethe is incapable of using language, that she rejects the distance of language, declines mediation between her body and her children, doesn't play fort"Giving Body to the Word: The Maternal Symbolic in Toni Morrison's *Beloved,*" p. 477.

88. Rodrigues, "The Telling of *Beloved,*" p. 159.

89. Caruth, "Introduction," p. 1.

90. Felman and Laub, *Testimony,* p. 58. Jean Wyatt, "The Maternal Symbolic in Toni Morrison's *Beloved,*" PMLA, 108, 3 (1993): 474–488, 477.

91. Spiegel, *The Last Trial,* p. 17.

92. Felman and Laub, *Testimony,* p. 58.

93. Morrison, *Beloved,* p. 104.

94. Felman and Laub, *Testimony,* p. 60. Nevertheless, his identification with the patient seems to come dangerously close, as if to say that he can speak for both, or to say that only Holocaust survivors can be effective analysts for other survivors: "The listener to the narrative of extreme human pain, of massive psychic trauma comes to be a participant and a co-owner of the traumatic event: through his very listening, he comes to partially experience trauma in himself" (p. 57).

95. Eleonora Lev, "Don't Take Your Daughter to the Extermination Camp," *Tikkun,* 2 (1988): 54–60, quotes from pp. 55 and 59.

96. Morrison, *Beloved,* p. 70.

97. Ibid., p. 6.

98. Caruth, "Introduction," *American Imago,* p. 2.

99. William J. Cromie, "Tests Reveal That Trauma Distorts Memory," *Harvard Gazette,* April 15, 1994, p. 5: people "experience nightmares and intrusive, repetitive flashbacks to the traumatic event." Vietnam veterans, victims of rape, are " 'stuck in time,' says Richard McNally, associate professor of psychology . . . 'Their inability to use memory robs them of details of their past and clouds their view of the future. The only clear thing in their minds is the trauma.' "

100. Morrison, *Beloved,* p. 58.

101. Felman and Laub, *Testimony,* pp. 57, 63.

102. Toni Morrison, " Unspeakable Things Unspoken: The Afro-American Presence in American Literature," p. 2.

103. Morrison, *Beloved,* p. 70.

104. Ibid., pp. 161, 46, 38.

105. Cornel West, *Race Matters* (Boston: Beacon Press, 1993), p. 19.

106. Morrison, *Beloved,* p. 164.

107. Carol E. Schmudde, "Knowing When to Stop: A Reading of Toni Morrison's *Beloved*," offers a moving interpretation, that nevertheless collapses the difference between tragedy and morality. It targets Sethe's (and the community's) excess (p. 131), her *hubris* (p. 126), as moral failures, and makes her inability to ask forgiveness the cause of being haunted by the baby. "Judging Sethe's action in all its stark extremity is in fact the crux of *Beloved*. Like a Greek tragedy, . . . The moral issue is not simple. Is the baby's death to be blamed on the inherent evil of a slave society?" p. 123. She points out that the white characters, slaveowner Schoolteacher and abolitionist Mr. Bodwin, absolve Sethe. But the blacks judge her critically, as a responsible agent.

108. Interview with Mervyn Rothstein, "Toni Morrison, in Her New Novel, Defends Women," *New York Times*, 26 August 1987, p. C17.

109. Claude Lanzmann, "Seminar on *Shoah*," *Yale French Studies*, 79 (1991): 82–99; p. 85.

110. Morrison, *Beloved*, pp. 271–272.

8. WHO CAN TELL?

1. Cirilo Villaverde, *Cecilia Valdés o la Loma del Angel, novela de costumbres cubanas*, foreword by Raimundo Lazo (Mexico: Editorial Porrúa, 1979), p. 57. Page references to the novel will be to this edition, in my translation. An English translation of the novel exists: *Cecilia Valdés or Angel's Hill: A Novel of Cuban Customs*, trans. Sydney G. Gest (New York: Vantage Press, 1962).

2. Imeldo Alvarez García, "Prólogo," in *Cecilia Valdés*, 2 vols. (Havana: Editorial Letras Cubanas, 1981), pp. 14–15. In 1855 Villaverde married Emilia Casanova, and she forced the family to leave Cuba for New York, given her outspoken criticism of Spain. Later, he wrote *Apuntes biográficos de Emilia Casanova de Villaverde*, about her continuing political work, courage, and intelligence.

3. Villaverde, *Cecilia Valdés*, p. 155.

4. See Norman Holland, "Fashioning Cuba," in *Nationalisms and Sexualities*, ed. Andrew Parker, Mary Russo, Doris Sommer, and Patricia Yaeger (London: Routledge, 1992), p. 147–156.

5. Villaverde, *Cecilia Valdés*, p. 112.

6. Ibid., p. 1.

7. Ibid., p. 103.

8. Arnaldo Cruz Malavé points this out in a letter to me of August 8, 1996, in which he mentions Vera Kutzinski's mistranslation of *maliciosa* as "malicious" in *Sugar's Secrets*.

9. Villaverde, *Cecilia Valdés*, p. 139.

10. Ibid., p. 150. "No entraban en el carácter, ni en las ideas de honor y dignidad de D. Cándido, el pedir a su esposa la explicación del misterio, menos a los hijos con quienes pocas veces hablaba, mucho menos a los criados, alguno de los cuales sabía más secretos de familia de lo que convenía a la paz y a la dicha del hogar."

11. Ibid., p. 112.

12. I am grateful to Gordon Hunter for pointing out a fascinating comparison with Villaverde's contemporary, Henry James. Significantly, James does not address the racial or ethnic obstacles to communicability, but he does meditate on the ultimate impossibility of "appropriating" another's experience or meaning in his Preface to the "Figure in the Carpet."

13. Miguel Barnet, "La Regla de Ocha: The Religious System of Santería," in *Sacred Possessions: Voudou, Santería, Obeah, and the Caribbean,* ed. Margarite Fernández Olmos and Lizabeth Paravisini-Gebert (New Brunswick: Rutgers University Press, 1997): p. 111. "[Yemagá] is 'jet black,' the babalochas say, which is why she is compared to the Virgin of Regla, who also looks to the sea, towards the bay. Multiple legends tell of a diligent Yemayá, understanding towards her children and conciliatory."

14. Villaverde, *Cecilia Valdés,* p. 239: "Temo mucho, temo todo. Los negros han de mirar primero como hablan."

15. See Roberto Schwarz, "Ideas Out of Place," in *Misplaced Ideas: Essays on Brazilian Culture* (London, New York: Verso Press, 1992). Legally, Cuban slaves had some recourse, since Spanish slavery was based on the combination of Roman law and Christian philosophy of the *Siete partidas* of Alfonso X. See Herbert Kline, *Slavery in the Americas: A Comparative Study of Virginia and Cuba* (Chicago: University of Chicago Press, 1967), p. 59. In practice, though, chattel had almost no personal rights, and Manzano complained that a slave was legally a dead body. See also Orlando Patterson, *Slavery and Social Death. A Comparative Study* (Cambridge, Mass.: Harvard University Press, 1982).

16. Villaverde, *Cecilia Valdés,* p. 239.

17. See the literature review by Imeldo Alvarez García, in "Prólogo." See also Roberto Friol, "La novela cubana del siglo XIX," *Revista Unión* (1968): 178.

18. Some provocative work in this direction is offered by Pierre Bourdieu, "Reading, Readers, the Literate Literature," *In Other Words: Essays Towards a Reflexive Sociology,* trans. by Matthew Adamson (Cambridge, UK: Polity Press, 1990), pp. 94–105, and by David Perkins, "Some Prospects for Literary History," *Modern Language Quarterly,* 54, 1 (1993): 133–139.

See especially Marianna Torgovnick, "The Politics of the 'We,'" *South Atlantic Quarterly,* 91, 1 (Winter 1992): 43–63. "I do not object to the 'we' voice in and of itself.

What I object to is the easy slide from 'I' to 'we' that takes place almost unconsciously for many users of the first-person plural or its equivalents—and is often the hidden essence of cultural criticism. This slide can make the 'we' function not as a device to link writer and reader, or as a particularized group voice, or even the voice of 'the culture,' but rather as a covert, and sometimes coercive, universal" (p. 48–49).

19. Cirilo Villaverde, "Prólogo del autor," in *Cecilia Valdés*, 2 vols. "Prólogo" de Imeldo Alvarez García, pp. 50–51.

20. George Steiner, *After Babel: Aspects of Language and Translation* (London: Oxford University Press, 1975), p. 355.

21. For the differences, see, for example, "Prólogo" by Imeldo Alvarez García. He quotes Domingo Del Monte's letter to the editor of *El Correo Nacional* in Madrid: "No extrañe usted que en esos cuadernitos sólo se hable del amor, pues a este estrecho límite está reducida lo que produce la aherrojada prensa habanera," p. 28. On pp. 36–37, he returns to the difference and also quotes José Varona: "Lo que había de ser en la primera intención, mera novela de costumbres, se convirtió, por la inmensidad de la emoción, la riqueza de los recuerdos . . . en exteriorización palpitante de la vida íntima de un grupo humano." See also pp. 28–29.

22. Cirilo Villaverde, *Cecilia Valdés o la Loma del Angel: Novela cubana*, vol. 1 (Havana: Imprenta Literaria, 1839), p. 26: "Que se te parece, como un huevo a otro.—No, que a ti. . . . A mí mucho menos, ni por cien leguas. Es la misma cara tuya y la de Leonardo.—¿Por qué se me ha de parecer a mí, a ti y a ti, y no a cualquiera otro de la calle? Hay tal tema de averiguar descendencias por la fisonomía?— A Leonardo no, que a papá.—A papá menos que a nadie. Papá tiene los ojos verdosos y ella los tiene negros; papá tiene el pelo rubio, y ella lo tiene como azabache.—Ya se ve que no se parecen en cuanto al color del pelo, y de los ojos, y de ... pero en cuanto a la expresión- . . . Además, aquella nariz, aquella frente . . . Vamos, es escrita.—Muchacha! ¿Parecerse a tu padre? (qué locura! ésta a mi entender hacía de tripas corazón.) ¿de a dónde? ¿en dónde encuentras esa semejanza?— Y en éstas y en estas otras, como sucede en las polémicas habidas y por haber de literato a literato en nuestros periódicos, . . ."

23. See Verena Martinez-Alier, *Marriage, Class and Colour in Nineteenth Century Cuba* (Ann Arbor: University Microfilms International, 1987). In 1776, the Crown passed a law, Pragmática Sanción, that prohibited "unequal" marriages. This was followed by an 1803 decree that required parental consent to marry, for men until the age of 23, for women until 25. And the Real Cédula of 1805 repeated the prohibition against pure-blooded whites marrying blacks or mulattos.

24. Villaverde, *Cecilia Valdés o la Loma del Angel: Novela cubana* (1839), p. 245.

"Por mi mulata santa, sería yo capaz de abandonar y despreciar todos los tesoros imaginables."

25. See Gerald Poyo, *"With All and for the Good of All": The Emergence of Popular Nationalism in the Cuban Communities of the United States, 1848–1898* (Durham: Duke University Press), p. 96.

26. The first published version is *The Life and Poems of a Cuban Slave* (London, 1840), ed. Richard Madden. It appeared in Spanish, ed. José Luciano Franco in 1937; this is the version reproduced in Juan Francisco Manzano, *Obras* (Havana: Instituto Cubano del Libro, 1972). Then Roberto Friol included several unpublished and relatively unknown works in his *Suite para Juan Francisco Manzano* (Havana: Editorial Arte y Literatura, 1977). See also Sylvia Molloy, "From Serf to Self: the *Autobiography* of Juan Francisco Manzano," in *At Face Value. Autobiographical Writing in Spanish America* (Cambridge, Eng.: Cambridge University Press, 1991), pp. 36–54, and Antonio Vera-León, "Juan Francisco Manzano: el estilo bárbaro de la nación," *Hispamérica*, 60 (1991): 3–22.

27. Sonia Labrador-Rodríguez; her field work in Cuba shows reluctance by intellectuals to acknowledge the publications.

28. Alvarez García, "Prólogo," p. 9.

29. Herbert Kline, *Slavery in the Americas; A Comparative Study of Virginia and Cuba* (Chicago: University of Chicago Press, 1967).

30. Gerald Poyo makes this point in *"With All and for the Good of All,"* which appreciates Villaverde the politician.

31. See Richard Rosas's brilliant reading in "Literatura y construcción de naciones: una lectura de los textos de Eugenio María de Hostos." (PhD. thesis, Harvard University, Cambridge, 1996).

32. See Julio Ramos, "The Repose of Heroes," *Modern Language Quarterly*, 57, 2 (1996): 355–367.

33. Herbert S. Klein, *Slavery in the Americas: A Comparative Study of Virginia and Cuba* (Chicago: University of Chicago Press, 1967), p. 211–225.

34. See Pedro Deschamps Chapeaux, "Autenticidad de algunos negros y mulatos de *Cecilia Valdés*," in *Acerca de Cirilo Villaverde*, ed. Imeldo Alvarez García (Havana: Editorial Letras Cubanas, 1982), p. 220–232.

35. Poyo, *"With All, and for the Good of All,"* p. 18.

36. José Martí, *Obras completas*, vol. I (Havana: Editorial Lex, 1946), p. 249.

37. Poyo, *"With All and for the Good of All,"* p. 9.

38. Cirilo Villaverde, "El Sr. Saco con respecto a la Revolución de Cuba," *La Verdad*, February 10, 1856. "El Sr. Saco aunque al principio de su carrera pública pareció consagrarse a la causa de la libertad e independencia de Cuba, después dedicó toda

su atención y sus talentos a la causa de una raza de sus habitantes, los negros, y hoy día solo sirve a los intereses de una clase . . . de unas cuantas familias cubanas." (my translation) I thank Rodrigo Lazo for this reference.

39. Poyo, "*With All and for the Good of All.*"

40. See George Handley, "Reading in the Dark: A Comparative Study of Creole National Imaginings," in *Theories of Colonialism in/of the Americas,* ed. Sylvia Spitta, forthcoming.

41. Imeldo Alvarez García, "Prólogo," p. 13: "La polémica sostenida con José Antonio Saco le resultó una derrota, porque en ella 'no llevó la mejor parte.' El hecho registra, no obstante, lo que sentía y pensaba *entonces* el novelista sobre la equivocada y funesta corriente política."

42. Martí on Villaverde, in *Patria,* October 30, 1894, in *Obras completas* I, pp. 833–835. Alvarez García, "Prólogo," p. 18.

43. Poyo, "*With All and for the Good of All,*" p. 68.

44. José Martí, *Nuestra America* (Havana: Rambla y Bouza, 1909), p. 308.

45. See Juan Gelpí's argument for Villaverde's control of characters and readers, "El discurso jerárquico en *Cecilia Valdés,*" *Revista Crítica Literaria Latinoamericana,* 34 (1991): 47–61.

46. Poyo, "*With All and for the Good of All,*" pp. 47, 48.

47. See my "Sab c'est moi," in my *Foundational Fictions: The National Romances of Latin America* (Berkeley: University of California Press, 1991), pp. 114–137.

48. For a similar observation, see Julio Ramos, "Faceless Tongues: Language and Citizenship in Nineteenth-Century Latin America," in Angelika Bammer, ed., *Displacements: Cultural Identities in Question* (Bloomington: Indiana University Press, 1994), pp. 25–46; p. 31. But Ramos assumes that Villaverde coordinates light color with mastery (that María de Regla is mulata, for example, when she is black), while he observes that Villaverde's mulatas were more voluptuous than verbal. (p. 33). See also his excellent piece on law and literature, "La ley es otra: literatura y constitución de la persona jurídica," *Revista de crítica literaria latinoamericana,* 20, 40 (1994): 305–335.

49. Villaverde's flair for writing in Cuban dialect, especially in *Excursión a vueltabajo,* is the focus of Antonio Benítez Rojo, "Cirilo Villaverde, Fundador," *Revista Iberoamericana,* 152–53 (1990): 769–779.

50. For the threat and anxiety this posed to marriage alliances, see Martínez-Alier, *Marriage, Class and Colour in Nineteenth Century Cuba.*

51. "La procreación de las castas mestizas [es] mil veces mas temible que la primera [raza pura africana], por su conocida osadía y pretensiones de igualarse con la blanca." From "Informe fiscal sobre el fomento de la población blanca en la

Isla de Cuba y emancipación progresiva de la esclava . . ." (Madrid: Imprenta de J. Martin Alegría, 1845), p. 33. Quoted from Julio Ramos, "La ley es otra."

52. Gertrudis Gómez de Avellaneda, *Sab*. I develop this reading in "Sab c'est moi."

53. Villaverde, *Cecilia Valdés*, p. 7.

54. Ibid., p. 104.

55. Juan Francisco Manzano, *Obras* (Havana: Instituto Cubano de Libro, 1972), p. 31. Julio Ramos reports that he could find no explicit law that prohibited slaves from writing. See his "La ley es otra." From the beginning, Virginians were more explicit; and by 1831, reading and writing were unlawful even for free blacks and mulattos. See Kline, *Slavery in the Americas*, p. 119; p. 246.

56. Villaverde, *Cecilia Valdés*, p. 103.

57. Ibid., p. 222.

58. Ibid., p. 239–240.

59. The author gives the following footnote to Part II, chap. 3, about a gala evening at the Philharmonic Society: "La relación que sigue la tomamos casi al pie de la letra de un semanario que se publicaba en La Habana en 1830, titulado *La Moda*," p. 82. The novel as well as those articles were dedicated to Cuban women.

60. Villaverde, *Cecilia Valdés*, p. 47. The heroine's race is written into her love of dances and drums: "en esto no desmentía la raza."

61. Ibid., p. 103. More precisely, this describes the whole Fair at La Loma del Angel, including the dances.

62. Ada Ferrer, "The Silence of Patriots: Racial Discourse and Cuban Nationalism, 1868–1898," paper given at Our America and the Gilded Age: Jose Martí's Chronicles of Imperial Critique, University California at Irvine, January 27–28, 1995, pp. 20–21.

63. I thank Enrico Mario Santí for this observation.

64. Villaverde, *Cecilia Valdés*, p. 38.

65. See Rebecca J. Scott, *Slave Emancipation in Cuba: The Transition to Free Labor, 1860–1899* (Princeton: Princeton University Press, 1985).

66. Villaverde, *Cecilia Valdés*, p. 279. Jay Kinsbruner pointed out the incongruity of an "alcalde mayor" in Havana of the 1820s. This was probably a provisional magistrate, not a mayor. See David Turnbull, *Travel in the West; Cuba, with Notices of Porto Rico and the Slave Trade* (rept. New York: Negro University Press, 1969), p. 246.

67. See my *Foundational Fictions*.

68. The liberating possibilities of free markets in general are suggested when, for example, the slave María de Regla learns how to negotiate to everyone's advantage from a street vendor. Villaverde, *Cecilia Valdés*, p. 267.

69. Ibid., p. 282.

70. Antonio Benítez Rojo, oral reminiscences.

9. GRAMMAR TROUBLE FOR CORTÁZAR

1. Julio Cortázar, "El perseguidor," in *Las armas secretas* (Buenos Aires: Sudamericana, 1959), pp. 149–313. To facilitate reading this essay, I avoid the redundancy (for bilingual readers) and eliminate the incomprehensibility (for the English reader) by quoting Cortázar's Spanish in the notes and Blackburn's English—sometimes adjusted to capture Cortázar's style—in the text. See "The Pursuer," translated by Paul Blackburn, in *Blow Up and Other Stories* (New York: Collier Books, 1985), pp. 161–220. When two page numbers appear, usually in parenthesis, the first refers to the translation, the second to the Spanish edition. Occasionally, for stylistic reasons, I include the Spanish original in text.

2. Could Bruno be "the brilliant André Hodeir?" quoted by Marshall W. Stearns? It seems plausible, given the respect Hodeir's book commanded upon its publication (a year before Parker's death), and his characterization of Parker as "the most perfect example" of the jazzman. *"L'oeuvre de ce genial improvisateur est l'expression la plus parfaite du jazz moderne."* A. Hodeir, *Hommes et problèmes du jazz* (Paris, 1954), p. 128; translated as *Jazz: Its Evolution and Essence,* trans. David Noakes (New York: Grove Press, 1956). See Stearns, *The Story of Jazz* (New York: Oxford University Press, 1956). Stearns concurs, "The giant of giants was saxophonist Charlie Parker," p. 227. See also James Lincoln Collier, *The Making of Jazz: A Comprehensive History* (Boston: Houghton Mifflin, 1978), and Frederick Garber, "Fabulating Jazz," in Krin Gabbard, ed., *Representing Jazz* (Durham: Duke University Press, 1995), pp. 70–103. "That pervasive uneasiness about jazz and its makers takes a revealing bitter form in another reading of Parker, Julio Cortázar's story "The Pursuer," an *histoire à clef* whose hero is plainly Bird. The unfolding of the tale reveals the complexities of the narrator's attitude toward Johnny Carter, on whom he has written a well-received book. It also reveals the depths of Carter's understanding of what he is pursuing. Bruno, the narrator, fears and envies Carter, whom he describes as a natural force . . . not only fear before Johnny's energy but fear of his understanding as well" p. 94.

3. "El compañero Bruno es fiel como el mal aliento" (p. 161; p. 149).

4. For one of many examples, see Collier, *The Making of Jazz,* pp. 356–57. "Parker . . . was already (1944) exhibiting the personality problems from which he suffered. He missed jobs; slept through others . . . [W]here Charlie Parker wasted his talent on the *pursuit* of the moment, Gillespie managed his career with intelligence and skill" (my emphasis). Collier calls Parker a "sociopath . . . who managed in a relatively short time to destroy his career, every relationship important to him,

and finally himself," largely through drugs and the arrogance that needed every desire fulfilled immediately (p. 363).

5. "Pienso en la música que se está perdiendo, en las docenas de grabaciones donde Johnny podría seguir dejando esa presencia, ese adelanto asombroso que tiene sobre cualquier otro músico" (p. 167; p. 255).

6. See pp. 164, 174, 179, 199; pp. 258, 263, 288, 291, 299.

7. See p. 163; p. 251.

8. Stearns, *The Story of Jazz*, p. 221. "Public interest in bop didn't last long—the musicians themselves seemed to go out of their way to discourage it—and the threat in bop soon became more psychological than economic. But the young and formerly admiring bop musician did not hesitate to tell the old-timer: 'If you don't dig these new sounds, man, you're real square.' In fact, he made a point of doing so—in a variety of ways—and many older musicians felt this hostility keenly. The revolt in bop was frequently revolting . . . The switch from 'hot' to 'cool' as the epithet of highest praise goes deeper . . . he refused to play the stereotype role of Negro entertainer, which he rightly associated with Uncle Tomism. He then proceeded to play the most revolutionary jazz with an appearance of utter boredom, rejecting his audience entirely."

In his review of the militant journalism that accompanied the "bebop" revolution, Martin Williams points out that the battle was pitched between those who claimed that bop had blasted everything else out of the field and those who claimed it was a passing aberration. See his introductory note to Ross Russel's 1948–49 articles in *The Record Changer* and *The Art of Jazz: Ragtime to Be-bop*, ed. by Martin Williams (New York: Da Capo Press, 1980, rept. 1959), p. 185.

9. "Bop Will Kill Business unless It Kills Itself First," *Down Beat*, April 7, 1948, p. 2.

10. See p. 208; p. 300.

11. P. 211; pp. 303–304.

12. P. 167; p. 256.

13. "Bruno, si un día lo pudieras escribir . . . No por mí, entiendes, a mí qué me importa" (p. 167; p. 256).

14. "[D]espués de la maravilla nace la irritación, y a mí por lo menos me pasa que siento como si Johnny me hubiera estado tomando el pelo" (p. 173; p. 262).

15. "Sonrío lo mejor que puedo, comprendiendo vagamente que tiene razón, pero que lo que él sospecha y lo que yo presiento de su sospecha se va a borrar como siempre apenas esté en la calle y me meta en mi vida de todos los días" (p. 173; p. 262).

16. Collier, *Making of Jazz*, p. 351: "The ideas of Parker and Gillespie were not so very novel from an academic viewpoint, and would have come into jazz anyway. By

the 1940s conservatory-trained musicians were beginning to enter jazz, and they were bringing with them similar ideas worked out by master composers in the previous century. . . . But Parker and Gillespie set about building a whole music around this concept, and, perhaps more important, they had the courage to insist that they were right." Parker, like Johnny, was reluctant to admit debts of gratitude and respect, even to mentor musicians (p. 365). See also Stearns, *The Story of Jazz*, pp. 218, 224.

17. "Como lo que era en el fondo: un pobre diablo de inteligencia apenas mediocre . . ." (p. 218; p. 311).

18. P. 220; p. 313.

19. Paul de Man, "Autobiography as Defacement." *Modern Language Notes*, 94 (1979): 919–930.

20. Emmanuel Levinas, *Ethics and Infinity: Conversations with Philippe Nemo*, trans. Richard A. Cohen. (Pittsburgh: Duquesne University Press, 1985) "Knowledge has always been interpreted as assimilation. Even the most surprising discoveries end by being absorbed, comprehended, with all that there is of 'prehending' in 'comprehending.' The most audacious and remote knowledge does not put us in communion with the truly other; it does not take the place of sociality; it is still and always a solitude . . . Sociality will be a way of escaping being otherwise than through knowledge" pp. 60–61.

21. "—Hace rato que no nos veíamos—*le he dicho* a Johnny—. Un mes por lo menos.—Tú no haces más que contar el tiempo—*me ha contestado* de mal humor. El primero, el dos, el tres, el veintiúno. A todo le pones un número, tú" (p. 162; p. 250, my emphasis).

22. "Johnny . . . seguía haciendo alusiones al tiempo, un tema que le preocupa desde que lo conozco. He visto pocos hombres tan preocupados por todo lo que se refiere al tiempo" (p. 250; p. 252).

23. Ralph Ellison, *Invisible Man* (New York: Random House, 1952), p. 11.

24. "Esto lo estoy tocando mañana . . . Esto ya lo toqué mañana, es horrible, Miles, esto ya lo toqué mañana" (p. 164; p. 253).

25. See pp. 201–204; pp. 293–295.

26. His other critics did that too. See Nat Shapiro and Nat Hentoff, who quote Parker: "I'd been getting bored with the stereotyped changes that were being used all the time . . . and I kept thinking there's bound to be something else. I could hear it sometimes but I couldn't play it.

Well, that night, I was working over *Cherokee*, and, as I did, I found that by using the higher intervals of a chord as a melody line and backing them with appropriately related changes, I could play the thing I'd been hearing. I came alive." Quoted in Nat Shapiro and Nat Hentoff, *Hear Me Talkin' to Ya* (New York: Rinehart, 1955), p. 340.

27. "No es víctima, no perseguido, sino perseguidor" (p. 196; p. 287).

28. These wonderful stories and others are collected in Julio Cortázar, *We Love Glenda So Much, and Other Stories,* trans. Gregory Rabasa (New York: Knopf, 1983).

29. See, for example, Lois Parkinson Zamora, "Movement and Stasis, Film and Photo: Temporal Structures in the Recent Fiction of Julio Cortázar," in *The Review of Contemporary Fiction* (Elmwood Park, IL), III, (Fall 1983): 51–64.

30. P. 178; p. 265.

31. P. 220; p. 313.

32. P. 212; p. 304.

33. The image strongly resembles the theme of Lacan's essay on "The Mirror Stage . . ." in *The Psychoses* (New York: Norton, 1993). In that essay, Lacan develops the idea of mirror images as fictional representations likely to cause paranoia in the onlooker who suspects that the coherent image knows more about him than he does himself. The scene also evokes "Author and Hero in Aesthetic Activity," by Mikhail Bakhtin, in *Art and Answerability: Early Philosophical Essays by M.M. Bakhtin,* ed. Michael Holquist and Vadim Liapunov (Austin: University of Texas Press, 1990), pp. 32–33.

34. That slime or "drool" is the same stuff that obsesses the photographer in "Las babas del diablo." Cortázar, *Las armas secretas,* pp. 61–78; "Blowup," in *Blowup,* pp. 100–118.

35. P. 192; p. 282.

36. "He leído algunas cosas sobre todo eso, Bruno. Es muy raro, y en realidad tan difícil . . . (sic) Yo creo que la música ayuda, sabes. No a entender, porque en realidad no entiendo nada" (p. 165; p. 254).

37. "Lo mejor es cuando te das cuenta de que puedes meter una tienda entera en la valija, cientos y cientos de trajes, como yo meto la música en el tiempo cuando estoy tocando a veces. La música y lo que pienso cuando viajo en el *métro*" (p. 168; p. 257).

38. Pp. 173–175; pp. 260–261.

39. "Bruno, si yo pudiera solamente vivir como en esos momentos, o como cuando estoy tocando y también el tiempo cambia . . ." (p. 173; p. 262).

40. Jay McShann, quoted in Robert Reisner's *Bird: The Legend of Charlie Parker* (New York: Da Capo Press, 1973), p. 149. Collier, *The Making of Jazz,* p. 353.

41. Ross Russell, "Bebop," in Martin Williams, ed., *The Art of Jazz: Ragtime to Bebop,* pp. 186–214. "Perhaps the most controversial aspect of bebop jazz is its rhythmic organization. Bebop rhythmics, or better polyrhythmics, are so revolutionary that they have been largely misunderstood and, since no jazz can exist without a solid beat, the new style has been suspect among many uninformed listeners" (p. 189).

Miles Davis has this telling memory of Parker revolutionizing the rhythm section: "Like we'd be playing the blues, and Bird would start on the 11th bar, and as the rhythm sections stayed where they were and Bird played where he was, it sounded as if the rhythm section was on one and three instead of two and four. Everytime that would happen, Max used to scream at Duke not to follow Bird but to stay where he was. Then eventually, it came around as Bird had planned and we were together again." Davis adds that Parker's "turning the rhythm section around" so frustrated him that for a while he would quit the group every night. Miles Davis quoted in *Metronome* (June 1955), p. 25. Stearns, *The Story of Jazz*, pp. 231–232.

42. Hodeir writes that Parker was the real leader of the bebop movement. Like Armstrong around 1930, Parker got jazz out of a rut. *Jazz: Its Evolution and Essence*, p. 101. Later the standard attribution was to Parker and Gillespie. See Leonard Feather, *The Pleasures of Jazz* (New York: Horizon Press, 1976).

43. From the liner to "Hampton Hawes Trio," Contemporary Records LP C3505, quoted by Lester Koenig (26 August 1955). Stearns, *The Story of Jazz*, p. 228. Hodeir had already made the point, "It is clear that he [Parker] created a school . . . But, as we shall see, the new generation has not completely assimilated his acquisitions, particularly in the field of rhythm." *Jazz*, p. 104.

44. P. 217; p. 310.

45. "Cuando la marquesa echa a hablar uno se pregunta si el estilo de Dizzy no se le ha pegado al idioma, pues es una serie interminable de variaciones en los registros más inesperados . . ." (p. 178; p. 268).

46. P. 211; p. 303.

47. André Hodeir describes Charlie Parker as a musical magician, "making appear and then disappear scraps of a melody that should have been rendered in full, hiding them up his sleeve." "The Genius of Art Tatum," *The Art of Jazz: Ragtime to Be-bop*, ed. Martin Williams, pp. 173–180; quotation from p. 175.

48. "([Y]o ya no sé cómo escribir todo esto)" (p. 210; p. 302).

49. Hodeir, *Jazz: Its Evolution and Essence*, 108.

50. P. 208; p. 300.

51. Toni Morrison, "Unspeakable Things Unspoken: The Afro-American Presence in American Literature," *Michigan Quarterly Review*, 28, 1 (1989): 1–34. Sula is "A modernity which overturns pre-war definitions, ushers in the Jazz age (an age *defined* by Afro-American art and culture), and requires new kinds of intelligences to define oneself," p. 26.

52. "Este no es el momento de hacer crítica de *jazz*, y los interesados pueden leer mi libro sobre Johnny y el nuevo estilo de la posguerra, pero bien puedo decir que el cuarenta y ocho—digamos hasta el cincuenta—fue como una explosión de la música . . ." (p. 176; p. 266).

For Stearns, "'bop' was a sudden eruption within jazz, a fast but logical complication of melody, harmony, and rhythm" (p. 218). World War II did a lot to break down the color line between black and white music: "by 1947–8, eager patrons formed queues around the block waiting to enter the Royal Roost, 'The Metropolitan Bopera House,' on Broadway." *The Story of Jazz*, pp. 219–220.

53. Domingo Faustino Sarmiento, "Biography is the most original kind of book that South America can produce in our times, and the best material we can offer history." *Recuerdos de provincia* (1850), in the appendix on biography.

54. P. 177; p. 266.

55. I find Jaime Alazraki unconvincing, for example, when he applauds Cortázar's fiction for maturing from an obsessive focus on plot to "more concentrated on characters, more vital and less dependent on plot"; but his partiality to character development is consistent with his appreciation for Cortázar's mastery as a writer of fiction. (See his "From *Bestiary* to *Glenda*: Pushing the Short Story to Its Utmost Limits," in *The Review of Contemporary Fiction* (Elmwood Park, IL), III, 3 (Fall 1983): 94–99. Cortázar, of course, kept mastery at enough distance to incite innovation. He always feared writing too easily or too well. Even if Alazraki is not wrong about the initial shift of focus,it is only one shift; and Cortázar is a moving target for his readers.

56. P. 174; p. 663.

57. Levinas's *Totality and Infinity* is an extended critique of the tradition of Western philosophy, a fundamentally ontological tradition that moves out in appropriative concentric circles from the subject. In its stead, Levinas appeals for an ethics based in the Other, the locutor who pre-exists the subject and constructs him as a necessary listener. Only an appreciation for the radical and inassimilable alterity, and primordialness, of the other can ground ethical relations.

58. See Adam Zachary Newton for the relevance of Bakhtin for Cortázar in his masterful *Narrative Ethics* (Cambridge, Mass.: Harvard University Press, 1995). Newton's focus is on the duration of the enabling engagement between author and hero.

59. "The Pursuer," p. 208–9. "Que los críticos son mucho más necesarios de lo que yo mismo estoy dispuesto a reconocer . . . porque los creadores, desde el inventor de la música hasta Johnny . . ., son incapaces de extraer las consecuencias dialécticas de su obra, postular los fundamentos y la trascendencia de lo que están escribiendo o improvisando." "El perseguidor," p. 300–301.

60. Bakhtin, "Author and Hero," p. 131.

61. See my "A Nowhere for Us: The Promising Pronouns of Cortázar's 'Utopian' Stories," *Dispositio*, IX, 24–26 (1986): 65–90. My focus is on his experiments with the very components of literary and common language; that is, on the arbitrarily pro-

duced linguistic signs which he shows to be constructed, changeable, flexible, and as unstable as the world they allegedly represent.

62. Cortázar, *We Love Glenda So Much, and Other Stories,* trans. Gregory Rabassa, p. 16. For the original, see *Queremos tanto a Glenda* (Mexico, D.F.: Editorial Nueva Imágen, 1980) "Queríamos tanto a Glenda que le ofreceríamos una última perfección inviolable. En la altura intangible donde la habíamos exaltado, la preservaríamos de la caída, sus fieles podrían seguir adorándola sin mengua; no se baja vivo de una cruz," p. 28.

63. Pp. 82–83 and p. 90.

64. Bakhtin, "Author and Hero," p. 56.

65. "Apocalypse at Solentiname," in *We Love Glenda So Much and Other Stories,* p. 265. "[L]o de siempre, por qué no vivís en tu patria, qué pasó que *Blow-Up* era tan distinto de tu cuento, te parece que el escritor tiene que estar comprometido? A esta altura de las cosas ya sé que la Ultima entrevista me la harán en las puertas del infierno y seguro que serán las mismas preguntas, y si por caso es chez San Pedro, la cosa no va a cambiar, a usted no le parece que allá abajo escribía demasiado hermético para el pueblo?" "Apocalípsis en Solentiname," *Alguien que anda por ahí* (Madrid: Ediciones Alfaguara, 1977), p. 95.

66. Bakhtin, "Author and Hero," Pp. 151, 26.

67. "Lo difícil es girar en torno a él sin perder la distancia, como un buen satélite, un buen crítico" (p. 197; p. 288).

68. Bakhtin, "Author and Hero," pp. 64, 81 and 88.

69. "En el fondo somos una banda de egoístas, so pretexto de cuidar a Johnny lo que hacemos es salvar nuestra idea de él . . . sacarle brillo a la estatua que hemos erigido entre todos y defenderla cueste lo que cueste" (p. 182; p. 272).

70. "[Q]ue se trepara a un altar y tironeara de Cristo para sacarlo de la cruz" (p. 204; p. 296).

71. P. 167.

72. "Deberías sentirte contento de que me haya portado así contigo; no lo hago con nadie, créeme. Es una muestra de cómo te aprecio. Tenemos que ir juntos a algún sitio para hablar . . ." (p. 181; p. 271).

73. P. 165; p. 254; and p. 213; p. 305.

74. "Y si yo mismo no he sabido tocar como debía, tocar lo que soy de veras . . . ya ves que no se te pueden pedir milagros, Bruno" (p. 212; p. 304).

75. "En el fondo lo único que ha dicho es que nadie sabe nada de nada, y no es una novedad. Toda biografía da eso por supuesto y sigue adelante, qué diablos" (p. 212; pp. 304–05).

76. P. 217; p. 310. P. 218; p. 310.

77. "[E]nvidio a Johnny, a ese Johnny del otro lado, sin que nadie sepa qué es exactamente ese otro lado. . . . Envidio a Johnny y al mismo tiempo me da rabia que se esté destruyendo por el mal empleo de sus dones . . ." (p. 180; pp. 269–70).

78. "[Y] quizá en el fondo quisiera que Johnny acabara de una vez, como una estrella que se rompe en mil pedazos y deja idiotas a los astrónomos durante una semana, y después uno se va a dormir y mañana es otro día" (p. 180; p. 270).

10. ABOUT FACE

1. Mario Vargas Llosa, *The Storyteller,* trans. Helen Lane (London: Faber and Faber, 1989); *El hablador* (Barcelona: Seix Barral, 1987), pp. 3, 7. Citations are given below with English translation page numbers first, followed by a semicolon, and original Spanish edition page numbers. Lane's translation is occasionally altered here; unless otherwise noted, all other translations are mine.

For a brilliant reading of Vargas Llosa's meditation on Peru confronting the limits of its national project, see Benedict Anderson's chapter, "El malhadado país," in *Specters of Comparison* (London: Verso, 1998).

2. Louis Althusser, "Ideology and Ideological State Apparatuses (Notes Towards an Investigation)," in *Lenin and Philosophy and Other Essays* (New York: Monthly Review Press, 1971), p. 162.

3. Emmanuel Levinas, *Totality and Infinity: An Essay on Exteriority,* trans. Alphonso Lingis (Pittsburgh: Duquesne University Press, 1969).

4. See pp. 3–4; p. 7.

5. Levinas, *Totality and Infinity,* p. 43.

6. Jacques Lacan, *Ecrits* (Paris: Seuil, 1966–1971), essay #2 on paranoia.

7. For an excellent summary of his ideological trajectory, from socialist sympathies in the early 1960s to increasingly authoritarian postures, see William Rowe, "Liberalism and Authority: The Case of Mario Vargas Llosa," in *On Edge: The Crisis of Contemporary Latin American Culture,* eds. George Yúdice, Jean Franco, and Juan Flores (Minneapolis: University of Minnesota Press, 1992), pp. 45–64. And for a recent example of Vargas Llosa's conservative animus, see his editorial "Jouer avec le feu," in *Le monde,* May 18, 1995, p. 17, opining that the recent confessions of the Argentine military leaders during the Dirty War do not show them to be more culpable than the revolutionaries who incited the army to terror.

8. The parallel with the author of the notoriously deployed slogan, "sendero luminoso," may be surprising. Nevertheless, Mariátegui was a model for the youthful Vargas Llosa, remembered in the novel (p. 78; p. 76).

9. J. C. Mariátegui, *El Alma matinal y otras estaciones del hombre de hoy* (Lima: Amauta, 1972), pp. 146–147, article of 1925; and pp. 192–193, article of 1929. Quoted in José Guillermo Nugent, *Conflicto de las sensibilidades: Propuesta para una inter-*

pretación y crítica del siglo XX peruano (Rimac: Instituto Bartolomé de las Casas, 1991), pp. 55–57.

10. See Debra Castillo's provocative reading, "Postmodern Indigenism: 'Quetzalcóatl and All That'" in *Modern Fiction Studies*, 41, 1 (spring 1995): 35–73.

11. See James Dunkerley's review, "Mario Vargas Llosa: Parables and Deceits," *New Left Review*, 162 (1987): 112–23, esp. pp. 118–19.

12. Enrique Dussel and Daniel E. Guillot, *Liberación Latinoamericana y Emmanuel Levinas* (Buenos Aires: Editorial Bonum, 1975), p. 9.

13. Pp. 98–99; pp. 96–97.

14. Mario Vargas Llosa, *A Writer's Reality* (Boston: Houghton Mifflin, 1991), p. 37.

15. Dussel, *Liberación Latinoamericana y Emmanuel Levinas*, p. 25: "*persona* is what makes a sound, and what makes a sound is the voice and the eruption of the Other in us; it does not erupt as 'the seen,' but as 'the heard.' We should no longer privilege the seen, but the heard."

16. Ilán Stavans, *Tropical Synagogues: Short Stories by Jewish-Latin American Writers* (New York: Holmes & Meier, 1994), p. 31.

17. Pp. 32–33; pp. 33–34.

18. *Historia de Mayta* and *Elogio de la madrastra* have the same structure, as Mary Berg and José Antonio Mazzotti remind me.

19. José Antonio Mazzotti confirmed this impression, in a letter of April 5, 1995. The Quechua-flavored Spanish appears, also importantly, in José María Arguedas' Andean stories, which Professor Vargas Llosa assigns to students. "—(El Wamani está ya sobre el corazón!—exclamó 'Atok' sayku', mirando . . . Ahistá en tu cabeza el blanco de su espalda como el sol del mediodía en el nevado, brillando." *Relatos Completos* (Madrid: Alianza, 1983). "La agonía de Rasu-Yiti," pp. 132–141; quotation from pp. 140–141.

20. For example, see *The Storyteller*, pp. 173, 181–182; pp. 168, 176.

21. See pp. 215–221; pp. 207–212.

22. P. 240; p. 229.

23. P. 240; p. 230.

24. Pp. 95–96; pp. 93–94. See also pp. 162–163; p. 157.

25. P. 34; p. 36.

26. P. 108; p. 106.

27. P. 242; p. 232.

28. Sendero Luminoso or the Communist Party of Peru, had been organizing and slowly building bases during the 1960s and throughout the 1970s, from its regional headquarters at the public University of Huamanga, near Ayacucho. It launched its military campaign against the state in 1980. See David Scott Palmer, ed., *Shining Path* (New York: St. Martin's Press, 1992).

345

29. Mario Vargas Llosa, "Homenaje a Javier Heraud, Paris, 19 mayo 1963," in *Contra viento y marea (1962–1982)* (Barcelona: Seix Barral, 1983), pp. 36–37.

30. P. 149–150; p. 144–145.

31. Angel Rama, "Introducción," in José María Arguedas, *Formación de una cultura nacional indoamericana,* ed. Angel Rama (Mexico: Siglo Veintiúno, 1975), p. ix.

32. The same speculation, though more elaborate and convincing, is put forth by Enrique Mayer, "Peru in Deep Trouble: Mario Vargas Llosa's 'Inquest in the Andes' Reexamined," *Rereading Cultural Anthropology,* ed. George E. Marcus (Durham: Duke University Press, 1992), pp. 181–219; p. 196. He cites a caricature of Arguedas published in the Senderista newspaper *El Diario* (cited in Carlos Ivan Degregori, *Ayacucho 1969–1979: El surgimiento de Sendero luminoso* [Lima: Instituto de Estudios Peruanos, 1990] p. 296): "Internationalism has to fight against magical-whining nationalism, whose fossilized remains we have had and continue to have in a chauvinist nationalism, whose promoter was none other than that writer who rejoiced in declaring himself 'purely apolitical,' but who, during World War II, was proud of his little Hitler moustache. His name: Jose María Arguedas, affable disciple and animator in Peru of Northamerican anthropology . . . Such is indiofilia zorra . . ." Mayer glosses this skewed picture of anthropological intransigence with, "The image of Zuratas again!"

33. See Rafael Humberto Moreno Durán, included in *Semana de Autor: Mario Vargas Llosa* (Madrid: Ediciones Cultura Hispánica, 1985), p. 82; and Mario Vargas Llosa, *José María Arguedas, entre sapos y halcones* (Madrid: Ediciones Cultura Hispánica, 1978). He continues to engage Arguedas, even if it is to disengage the writer from the ideologue. For example, all of the undergraduate course he taught at Harvard University in the Fall of 1992 was dedicated to Arguedas.

34. For criticism of American anthropology in Peru, see Orin Starn, "Missing the Revolution: Anthropologists and the War in Peru," in George E. Marcus, ed., *Rereading Cultural Anthropology,* pp. 153–180.

35. Mayer, "Peru in Deep Trouble," pp. 190–91. The line goes from the 1930s, with Julio Tello and Luis Valcárcel (both ministers of education), Arguedas himself (head of the National Institute of Culture), and Mario Vázquez (designer of agrarian reform in the 1960s).

36. David Stoll, *Fishers of Men or Founders of Empire?: The Wycliffe Bible Translators in Latin America* (London: Zed Press, Cambridge, Mass.: Cultural Survival Inc., 1982), p. 7.

37. Ibid., p. 2.

38. Ibid., p. 201.

39. "The Schneils, like all the other linguists, had degrees from the University of Oklahoma, but they and their colleagues were motivated above all by a spiritual

goal: spreading the Glad Tidings of the Bible. I don't know what their precise religious affiliation was, since there were members of a number of different churches among the linguists of the Institute. The ultimate purpose that had led them to study primitive cultures was religious: translating the Bible into the tribes' own languages so that those peoples could hear God's word in the rhythms and inflections of their own tongue. This was the aim that had led Dr. Peter Townsend to found the Institute. He was an interesting person, half evangelist and half pioneer, a friend of the Mexican president Lázaro Cárdenas and the author of a book about him. The goal set by Dr. Townsend still motivates the linguists to continue the patient labor they have undertaken." (ibid., p. 85).

40. Pp. 96–97; pp. 94–95.

41. Mario Vargas Llosa, *Historia secreta de una novela* (Barcelona: Tusquets, 1968).

42. Edward Said, "Representing the Colonized: Anthropology's Interlocutors," *Critical Inquiry*, 15 (Winter 1989): 215.

43. Kristin Herzog, *Finding Their Voice: Peruvian Women's Testimonies of War* (Valley Forge, Penn,: Trinity Press International, 1993) pp. 145, 156.

44. Vargas Llosa's unacknowledged debt to Catholic missionaries is the subject of an angry editorial by Domiciano García Benito, Superintendent of Catholic Schools in the Diocese of Caguas, Puerto Rico. "Truenan contra Vargas Llosa," *El Nuevo Día*, Puerto Rico, Feb. 22, 1995.

45. P. 72; p. 71.

46. Stoll, *Fishers*, p. 205.

47. Nevertheless, anthropologist Luis Millones expresses dismay at the novelist's careless and prejudiced portrayals of Andean culture. See Luis Millones, "Vargas Llosa y la mirada de Occidente: *Lituma en los Andes,*" *El Peruano*, "Opinión," Lima, Jan. 12, 1994.

48. Sigmund Freud, "Notes Upon a Case of Obsessional Neurosis (1909)," in *Collected Papers: Vol. 3,* trans. Alix and James Strachey (New York: Basic Books, 1959): p. 376, and "Screen Memories (1899)," in *Collected Papers: Vol. 5,* pp. 52–53.

49. P. 100; p. 98.

50. Pp. 161–162; pp. 155–156.

51. P. 181; p. 175.

52. P. 9; p. 10.

53. Stanley Cavell, "The Avoidance of Love: A Reading of *King Lear,*" in *Must We Mean What We Say: A Book of Essays,* (Cambridge, Eng.: Cambridge University Press, 1969), pp. 267–353. Rael Meyerowitz reminds me that this is a sweeping simplification of Cavell's position. He also approves of American "onwardness," what Emerson calls "abandonment." For an excellent reading of Cavell's subtle and

humane balancing acts, see Rael Meyerowitz, "Welcome Back to the Republic: Stanley Cavell and the Acknowldgement of Literature," *LIT,* 4 (1993): 329–352.

54. P. 34; p. 36.

55. Betty Elkins de Snell, *Cuentos folklóricos de los machiguenga* (Yarinacocha: Instituto Lingüístico de Verano, 1979).

56. See pp. 33, 73–74, 78, 90, 94, 236–246; pp. 35, 72, 77, 88, 92, 225–235.

57. Two recent and provocative explorations are Paul Ricoeur's *Oneself as Another* (Chicago: Chicago University Press, 1992) and Julia Kristeva's *Strangers to Ourselves,* Leon S. Roudiez, trans. (New York: Columbia University Press, 1991).

58. Emmanuel Levinas, *Otherwise Than Being, or Beyond Essence,* translated by Alphonso Lingis, (Dordrecht: Kluwer Academic Publishers, 1991) p. 11.

59. Levinas, *Totality and Infinity,* p. 43.

60. Ibid., p. 44.

61. Stanley Fish, *Surprised by Sin: The Reader in Paradise Lost* (Berkeley: University of California Press, 1967), throughout. See, for example, p. 208, quoting C. S. Lewis on the "blind alleys" pursued by readers of *Paradise Lost.* "How are we to account for the fact that great modern scholars have missed what is so dazzlingly simple?" from *A Preface to Paradise Lost* (Oxford, 1942), pp. 69–70. See also Cavell, *The Avoidance of Love,* whose very title announces a brilliant development of the theme (New York: Macmillan, 1967).

62. P. 240; p. 229.

63. Levinas, *Totality and Infinity,* p. 44. My emphasis.

64. P. 16; p. 19.

65. Dussel and Guillot, *Liberación Latinoamericana y Emmanuel Levinas* p. 29.

66. P. 6; p. 10.

67. P. 173; p. 168. Reflecting later on his obsession with that role, the narrator remembers how he hounded his Irish friends to introduce him to an equally untranslatable "*Seanchaí:* 'teller of ancient stories,' 'the one who knows things,' as someone in a Dublin bar had off-handedly translated the word into English" (p. 165; p. 159).

68. Walter Benjamin, *Illuminations,* ed. Hannah Arendt, trans. Harry Zohn (New York: Schocken, 1969). *The Storyteller,* pp. 83–109.

69. P. 209; p. 201.

70. Mario Vargas Llosa, "En torno a los derechos humanos" Lima, dated at the end of the essay on 19 de Septiembre de 1978. First published in *Premio Derechos Humanos, 1977* (Lima: Asociación Judía del Peru, 1979) p. 5, my translation. The speech was reprinted as "Ganar batallas, no la guerra," in *Contra viento y marea (1986–1990)* (Barcelona: Seix Barral, 1991), pp. 309–323.

71. Vargas Llosa, "En torno," p. 6. My emphasis.

72. "Likewise, a photograph, for example, of Holocaust victims might be inappropriate for display in the entrance of a museum where all would have to confront it, whether they chose to or not." Quoted in Andrea Liss, "Trespassing Through Shadows: History, Mourning, and Photography in Representations of Holocaust Memory," *Framework* 4, 1 (1991): 29–41. See also Marianne Hirsch, "Family Pictures: *Maus*, Mourning, and Post-Memory," *Discourse*, 15, 2 (Winter 1992–93): 3–29.

73. Vargas Llosa, "En torno," p. 17.

74. Oral information on immigration supplied by Judith Laikin Elkin.

75. P. 99; p. 97. When Mario suggests that Mascarita's deformity is felt in exclusions, and allies him to the excluded tribes of the Jungle, Saúl answers, "still laughing, he told me that Don Salomón Zuratas, being sharper than I was, had suggested a Jewish interpretation. 'That I'm identifying the Amazonian Indians with the Jewish people, always a minority and always persecuted for their religion and their mores that are different from those of the rest of society . . . Okay . . . Suddenly being half Jewish and half monster has made me more sensitive to the fate of the jungle tribes than someone as appallingly normal as you'" (pp. 28–29; p. 30).

76. P. 78; p. 76.

77. P. 243; p. 233.

78. José Antonio Mazzotti provided this clear formulation.

79. Mario Vargas Llosa, *Historia secreta de una novela*, 8–9.

80. From a conversation with Mario Vargas Llosa on October 23, 1993, during his teaching semester as Robert Kennedy Professor of Latin American Studies at Harvard University.

81. See Mario Vargas Llosa, "Inquest in the Andes," *The New York Times*, 31 July 1983.

82. Enrique Mayer, "Peru in Deep Trouble," p. 187. Mario Vargas Llosa, "Informe de la comisión investigadora de los sucesos de Uchuraccay" (Lima: Editora Peru, 1983), pp. 202–203. Ventura Huayhua was later removed, for "mistrial," but not before he garnered immense popular support.

83. See Mayer, ibid., for documentation of the gory details (likewise remembered by Julio Ortega and José Antonio Mazzotti), and for facts that don't fit the commission's report.

84. Vargas Llosa, "Inquest," 1983, p. 23 (cited in Mayer, p. 187).

85. Mario Vargas Llosa, *Lituma en los Andes* (Barcelona: Planeta, 1993).

86. The story of repression against Jum, a chief of the Aguaruna, starting with his refusal to be robbed by a local rubber boss, to Indian resistance and a general vengeance by the whites and mestizos, is told in Mario Vargas Llosa, *The Green House*, trans. Gregory Rabassa (New York: Avon, 1968), pp. 49–50, 119–120, 156, 172, 231, 252–3, 271, 281–4, 324, 339–41. *El hablador* summarizes: "But in Urakusa, besides

the copper-colored bodies, the dangling tits, the children with parasite-swollen bellies and skins striped red or black, a sight awaited us that I have never forgotten: that of a man recently tortured. It was the headman of the locality, whose name was Jum . . .

The ostensible reason for this savagery was a minor incident that had taken place in Urakusa between the Aguarunas and a detachment of soldiers passing through" (pp. 74–5; 72–3).

87. For a responsible history in English, see Sabine MacCormack, *Religion in the Andes: Vision and Imagination in Early Colonial Peru* (Princeton: Princeton University Press, 1991).

88. One of the anthropologists who collaborated in Vargas Llosa's Commission to investigate Uchuracay, writes that the novelist should have known better. See Luis Millones, "Vargas Llosa y la mirada de Occidente: *Lituma en los Andes.*"

89. To Vargas Llosa's arguments about Mayta's inability to fit into society, a Brazilian interviewer repeatedly asks, "Mas por que tambén homossexual?" Ricardo A. Setti, *Conversas com Vargas Llosa* (Sao Paulo: Editora Brasiliense, 1986), p. 59.

90. Mario Vargas Llosa, "Cruzados del Arcoiris," in *Desafíos a la libertad* (Madrid: El País / Aguilar, 1994), pp. 229–234. 234.

91. Reinaldo Arenas, *Antes que anochezca (Autobiografía)* (Barcelona: Tusquets, 1992) translated as *Before Night Falls: A Memoir,* trans. Dolores M. Koch (New York: Penguin Books, 1993), p. 106.

92. Mario Vargas Llosa, "El pene o la vida," *Desafíos,* pp. 301–306.

93. Mario Vargas Llosa, *Lituma en los Andes* (Barcelona, Planeta, 1993), p. 311.

94. Mary Berg pointed out these parallels.

95. Kristin Herzog, *Finding Their Voice,* p. 83.

96. From Garcilaso de la Vega, El Inca, *Royal Commentaries of the Incas and General History of Peru,* trans. Harold V. Livermore, (Austin, University of Texas Press, 1966), bk. 1., chap. 18.

97. Vargas Llosa, *Lituma,* p. 312.

98. Garcilaso, *Royal Commentaries,* bk. 1., chaps. 11 and 13.

99. Ibid., bk. 1, chap. 11.

100. Vargas Llosa, "En torno," p. 16.

101. See Efraín Kristal, *Peruvian Indigenismo Narrative and the Political Debate about the Indian* (Dumbarton Oaks, 1985; Ann Arbor: University Microfilms, 1997).

102. Mario Vargas Llosa, "Questions of Conquest," *Harper's* (Dec. 1990): 45.

103. Mario Vargas Llosa, "Novels Disguised as History: The Chronicles of the Birth of Peru," *A Writer's Reality* (Boston: Houghton Mifflin, 1991), pp. 21–38.

104. Vargas Llosa, "Questions of Conquest," p. 45.

105. Vargas Llosa, *A Writer's Reality,* p. 46.

106. Ibid., pp. 35, 34.

107. Ibid.., p. 37.

108. See William Rowe, "Liberalism and Authority: The Case of Mario Vargas Llosa," in *On Edge: The Crisis of Contemporary Latin American Culture,* ed. George Yudice, Jean Franco, and Juan Flores (Minneapolis: University of Minnesota Press, 1992), pp. 45–64. He cites and agrees with Mirko Lauer, Julio Ortega, James Dunkerley, Julio Cotler, Gerald Martin (who comes to the defense as well), and Elizabeth Farnsworth. Rowe himself points out that, "Along with the globalizing attitude that flattens out historical differences, the language tends to solidify into imperviousness, losing referential accuracy and analytical precision . . ." (p. 49).

109. Ibid., p. 50.

110. Mirko Lauer, "Vargas Llosa: Los límites de la imaginación no liberal," *La República* (Lima), April 15, 1984, p. 30.

111. Mayer, "Peru in Deep Trouble," p. 207.

112. Vargas Llosa, *A Writer's Reality,* p. 36.

113. José Antonio Mazzotti names them: Manco Inca, Sayri Túpac, Titu Cusi Yupanqui, and Túpac Amaru I, who fought in Vilcabamba until 1572. Letter to me.

114. Vargas Llosa, *A Writer's Reality,* pp. 29, 32, 33–34 (my emphasis).

115. Levinas, *Totality and Infinity,* p. 43.

116. One simplified version of the impatience Vargas Llosa's novel elicits, along with his fiction in general, among educated Peruvian readers, is presented by Mirko Lauer in *El sitio de la literatura: Escritores y política en el Perú del siglo XX* (Lima: Mosca Azul Editores, 1989), pp. 97–119. His fundamental objection is that the novelist fails to maintain an ethical and coherent position. I prefer to think of this in Julio Ortega's terms of holding a position that is open to doubt, rather than one that is dogmatic and orthodox. See Julio Ortega's review of *El pez en el agua,* "El pez en la sartén," *La Jornada,* Mexico, June 9, 1993.

117. P. 94; p. 92.

118. Vargas Llosa, *A Writer's Reality,* p. 25.

119. Pp. 96–97; p. 95.

120. Vargas Llosa, *A Writer's Reality,* p. 33.

121. See Helen Rand Parish on polemical Las Casas, who wrote, in addition to the *Brevísima relación de la destrucción de las Indias,* the less well known *Brevísima relación de la destrucción de Africa.* Rand Parish, *Las Casas en México: Historia y obras desconocidas* (Mexico: Fondo de Cultura Económica, 1992).

Andrés Bello, "Autonomía cultural de América" (1848), in Carlos Ripoll, ed., *Conciencia intelectual de América* (New York: Eliseo Torres, 1966), pp. 48–49. An editor's note informs that the present title "has been used in various Anthologies to present this piece."

122. See Mayer's essay, especially the section "Anthropological Authority," pp. 190–200.

123. Rowe, "Liberalism and Authority," p. 61, represents this tendency.

124. Stanley Fish, *Is There a Text in This Class?: The Authority of Interpretive Communities* (Cambridge, Mass.: Harvard University Press, 1980), p. 3.

125. P. 245; p. 234.

126. Pp. 245–246; p. 235.

127. See Marc Shell, *Children of the Earth: Literature, Politics, and Nationhood* (New York: Oxford University Press, 1993).

128. Vargas Llosa, *A Writer's Reality*, p. 35.

129. Mario Vargas Llosa, "El Preso 1.509," in *Desafíos a la libertad*, p. 153. José Antonio Mazzotti points out that Aníbal Quijano coined the term "dualismo medular" to describe Peruvian society as irreconcilably diverse, so that some pieces have to be sacrified.

130. P. 246; p. 235.

ACKNOWLEDGMENTS

Of the many people who supported and guided this book, Sacvan Bercovitch has been the most enthusiastic about its possibilities and the most insistent that I realize some of them. I thank him profoundly. For generous financial support, I thank the John Simon Guggenheim Foundation, the ACLS, and Harvard University. I am also grateful to Adam Zachary Newton for early and lasting lessons in narrative ethics; to Rubén Ríos Avila for instruction in reflexivity; Arnaldo Cruz-Malavé for detailed engagements; Hilary Putnam for readings of Wittgenstein and Levinas; Bonnie Honig for legal discourse advice; Efrain Barradas for reminding me that Garcilaso was worth rereading; and to Benedict Anderson for nudging me beyond at least some clumsiness of thought and expression. Heartfelt thanks, that I gratefully acknowledge here, also go to Ana María Amar Sánchez, Begoña Arextaga, Amrita Basu, Daniel Bell, Seyla Benhabib, Antonio Benítez Rojo, Mary Berg, Lawrence Buell, Homi Bhabha, Alicia Borinsky, Bruno Bosteels, Marshall Brown, Luisa Campuzano, Sara Castro-Klarén, Michel Chaouli, John Coatsworth, Tom Conley, Marianne Constable, Joseph Dan, Román de la Campa, Arcadio Diaz Quiñones, Wai Chi Dimock, Jorge I. Domínguez, Brad Epps, Luis Fernández Cifuentes, Juan Flores, Diana Fuss, Henry Lewis Gates, Jr., Mary Gaylord, Eduardo González, Robert Gooding-Williams, Beatrice Hanssen, Regina Harrison, María Herrera-Sobek, Marianne Hirsch, Shannon Jackson, Djelal Kadir, Allen Kaufman, Anna Sommer Kaufman, Sara Sommer Kaufman, Susan Keller, Miri Kubovy, Joan Landes, Leo Ou-fan Lee, Scott Mahler, Francisco Márquez Villanueva, J. Lorand Matori, David Maybury-Lewis, José Antonio Mazzotti, Rael Meyerowitz, Walter Mignolo, Sylvia Molloy, Julio Ortega, Francisco Ortega, Juan Otero-Garabís, Marvette Perez, Mary Louise Pratt, Julio Ramos, Mary Beth Rhiel,

Kerry Ridich, Carlos Rincón, Ileana Rodríguez, Richard Rosa, Susana Rotker, Anita Safran, Henry Schwarz, Greta Slobin, Reynolds Smith, Werner Sollors, Ilan Stavans, Mary Steedly, Ann Stoler, Marcelo Suárez-Orozco, David Suchoff, Susan Suleiman, Diana Taylor, Michel-Rolph Trouillot, Betty Tzafrir, Mario Valdés, Nelson Vieira, Lindsay Waters, Cornel West, and Ken Wissoker. Their generosity of spirit and intelligence cannot be measured by this book, which is necessarily bounded by my own limited faculties. Boundless only is my gratitude for their efforts.

I am grateful to Editorial Letras Cubanas for permission to use the engraving "Cecilia Valdés" by Antonio Canet, *Grabados en xilografía y linóleo* (Havana, 1983). My thanks also to the publishers of earlier versions of some of the chapters in this book: "Grammar Trouble: Cortázar's Critique of Competence," *Diacritics,* 25:1 (Spring 1995):21–45, published by the Johns Hopkins University Press; "Taking a Life: Hot Pursuit and Cold Rewards in a Mexican Testimonial Novel," *Signs,* 20:4 (summer 1995):913–940, published by the University of Chicago Press; "Who Can Tell? Filling in the Blanks for Villaverde," *American Literary History,* 6:2 (1994):213–233, published by Oxford University Press; "Cortez in the Courts: The Traps of Translation from Newsprint to Film," in *The Dissident Spectator,* ed. Marge Garber (New York: Routledge, 1993); "No Secrets," in *The Real Thing: Testimonial Discourse and Latin America,* ed. Georg Gugelberger (Durham: Duke University Press, 1996); "At Home Abroad: El Inca Shuttles with Hebreo," in *Creativity and Exile,* ed. Susan Suleiman, special issue of *Poetics Today* (1997), published by Duke University Press; "About Face: The Talker Turns," *Boundary,* 23:1 (spring 1996):91–134, published by Duke University Press.

INDEX